# UNLIKELY WARRIOR

# UNLIKELY WARRIOR

## A Pacifist Rabbi's Journey
## from the Pulpit to Iwo Jima

### LEE MANDEL

PELICAN PUBLISHING COMPANY
GRETNA 2015

*The word "Pelican" and the depiction of a pelican are*
*trademarks of Pelican Publishing Company, Inc., and are*
*registered in the U.S. Patent and Trademark Office.*

Library of Congress Cataloging-in-Publication Data

Mandel, Lee.
  Unlikely warrior : a pacifist rabbi's journey from the pulpit to Iwo Jima
/ by Lee Mandel.
     pages cm
  Includes bibliographical references and index.
  ISBN 978-1-4556-1987-0 (hardcover : alk. paper) — ISBN 978-1-4556-1988-
7 (e-book)  1.  Gittelsohn, Roland Bertram, 1910-1995. 2.  Iwo Jima, Battle
of, Japan, 1945. 3.  Rabbis—United States—Biography. 4.  United States.
Marine Corps. Marine Division, 5th—Biography. 5.  United States. Marine
Corps—Chaplains—Biography. 6.  United States. Navy—Chaplains—
Biography. 7.  World War, 1939-1945—Chaplains—United States. 8.  World
War, 1939-1945—Participation, Jewish. 9.  Military chaplains—United
States—Biography. 10.  Pacifists—United States—Biography. 11.  Pacifism—
Religious aspects—Judaism. 12.  Jews—United States—History—20th
century. I. Title. II. Title: Pacifist rabbi's journey from the pulpit to Iwo Jima.
  D767.99.I9M26 2014
  940.54'78092—dc23
  [B]

                              2014006427

Printed in the United States of America

Published by Pelican Publishing Company, Inc.
1000 Burmaster Street, Gretna, Louisiana 70053

*This book is dedicated to all of the chaplains who served in our military forces in World War II and to all members of that Greatest Generation who fought in the war. We owe them a debt that we can only hope to repay.*

# Contents

# Acknowledgments

There are several people and organizations without whom *Unlikely Warrior* would not have been possible. I am greatly indebted to the archival staff of the American Jewish Archives at the Jacob Rader Marcus Center in Cincinnati for their assistance in helping me obtain Roland Gittelsohn's private papers. I especially want to acknowledge archivist Michelle Detroit for her efforts on my behalf. David Gittelsohn and Judith Gittelsohn Fales were gracious enough to talk with me on several occasions and share memories of their father, as well as provide me with photographs. Their recollections are priceless, and many of their stories and anecdotes about Roland Gittelsohn are included in the book. I would like to thank Pelican Publishing for believing in the book, especially my editor, Erin Classen, who was a great mentor to me and a pleasure to work with. Lastly, but certainly not least, I would like to thank my wife, Ann, for her patience and support throughout the entire writing of this book.

# Introduction

In the spring of 2012 I received an invitation from my alma mater, Washington and Jefferson College, to take part in the upcoming homecoming weekend scheduled for October. At each homecoming there is a Veteran's Memorial Service, and I was asked to be the speaker at the ceremony. This was my fortieth reunion and knowing that maybe a dozen of us from the class of 1972 had served in the military, I was sure that at this point I was the only member of the class still on active duty. I was a captain in the United States Navy.

After studying several of the previous year's speeches, I was looking for some particularly inspiring words to frame my presentation on. As a historian, I remembered reading about a famous speech—a sermon, actually—delivered by a Navy chaplain at the end of the Battle of Iwo Jima. I checked my sources and found out that his name was LT Roland Gittelsohn, a rabbi from New York. He was the first rabbi ever to be assigned to the United States Marine Corps. The strong objections of his fellow Christian chaplains nearly prevented Gittelsohn from delivering his sermon, now known as "The Purest Democracy." It made for very interesting reading to learn of the infighting behind the scenes in the time leading up to the dedication of the Fifth Marine Division Cemetery on Iwo Jima on March 21, 1945, the site of Gittelsohn's sermon. Within a month, most of the free world knew of "The Purest Democracy," a speech that in various circles has been referred to as the Gettysburg Address of World War II.

I read the entire speech and was impressed by the power and the passion of that Navy chaplain's words. As a result, I became very interested in Roland Gittelsohn and began researching his background. I quickly learned that he was an outspoken pacifist in the 1930s who opposed all wars and frequently preached against the United States' entanglement in future European wars. Yet Gittelsohn actively sought and received a commission in the United States Navy in 1942. This seemed amazing to me: a longtime, outspoken pacifist who *volunteered* to join the Navy, became the first Jewish chaplain in the history of the United States Marine Corps, and finally ended up in combat on Iwo Jima. As the expression goes, "you can't make this stuff up!" My interest in the man only accelerated at that point.

Gittelsohn was a prominent rabbi both on Long Island, New York, and in Boston. He was a leader in the Reform Judaism hierarchy and after the war served on President Truman's Committee on Civil Rights. He was a prolific writer, having authored over a dozen books. To my delight, I discovered that he was also a meticulous documenter and kept voluminous personal files. In 2002, his son David Gittelsohn and daughter Judith Gittelsohn Fales, donated all of his personal papers to the Jacob Rader Marcus Center of the American Jewish Archives. The Marcus Center is located on the campus of the Hebrew Union College-Jewish Institute of Religion in Cincinnati, where Roland Gittelsohn went to rabbinical school. The Gittelsohn collection contains sixty-four boxes of his personal papers, each organized into multiple folders. It is a researcher's treasure trove. With the assistance of the staff at the American Jewish Archives, I was able to obtain many of Rabbi Gittelsohn's notes.

Roland Gittelsohn was a brilliant, opinionated man and was clearly one of the most well-read people of his generation. Studying him and his life provides not only insight into a truly remarkable individual but also an excellent framework in which to study several world events and significant movements of his time. The Jewish immigration from tsarist Russia around the turn of the century, the ever-expanding anti-war movement that followed World War I and the so-called "lessons of the World War," the transformation of America with Franklin D. Roosevelt's New Deal, the rise of Nazi Germany, the entry of the United States into World War II, the chaplaincy in the United States military, the United States Marine Corps, and, of course, the battle for Iwo Jima; to tell Roland Gittelsohn's story is to also tell the story of these events. Gittelsohn was a product of this historic time, the events of which would ultimately transform a short, scholarly, pacifist rabbi into a highly effective chaplain serving with the United States Marine Corps at Iwo Jima. To be certain, he would remain an outspoken opponent of war until he passed away in 1995. But from that point on, Gittelsohn would speak not as a theorist who was well-read about war but with the authority of one who had lived through the hell of the bloodiest battle in the history of the United States Marine Corps.

# Prologue

The message provided a rare moment of joy in a world of pain and horror. It arrived just before darkness, as mortar shells exploded around him and rifle and small arms fire crackled overhead. Chaplain Roland Gittelsohn read the telegram that had been sent by the wife of Herman, one of his fellow Marines in the Fifth Marine Division. Because the Red Cross was unable to clear cables to men in active combat, she had arranged for the telegram to be sent to his chaplain so he could convey her joyous news: she had given birth to a baby girl. There in the carnage that was Iwo Jima, Lieutenant Gittelsohn actually felt a glimmer of hope as he reread the telegram. Maybe, just maybe, they would survive to go home and to resume the lives they led before the war. In the morning he would track down Herman and deliver the wonderful news from home.

Gittelsohn had reported to the Fifth Marine Division the previous May. Upon reporting in, he learned that, because he was the division's only Jewish chaplain, he was being assigned as the assistant division chaplain. Like all military chaplains, he ministered to men of all faiths while in the field; and like all effective chaplains, he became a counselor, mentor, and father figure to many of the young Marines like Herman. A short, balding, scholarly man, Gittelsohn was somewhat older than many of the Marines in the division, and at the age of thirty-four he no doubt reminded many of the young men of their high-school teachers and college professors. In the same vein, he forged a bond with many of his fellow Marines through the weekly discussion groups he established in Hawaii to foster conversation on war goals and visions for peace after the war ended. While the division was training in Hawaii, Herman learned that his wife was pregnant with their first child and had shared the news with his chaplain.

After months of arduous training in San Diego, Hawaii,

and Saipan, the Third, Fourth, and Fifth Marine Divisions that comprised the Fifth Amphibious Corps departed for their ultimate destination, which had been kept a secret from them until their departure. They would be landing on a small, heavily defended volcanic island called Iwo Jima. The Marines were trained and ready. Emotions ran high, and the night before the invasion began all of the chaplains made themselves available to their Marines for last-minute spiritual needs. Gittelsohn was surprised to see so many young men come to see him, knowing that many were not Jewish. Later that night, he compared notes with a Christian chaplain and the two realized what the men were doing. Many were going to visit all of the chaplains of different faiths to "cover their bases." They would carry a variety of religious icons and items with them into combat: crosses and crucifixes provided by the Protestant and Catholic chaplains, mezuzot provided by Gittelsohn, and even pocket Bibles given to them by Gittelsohn and the Christian chaplains.

Since landing on the beaches of Iwo Jima on February 19, seventy thousand United States Marines were pitted in mortal combat against twenty-two thousand well-entrenched Japanese defenders who were under orders to fight to the death—and to each kill at least ten Americans before they died. On a daily basis, Gittelsohn and his fellow chaplains ministered to Marines in combat and comforted the dying. In addition, Gittelsohn was in charge of the Fifth Marine Division Cemetery. Each day, scores of young Marines killed in combat were brought to the cemetery for identification and burial. It was emotionally devastating work. The telegram that Gittelsohn had received from Herman's wife was like a ray of sunshine in an overcast, stormy day. To the young rabbi, it represented an affirmation of life over death.

Gittelsohn set out the next morning on his mission. Herman had been recently transferred to a new unit and proved difficult to locate. Gittelsohn spent the entire morning searching as the fighting raged on around him. It was nearly noon before the chaplain finally found his friend. Herman had just been brought to the Fifth Marine Division Cemetery. He had been killed that morning and, along with other new combat casualties, was awaiting burial.

He never knew that he had just become a father.

# UNLIKELY
# WARRIOR

Part I

# Pacifist

*And he shall judge among the nations, and shall rebuke many people: and they shall beat their swords into plowshares, and their spears into pruning hooks: nation shall not lift up sword against nation, neither shall they learn war any more.*
—Isaiah 2:3-4

*I will fight no more forever.*
—Chief Joseph of the Nez Perce

# Chapter One

# Origins

Roland Gittelsohn was only able to trace back his family heritage with any certainty to his grandparents. His grandfather, Rabbi Benjamin Gittelsohn, was born in Russia in 1852 or 1853. (The exact date is unknown.) A few weeks before he died, Rabbi Gittelsohn shared a fact with his son Reuben, Roland Gittelsohn's father. His research indicated that the family was descended from Isaiah Horowitz, a renowned sixteenth-century rabbi who lived in Poland. Rabbi Horowitz was known for his scholarship and, like most great rabbis of those times, was identified by the name of one of his books, which had made him famous. This major work was entitled *Sh'nay Luchot Habrit,* or *Two Tablets of the Covenant.* Horowitz's contemporaries took the first letter of the three-word title and created an abbreviated title: *Shelah.* When they referred to the author himself, they called him Shelah Ha-kodosh, or the Shelah. Reuben Gittelsohn would note of his ancestor, "From such titles you could see that he was considered a great and holy man."[1] This familial linkage was impossible to corroborate, but it remained a part of the Gittelsohn family tradition on his father's side.

In fact, research showed that the Gittelsohn family name extended back only as far as Benjamin. Reuben would recall that, like most European Jews of the era, Benjamin Gittelsohn's father probably didn't have a family name at all. The draft law that Tsar Nicholas I promulgated in 1827 that for the first time allowed male Russian Jews to serve in the army would lead to the creation of many family names in the Jewish community. Among the stipulations of the law was the requirement that all Jews must adopt family names. This bureaucratic requirement was likely enacted for record-keeping purposes.

While the permitting of Jews to serve in the army may, at first glance, seem to have been a new measure of social equality, it was in fact an effort to detach Jews from their own society and to force them to convert to Christianity. The law required all Jewish males between the ages of twelve and twenty-five to be drafted into the army and to serve for twenty-five years. One of the results of the law was a scramble among Jews to acquire created family names, for the draft law had a loophole that many families took advantage of.

According to the law, an only son was exempt from the draft. As such, in a family that had several sons, each one would adopt a different name and register as the only son of another family, real or factitious. [2] This was the method used by Benjamin Gittelsohn; his other two brothers had different family names: Kaplan and Cohen. Reuben would later write to his son Roland, "I spoke to A.D. about the history of the family tree and he is of the opinion that grandfather's original name was Kaplan. He agrees with me that father changed his name on account of the draft, as I said before. Why he assumed the name Gittelsohn, we don't know. It is funny that we never discussed the matter with him. At any rate, the consensus of opinion is that there are no other Gittelsohns in the family."[3]

Other Jews adopted different strategies to avoid being drafted. Some used their father's or mother's first name, in the form of Abramson, Isaacson, Jacobson, Gittelsohn, etc. Others chose to take the names of well-known cities, such as Berlin, Manheim, Hamburger, or Frankfurter, while another group opted for the names of certain birds or animals, or of professions or businesses that they were engaged in at the time. Examples of the latter category include such well-known names as Gold, Goldsmith, Goldstein, Goldman, Goldberg, etc.[4]

---

Benjamin Gittelsohn was born in the northwestern part of Russia, now Lithuania, in the area known as Samogitia—or as he referred to it in Yiddish, Zamet. The area was part of the Pale of Settlement, the only part of Russia where Jews could legally live. Established by Catherine the Great in 1791 as an area to where Jews could be exiled to rid cities like Moscow of Jewish business competition and to shield Russians from "evil" Jewish influences, the area was comprised of parts of present-day Latvia, Poland, Lithuania, Ukraine, and Belorussia.

When Benjamin was only eight years old, his father died; the young boy, who was the oldest child in his family, went out on his own. He traveled around the area, spending a few years in different Orthodox Jewish schools—*yeshivas*—and eventually ended up in the town of Slonim, in the Grodno province of Lithuania. It was in Slonim that he met Celia "Sippa" Alenik, who he married shortly after. The newlyweds settled in with Sippa's family, who supported the couple while Benjamin continued his Talmudic studies. This arrangement, known as *kest*, was a common practice of the times. During this time, Benjamin and Sippa began their own family and eventually had twelve children. After several years of schooling, Benjamin was confirmed as a rabbi and the Gittelsohn family moved on from Slonim.

In 1878, Benjamin and Sippa settled in the town of Avanta, located in the Kovno province of Lithuania. It was there that their son Reuben was born. After serving as the town's rabbi for several years, Benjamin relocated his family to another town in the Kovno Province, Trashkun, in 1883. The family would remain in Trashkun until they immigrated to the United States several years later. Their life in Trashkun was typical of the Jews in the Pale of Settlement. Grinding poverty and discrimination from other areas of Russian society were parts of the daily norm. In addition, a somber fact of life for Jews living in the Pale was the frequent instigation and approval of *pogroms*, or anti-Jewish riots, by the government.

Reuben Gittelsohn would carry memories of his youth in Trashkun with him for the rest of his life. In the frequent letters he would write to his son Roland and his daughter Natalie, he would vividly describe what their life was like, while contrasting it to the comparably wonderful life that they were living in the United States. "I want you to save these pictures and to note especially the reminiscences of my childhood days, in order to get acquainted with that kind of life. In later years,—and I hope it won't be too much later,—when you travel to Europe, don't forget to visit those small towns. The further away they are from a railroad station, the further away from civilization, the better; because it is there that you will find the real old-fashioned Jewish life, the kind of life that has been lived in the same rut for centuries."[5]

Each little village consisted of about two hundred houses. The houses would be built adjoining two major intersecting streets, and each featured a small fenced garden in the back where the owners would grow vegetables. Most of the houses were built of rough, rounded logs, "on the order of the log cabin where Abe Lincoln lived."[6] The ceilings were flat, wooden boards covered with straw. The difficult task of constructing the roof was accomplished by the *goyim*, non-Jews from neighboring villages. There might have been three or four windows in the Gittelsohn house, but Reuben would recall never seeing a clean one. Attempting to keep windows clean in that environment was an exercise in futility. In addition, the grime on the windows cut down on the brightness inside of the house and was easier on the residents' eyes.

Taking a large part of the floor space was the wood-burning brick oven. The oven served two purposes—both cooking as well as providing heat. Hence, there were piles of wood alongside the house all year round. The floors were bare dirt.

Benjamin Gittelsohn was one of two rabbis in Trashkun, head of the Misnagdim congregation. As such, he and his family lived in the synagogue building itself. The building was rectangular, and about one-sixth of the room on the left of the entrance corridor was partitioned off as the rabbi's family residence. An equal-sized room was partitioned off on the other side of the entrance corridor to serve as the *Beth Hamidrash*, or study hall, also used for daily services. The small residence that Reuben would jokingly refer to as their "mansion" was home to the rabbi, his wife, and their twelve children. In addition, on cold nights, the family's goat would be brought into the residence and slept next to the oven.

About one third of the rabbi's residence was partitioned off into a second room. This smaller room "served as my father's office, study, library, Beth-Din (rabbinical court), meeting place of the town nobles, reception room for out-of-town Rabbis who visited us occasionally and . . . my bedroom!" Reuben once wrote.[7] In this room, he would have access to all of his father's books in a library that was considered immense by the town's standards. In this library he would discover a book on Kabbalah and, much to his astonishment, a copy of the New Testament. This was unheard of in the Russian Jewish community; Roland Gittelsohn would later write about the incident when reflecting on his grandfather, stating, ". . . his incisive mind insisted that he could not defend Judaism, could not protect it against hostile invasion, unless he knew and understood the source of such invasion."[8]

Like all young boys in Trashkun, the whole focus of Reuben Gittelsohn's life was the study of Judaism. In numerous letters to his children, he would describe the stress of those days, although he would often look back with nostalgia on his childhood. He would attend school at the local *cheder*, or elementary Hebrew school. He and his friends would attend school at the cheder for up to ten hours a day, six days a week, for forty-eight weeks a year. There they would study Hebrew, Yiddish, and Aramaic. In addition, the curriculum contained study of the "Bible, Midrash, and the Talmud; rabbinical commentaries and codes; probably a smattering also of modern Hebrew literature. None of their education was secular, for intellectually and culturally the world was limited to Judaism and Jews. Russian government authority dictated it that way; the Jews of Trashkun acquiesced."[9]

Although he would grow up to become a man of science and medicine, it was during his childhood in Trashkun that Reuben developed his lifelong belief in the supernatural—a belief in ghosts and spirits. In several of his letters to his children he told of the ghosts from his days in Russia. Describing the dark dreariness of Trashkun in an early letter, he wrote, "However, the worst part of it was that our town was infested, yes, literally infested with hordes of spirits and ghosts and devils or, as we used to call them in Yiddish, *shaydim*. They used to roam around freely through our crooked streets and narrow alleys, making all kinds of weird noises to scare the life out of us poor kids."[10] Knowing the cynicism that this would elicit from Roland and Natalie as they read the letter, he went on to say, "I hear the doubting-Thomas sort of snickers from you, as much as to say: 'Do you really expect us to believe it?' Well, you can take my word for it. I really have seen it with my own eyes. I have seen it again and again on those dark, cold, wintry nights as I used to run home from the cheder."[11]

In a letter written nearly two years later, Reuben described an incident that might have been the genesis of his belief in ghosts. One night, Reuben spent the night in the synagogue with the *Shamos*, the assistant synagogue manager. One of the Shamos' duties during the beginning of the High Holiday season was to arise at 3 o'clock in the morning and awaken all the Jews in the village from their slumber to prepare to go to synagogue. The Shamos was afraid he'd fall asleep and not complete his task, so he invited young Reuben to spend the night in the synagogue with him to prevent this from happening. Reuben gladly accepted.

They each brought books to study, but soon tired of this and began to talk. The Shamos talked mainly about the dead and the ghosts that were all about in Trashkun. He explained to his young colleague that dead people don't stay in their graves all the time, particularly at night, when they come out to the synagogue and pray until dawn. "As to the ghosts (shaydim) they roam around in all the dark streets and alleys. They usually appear in the form of a large, black goat with a long beard and long, twisted horns, but sometimes they disguise themselves and appear as a black dog or an old woman dressed in black, standing in a dark corner and talking to herself incoherently.

"The Shamos lit his lantern, picked up his cane and went out into the dark night. Meanwhile, I—the only living, wide-awake person in the whole dark and slumbering world—was left alone in my room, with all the stories about maysim and shaydin dancing before me . . ."[12] Again, as if to ward off the skepticism of his children, he added, "You children, products of a modern, unbelieving world, who were born and educated in this country, may not believe these stories. But I am talking about 'facts': things that I have seen with my own eyes and heard with my own ears. . . . On such nights as I happened to lay awake on my bed near the wall that separated me from the synagogue, I could hear the dead people come in, one by one; I could hear them open the Ark, I could hear them pray in mournful, crying tones. I could hear their voices rise and fall, synchronous with the howling of the wind and the barking of the dogs, and on one or two occasions I could even discern the voices of somebody who had died a short time before and whose memory was still fresh in my mind."[13]

———•———

The first Jewish settler in Cleveland was Daniel Maduro Peixotto, a physician who joined the faculty of Willoughby Medical College in 1836. The next year, Simson Thorman, a hide trader from Unsleben, Bavaria, settled in the area. With the expanding economic opportunities being offered by the opening of the Ohio and Erie canals, nineteen residents of Unsleben departed for the United States aboard the SS *Howard*, and fifteen of them left New York City and settled in Cleveland. The group brought with them a message and a prayer written by their teacher Lazarus Kohn imploring them to remember their heritage and not to abandon their religion in their new country.[14] They brought with them a *Sefer Torah* (a hand-written Torah) and one of the men, Simson Hopferman, served as a *hazzan* (cantor) and *shohet* (a person trained to slaughter animals for food according to Jewish traditions).

By 1839, they had enough men to form a *minyan* and proceeded to establish the Israelitic Society. Within two years, internal bickering led to the formation of a second temple, Anshe Chesed. After reuniting briefly, the groups split again in 1850 and a new congregation was formed, Tifereth Israel. In addition, six communal organizations were formed before the Civil War. By the time of the war's outbreak, the Jewish population of Cleveland was approximately one thousand, with 78 percent of them from the German states (primarily Bavaria) and 19 percent from the Austrian empire (primarily Bohemia). During this first period of Jewish immigration to Cleveland, known as the German era (1837-1900), the immigrants were businessmen and shopkeepers who prospered in their adopted country. They embraced Reform Judaism as they attempted to minimize the difference between them and their Christian neighbors. During this first immigration period, Cleveland became the second-largest garment manufacturing area in the country behind New York City, with many firms making uniforms for the Civil War soldiers.[15]

This period contrasted with a second, overlapping immigration period known as the East European era that ran from 1870 to 1924. Compared to the earlier German era of Jewish immigration, the new arrivals were primarily from Russia, Poland, and Romania. Unlike the immigrants from the German era, immigrants of the East European era were generally East European Jews who were fleeing pogroms and dire poverty. They arrived in America to find that their German Jewish predecessors were often affluent and had more in common with their Protestant neighbors than with their newly arrived co-religionists. In Cleveland, the differences between the two groups embarrassed the German Jewish leadership and enraged the new immigrants.[16]

While the exact date of his arrival is unknown, it was during this period of religious turmoil in the Cleveland Jewish community that Benjamin Gittelsohn came to America. Different sources provide different dates for his arrival to Cleveland: The United States Federal Census Record of 1900 lists 1890 as the year that he arrived in the United States. That census record lists 1891 as the year that Sippa and the children, including Reuben, arrived in America. In subsequent census reports, the years of their arrival vary slightly from the 1900 report. Their home was listed as Cleveland Ward 16, Cuyahoga, Ohio.[17] Despite this discrepancy in dates, it is known positively that Benjamin Gittelsohn was a highly regarded Orthodox Jewish scholar and was asked to immigrate to Cleveland to become a leader in the Orthodox Jewish community.

There are also somewhat-conflicting records of the synagogues where Benjamin served as rabbi. Records of Congregation Oer Chodosh Anshe Sfard state that this Orthodox Jewish synagogue was founded in 1894 and "the founding rabbi was Benjamin Gittelsohn."[18] The Encyclopedia of Cleveland History records that in 1890 Gittelsohn was asked to settle in Cleveland by the growing community of Lithuanian Jews in the city; he became rabbi at Beth Hamidrosh Hagodol, serving that congregation until 1901. He then assumed the pulpit at Oer Chodosh Anshe Sfard and remained its rabbi until his death on January 7, 1932. He was ninety years old.[19] It is best stated that Rabbi Benjamin Gittelsohn's religious knowledge as Cleveland's first rabbinic scholar led him to become the spiritual authority for a number of other small congregations in Cleveland, such as Shaare Torah and Agudath Achim.[20]

Roland Gittelsohn would have very fond memories of his grandfather. Benjamin never learned to speak English, instead conversing only in Yiddish. Roland spoke English and had learned to speak Hebrew. His grandfather, however, would not communicate in Hebrew because for most Orthodox Jews of that era it was a tongue for sacred conversation with God, not for ordinary discourse with people. Despite this barrier, Benjamin would listen to his own grandchildren speak to him in Hebrew with undisguised pride. "But emotion often leaps the barriers of language. I remember the smell of Grandpa's beard when he kissed me . . .," recalled Roland. "Closing my eyes at this very moment, I still see the combination of regal dignity and paternal love on his face as he conducted the yearly Seder. My heart is tempted to beat wildly again today as I recall standing next to him on the pulpit of his synagogue for my Bar Mitzvah."[21]

Shortly after his arrival in the United States, Benjamin was quoted as saying, "Here too I found no ease or repose, nor did I have joy or pleasure, [but] thank God who brought me here, I have just a little bit . . ."[22] Roland would theorize that his grandfather's initial lack of joy may have been due to the fact he perceived that very little attention was given to his learned accomplishments.[23] This perception would soon be altered, because in Cleveland, Benjamin Gittelsohn's prominence as a scholar would soon be widely acknowledged. A distinguished writer, he published two renowned works of Hebrew scholarship after he immigrated to the United States. *Ha-Poteah ve-ha-Hotem* was a collection of Talmudic discourses, most of which he had delivered to his congregations, and *Seder Haggada shel Pesah 'im Be'ur Nagid ve-Nafik* was a detailed commentary on the Passover Haggadah. Despite his exalted status for his scholarship and his spiritual guidance, he remained a modest and grounded man. On multiple occasions he was urged by his followers and admirers to assume the title of chief rabbi in Cleveland. Each time, he refused. Titles meant little to him. He was happy to accept the authority earned by his courageous leadership and several brilliant books, but he wanted no other.[24]

Orthodox rabbis of that era were scholars, teachers, and judges; they rarely preached in synagogue. Rabbi Gittelsohn only preached about four times a year, but he was a very mesmerizing and powerful orator. Reuben Gittelsohn described the power of his father's sermons: "You have never seen or witnessed such a sight. Imagine a large group of men, old and young, breathing heavily, sobbing, with tears running down their cheeks into their beards; and the women upstairs crying so loud that one could hear them across the street. That was a sight never to be forgotten, and an art on my father's part that very few preachers could have equaled."[25]

Benjamin Gittelsohn had one fervent belief that set him apart from his fellow Orthodox rabbis. His arrival in America coincided with the beginnings of modern Zionism, and most of his peers strongly opposed the concept of a Jewish homeland being championed by Theodore Herzl. They believed that in His own good time, God would reconstitute the Jewish commonwealth through the agency of the Messiah. To "push the end" by human means was to be guilty of utmost arrogance.[26] While he believed in the Messiah, Gittelsohn believed that the partnership of God and man would be the means of fulfilling God's purpose for the Jewish people. Hence he became one of the first Orthodox rabbis to embrace wholeheartedly the concept of Zionism. Roland Gittelsohn proudly cited in his autobiography a note from a history of the Zionist movement that stated, "On October 20, 1897 Herzl was told that at a Zionist meeting in Cleveland, where Rabbi [Benjamin] Gittelsohn and S. Rocker spoke, many members were signed up."[27]

————•————

Like his father, the exact date of Reuben Gittelsohn's birth is unknown. The 1900 census report lists his date of birth as "August, 1876." His draft card, issued during World War I, lists his birthday as August 15, 1878. Roland Gittelsohn was only able to estimate that his father was about eighteen or nineteen years old when he came to America. Even the date of his emigration from Russia is a source of conflict. The 1900 census reports his arrival to America as taking place in 1891, whereas the 1910 and 1930 census reports state he arrived in 1893. Arriving in Cleveland as a shy teenager who spoke no English proved to be very difficult for young Reuben.

The years of living in extreme poverty with constant threats of pogroms and discrimination no doubt took a toll on the development of his personality. His shyness and lack of assertiveness, coupled with his small physical stature, served to greatly diminish his self-confidence. Writing to his son, he lamented his lack of a proper public school education, stating, "Had I had that chance, I would perhaps be a different man now. I would perhaps have followed a different vocation. Not that I would have been more of a success than I am, because to be truly successful one must have those all-important qualities, 'push and pull,' born into him; and I am rather lacking in them."[28]

Reuben went on to profess his admiration for people who could stand up in front of an audience and inspire them to noble causes. "This is where my inferiority complex comes in: I know my shortcomings. I could never be a leader because I wasn't born to be one. I could never be a shepherd because I wasn't trained to be one. I was born to be a poor sheep, a member of a large flock, a follower, that's all."[29] Although he would go on to a successful career in medicine, he would always regret that he didn't have the personality or the oratorical skills to become a rabbi. He would be absolutely delighted when his son made the decision to pursue the rabbinate and, to a degree, lived vicariously through him in that regard.

Determined to build a new life for himself while, at the same time, proudly maintaining his Jewish heritage, Reuben went to work in a cigar-making factory in Cleveland. Knowing the critical importance of language skills, he was determined to learn English. Accordingly, he attended night school for a year and supplemented his studies with private lessons in English twice a week for at least a summer.[30] All the while, the only language spoken in the Gittelsohn household was Yiddish. He would admit to his children that he was always self-conscious that he had not attended a liberal arts college where could have obtained the skills he so desired in language, writing, and literature. As he would note with a mixture of regret and pride, "I acquired all my preliminary education through my own plugging."[31]

Reuben would eventually become the only one of the twelve Gittelsohn children to become a professional. Realizing that he had neither the personality nor the oratorical skills to become a rabbi, he set his sights on a career in medicine. At the time, the requirement to enter medical school was either to have obtained a high school diploma or the ability to pass a rigorous official entrance examination that covered certain high school subjects. Reuben arranged with Professor John White, principal of Central High School on East 55th Street, to take the examination. There was only one problem—the exam was scheduled to be given on Yom Kippur, the holiest day of the year.

It would be scandalous for the son of the Orthodox synagogue's rabbi to not be in the synagogue all day on Yom Kippur. Somehow, Reuben managed to leave the service without attracting his father's attention; or, as Roland would explain, "perhaps Grandpa noticed this as he did so many things of which he pretended to be oblivious."[32] Reuben got away to Central High School, took his examinations, and returned to resume his worship several hours later.

At Central High School, the first test that Reuben had to complete was a lengthy essay chosen from any topic on a list that was given to all of the prospective medical students. He selected "Why I Want to Study Medicine." He was pleasantly surprised that he did quite well, receiving a compliment from Dr. White that his "composition was excellent."[33] While recalling this moment of achievement to his grandchildren, Reuben again bemoaned his lack of a better education, stating, "I deplored the fact that I didn't have the opportunity of getting a proper preliminary education, in which case I might have selected a different profession altogether, with somewhat greater success."[34]

Reuben did well enough on his entrance exams to be accepted into Ohio Wesleyan University's Cleveland College of Physicians class of 1905. His junior year class roster lists his birthplace, along with that of two other students, as "Russia." To afford the tuition for his studies, he continued to work at the cigar factory until he graduated. He became a general practitioner, making frequent house calls and serving his community with devotion. Reuben would continue to practice into his eighties. Roland would recall the type of physician his father was thusly: "He never failed them. Nor any of his patients. A general practitioner, he made house calls at the most ungodly hours, responding from his badly needed sleep to those who hadn't paid their bills, even to those whom he knew to be hypochondriacs. His purpose in life was to help people, not to tell them from some lofty perch that they didn't really need help."[35]

Despite his important and satisfying medical practice, Reuben's heart never drifted far from his probable first career choice: to become a rabbi. He never stopped studying Judaism and was a voracious reader in English, Yiddish, and Hebrew. He began every day the same: after breakfast he would read six or more chapters from the Hebrew Bible. His self-imposed schedule called for completion of the entire biblical text once each year.[36] This routine continued into his later years, and his joy of reading the Bible never diminished. Roland would recall visiting him when he was living in a nursing home towards the end of his life. Invariably he would pick up his Hebrew Bible, read Roland a few verses and say: "You know, Roland, I must have read these words a thousand times, but when I encountered them yesterday a new interpretation came to me."[37]

Roland would inherit other passions from his father in addition to his love of Judaism. One was his passion for the underdog, for the equality of all men. After Reuben's medical practice began to flourish, he took his first trip to Washington, DC. He had developed a great love and sense of patriotism for America, his adopted country, which had given him the opportunities he could only dream of as a boy back in Russia. On the first day of his visit to the nation's capital, he took his first trolley ride and made an unknowingly innocent mistake that would have a profound effect on him. He took a seat in the back of the trolley car.

As he sat, looking out the window, he was approached by the conductor. He was informed that he was sitting in the rear of the trolley car where only blacks were supposed to sit. He was invited to move up to the front section that was, of course, restricted to white trolley riders. Reuben was stunned—this was his first experience with discrimination against another minority. It surely must have immediately recalled to him the years of discrimination and maltreatment that he had experienced during his childhood in Russia. He did not move to the front of the car. Rather, he got off the car entirely. For the remainder of his visit to Washington, he would walk to his destinations rather than ride the streetcar. Roland inherited this sense of outrage against discrimination toward all minority groups, especially black Americans. His outspokenness on this issue would cause much turmoil in the later years of his life, but Roland would never retreat from the controversy or tone down his strong feelings on the subject.

Another topic that Reuben was passionate about was Zionism. As Roland would recall, "My sister and I were weaned on Zionism. *Palestine* was a sacred word in our household. Dad read or told us stories about the destruction of the Temple in Jerusalem—how the birds carried the burning embers in their effort to quench the conflagration, how the priests threw the Temple keys heavenward as they apologized to God for having failed to protect the Holy Place, returning the responsibility to Him."[38]

Reuben truly saw Zionism as the ultimate culmination of Jewish nationalism.[39] In Roland's first year as a rabbinical student, Reuben charged his son "to spread the holy gospel of Jewish nationalism." Writing to Roland in 1931 on the eve of *Tisha B'Av*, the holiday that commemorates the destruction of the ancient Temples of Jerusalem, Reuben wrote, "We never forgot Jerusalem. We always remembered Palestine. And now, after the long night of exile, we of the present generation have the greatest privilege of witnessing the beginning of the fulfillment of our sweet dream."[40] Roland would recall in his autobiography that next to the birth of his children, May 15, 1948—the day that the State of Israel was proclaimed a nation—was the most glorious day of his father's life.[41] The desire for an independent Jewish state was a dream shared by the three generations of Gittelsohn men—from the poverty-stricken, Russian-born rabbi; to his son, the struggling immigrant who became a doctor; to his grandson, a scholarly, outspoken, and prominent rabbi. The dream became a reality in 1948.

In later years, Roland Gittelsohn would recall his mother, Anna Manheim Gittelsohn, as a unique and somewhat troubled woman. Like Reuben, she was born in Russia around 1887. (The exact date is uncertain.) Her family immigrated to the United States when she was only six months old and, in a very unusual move for Jewish immigrants of that era, settled in Montana. Her father became a merchant in both Washington and Montana.

Anna's childhood was unique. The Manheim family household kept kosher, which was not an easy thing to do in Missoula, Montana, a city that had only seven Jewish families. Anna had an Orthodox Jewish upbringing. Years later, she shared with Roland how lonely and insecure she was as a child. There was no Jewish community in Missoula, and Jews were largely ostracized from society.[42] She was so desperate in her need for companionship and acceptance that at one point—with no perception at all of its theological significance—she secretly joined the Salvation Army. As Roland recalled, "When her parents discovered what she had done, their punishment must have painfully reinforced her innate sense of loneliness and alienation."[43]

In 1905, Anna traveled to Cleveland to visit a cousin. It was there that she met a scholarly, shy medical student named Reuben Gittelsohn. It was pretty much a case of love at first sight. Reuben and Anna got engaged several months later and were married in Cleveland on March 27, 1906. His age was listed on the marriage certificate as twenty-eight, hers as nineteen. Rabbi Benjamin Gittelsohn performed the wedding ceremony. Interestingly, on Cuyahoga County wedding license application 46063 dated March 24, the bride-to-be's name was listed as "Emma E. Manheim." On the wedding certificate portion at the bottom of the application confirming the wedding on March 27, it lists the bride's name as Anna E. Gittelsohn. All other census documents in existence list her name as Anna.

Being married to a dedicated young physician who was busy making house calls at all hours and was frequently missing meals at home soon proved to be stressful for the young bride. Roland would describe her as an emotionally frail person who was quite incapable of carrying the full responsibilities of marriage and family. It was not long after she and Reuben were married that she suffered the first of a series of mysterious "breakdowns" and went off to live for a few weeks with her married sister in nearby Canton, Ohio. Observing these episodes throughout his youth would, in a sad sense, prepare Roland for the trials and tribulations that a rabbi must deal with in his role as a counselor and mentor to his congregants. It was also a harbinger of things to come in his own married life.

Reuben would find it difficult to deal with his wife's breakdowns, vacillating "between tender patience and peevish irritation. Depending on the season, he would brood silently in the living room easy chair or on the porch swing." Seeing a glimpse of the positive in his father's marital stress, Roland noted, "I suspect that his problems at home probably made him more sensitive to the emotional ills of his patients, more ready to empathize with their families."[44]

Anna Gittelsohn did have many positive influences on her husband's life, in spite of her emotional instability. Having come to her adopted country as a baby, she was certainly more "Americanized" than her husband. Roland would note that his father was the most urbane and Americanized of all of the twelve Gittelsohn siblings, and he attributed this fact largely to his mother's influence. It was Anna who insisted that their children be allowed to go to summer camp and that they be exposed to many cultural opportunities, such as piano lessons.

Perhaps her greatest influence on Reuben was her religious sway. Both Reuben and Anna were raised as Orthodox Jews. However, having grown up in Montana, Anna had no sense of Orthodox community roots. Despite his Orthodox upbringing, Reuben was now an American and was taking advantage of all that his new country was able to offer him. He remained a devout Jew

until the day he died, but he was no longer in the *shtetl* in Russia—
he was in Cleveland, Ohio, an up-and-coming American physician.
Roland felt that his father was ready to depart from Orthodoxy
on his own, but clearly his mother accentuated his religious
restlessness.[45] It was Anna who encouraged him to join a Reform
synagogue and to send their children to a Reform religious school.

Roland would look back on the type of parents that Reuben
and Anna were to him and his sister, Natalie. He was much more
reflective on his father. Despite his obvious love and admiration
for Reuben, he noted that he was not a perfect parent. Both Roland
and his sister bitterly resented the times when family plans were
aborted at the last minute due to medical emergencies that Reuben
got called away for. "Many times I wished he had been interested
in baseball, as my friend's fathers were," Roland wrote.[46] One of
the joys of his childhood was time spent accompanying Reuben
on his house calls, "relishing his company and conversation as we
drove from house to house, reading in the car while he attended to
a patient."[47]

One area that Roland found his father lacking in was that of sex
education. In his autobiography, he specifically mentioned that
Reuben provided no parental guidance to him when he was an
adolescent. At Anna's insistence, he simply gave Roland several
pamphlets on sex to read while he waited in the car for him to
finish his house calls. When he returned, he asked if his son had
any questions. That was the sum total of information on sex that Dr.
Reuben Gittelsohn provided to his young son.

In his autobiography, Roland would ponder if his father lived
a happy life. His thoughtful analysis attempted to answer that
difficult question. "Through placidity and peace, no. Through
the achievement of either psychological or financial security,
no. Through his children and grandchildren, yes. . . . Above all,
through the satisfaction of knowing that he as an individual had
substantially served purposes larger than himself, yes, in that
respect too, my father was happy."[48]

Roland's recollections of his mother were much more limited
and restrained. As mentioned, she had some positive influences on
Reuben and was a dedicated homemaker to the Gittelsohn family.
However, Roland would summarize his feelings thusly: "Mother
did her best. At times she succeeded, but mostly failed."[49]

# Chapter Two

# Gifted Student

On Friday, May 13, 1910, Anna Gittelsohn gave birth to their first child. Their new son arrived prematurely; they named him Roland Bertram Gittelsohn. As is Jewish tradition, he was given a Hebrew name to keep alive a deceased relative's name, in this case his maternal grandmother.

Interestingly, Roland Gittelsohn would claim to have "very few memories of early childhood, almost none."[1] Most significantly, what childhood memories he did harbor centered on humiliation and failure. He was in many ways like his father. Small in stature and abnormally thin, he felt himself to be a very homely child. But unlike Reuben, Roland was a native-born American and was a very eloquent individual. He differed from his father in another significant way—he was an outspoken boy who grew up to be an outspoken adult. Never afraid to speak his mind, Roland would become the leader that his father never could dream of becoming. Like both his father and grandfather, he also became a first-rate scholar with a brilliant, analytical mind.

After a lifetime of counseling congregants and serving numerous organizations as a compassionate clergyman, he would reflect back on his childhood and realize that his selective recall of only episodes of failure or humiliation bespoke a great deal of his youthful insecurity.[2] He was very conscious of his perceived shortcomings. Young Roland was a clumsy boy with very little athletic prowess. When he was eleven years old, he had an appendectomy. In high school, he would still use the appendectomy as an excuse to get out of gym activities that he despised. So great was his insecurity that when he would telephone a girl for a date, he would prepare in advance an outline of proposed conversation, lest there be an embarrassing silence. If a girl should turn down his invitation, he would "suffer a severe sense of rejection."[3]

In his youth and early in his professional career, Roland suffered from many recurrent dreams involving stressful, embarrassing situations. In a typical dream, he would be standing at the pulpit getting ready to deliver a sermon—and then realize he forgot his notes. A variant would be him attending a convention and being unable to find which room an important meeting was supposed to take place in.[4] Any psychologist would note that dreams such as these are fairly typical for driven, intellectual achievers and that, with the passage of years, Roland would come to realize these dreams and his accompanying insecurities were not unusual; Roland's dreams could be pinned to the nature of adolescence. These experiences would also add considerably to his personal skills in dealing with young people when he became a rabbi. He once noted, "Openly sharing with them in retrospect my own adolescent turbulence has probably helped more of them than any other technique I might have used."[5]

At an early age, Roland demonstrated the verbal prowess and outspoken nature that he would become known for. When he was fourteen years old, he was attending the Hebrew School at Euclid Avenue Temple, a Reform synagogue. As always, he was a superb student with a flawless attendance record, and his behavior was exemplary. Yet he was nearly thrown out of his confirmation class: "Because then, as now, I was given to vehement argumentation. Alone among my fellow students, I disputed Rabbi Louis Wolsey's views on Zionism."[6] Displaying the typical attitude of Reform rabbis of the time, Rabbi Wolsey was opposed to Zionism. He was quite taken aback when his ninth-grade star student—the son of a prominent member of the synagogue who was a respected physician in the community and, likely unbeknownst to Rabbi Wolsey, the only avowed Zionist in the congregation—proceeded to debate him in front of the class. This was possibly the first public exhibition of Roland Gittelsohn's considerable debating skills, a talent for which he would become very well known.

It is not known whether it was his academic excellence or his outspoken nature that first attracted the attention of one of his classmates. She was a shy girl who also did well in school. In addition, she had an artistic nature that attracted young Roland. Her name was Ruth Freyer, and they would become sweethearts during the rest of their school years. Graduating in the same confirmation class, they were destined to go to the same university, where their futures would be ultimately entwined.

Roland's childhood stood in marked contrast to both his father's and grandfather's. He would never experience the grinding poverty of Russia as they had. He was supported by a very strong, loving family unit that was increased on August 13, 1914, with the birth of his sister, Natalie. He was very close to his parents and grandparents, who encouraged his academic pursuits and his interest in the rabbinate. His father was a busy physician; and although the obligations of the medical profession frequently had an intrusive effect on the family, Reuben was apparently a financially successful general practitioner. (The 1920 federal census report lists nineteen-year-old Eva Curni from Hungary as living at the Gittelsohn household as their servant.)

Youthful insecurities aside, Roland Gittelsohn had many strengths that he was blessed with and utilized them to the utmost. While dealing with his youthful angst, he was balancing these youthful tribulations with the God-given talents that he possessed. He was a superb student and his intellectual prowess made it possible for him to skip an entire year of elementary school. To a degree, this laudable achievement further fueled his insecurity. From that point on, he was a year younger than his classmates, which all the more accentuated their differences in physical size and athletic prowess. "I would have given almost anything," he later wrote, "to exchange my talents for those of the school's most acclaimed athletic star, who quite probably felt as inadequate in my arena as I did in his."[7]

At Cleveland Heights High School, Roland was elected to the National Honor Society. The skinny, homely boy obviously made quite a positive impression on his high school classmates because they elected Roland president of the senior class. In addition, he was captain of the debate team and was winner of a statewide extemporaneous speaking contest. "Looking back," he would recall, "it all seems silly. In terms of long-range values, the areas in which I was clearly superior far outweighed those in which I was lacking."[8]

Beginning in his junior year of high school, debating became a major part of Roland's life. At Cleveland Heights, he was coached in speech and debate by Clarence P. Drury who himself was a former intercollegiate debater at Bates College. Drury was a disciple

*Roland Gittelsohn, age 13, with his mother, Anna, and sister, Natalie* (Courtesy David Gittelsohn and Judy Gittelsohn Fales)

of Professor Howard Woodward, who was a leader in the field of speech and the former president of the National Association of Teachers of Speech.[9] Professor Woodward would become Roland's debate coach in college. Both coaches stressed the importance of evidence and logic, and neither allowed their debaters to write out their speeches for memorization.[10] Roland would recall: "We were forced to think on our feet, to scrap what we had prepared, if necessary, in order immediately to counter an opponent's argument."[11]

Roland would look back years later and realize that, although he had a passion for debating and loved the intellectual challenge it always presented to him, it probably had a negative effect on his personality development. Debate encouraged him to see issues as absolutes—as black and white, as right and wrong, or true and false. A debater either won or lost the argument; compromise indicated defeat. As he began to realize that this worldview was flawed, he "had to discipline [himself] severely to recognize that in most controversies neither extreme view is wholly correct, that an aspect of truth inheres in each."[12]

Roland would also perceive a second disadvantage that resulted from his debate training: he came to depend too exclusively on reason and logic and too little on emotions. Always considering himself a rationalist, he viewed emotion without the control of reason as "a terrible danger." On the other hand, he felt that reason without emotion was too sterile. In his future counseling work, he became fond of saying that the longest distance in the universe is that which separates the heart from the mind. "In the human search for God, too, reason and fact, while indispensable, are by themselves not enough. To experience human life in its fullest dimension, we must think and feel together."[13]

———————

After graduating from high school in 1927, Roland began his college studies at Western Reserve University, which traced its roots to Western Reserve College, a small school founded several miles from Cleveland in 1827. It was the first institution of higher learning in northern Ohio. (In 1882, the school moved to Cleveland and changed its name. In 1967, the school would merge with the

Case Institute of Technology to become Case Western Reserve University.)

Roland Gittelsohn continued to excel in his academic studies in college. As he did in high school, he joined the debate team and soon became its captain. At Western Reserve, Professor Howard Woodward continued to hone his student's debating skills. Roland would be acknowledged for his debating skills at graduation with a Delta Sigma Rho key for forensic excellence.

While at Western Reserve, Roland earned tuition money mainly by giving private Hebrew lessons. By all accounts, he thrived in college, excelling in virtually everything he attempted. By the end of his third year, he had all but officially decided on his life's work. When Roland was a teenager, his father once asked him if he would ever consider becoming a physician. The son's answer was an emphatic "no!" At the time, he was unsure of his career plans, but he informed Reuben, "I'll tell you one thing for sure: it's going to be an occupation where my time will be my own, not like your life!"[14] His career choice was not what he had originally planned on. When he was younger, Roland imagined he would become a lawyer. Given his eloquence and debating skills, this is not surprising. However, he was interested in becoming a crusading attorney along the lines of one of his heroes, Clarence Darrow; much to his chagrin, Roland learned that in reality most lawyers sat at their desks for hours busied with dull paperwork.[15] This was not the life he envisioned for himself. Ironically, he ultimately decided on a career that would cut into his time probably as much as his father's work did.

He did not choose to join the rabbinate to please his father and grandfather, although they were delighted with his career choice. In addition, there was nothing explicitly theological about his decision to become a rabbi. "I received no 'divine call'; neither, so far as I knew, did any of my classmates. We would have laughed uproariously had any of them made such a claim."[16] To Roland, Judaism's uniqueness accounted for his decision to join the rabbinate. "We constitute a religion, yes; but not a religion, period. Strands of ethnicity and culture, of peoplehood and nationality, are woven—together with those of religion—into the total fabric of Judaism. To pull out one color or thread would unravel the entire tapestry."[17] His love of God, his love of Judaism, and his love of people, coupled with the desire to help his fellow man, all factored into his career decision. It is not surprising, then, to learn that when he was asked at his first interview for admission to the Hebrew Union College why he wanted to become a rabbi, he replied that he loved the Jewish people and felt that becoming a rabbi was the most constructive way he could serve them.[18]

As he began his senior year, word began to spread in Cleveland's Jewish community that Rabbi Benjamin Gittelsohn's grandson would be following in his footsteps and would enter rabbinical school. Reuben Gittelsohn was absolutely delighted with his son's decision and the realization that he would then be able to live out his repressed desire to become a rabbi vicariously through Roland. However, Rabbi Gittelsohn's Orthodox congregation was very upset when they learned Roland's plans. Roland would be enrolling at the country's major school for educating *Reform* rabbis—the Hebrew Union College in Cincinnati. Certainly, they felt, as the pillar of the Orthodox community Benjamin Gittelsohn must also be outraged that his grandson was planning on entering what they called "the rabbi factory."[19] They demanded to know what their leader intended to do about it.

Benjamin had total faith and trust in his grandson's decision to attend Hebrew Union College. As recreated by Roland, he replied to his scandalized congregants thusly: "Orthodox Judaism is the only kind possible for you and for me. Knowing, however, my grandson's home background and education, if he were to tell me he planned to become an Orthodox rabbi, I would suspect him of hypocrisy. I want him to become the kind of rabbi he can honestly be."[20]

In the spring of 1931, Roland Gittelsohn graduated with honors with a bachelor of arts degree from Western Reserve University. In recognition of his academic achievements, he was elected to Phi Beta Kappa. That fall, he began five years of graduate study at Hebrew Union College in Cincinnati.

Throwing himself into his studies, young Roland continued to excel academically. After he wrote to his parents that he successfully completed his first set of examinations, Reuben wrote back to Roland expressing both pride and lack of surprise in his son's accomplishment. In his letter, Reuben also expressed his future expectations for his son:

I hear Dr. Morgenstern told you that you came highly recommended and that he expects a lot from you. Well, son, to us you came highly recommended twenty-one years ago, and we also expect a lot from you. Only our expectations embrace a much wider field than those of Dr. M. Whereas he expects you to become a successful rabbi, we expect you, in addition to all that, to also be a good man and a good Jew. Our people need you, son. Our people need new blood, the kind of blood that flows through your veins and in the veins of your colleagues at H.C.C. I hope that the small group of intelligent young men with whom you will live for the next four or five years will blossom forth into a group of Jewish leaders who will exert all their energies to reawaken the Jewish self-consciousness, and who will go out into the world with a strong determination to spread the holy gospel of Jewish nationalism.[21]

Expressing joy over his son's chosen field for his life's work as well as admiration and perhaps a bit of vicarious projection, Reuben felt that he and Anna had been successful in instilling into their children a love for everything Jewish. "If that should happen to be my only achievement during my short stay on this planet, I shall be satisfied," he wrote.[22]

—————•—————

World War I was supposed to be the "war to end all wars." In the United States, it was said that the country entered the war "to make the world safe for democracy." When the armistice was signed in November of 1918, it quickly became apparent that the world was in many ways worse off than before 1914. The price worldwide in blood and treasure was enormous. Over sixteen million people were killed and nearly twenty-two million people were wounded. The economy of Europe was wrecked, and Russia descended into a civil war that ended with the Bolsheviks taking control of the government. Worldwide, many people looked back with bitterness over what was perceived as the futility of the entire war and the futility of war in general. Many came to the conclusion that there must never be another war, that there had to be a rational alternative to resolving nation's disputes.

While not new, the concept of pacifism started to take hold around the world, including in the United States. In 1923, the War

Resisters League was founded in New York City by Jessie Wallace Hughan, an educator, socialist activist, and radical pacifist. The War Resisters League was an offshoot of the London-based War Resisters International. The organization's core principles were opposition to the military and total opposition to war. It preached a radical brand of pacifism condemning all forms of violence, and activism in renouncing war as a means of resolving international disputes. Their strident message of active resistance to war started to make an impression on a young teenager in Cleveland, Ohio, by the name of Roland Gittelsohn.

Gittelsohn would write, "Through my years of high school, college, graduate study and even into the initial stage of my professional life, absolute pacifism was one of my most cherished — and I thought inviolate—ideals."[23] Granted, he was small in stature, and he was able to fight with words, but Roland truly believed that pacifism represented one of Judaism's highest ideals. He quoted Zechariah: "Not by might, nor by power, but by My spirit- said the Lord of Hosts!"[24]

Born shortly before the Great War had begun, "[Roland] was too young during World War I to sense much of what was going on." Still, the conflict left a lasting impression:

> I do remember the fascination and pride with which I listened later to my two closest uncles telling of their experiences in the army and navy. The fascination, the pride . . . and the fear. What would I do if ever I had to be a soldier or sailor? This dread was reinforced a few years afterward when I was repulsed by gory photographs of battlefield atrocities. In any event, for whichever reasons, war became for me the ultimate immorality, to be shunned at all cost.[25]

Several leaders in the world pacifist movement would have a great effect on young Roland. One of them was the famous physicist Albert Einstein. Living in Berlin when the war broke out in 1914, Einstein was shocked by the development. "Europe in her insanity has started something unbelievable," he wrote. "In such times one realizes to what a sad species of animal one belongs."[26] He helped draft an anti-war statement, "Manifesto to Europeans," that condemned the war, arguing that "national passions cannot excuse this attitude which is unworthy of what the world has heretofore called culture."[27] Einstein would continue with his anti-war, anti-military message throughout the 1920s and the 1930s. In 1930, he immigrated to the United States.

Later that year, Einstein was invited to address a meeting of the New History Society, an offshoot of the pacifist Baha'i religious movement. On December 14, he delivered a speech that has come to be known as the "Two Percent Speech." In it, he suggested the means to end future wars "is uncompromising war resistance, refusal to do military service under any circumstances." Einstein went on to make a key point: "For the timid who say, 'What's the use? We might be shut up in prison,' I add: even if only two percent of those supposed to perform military service should declare themselves war resisters and assert, 'We are not going to fight. We need other methods of settling international disputes,' the government would be powerless—they could not put such masses into jail."[28] These words would resonate with young Roland. For years he would wear a "2 percent pin with pride, almost defiantly."[29] In addition, he became a member of the War Resisters League.

Another great influence on Roland Gittelsohn's pacifist beliefs was Rev. Harry Emerson Fosdick. Fosdick was a Baptist minister who in earlier years had been a staunch supporter of America's entry into World War I. Speaking in pulpits around the country, he exclaimed, "Sad is our lot if we have forgotten how to die for a holy cause!"[30] Later on, after the United States entered the war, he toured the trenches in Europe and observed firsthand the horrors of the war. Within a short time he became increasingly disappointed in war's inability to unite the world.

By 1921, Fosdick had started to change his views. Ruefully he concluded, "We cannot reconcile Christianity with war any more [sic]."[31] By 1923, he had completely embraced a commitment to peace. Preaching at the interdenominational Riverside Church in New York City on November 12, 1933, he delivered a sermon entitled "Apology to the Unknown Soldier." In it, he articulated his pacifist position, which had been evolving since the end of World War I. With the passion of a true believer, he concluded his sermon by saying, "I renounce war and never again, directly or indirectly, will I sanction or support another!"[32]

Roland Gittelsohn would find much inspiration in the words of Harry Emerson Fosdick. In his future sermons and writings, he would reference and cite Fosdick's example of active pacifism. Fosdick's opposition to a military draft and to allowing ROTC units on college campuses—as well as his belief in disarmament, even if unilateral—were perfectly in consonance with his own evolving beliefs. He also shared Fosdick's vision, which eschewed isolationism and advocated a spirit of international cooperation. The views of Fosdick, Einstein, and other peace advocates were shaping the pacifist beliefs of young Gittelsohn. By the early 1930s, he "was a pacifist. Not just a peace-lover who misunderstood or misused the word, but a complete pacifist,—a complete, convinced, literal, unreasonable, dogmatic, unchangeable pacifist! If there was one 'absolute' in my personal credo, it was the 'absolute' of pacifism."[33] He would also state, "I read Harry Emerson Fosdick's magnificent 'Apology to the Unknown Soldier' regularly from my pulpit, and felt as if Dr. Fosdick had written it especially for me."[34]

# Chapter Three

# War No More

Roland Gittelsohn was a product of his times, but his early embracing of the causes of social justice and pacifism marked him as precocious in comparison to his age/peer group. Throughout the 1920s and into the early 1930s, the student bodies on virtually every college campus in the United States were on the whole both conservative and apolitical. The major issues that concerned students were football, fraternities, and parties. Up to and during the first two years of the Great Depression, most college students were middle to upper class and were shielded from the effects of the depression. This all began to change in 1931, and the change began in New York City.

The birthplace of student activism was the City College of New York (CCNY). In the fall of 1931, the New York Student League, soon to be called the National Student League (NSL), was founded at CCNY, and one of the first scathing editorials to be featured in its newsletter, *Frontiers,* was a call to ban ROTC from the campus. University president Frederick C. Robinson responded by attempting to confiscate all copies of the journal and then suspending ten of the members of the NSL. The NSL proceeded to organize a city-wide protest over the attempt at censorship, forcing Robinson to yield to public opinion and back down. In addition, all of the suspended students were reinstated.[1]

The NSL held its first convention in March of 1932, and twenty-five colleges, all of them from the east coast, sent delegates. The League quickly attracted members from other New York City schools, as well as from schools in the Deep South. Drawn to the NSL were members of the Young Communist League who were attracted to its overall agenda of social justice and pacifism, and many of them assumed leadership positions in the various chapters. The YCL "factions" became highly influential in the NSL. Prominent in the NSL national plank was the praising of the Soviet Union and the calling for emulation of the Soviet Union as an example of an "inspiration and guide to us in other parts of the world who are witnessing the social and economic evils which accompany Capitalism."[2] As a communist-influenced organization, the NSL was unusual in that its birth was not dictated from above—by the Communist Party or by national Young Communist League leaders. Rather, it evolved from below, out of the agitation of communist rank and filers and communist sympathizers in the wake of the CCNY free speech fight.[3] The NSL, especially the YCL factions, were initially opposed to any dealings with the rival League for Industrial Democracy (LID).

The LID was founded in 1905 and was a socialist movement, embodied by the leadership of its founder, muck-wracking journalist Upton Sinclair. By the 1920s, the LID had become somewhat moribund, despite the leadership of national figures such as Norman Thomas, who would run for the presidency in 1932 as the Socialist Party candidate. Their movement initially had no student involvement. Rather, their philosophy was that of educating the young students, resulting in an almost paternal relationship where the students were expected to learn from their teachers and then go on to become educators themselves, spreading the gospel of socialism. The LID quickly realized that their relevance was being supplanted by the burgeoning student movement created by the NSL.

By the spring of 1932, students on many campuses shook off their apathy and became involved in social causes. This involvement was exemplified by the Columbia University students who traveled to Harlan County, Kentucky, twice that spring to show support for the striking coal miners. The students were harassed and beaten by Kentucky law officials and, while they were unable to provide any real aid to the striking miners, the national news coverage of the brutal treatment of the students struck a chord with many readers nationwide.

Realizing the great unifying potential of the anti-war issue, the student activists in both the NSL and the LID joined forces in December of 1932. Meeting in Chicago, they convened the Student Congress Against War. It was the largest national meeting of student activists since the beginning of the Great Depression: it attracted 680 delegates from eighty-nine colleges and universities in thirty states.[4] The inspiration for the meeting came from overseas. In August of 1932, the NSL sent a delegate to Amsterdam to attend the communist-sponsored World Congress Against War. Leaders of the American delegation, such as novelist Sherwood Anderson, were so impressed that they contacted the NSL, asking it to organize a similar conference in the United States directed at the student movement.

The meeting of the Student Congress Against War did not go smoothly. The communist factions of the NSL, already wary of the socialists of the LID, felt that the NSL was too accommodating to the socialists. The communist leadership was very vocal in its criticism of both the socialists and the NSL members whom they felt were too compliant. In the end, the NSL's official account of the Congress boasted that the meeting had established a "basis of united action of all students and groups represented at the Congress." The account also mentioned that the socialists and the LID were part of this united front.[5]

A crucial schism developed at the Congress that would go far in defining pacifist core values in the coming years in a way that none of the delegates, including those of young rabbinical student Roland Gittelsohn, could have anticipated. The conflict was not between the socialist and communist delegates but between the leftist and pacifist delegates.[6] The pacifists had embraced the anti-war movement largely because of their religious principles; they opposed all forms of war and violence. The leftist delegates, while opposing war in general, had no problem with class warfare and anti-colonial wars. This schism produced intense and heated debate and was never truly reconciled. In the end, the pacifists issued a minority report stating, "We believe that war is not right, even if used in trying to reach a worthy goal."[7]

Despite the frequent and stormy disagreements, the Congress was a success, and a unified program was issued as a result of the debate. The opposition to an American military buildup and opposition to the interventionist policies that culminated in the First World War were key position points. The Congress also called for a nationwide campaign on college campuses to promote anti-war meetings and regular college peace meetings, as well as for the abolition of ROTC units. The goals of the Student Congress Against

War were about to get a major boost in the United States as a result of a debate that was held two months later in Great Britain.

———•———

On February 9, 1933, a debate was held at the Oxford Union, the debating society of Oxford University. At the conclusion of the debate, the students voted 275 to 173 in favor of a motion stating ". . . that this house will in no circumstances fight for its King and country."[8] The motion produced a firestorm of criticism and controversy around Great Britain, but shortly after, students from all over the kingdom were adopting the "Oxford Pledge." During that same semester, an Americanized version of the Oxford Pledge swept campuses across the United States. It was during his second year of rabbinical studies at Hebrew Union College when Roland Gittelsohn, along with thousands of other American students, first heard of the Oxford Pledge. The influence of the First World War on American student supporters of the Oxford Pledge was so strong that they seemed unable to give a speech or make an argument about foreign affairs without referring to that war and its "lessons."[9] Those "lessons" would figure prominently in Gittelsohn's future sermons.

The Oxford Pledge became a major factor in promoting the American anti-war movement on college campuses, but the wording had to be retooled for use in America to accommodate both the pacifist and leftist branches of the movement. As previously noted, the leftist members of the anti-war movement had no problem with anti-colonial wars, and this went against the spirit of the Oxford Pledge, which espoused total pacifism. Accordingly, the wording of the Americanized version declared intent to "refuse to support the government of the United States in any war it may conduct." Since the Marxist position maintained that the only type of war the American government could wage would be an imperialist war, members of the NSL and other leftist students felt they could support the pledge because it was a rejection not of all war but only imperial war.[10]

The NSL would soon organize national student strikes against the war. The first, held on April 13, 1934, drew twenty-five thousand students, mainly from the East Coast. The second,

Student Strike Against War in 1935, was far larger, drawing about one hundred seventy-five thousand students, this time from all around the country, including Ohio State and Oberlin College. The year Roland Gittelsohn took the Oxford Pledge is not clear, but he certainly embraced it completely. While he appeared to support the religious pacifist view that all war is evil and cannot be supported, in the future he would embrace the position consistent with that of the leftists in the anti-war movement, which justified some wars. His changing support, however, was ironically due largely to religious principles, which in the early 1930s may have appeared wildly inconsistent. His conversion would involve his "spiritual schizophrenia," which he would later write about.

Like virtually all of the young anti-war activists of the 1930s, Gittelsohn believed that the United States' involvement in World War I in 1917 was motivated primarily by economic factors. Despite President Wilson's lofty rhetoric and his claim that we entered the war to "make the world safe for democracy," it was really done to protect the profit margins of American capitalists.[11] In addition, another "lesson" learned was to be wary of the propaganda produced by the government to generate war support. The demonization of the German people was largely the work of the media supporting the country's entry into the war. Convinced that history tends to repeat itself, student anti-war activists took these lessons about economics, war guilt, and the origins of World War I and applied them to the turbulent international scene of the 1930s.[12] They thought that their understanding of these "lessons" learned from the World War would help them understand and appropriately respond to the world issues developing in the 1930s. The cliché about generals always fighting the last war was applicable here to the campus peace movement and to the pacifist movement in general. The student anti-war activists in 1933-35 still had their heads in 1917; and in a sense, as NSL leader Joseph Clark recalled, they "relived an era . . . which no longer existed."[13]

Activists such as Gittelsohn would bemoan the growing military and increase in defense budgets as an indication of the country's expansionist tendencies and willingness to be embroiled once again in foreign conflicts. In fact, in the early- and mid-1930s, there was a strong isolationist movement in the country and an overall disinclination to once again be drawn into a foreign conflict. This is evidenced by the fact that at the outbreak of the Second World War in 1939 the United States had the eighteenth largest military in the world, behind such countries as Poland and Belgium. By honing in on the "lessons," largely economic, that they gleaned from their study of World War I, activists failed to assess the nature of the coming storm in Europe, a conflict not defined by capitalist protection but by one of combating Nazi totalitarianism.[14] While American students were taking the Oxford Pledge, students in Nazi Germany were burning pacifist books. As they struck for peace on those World War I anniversaries, marched against Wilsonian slogans of 1917, and championed anti-interventionalism, students in the United States, including Roland Gittelsohn, remained captives of the past, opposing the wrong war at the wrong time.[15]

As he continued his studies at Hebrew Union College, Gittelsohn vigorously embraced the growing pacifist movement. He had believed the tenets of total pacifism for years, long before the average student had embraced it. Roland had established his bona fide credentials: he proudly wore his two percent pin and was a member of the War Resisters League. While still a rabbinical student, he would greatly refine his credentials and become a well-known, outspoken advocate of peace throughout the Jewish community.

———•———

In the latter half of 1931, during the first year of his rabbinical studies, Roland and his longtime sweetheart Ruth Freyer decided that they would marry. Ruth was the same age as Roland and was a student at Flora Stone Mather College—the women's school of Western Reserve University. Like Roland, she was born in Cleveland, the daughter of Solomon Freyer and Eva Cohen Freyer. Solomon was a garment worker who was born in New York City in October of 1872; Eva Cohen was born in England in September of 1879. The Freyers lived in East Cleveland, the Gittelsohns in Cleveland Heights.

After getting engaged, Roland approached his grandfather and posed a potentially awkward dilemma for the rabbi. Both Roland and his family and Ruth and her family were members of the Euclid Avenue Temple, a Reform synagogue. Would Orthodox

Rabbi Benjamin Gittelsohn be willing to officiate at their marriage ceremony along with Rabbi Barnett R. Brickner of Euclid Avenue Temple? His answer was "We'll see." Roland clearly understood that his grandfather was telling him, "If you observe such essential Orthodox marriage rites as covering your heads and reciting the appropriate formulae and including the traditional seven wedding blessings, yes."[16]

Rabbi Gittelsohn never was able to co-officiate at his grandson's wedding. By late 1931 he was in failing health and was living in a nursing home. On January 7, 1932, he died at the approximate age of ninety.

On September 25, 1932, Roland Gittelsohn and Ruth Freyer were married at the Euclid Avenue Temple. Rabbi Barnett Brickner performed the wedding rites for the young couple. Both of the newlyweds resumed their studies after the wedding. In 1934 Gittelsohn received his bachelor of Hebrew studies degree from Hebrew Union College. Ruth Gittelsohn would receive her bachelor of arts degree from Western Reserve University on June 12, 1935. The following year, after additional postgraduate work, Roland would be ordained as a rabbi.

———•———

The first public airings of Gittelsohn's views of pacifism and social justice, two subjects that would dominate his thinking and action for the rest of his life, took place in the years between the completion of his bachelor's degree and his ordination. The pulpits of the various synagogues that he would be preaching from provided the forum for his views on war, pacifism, injustice, and the world's situation in general.

For the sermon that he delivered on the Jewish New Year, Rosh Hashanah, in 1934, Roland delivered a message entitled "More Human Bondage." This sermon, expounding his views on war and pacifism, was one he would deliver several times with modifications in the near future: on November 16, 1935, and again after his ordination on Rosh Hashanah eve in 1936. That night he began his speech by relating the story of Abraham on Mt. Moriah, using it as a metaphor for mankind, the Jewish people, and the advancing concepts of the sanctity of life, saying, "and so we might

*Roland Gittelsohn as a rabbinical student, approximately 1932* (Courtesy David Gittelsohn and Judy Gittelsohn Fales)

go on and see that almost every incident in the life of Abraham is symbolic of some great advance in the life of his people."[17] God had called to Abraham, asking that he sacrifice his only son, Isaac, the boy whom his entire life was centered around. This was not an unusual request, as in the religions of antiquity human sacrifice was the noblest and highest of all rites.[18] Dutifully, Abraham obeyed God's request and prepared to sacrifice Isaac. Just as Abraham raised his knife, preparing to take Isaac's life, an angel called out, crying: "'Abraham, Abraham . . . Lay not thy hand upon the lad, neither do thou anything to him.' Lay not thy hand upon human life, said the voice to all mankind. The days of human sacrifice were to be ended."[19]

Gittelsohn next related a question that ancient rabbis had debated: Why had the angel called out Abraham's name twice? "Wouldn't one Abraham have been enough, asked the rabbis? Their answer is important. The first Abraham was for that very one who stood there, knife raised aloft, ready to slay his son. The second Abraham, said the wise old rabbis, was for all the Abrahams to come. In other words, the great message given to Abraham on Mt. Moriah was not intended for him alone. It came, through him, to Jews of all time." Noting that from that point on human sacrifice was not part of official Judaism, Gittelsohn asked: What about those to whom the second Abraham was addressed? "Have we too heeded the message and stopped sacrificing human life? Oh, if only the answer in our case could be the same! . . . What we do in war speaks too loudly for any sane answer to the question of human sacrifice to be heard."[20]

Gittelsohn then spoke about one of the exhibits currently being displayed at Chicago's Century of Progress International Exposition. Describing a miniature model of the United States Treasury Building, he noted that it had a long, continuously-looping belt in lieu of steps, down from which came a continuous stream of gold coins. A sign above the belt explained the meaning of the display of coins: it showed that of every dollar taken in by the federal government, eighty-two cents went for war. One can envision the rising anger in Gittelsohn's voice as he exclaimed, "Think of it! People still starving, tired feet still pounding pavements in search of work where there is no work, unemployment, misery, squalor, slums— and still our government spends 82 cents out of each dollar to pay for the last war, which nobody admits starting, and the next war, which nobody admits wanting."[21] Imagine, asked Gittelsohn, how much more terrible the exhibit would be if, instead of coins being displayed on the belt, there were instead the ten million bodies of the men killed in the last war.

Reflecting on those millions killed in World War I, he rhetorically asked, "And for what? At least primitive man, in sacrificing his own flesh and blood to a god, expected some benefit in return."[22] Riches? Freedom? Democracy? Roland asked cynically. Had any of these things been achieved? "We sacrificed ten million souls in a war to end war, and what have we today? More war, more hate, more suspicion, more death," he passionately declared.[23] Greater than the cost in blood and treasure to Gittelsohn was the thought that these men had died in vain. This was the ultimate mockery, that they may have died for nothing. This was intolerable to him. To his congregation he posed the question: What are we going to do about it?

The first concrete step to be taken, he lectured, was to disarm. He proceeded to reference a speech that Pres. Franklin D. Roosevelt made the year before in which Roosevelt stated: ". . . that the invasion of any nation or the destruction of a national sovereignty can only be prevented by the complete elimination of the weapons which make such a course possible. The only way to disarm is to disarm."[24] Yet a year after Roosevelt made this speech, Gittelsohn pointed out, a leading periodical commented on legislation Roosevelt promoted that contradicted his statements of the previous year. The source stated, "After President Roosevelt took office, building of warships began on such a scale as the Navy had never before known in peacetime."[25] This, noted Gittelsohn, from that man who said "the only way to disarm is to disarm." To him, the hypocrisy was thoroughly distasteful.

Like many of the pacifists of the era, Gittelsohn pointed to the real possibility of disarmament by citing the example of the United States-Canadian border. He specifically noted the efforts of Acting Secretary of State Richard Rush after the War of 1812 that resulted in the Rush-Bagot Treaty, which effectively demilitarized the border between the two nations. With admiration, Gittelsohn pointed out, ". . . for more than 100 years there hasn't been a single piece of armament on a borderline more than three thousand miles in length, and in all that time, not one single war! Isn't it about time for the rest of the world to sit up and take notice?"[26] Quoting the French philosopher Edmond Fleg, Gittelsohn proclaimed, "Peace will not be achieved by conferences nor by treaties. There will be peace when men are willing to die for peace."[27] There can be no compromise, he insisted. "That's the trouble with most of our pacifists. Even they are willing to fight just one more war. Communists want one more war for Communism. Fascists want one more war for Fascism. But if we are ever to reach peace, then we must sacrifice Communism and Fascism and every other 'ism' to the greatest of all, Pacifism."[28]

How many in the synagogue, he asked, had ever done anything to truly oppose war? How many of them had questioned candidates for office on their positions on peace? How many of them protested when Congress appropriated billions of taxpayer dollars to build more warships? Noting that it took a long time for religion to grow out of human sacrifice, he cautioned that it may well take a long time for them to achieve peace. But he reminded them that everyone in attendance that day could do something, be it ever so humble, in the fight for peace. "If we do," he assured them, in future generations, "men will tell how we were commanded by the Great God War to sacrifice millions of our sons on his altar . . . And they will tell how a voice came forth from the heavens and said to us: 'Abraham, Abraham, lay not thy hand upon thy sons, neither do thou anything to them, for I the Lord thy God am a God of peace.'"[29]

When Gittelsohn next delivered "More Human Bondage" on November 16, 1935, he had embellished on several points, making his message more urgent and more strident in its tone. Once again he began with the story of Abraham and Isaac on Mt. Moriah. Abraham, he reasoned, was willing to give up the most important thing in his life—his son Isaac—in support of his beliefs. To his congregation he asked: how about ourselves? "How much are we really willing to sacrifice, if need be, to achieve that peace?"[30] Sure, people may protest and preach, but how many people would be willing to sacrifice "their Isaac?" How many of them would give up their wealth, social standing, and approval—and perhaps even life itself? This, he stated, was the key to all of their failure. The soldier is often willing to die for his beliefs, so he asked, "How can we, who pretend to love peace, do less than the soldier who is willing to go forth into battle and possibly lose his life in support of that in which he believes?"[31] Once again quoting the French philosopher Edmond Fleg, Gittelsohn claimed, "Peace will not be achieved by conferences nor by treaties. There will be peace when men are willing to die for peace."[32]

To those who might wonder why his rhetoric was so strident and so urgent, Gittelsohn exclaimed that they could not afford to be patient any longer. "We cannot afford to wait patiently for peace. We have no other choice than to be extreme . . . We have no time for patience."[33] Comparing everyone to passengers in a car being driven by a drunk driver, he pointed out that they had to take the wheel from the driver; they had no time to attempt to teach the intoxicated driver lessons in safety. Immediate action was required. "Either we grab the wheel from his hands and save ourselves, either we are sudden and extreme, — or else we meet that train and another war destroys us and our civilization. This is our only choice."[34]

In closing, he once again referred to the story of Abraham on Mt. Moriah preparing to sacrifice his beloved son, Isaac. When the call came to Abraham, he responded, "Here I am, ready, if need be, to lose that which I love most."[35] Soberly, Gittelsohn stated, "That was the answer of the first Abraham, and it must be the answer of the others, of ourselves, too."[36] His closing paragraph was identical to his Rosh Hashanah sermon given the year before.

———•———

Ten days later, on Yom Kippur eve 1934, Gittelsohn delivered another sermon where he continued to share his strong views, this time speaking on the concept of social justice. In this sermon, entitled "The Fast That We Have Chosen," he used the occasion of the holiest day of the Jewish year, the Day of Atonement, to frame his vision of what meaningful atonement should entail. He began by noting that the Day of Atonement had been referred to by many Jews and non-Jews as a convenience and that its value had been doubted, that its existence led to a sort of moratorium on morals. "How perfectly simple it all is," he gave as an example of a non-Jew commenting on the observance of Yom Kippur, "you Jews can sin as you please all through the year confident that this one day will restore you in the good graces of God."[37] To Gittelsohn, these skeptics likened Yom Kippur to a little boy being caught misbehaving and then assuring his mother that it was alright because he promised to be sorry the next day.

Even worse, he claimed, enemies of Judaism had often taken the Kol Nidre prayer, the traditional prayer recited in the synagogue on the eve of Yom Kippur, and tried to make of it something mean and contemptible. "They say," he claimed, "that we purposely connived this day and the Kol Nidre prayer that goes with it in order to cheat and deceive the non-Jewish world. Yom Kippur, they say, is a cunning device which enables the Jew to escape all his vows and obligations of the year."[38] He pointed out that this thinking represented a total misunderstanding of the meaning of Yom Kippur to the Jew, and it certainly was not a recent development. The ancient rabbis who had compiled the Mishnah, the first written revision of the oral traditions of Judaism that had been first written nearly two thousand years before, had dealt with the same accusations. "Listen to what they decreed," instructed Gittelsohn. "He who says, 'I will sin and later repent,'—he will not be given a chance to repent. He who says, 'I will sin and the Day of Atonement will wipe out my sin,'—in such a case, the Day of Atonement will not wipe out his sin."[39]

But in his next statement, Gittelsohn delivered the crux of his meaning of atonement as described in the Mishnah. "Yom Kippur wipes out the sins between men and God: it does not wipe out the sin which men commit against men until they have first become reconciled with each other!"[40] This was the basis of the Yom Kippur sermon that he passionately preached to his congregation. "What a noble statement!" he exclaimed. "Man's sin against his fellowman is more grievous than his sin against God. This is not the easy way out charged by our critics. This makes Yom Kippur a stimulant instead of a salve, a challenge, demanding man's noblest conduct toward his fellowman. This means in order to have a Day of Atonement, we must live a year of atonement."[41] He drove home this concept by relaying the prophet's description from ancient times of when the people wondered why their prayers had not been answered, despite having fasted on Yom Kippur. True, Gittelsohn noted, they had fasted, but ". . . even while they fasted to atone for the sin of yesterday, they were planning the sin of tomorrow."[42] The prophet then asked the people, "Is such the feast I've chosen?" Does simply bowing one's head and praying make one acceptable to God? he asked. No, he countered with a different interpretation of atonement, alternatively asking, "Is not this the fast that I have chosen? To loose the fetters of wickedness, to undo the bands of the yoke, and to let the oppressed go free, and that ye break every yoke? Is it not to deal thy bread to the hungry, and that thou bring the poor that are cast out to thy house? When though seest the naked, that thou cover him, and that thou hide not thyself from thine own flesh?"[43]

Looking out on his congregation, Gittelsohn asked them which alternative they had chosen. "Do we use this day as a moral cathartic, or do we answer the prophet's challenge? 'To loosen the fetters of wickedness, to undo the bonds of the yoke, and to let the oppressed go free . . .'"[44] Having described a framework for true atonement consistent with the writings of the ancient prophets and rabbis, he proceeded on to describe current-day examples of man's injustices to his fellow man, examples that would showcase, possibly for the first time in a public forum, Gittelsohn's outspoken and often controversial views on social justice.

Gittelsohn chose to begin his discussion of social injustice with the story of Tom Mooney, a political activist and labor leader who was languishing in prison since 1916. Mooney had been convicted of the bombing of the San Francisco Preparedness Day march on July 22, 1916, that had killed a total of ten people. Many believed that Mooney, a known socialist, had been framed. For years there was a continuing campaign to demand Mooney's release from prison. Roland Gittelsohn was a passionate believer in Mooney's innocence. To his congregation he stated, "Tom Mooney loved peace; the powers that be were dependent on war:—therefore Tom Mooney was thrown in jail. Tom Mooney loved his fellowmen so much that he opposed a government which denied them freedom. Therefore, that government committed him to prison. That was in 1916."[45] Citing multiple examples of perjured testimony as well as suppression of evidence that would have exonerated Mooney, Gittelsohn noted with disgust that Mooney remained in jail in 1934 for a crime he didn't commit in 1916. (Tom Mooney was eventually pardoned and released from prison in 1939.)

The next paragraph from his sermon notes are revealing. "Please don't misunderstand me," he cautioned the audience. "Tom Mooney is a communist," he erroneously stated. Mooney was a socialist. "Not long ago when I mentioned his name from a pulpit, at least one woman left the Synagogue thoroughly convinced that since I defended him, I must be a communist too. It happens that I am not."[46]

In the future Gittelsohn would be accused of being a communist on several occasions due to his leftward leanings, but he was never a member of the Communist Party. (The issue would even surface towards the end of World War II, after the battle of Iwo Jima.) And his views on the Soviet Union were often ambivalent, as will be demonstrated. But his point was this: true freedom from oppression means freedom for those who disagree with us. "This is the only freedom ever threatened; therefore it is the only freedom worth having. Why, to my mind one of the noblest sentiments ever uttered by the human tongue was that spoken by Voltaire when he said: 'I cannot agree with a thing you say, but I'd die for your right to say it.'"[47] The precious freedom of speech, the right of dissent—these were critical American values that Roland Gittelsohn cherished and believed were the right of every American. The case of the injustice suffered by Tom Mooney was illustrative of his example of the fast we have chosen; of wiping out the sin we commit toward our fellow men before we can wipe out the sin between men and God. "But so long as Tom Mooney and others like him remain in jail," he declared, "we *haven't* loosened the fetter of wickedness, we *haven't* undone the bands of the yoke, and we *haven't* let the oppressed go free."[48]

Gittelsohn proceeded to next discuss a second area of social justice that would need to be reconciled among mankind in order for true atonement to be achieved: racial equality. This would also be a lifetime quest for him. He informed the congregation of a book that he had discovered entitled *The Negro a Beast; or In the Image of God*, written by an author named Charles Carroll at the turn of the century. With absolute disgust, he revealed to them that the publisher of the book was the American Book and Bible House. In addition to reviewing several examples of discrimination against black Americans, he decried the economic and educational disparities between black and white America. "Eight Southern states average $44 per year for education of each white child," he pointed out. "For each negro child they average $12.50. And the inhabitants of those very states dare to speak of the negro's low level of culture."[49]

The last area of social justice that he would discuss that day was poverty. Gittelsohn attacked the naïve assumption that there was no such thing as a hungry, unemployed person in America before the stock market crash of 1929 that led to the Great Depression. Along with this assumption was another naïve belief of some that as a result of the New Deal, the country had returned to a state of prosperity. This was total nonsense, he declared. Before the stock market crash there were four million unemployed Americans. Now, after two years of the New Deal, there were close to ten million unemployed. Children were living in poverty on a daily basis. "How many of us, have," he asked, "burned deeply on our conscience and heart, the cry of a child without clothes for its naked body or food for its empty stomach?"[50] In contrast to this striking scenario, he pointed out that in 1931 the Electric Bond and Share Company made profits of 103 percent while millions of such children starved. The following year the Bank of Manhattan made record profits while many Americans were living in dire poverty. "What shall we say of our generation's method of dealing bread to the hungry?" he asked. "This is the challenge of Yom Kippur. How have we answered it?"[51]

To draw together the threads of his sermon into a defining statement, Gittelsohn went on to describe the short story written in 1866 by Leo Tolstoy entitled *How Much Land Does a Man Need?* In it, Tolstoy tells the story of an ignorant Russian peasant named Pahom. Although on a daily basis Pahom would toil in a backbreaking manner over the land of his master, he was a happy individual. But when his master died and left the little strip of land to Pahom, his days of contentedness were over. From that point on he wanted more and more land. After learning of the proposed giveaway of large tracts of land in Siberia, Pahom, craving more land, sold his home and everything in it and with his one faithful servant headed out to Siberia.

Once there, Pahom entered into an agreement whereby he would acquire all the land he could surround in one day by foot, provided he returned to the starting point by sunset. Readily agreeing to this, by midday he had acquired a large tract, but his craving for more and more land led him to keep going. Racing against time to return by sunset, he ran past the point of exhaustion. Returning to the starting point just as the sun's last rays were fading behind the hills, Pahom collapsed.

His servant shouted out congratulations that he had won. But looking at his master lying there with blood trickling from his mouth, he realized that Pahom was dead. "Then the faithful servant of Pahom took his spade, and with it dug a space 7 feet long, and there laid his master to eternal rest. And that, said Leo Tolstoi [*sic*], answers the question, How much land does a man need?"[52]

It was at this point that Gittelsohn provided the answer to this question: why haven't we been able to answer the challenge of Yom Kippur? According to him, ". . . we've become a generation of Pahoms, blindly killing ourselves as well as others, in a desperate effort to acquire land and wealth which we didn't need." In a controversial summary that sounds very much like the rhetoric of Karl Marx melded into his own socialist-leaning views, Gittelsohn announced what needed to be done.

> The creed we must adopt is simple: First, the needs of all; second, the luxury of a few. Only after *every man* has what he *needs* can *any man* have what he *wants*!
>
> This is the fast that we must choose. It is the only way to change Yom Kippur from convenience to challenge. With it, our fasting and prayer on this day have meaning. Without it, every hour we fast and every prayer we utter is hypocrisy and sham. Let us, then, fill this day with meaning by consecrating ourselves to a year of ceaseless effort for those who are oppressed and hungry. We must defend the man who seeks to speak what he calls the truth, even if we think it false. We must protect the man whose skin is black even if our own is white. And we must feed the hungry and clothe the naked, even if it means less luxury for us. [53]

Thus, with two sermons delivered over the High Holidays in 1934, Roland Gittelsohn laid out his vision of America. The activist rabbi envisioned a world where the United States of America would refuse to ever be drawn again into a war; war driven by false propaganda that touted making the world safe for democracy when he believed it was to make the world safe for corporate profits. He envisioned a United States where justice would prevail to all, where freedom of dissent was tolerated and where racial equality was among the noble goals that our country could achieve. His views would remain consistent over the years, although his vision of pacifism at all costs would be greatly challenged within the decade, as it would for many committed pacifists of the 1930s.

# Chapter Four

# Discovery

Prior to 1913, women of Reform Judaism were organized in independent, local synagogue sisterhoods that had been founded in the 1890s and 1900s. At the request of the Union of American Hebrew Congregations, Reform sisterhood members met at the Sinton Hotel in Cincinnati in January of 1913. One hundred fifty delegates representing forty-nine different sisterhoods were in attendance. It was there that they formed the National Federation of Temple Sisterhoods on January 21. The purpose of their new organization, as stated in the preamble to the minutes of their first meeting, was "that the increased power which has come to the modern American Jewess ought to be exercised in congregational life and that the religious and moral development of Israel will be furthered by this co-operation."[1] The NFTS not only aimed to strengthen temple sisterhoods already in existence but also to translate women's roles in the home to a larger and more public sphere.[2]

The NFTS elected Carrie Obendorfer Simon as their first president, and from its inception, the organization played an activist role that complimented the Union of American Hebrew Congregations. Its emphasis was the expanding role of women in the synagogue that transcended domestic responsibilities beyond the home. Education of children and youth and promoting religion in the community were priorities of the organization. Providing scholarships for rabbinical students, as well as providing housing for the students, became part of the NFTS mission. Cooking, entertaining, and serving as hostesses for temple fundraisers were all embraced by the NFTS.

For many years, the NFTS walked a fine line between its commitment to Reform Judaism and its interest in general philanthropic work and contemporary political issues. NFTS presidents, such as Hattie M. Wiesenfeld, urged members not to overextend the sisterhood by venturing into social service and political avenues best left to other organizations.[3] While there were several prominent Jewish women who were social activists and activist women's groups that became involved with social and political issues around the turn of the century, after World War I such work was seen as inappropriate for middle class Jewish women. As such, it was turned over to professional social workers who were mostly men.[4] Nevertheless, NFTS leaders always considered certain issues, notably peace work and separation of church and state in the public schools, at the center of the sisterhood's religious mission.[5]

Their growing anti-war sentiment was expressed in a policy statement "Resolution on Peace" passed at their 1931 annual meeting.[6] It cited the extensive military buildup taking place both in Europe and America, noting that these actions were "in direct opposition to the solemn pledge made by the fifty-eight nations who signed the Kellogg-Briand Pact never again 'to use war as an instrument of national policy . . . '" It went on to state the critical importance of organized groups unequivocally opposing the support of and the participation in war. The resolution concluded with "*Resolved*, that this National Federation of Temple Sisterhoods in Convention assembled go on record as endorsing only pacific settlements of international disputes, so that the spiritual values for which Jews have sacrificed during their long history shall be preserved." The NFTS's component committee, the National Committee on Peace, had a proactive, energetic chairman in the person of Jennie L. Kubie of New York City. With the exception of a two year period, Kubie would chair the peace committee for the entire 1930s.

At the meeting of the NFTS held in New York City on March 1, 1933, Kubie delivered the Report of the National Committee on Peace, in which she offered two key recommendations. She directed that every sisterhood determine to further its peace work through establishment of a peace budget. Her next recommendation would have a lasting impact on the member sisterhoods. She insisted that peace study groups be organized in the member sisterhoods with the special purpose of developing peace leaders.[7]

Later that year, at an executive board meeting of the NFTS held in Chicago on June 17, 1933, the board considered a proposal that it had received to establish a Sisterhood Publication Fund. "It was moved, seconded, and carried that the Executive board recommend to the Assembly that a Sisterhood Publication Fund, not to exceed $4,500 annually, be created for the exclusive purpose of publishing new books to be used in Jewish Religious Schools."[8]

Involvement in peace work would become a much more sharply focused interest of the organization when Jane Evans, known as "the first lady of Reform Judaism," became the first full-time executive director in 1933. Evans, an outspoken advocate of women's rights, was a keen observer of contemporary affairs and a religious pacifist who immediately began to push the organization beyond its original mandate of service to the congregation, religious school, and community.[9] She insisted that Reform Jewish women not only voice their opinions on issues pertinent to Reform Judaism but also on important political issues. During her forty-three year tenure as executive director of NFTS, the organization would sponsor resolutions on civil rights, birth control, child labor laws, and immigration reform and would consider the question of ordaining female rabbis.

However, Jane Evans was especially interested in the concept of pacifism and world peace. Under her leadership, the NFTS passed the resolution entitled "World Peace" at its 1935 annual meeting, proclaiming:

> We, The Executive Board of the National Federation of Temple Sisterhoods, in annual meeting assembled, are deeply aroused by the grim spectre of war, which once again threatens the world. Stirred as American Jewesses, and loyal to the lofty teachings of our Hebrew prophets, who first proclaimed the Fatherhood of God and the brotherhood of all men, we must now, as perhaps never before, imbue the hearts of men with the teachings of truth, love, justice and peace. The time has now come to declare our firm opposition to war and our determination to aid and to support every effort in the up building and the strengthening of those forces that shall make for world peace.[10]

Together, Jane Evans as executive director and Jennie Kubie as chairman of the national committee on peace proved to be a very effective team in the movement for world peace. In the Report of the National Committee on Peace that Jennie Kubie delivered in New York City on May 15, 1934, she discussed several of the committee's accomplishments.[11] Among these was the formation of peace study groups. "Your chairman has repeatedly urged the formation of study groups touching matters of present-day national and international importance," Kubie began. "A number of sisterhoods and National and District Federations have followed this suggestion." With pride, she pointed out that a study group created for the development of peace chairmen, or leaders, had been organized. Kubie also reported the creation of "Peace News Flashes," intended to provide up-to-date information on worldwide peace developments for all peace chairmen. She also advised that the peace study groups closely follow the outlines that would be soon issued by the National Chairman in cooperation with the programs that were being formulated by the National Peace Conference.

Jane Evans' address, "Report of the Executive Director," was delivered in Cincinnati on March 8, 1935. It was read at the Eleventh Biennial Assembly of the NFTS in Washington, DC, on March 22, 1935, and contained a very interesting announcement by Evans: "In the report of 1934, we promised for last fall, new educational programs. Due to a number of unforeseen circumstances, these programs were not forthcoming at the time stated. But at this convention, we have on display for you in the Exhibit Room, the first two of our series, namely: *Dramatic Moments in Jewish History* by Dr. A. L. Sachar, and *The Jew Looks at War and Peace* by Roland Gittelsohn."[12]

It is not known whether Jane Evans was actually in attendance that Rosh Hashanah in Cincinnati when Roland Gittelsohn delivered his sermon entitled "More Human Bondage" as a young rabbinical student. More likely, it was a group of members of the local sisterhood who were in the congregation that day. So impressed were these women with the message they heard that they reported it to the national headquarters of the NFTS, where Jane Evans would have learned of it if she was not present that day. Evans quickly realized that the views of this young rabbinical student and the passion with which he expressed them were exactly what the NFTS needed to anchor its peace study groups organization-wide. And it was only the year before that the group had created the

Sisterhood Publication Fund. In late 1934, Jane Evans approached Gittelsohn with a request that he bring his message to various chapters of the NFTS. She commissioned him to write a book that would become his first copyrighted work.

Published by the NFTS in 1935, *The Jew Looks at War and Peace* is a study guide that was intended to foster the message of peace and pacifism espoused by the organization. It was actually a series of five pamphlets, each about twenty pages long. Each pamphlet was organized into four sections: a) a short lecture, b) a series of questions to facilitate discussion; these were presented in pro and con format to stimulate debate, c) suggestions for individual reports and activities, and d) a bibliography.

Pamphlet I was entitled "Balancing our War Books." In his introduction, Gittelsohn revealed to all potential study group leaders his style of teaching and reasoning through issues that he learned from his debate teachers and also his instructors at Hebrew Union College. "First give the group members every opportunity to think problems through for themselves and express themselves. If some member of the group thinks her way through to an answer given here, the result is many times more profitable than if she simply hears it presented by someone else."[13] He ended the introduction by offering, "My grateful thanks are due Miss Jane Evans, Executive Secretary of the N.F.T.S., who originally suggested this series, who consistently helped during its writing, and who waited patiently to have it completed."[14]

"Balancing our War Books" is essentially a repeat of Gittelsohn's sermon "More Human Bondage," using virtually every part of the original sermon. He finished the lecture section with an even more passionate expression of the obligation that all pacifists must achieve.

There can be no more compromise. Communists want one more war for Communism. Fascists want one more war for Fascism. But if we are to have peace, we must sacrifice Communism and Fascism and every other "ism" on the altar of pacifism. We have played too well the part of the drunkard who always wants "one more drink" before quitting. And right now "one more drink" may be all that is needed to finish for all time a civilization that is already staggering in drunken delight. Men must stop playing with the idea of peace as if with a hobby, and must make of it a life and a work.[15]

Balancing our war books today, according to Gittelsohn, was impossible. But it was to the future that mankind must look. Balancing the war books would be a possibility for tomorrow, he reasoned, but it would only be possible if mankind made it possible.

Pamphlet II, entitled "Religion on Trial," was a discussion about religion in general, not solely Judaism. Gittelsohn began the lecture with two examples of clergymen who displayed courage in their support of pacifism, much in the same way that Sen. John F. Kennedy would describe the political courage of several members of the United States Senate in his book *Profiles in Courage* nearly twenty years later. Both Christian clergymen described by Gittelsohn suffered greatly for their opposition to the World War.

He described the one place where religion was needed the most during the war; it was the one place where men were taught to hate and to kill—namely the army. Here, religion should have been able to teach the men to love and to heal. Yet it was here that the clergy failed greatly. He quoted the experience of Norman Thomas, who noted, "I think it was a most common experience of conscientious objectors that their most bitter and intolerant enemies in the army were the chaplains and the Y.M.C.A. men . . . and they found that they were less understood and more contemptuously despised by these men than even by veteran soldiers who made no profession of allegiance to the principles of Jesus."[16] There was no doubt in Gittelsohn's mind—religion was on trial during the Great War, and religion had failed miserably.

He feared that there was truly a danger of religion becoming a "pious irrelevancy" should war ever again come between nations. "If the peace religion preaches, is again to disappear when it is needed most, the danger is grave that with it religion too will disappear."[17] Having religious services dedicated to peace was not enough. "The houses of organized religion must declare now and forevermore that under no circumstances will they ever again support war."[18]

Gittelsohn ended the lecture in Book II with the story of Harry

Emerson Fosdick. Although he erroneously stated that Fosdick was a pacifist long before 1917, his admiration for the man was obvious. He told the story of Fosdick's 1923 sermon "Apology to the Unknown Soldier" and spent an entire page quoting from the speech. The passion built to Fosdick's final words: "I renounce war and never again, directly or indirectly, will I sanction or support another! O Unknown Soldier, in penitent reparation I make you that pledge."[19]

Gittelsohn solemnly ended the lecture by saying, "May all religions make the same pledge."

In Pamphlet III, "Are Jews Pacifists?," Gittelsohn attempted to answer the question with a definitive "yes." To support his position, he went back to the time of Alexander the Great and related the story of Alexander's dealings with Jerusalem. According to the Talmud, Alexander sent emissaries to Jerusalem to obtain food supplies for his massive armies. At the time, the city was under the rule of Persia and the residents feared offending the Persians if they complied with Alexander's request. Accordingly, they refused. Furious with their response, Alexander announced that they would march on Jerusalem in three days and destroy it.

Panic began to set in among the residents of Jerusalem. No one seriously believed that they could defend their city against the mightiest army in the world. It was the high priest, Jaddua, who came forward with the plan. "It was a strange one," noted Gittelsohn, for it entailed no armies or plans for battle. "My plan," said Jaddua, "is to meet the great Alexander with peace. Let us march out of the city to welcome him in friendship; that is our best defense."[20]

In spite of their fear and doubts, the residents of the city complied with the plan of Jaddua. Wearing their most festive clothing, they marched out of the city to meet the armies of Alexander with Jaddua leading the way. Alexander was astonished when he came upon the approaching throng. He had never experienced this—instead of weapons, they approached him with gifts and celebration. "Then Alexander did a strange thing. He descended from his horse and bowed before the Jewish Priest Jaddua. To his astonished soldiers he said: 'When I saw not a spear nor a sword nor even an axe, I could not raise my hand against them. This is the only people that has met me peacefully instead of with arms. The more glory to their leader, Jaddua, who was brave enough and wise enough to do this."[21]

To Gittelsohn, the story was typical of many in Jewish lore. For him it exemplified that all men are brothers, descended from one man that God had created. Why, wondered the ancient rabbis, did God, with all of His powers, create only one man? Pointing out that the dust out of which Adam was formed was collected from every land in the world, it was clear to Gittelsohn that God's plan to create one man from whom all others would descend reflected his intention that no group of men would ever fight against another group, being that they were all brothers.[22]

Gittelsohn explained why Jews hate war and want peace. The Jew could never rejoice over the plight of the vanquished. Noting that "we have always been a hated minority," he stated: "We know the effects of force too well to use force against others. Wars are not kind to strangers, and we are strangers in many lands. Therefore we hate war and love peace."[23] He stated that "our experiences as a people have given us an all-consuming love of life." In spite of discrimination and the difficult lives they had often lived, Jews had learned to love life. It is war that destroys life; therefore the Jew hates war and wants peace.

He concluded by describing Jews as "an international people." Emphatically, he declared, "we, more than any other people, should be lovers of peace. And loving peace, we must pursue it. We must continue to meet the force of Alexander with the peace of Jaddua, that our efforts may help bring about the day envisioned by our own prophet, a day when—'they shall beat their swords into ploughshares and their spears into pruning hooks; Nation shall not lift up sword against nation, Neither shall they learn war any more.'"[24]

In Book IV, Gittelsohn posed a crucially important question with his title: "Can Jews Afford to Be Pacifists?" Surely at no time, he began, has it ever been an easy thing to be a pacifist. For "to be a Jew and a pacifist is challenge enough for the strength and skill of Hercules."[25] To graphically illustrate this dilemma, he related the story of Pres. David Israels, the factitious Jewish president, in Frank Copley's novel entitled *The Impeachment of President Israels.*

In the novel, Israels was the first Jewish president, elected before the World War on a strong pacifist platform. After his election, tensions arose between the United States and Germany, and Israels resisted all calls to increase American armaments and prepare for war. Shortly after, an American ship was sunk in German waters with the resultant loss of three American lives. The overwhelming majority of Americans demanded a declaration of war, which Israels refused to pursue. He instead counseled patience, believing that the German population was also being spun up in a patriotic fervor. Without restraint, Israels believed that a war was inevitable, but he let it be known both at home and overseas that he had confidence in the German government and would take no rash steps against it. Germany, he was sure, would realize that the sinking was a terrible accident and would apologize to the United States and end the war tensions.

Unfortunately, several months before, Israels had committed to send the American fleet to the Mediterranean to participate in an anniversary celebration for the Republic of Turkey. The president now faced a dilemma. The country was clamoring for him to send the fleet against Germany instead. To cancel the participation in the Turkish celebration would offend our Turkish ally, and at the same time it would belie the confidence he had expressed toward Germany and further fan wartime passions in that country. President Israels decided to send the fleet to Turkey and was promptly impeached. In addition, anti-Jewish sentiment through the country was exacerbated by his actions. "People everywhere blamed not only him, but his people too," explained Gittelsohn. "What else could one expect from lily-livered Jews? One grants them freedom and liberty only to be stabbed by them in the hour of need!"[26]

To Roland Gittelsohn, David Israels served as a metaphor that represented the Jewish pacifist. The quandary that faced him was the dilemma that every Jew who loves peace must face. "What would happen to our people," asked Gittelsohn, "if we should be consistent pacifists? If another war were to start and every Jew in this country refused to fight? The answer is frequently given that by such action we should be risking pogroms and massacres and death. How, then, can we afford to be pacifists?"[27]

Before an intelligent answer could be provided, Gittelsohn insisted that one must look at it from the Jewish point of view and ask—what does war mean to the Jew? Reflecting back on the Great

War, it was easy for him to recall the horrible toll that that the Jewish community in Europe suffered. When the Germans entered Poland, they accused the Jews of being Russian agents; when the Russians took the country, the Jews were accused of being German agents. All told, he recounted that 215 pogroms against Jews took place in Poland during the war. "Whatever the Jew did, he was wrong. And being wrong, he was persecuted and oppressed."[28] In Russia, many Jews willingly joined the army, only to have their loyalty repaid with further discrimination and persecution.

Gittelsohn recounted a conversation that took place at the Paris Peace Conference in 1919 between President Woodrow Wilson and Polish Prime Minister Ignace Paderewski. Paderewski was urging Wilson and Prime Minister Clemenceau of France to grant certain concessions to Poland. "If these claims are not granted," said Paderewski, "the Polish people will be so furious that they would massacre all the Jews." Wilson naively asked what would happen if they agreed to grant the claims. "Ah," replied Paderewski with a smile, "that will be different. In that case the Polish people will be so delighted that they will massacre all the Jews."[29] Sadly, Gittelsohn noted that "Klansmen and Nazis, Endeks and Cuzists, — all of them were revived, if not actually founded by the war to make the world safe for democracy!"[30]

All of this led Gittelsohn to answer his question "Can Jews afford to be pacifists?" with a resounding "We *must* be pacifists!" Are there difficulties with this mission of peace? Of course, he acknowledged. But as he had pointed out the horrendous burdens that war wreaked on mankind, it was worse for the Jews. "If these burdens are hell for the whole of humanity they are infinitely more fiendish for the minority groups upon whom is heaped the unmerited blame.

"We *must* be pacifists. With all the vision of our dreamers and prophets, with all the wisdom of our wise men and sages, and with all the courage of our heroes and martyrs, we Jews of today must work for peace, live for peace, and if need be die for peace, until the lips of all men echo the undying wish of the Jew: Shalom! Peace!"[31]

The last book of *The Jew Looks at War and Peace*, Book V, was directed at the target audience that the NFTS intended to reach specifically. Entitled "If Women Wanted Peace," it spoke to the very essence of what Jane Evans and her newly discovered spokesman believed possible in the peace movement worldwide.

Without mentioning it by name, Gittelsohn began by describing *Lysistrata*, the ancient Greek play by Aristophanes. In the play, the women of Greece, tired of war, threatened to withhold sex from their husbands until war had ended and peace had returned to Greece. "No sooner had the men discovered that their wives meant what they said than the war *did* end and peace *did* begin. Women succeeded where diplomacy and statecraft had failed."[32]

In primitive tribes, Gittelsohn noted, it was the men who made war, but it was the women who were the guardians of peace. It was the women who decided when the fighting had proven futile, and their word was law. This illustrated the potential role of women as makers of peace. However, many women had lost their way during the World War and supported it wholeheartedly. "They cheered the warrior and jeered the pacifist. They hated the 'enemy's' women, forgetting that they too had nursed sons, that they too suffered bereavement, and that their hearts too knew the ache of silent sorrow."[33] In Gittelsohn's view, it was women who largely urged that American citizenship be refused to Hungarian peace activist Rosika Schwimmer during the World War.

He did note that there were exceptions to female support for the war. He specifically noted the efforts of Schwimmer, Jane Addams, and Carrie Chapman when they met at the Hague Congress of Women in 1915. There, women of twelve countries, including England and Germany, met in their quest for peace. What did they accomplish? "The very fact that it met at all was accomplishment enough. What international group of men met in the heat of hostilities? We rejoice that *some* women succeeded; we are grieved that *most* women failed."[34]

But Gittelsohn was emphatic that they could not fail again because civilization would fail with them if they did. Men had failed in the quest for peace in the past. It now rested in the hands of women. He quoted Albert Einstein when he said at the Disarmament Conference of 1933, ". . . since men have so utterly failed in what seems to be so simple to achieve, it is high time the women took a hand in the affairs of this world. They at least would not talk about the size of cannons and the wing-spread of bombing planes. They at least would not talk so callously about men's lives and the lives of children."[35] Women cannot fail, Gittelsohn reiterated, because men have.

Women also could not fail, he explained, because their own happiness hung in the balance—the happiness that was taken from women when they became war widows. Failure would also destroy their own welfare, as war breeds a colossal contempt for women. Gittelsohn cynically pointed out that, in times of war, women are needed to make munitions and keep industry running when men go off to fight. And when the war is over, they are then sent to "breed more sons for the next war . . . There is no room for women in the social scheme of Mussolini or Hitler, because there is no room for women in the social scheme of war."[36] His cynicism was accentuated by quoting the philosopher Oswald Spangler, who said, "Women are for breeding, and men for cannon fodder." Again, stressed Roland Gittelsohn, "women must succeed."

And how could women succeed in their endeavor for peace in the world? Gittelsohn listed several steps for women to take to achieve the goals of pacifism. First, they must never condone war. There was nothing good, beautiful, or noble in war—only ugliness. "When once we have convinced ourselves of that, when once we have sworn never again to open our lips except to damn war, then we can first start to bring peace."[37]

And how might they bring peace about? Gittelsohn's next suggestion was the boycott. As an example, he suggested that if every woman in American vowed not to purchase any silk from Japan, the economic ramifications might well affect conditions in the Far East. While men held predictably worthless peace conferences, "women, who do most of the buying, could use [their] power to enforce peace."

Gittelsohn urged women to use the power of the voting ballot to achieve peace. Women should learn the voting records of the candidates in regard to their views on war and peace. With disdain, he mentioned what he considered the hypocrisy of Franklin D. Roosevelt in proclaiming, "The only way to disarm is to disarm," and then six months later signing one of the largest United States Navy funding bills in history. Women should, thought Gittelsohn, adopt the following idea: "We it is who, with our new-won power to vote, can insist that the candidates who speak for peace also work for peace. We should know the peace record of every candidate for every office. And in voting, we should let those records be our guide."[38]

Lastly, Gittelsohn stressed the importance of women educating their children in the concept of peace. He noted that women were responsible for about 90 percent of all of the training that children receive at home. In addition, it was the women who helped shape the policies of the Temple Schools. "Therefore we are the ones who must educate for peace . . . We must teach our children that in the nursery and schoolroom, as well as in the larger areas of life, right is far stronger and nobler than might. These things we must do if we would not fail again."[39]

Gittelsohn concluded this last book by quoting the horrific wartime experiences recorded by nurse Kathleen Norris. This was the hell, he claimed, that women must end. It would require courage and strength, and he repeated an oath written by a Swedish female novelist. The oath ended with the quote, "I shall work for the sake of peace, though it cost me my life and happiness." He then ended the five-book series by stating, "If we take this oath and meant it, tomorrow's world will be shaped by our hands."[40]

---

Roland Gittelsohn's affiliation with the NFTS established him as a prominent spokesman for pacifism in the Jewish community. *The Jew Looks at War and Peace* quickly became a much-used teaching guide in temple sisterhoods around the country. New committee chairwoman Hortense L. Fox was concerned that the book would be used solely as material for programs on peace and expressed both her concern and advice in her Report of the National Committee on Peace that she delivered in Chicago on December 15, 1936. "The material provided by the National Office for study class material (I refer to 'The Jew Looks at War and Peace' by Roland Gittelsohn) seems to be used more as program material than as class material. I suggest that the Sisterhoods go thoroughly into the possibilities that these outlines offer for both study and for program material before discarding their use."[41]

So influential was Gittelsohn's book that in 1937 one sisterhood member was inspired to write a play based on it. In the Report of the National Committee on Programs delivered in Columbia, South Carolina, on December 15, 1937, committee chairwoman Helen Kohn Hennig reported, "Adding to this list of published material, the committee had this season presented *A Playlet based upon The Jew Looks at War and Peace*, written by Mrs. Arthur L. Reinhart."[42] The NFTS would publish an additional book by Roland Gittelsohn in the summer of 1937 entitled *The Jew Faces His Problems*.

Thus with a fiery sermon entitled "More Human Bondage," written for Rosh Hashanah in 1934, Roland Gittelsohn launched a career as a dedicated spokesman for world pacifism. He would deliver essentially the same sermon in November 1935, as well as for Rosh Hashanah in 1936, his first High Holidays sermon after his ordination as a rabbi. In addition to his eloquence and his Talmudic reasoning and logic, he was also a member of the War Resisters League, had taken the Oxford Pledge, and would defiantly wear his two percent pin. Like many young Americans of the 1930s, he would have preferred to go to jail than go into the military and fight a war. Even though the events in Europe were first beginning to cause a sense of uneasiness for him and other Reform rabbis in particular, his mind was settled—he would never go to war under any circumstances.

Chapter Five

# The New Rabbi

In the fall of his last year of rabbinical studies, Roland Gittelsohn delivered a Rosh Hashanah eve sermon that picked up on the pacifist themes he had espoused in "More Human Bondage" and further embellished them. Speaking at Beth Abraham Synagogue in Zanesville, Ohio, the tone of his message was both dark and strident. He began the untitled sermon by reminding the congregation that the ten days between Rosh Hashanah and Yom Kippur are distinctive and are known as *Yomin Noraim* — the dreadful days, the days of awe. According to ancient tradition, on Rosh Hashanah our destinies for the year were written and on Yom Kippur our destinies were sealed. And it was here, at the beginning of the year, that Gittelsohn described the near future for them as if they were standing at an entrance to a dark tunnel, fraught with uncertainty.[1]

The crux of the uncertainty was the distinct possibility that war would once again erupt in Europe. And when war in Europe came, as Gittelsohn felt it probably would in the course of the very year which was then starting, would the United States once again be drawn into it? Gittelsohn went on to attempt to answer that question by posing a more thought-provoking question: "What were the causes of our being forced into the World War? We had a dream of peace in 1914 and 15 and 16. What caused that dream to become a nightmare?"[2] He challenged the congregation to consider the causes of the United States entering the war and to consider if those causes still existed at the present time.

To Gittelsohn, there were clear-cut answers to the questions he posed. The first had to do with what he referred to as the "armament conscious" mindset of the United States. It was present before 1917 when we spent more money on weapons than ever before in our history. "We were definitely, consciously preparing for war. Therefore we soon had war."[3] It was no different in the present time (1935). Referencing figures provided by the Foreign Policy Association, he noted that the 1936 budget for direct Army and Navy expenses was eight billion dollars—nearly four times the amount of the 1913 budget. What was galling to him was that in the five years of the Depression thus far, the government had spent eight billion dollars on welfare and relief. Yet, in the eighteen months that the United States participated in the World War, the government spent thirty-seven billion dollars. Angrily, Gittelsohn pointed out that we spent "Fifteen times as much for breaking men as we are willing to spend building men!"[4] Clearly, he noted, the first cause of our entry into the World War was armaments.

But armaments are just inanimate objects of steel. Without human beings to use them, they aren't a threat. This was the next cause of the United States' entry into the World War that Gittelsohn pointed out. The people had to be made to want war. "There had to be a way; it was the way of propaganda. And the same men who made the armaments controlled the press and the screen and every means of communication. Every cheap, miserable, petty lie was used to whip this people into frenzied madness."[5] He honed in on those who he considered to be the culprits of this outrage: the Morgan interests and the banks. He reported a charge issued on the floor of Congress that as early as March of 1915 the Morgan interests had enlisted twelve publishers and 197 newspapers to persuade public opinion in favor of the United States joining the Allies. He also cited the influence of French historian and politician Gabriel Hanotaux, who worked with Morgan interests to foster a fear campaign that was intended to influence the American public into supporting entry into the war.[6] "And all the while that we dreamed of peace, all the while that our president promised to keep us out of war, these men were coldly, calmly plotting to increase business by destroying life."[7]

As his prime example of how propaganda worked, he offered the sinking of the RMS *Lusitania* by a German U-boat on May 7, 1915. Over eleven hundred passengers lost their lives, including 128 Americans. Germany had issued a proclamation that the seas around the United Kingdom were to be designated a war zone and that they would be stepping up submarine warfare in those waters. Despite all warnings, the *Lusitania* sailed from New York

Harbor on May 1. The *Lusitania* was a non-military ship, and hence international law required that the crew and passengers should be allowed to evacuate before it could be fired on. The attacking U-boat gave no such warning, as the Germans believed that the ship was carrying munitions and was therefore a legitimate military target. As a result of the torpedoing, anti-German passions flared in the United States. Newspapers screamed for vengeance against Germany, claiming our neutrality had been violated, and that our women and children had been ruthlessly murdered by the "Huns." Judging the anti-German hysteria from overseas, many in Great Britain hoped and assumed that the Americans would enter the war.

It soon came out that the *Lusitania* was indeed carrying munitions in violation of international law, despite efforts to cover up the facts. One can almost picture Roland Gittelsohn on the pulpit, exclaiming with intense emotion, "We violated our neutrality, not Germany! Why weren't we told these facts at the time? Because we were dupes of propaganda."[8] Interestingly, in his original notes for the sermon, he crossed out the following quote from British politician Arthur Ponsonby: "In war-time, failure to lie is negligence, the doubting of a lie is a misdemeanor, the declaration of the truth a crime."[9]

After pointing out that propaganda is the second condition that would set the stage for American intervention in the next war, Gittelsohn rhetorically asked if there had been any change since the World War. Emphatically not, he declared. The DuPonts and William Randolph Hearst were two examples he cited to show that the same controllers of media thought were still in charge and still had vested interest in US military ventures. In Gittelsohn's view, media manipulation would be just as intense and dishonest as it had been in the run-up to our country's entry into the World War.

The third condition that Gittelsohn pointed out was wartime profiteering. "The first two, in a sense, merely set the stage for our entrance," he said, "the third actually dragged us in. We entered the World War because private capital and industry demanded it!"[10] Acknowledging to the congregation that he could see on their faces that many didn't believe his last claim, he cited several illustrative examples. The Naval Disarmament Conference of 1927 was a colossal failure, he claimed, because of the work of William Baldwin Shearer. Shearer, bankrolled by several shipbuilding firms and backed by the Daughters of the American Revolution, worked proactively to ensure that the conference and all subsequent meetings would fail. According to Gittelsohn, by 1932 the disarmament meetings had been wrecked. "You may not know, however, that almost every prominent armament firm in the world had its representative there to wreck it! What chance will there be for our nation when these forces commence their work?"[11]

Even more damning was his reading from a cablegram sent from US Ambassador to Great Britain Walter Hines Page to Pres. Woodrow Wilson on March 5, 1917. Gittelsohn pointed out that one month after the cablegram was sent, the United States entered the war. Page informed Wilson, "If we should go to war with Germany, all the money would be kept in our country, trade would be continued and enlarged until the war ends, and after the war Europe would continue to buy food and would buy from us also an enormous supply of things to re-equip her peace industries. We should reap the profit of an uninterrupted, perhaps enlarging trade, over a number of years and we should hold their securities in payment. . . . Perhaps going to war is the only way in which our present preeminent trade position can be maintained and panic averted."[12]

After reading the Page cablegram, Gittelsohn asked the congregation if any of them lost a loved one in the war, or if they knew any of the soldiers permanently maimed in the war. "Be comforted, then," he caustically declared, "with the thought that they died to 'maintain our present preeminent trade position' . . . that they made their sacrifice in order that we might reap the profit of an uninterrupted, perhaps enlarging trade."[13] He finished this section of the sermon by reciting several examples of the almost giddy reaction of various American businesses to the news that the United States was entering the war in April of 1917.

As he neared the end of his sermon, Gittelsohn was somber and almost pessimistic. "Nothing short of a miracle," he concluded, "can prevent the outbreak of war in our year 5696 (fall 1935-fall 1936), which starts tonight. The last time a major war was waged, we were forced in because of three conditions. Now, all three are even more dangerous."[14] Was there no hope? "There is hope, my friends, only if we insist that our nation and every other nation disarm."[15] He called for a letter-writing campaign targeting the president and all legislators, demanding they vote to disarm, and supporting only those politicians who were one hundred percent against armaments. Next, he called for all Americans to refuse to believe the propaganda that the armament industry would assuredly create to generate war support. Lastly, he declared that there is hope "only if we dedicate our lives to the building of a new society, one where no few men can have enough financial control to kill the rest."[16]

Gittelsohn dramatically ended his sermon by urging the congregation to take the vow written by the nineteenth century American pacifist Thomas Grimke, which Gittelsohn personally pledged before them: "I, at least, have resolved, and may God give me the strength to abide by that Holy Purpose, that come what may, I shall never bear arms in a civil combat . . ."[17]

As his days at Hebrew Union College drew to a close, Roland Gittelsohn was becoming a rising authority in the anti-war movement. Pacifism was clearly his most passionate issue, and while it might appear that his involvement in a secular, seemingly non-religious worldly concern would not be within the realm of a rabbi's purview, he had no problem reconciling this potential conflict. It all went back to his concept of the rabbinical duties and how the roles of a rabbi had evolved throughout history. There were no rabbis until after the time of Jesus—priests and prophets, but no rabbis. The province of the priest was to implement the sacerdotal practices of the ancient Temple. The prophet was a moral guide and goad. The priest's purview, according to Gittelsohn, was easy to understand; the prophet's was far more difficult and complex. "I needed to appreciate both, for as a modern rabbi my responsibilities would encompass the boundaries of both."[18]

As his twenty-sixth birthday and his ordination were approaching, he was every bit the committed, outspoken activist, determined to reshape the world. Like most of his peers, he had a leftist view of societal issues that frequently called for exposure of the darker sides of a capitalist economy and the "few" villains, mainly bankers and armament manufacturers and dealers, who were no doubt working to embroil citizens into another war purely for profit. Like most of his peers, he had a black and white view of these issues and appeared to be completely obsessed with the First World War and the "lessons" that had to be derived from it. It was almost as

if the radical pacifist proponents could not possibly envision a situation—like the one that was slowly developing in front of their
eyes—that might well justify the United States' involvement in yet
another conflict. They did not recognize the new cause for entering
into war: combating the pure evil of some societies and the evil that
man is capable of. The pacifists behaved as if all people were rational, pragmatic individuals like themselves and that surely their
arguments and their teaching of the "lessons" of the World War
would make all nations realize that war was futile and that peace
was the only answer. While they were espousing this approach,
Japan had already invaded Manchuria and was murdering Chinese
citizens by the thousands. In Germany, Nazism had taken hold of
the country, and in 1933 Adolf Hitler had become chancellor. Had
many of them they read Hitler's 1924 manifesto *Mein Kampf,* they
could have easily seen that the "lessons" Hitler learned from the
First World War were quite different than the ones they preached.

---

May 23, 1936, was a stiflingly hot day in Cincinnati. On the campus of the Hebrew Union College, the graduating rabbinical candidates stood in line, waiting for the cue to begin their processional
into the chapel. Like his fellow candidates, Roland Gittelsohn could
not wait to get inside and escape the powerful rays of the sun that
made his necktie seem like it was strangling him. Finally, at 2:30
p.m., the signal came and they solemnly marched into the chapel
and took their seats. At the bimah, the synagogue's holy lectern,
stood the president of the college, Dr. Julian Morgenstern, who of-
ficiated over the ordination ceremony. For virtually all graduates of
Hebrew Union College, Dr. Morgenstern would have a profound
influence over their lives.

Dr. Morgenstern held his hands solemnly over each student's
head individually as he pronounced the words of Jewish tradition
that were already inscribed on their diplomas. "*Yoreh, yoreh, yadin,
yadinp*—he may surely teach, he may certainly judge." These were
the succinct terms of a rabbi's responsibilities through the centuries,
and they would now be carried out by the newly ordained students.[19]
Like his grandfather, Roland Gittelsohn was about to embark on a
lifetime journey of teaching and judging. In addition, it was to be

a lifetime of study, social crusading, and oftentimes one of intense controversy. After an hour, the newly ordained rabbis departed the chapel, each headed for their first rabbinical postings or for further studies. For Rabbi Gittelsohn and his wife, Ruth, it was time to pack their household goods as they departed from Ohio and started out to begin their new life on Long Island, New York.

On the evening of December 30, 1935, fifty-eight Jewish families met at the Milburn Country Club in Baldwin, Long Island, New York. They shared a common vision and that night would enact a plan to transform that vision into a reality. Presented to the group was a plan to establish a Reform Jewish congregation for their immediate region. The idea was enthusiastically approved by all and a provisional committee was established to organize the proposed synagogue. The committee members immediately and enthusiastically proceeded to carry out their mission.

Their first task was to acquire a temporary site in which to hold both Friday night worship services as well as Sunday religious school instruction. They accomplished this by acquiring a building with a decidedly non-Jewish sounding name: the McIntosh Studio. The first Friday night worship service of the newly established Central Synagogue of Nassau County was held on February 13, 1936. This initial service would be the true test for the visionary group of families that had met only six weeks before at the country club—would the Jewish community attend the initial worship service and support the fledgling synagogue?

The turnout for the first service was described as "electrifying," more than justifying the efforts of the founding families.[20] It clearly displayed the need for the establishment of the synagogue. The Union of American Hebrew Congregations responded with great enthusiasm and encouragement, providing leading metropolitan rabbis for the pulpit through May of 1936.[21] Shortly thereafter, the congregation moved to the Masonic Hall Lodge on nearby Lincoln Avenue.

Earlier in February, the first Synagogue School was established, enrolling thirty students. The enrollment would very soon rise to sixty-two students. Towards the end of the month, the

Woman's Group of the Central Synagogue was founded with an initial membership of thirty women. Concurrent with this rapid growth and organizational evolution, official incorporation of the synagogue took place in March. On April 21, 1936, the first regular meeting of the board of trustees, with William Godnick as president, was held.[22] The new organization was up and running and was fully embraced by the Reform Jewish community. Its rabbinical needs were being temporarily supported by the Union of American Hebrew Congregations. A permanent rabbi was needed to fully establish the synagogue and direct its future. To fulfill this need, the board of trustees looked toward the largest Reform rabbinical school in the nation, Hebrew Union College. Specifically, they sought out an outspoken young rabbi with a reputation of having a brilliant analytical mind: Rabbi Roland Gittelsohn.

———————

In June of 1936, Roland Gittelsohn began what would be a seventeen-year tenure as rabbi to the Central Synagogue of Nassau County. During that timeframe, membership in the synagogue would increase from the original fifty-eight founding families to over nine hundred families. A steady campaign of building and expansion would also take place during Gittelsohn's tenure. However, he would acknowledge that despite all the apparent successes, there were some difficult times and issues that were faced while he was at the temple.

When he took the job, he knew that very few of the families had ever belonged to a synagogue. From the start, the founders appeared to have mixed expectations of their new rabbi. "Many were not quite sure whether they wanted a rabbi who would lead or one who would cater to all their wants," he quickly learned.[23] Gittelsohn had already formed definite opinions of the role of the rabbi as both priest and prophet. Some members of the temple seemed to want a rabbi who would perform only "priestly" functions and would otherwise not involve himself with other more operational and social issues that would fall under the "prophet" role. From the beginning, Gittelsohn made it clear that he would be performing both the priest and the prophet roles as he carried out his rabbinical duties.

Early conflicts arose between the congregation and their new rabbi. Gittelsohn was never one to take criticism very well if he felt it was unjustified, and he was never one to back off in a conflict or difference of opinion. Perhaps the excellent debater within him made it more difficult to compromise at times. "From time to time," he noted, "they contested my judgment on matters clearly within my field of expertise. I therefore had to remind them that just as a physician must be presumed to possess more knowledge of medicine than a patient and an attorney more background in law than a client, so I was the expert on Judaism."[24]

Later in life, he would think back to the early years at Central Synagogue and realize that he probably should have been more diplomatic on some issues and not approach every disagreement as a debate competition to be won or lost. It was not simply principle that always drove his competitive arguments when he disagreed with policies or procedures; he also realized that his own insecurities were a factor. "Like many young clergymen," he reflected, "I was in the beginning not yet secure enough within myself always to yield where I should."[25] Still, he would look back over his tenure at Central Synagogue with pride, noting the impressive growth of the temple's membership, citing it as a "testament to a reasonably balanced relationship, though some tension persisted to the very end."[26]

The congregation would quickly see the passion of their new rabbi displayed in his High Holiday sermons, beginning on Rosh Hashanah eve, September 17, 1936. Certainly there would be no doubt after the services that he intended to be both priest and prophet in the fulfilling of his rabbinical duties. As they sat attentively in the Masonic Hall Lodge, Rabbi Roland Gittelsohn delivered the powerful sermons that he originally delivered in Ohio two years before: "More Human Bondage" and "The Fast That We Have Chosen."

For his initial High Holiday sermons as Central Synagogue's new rabbi, Gittelsohn chose to tone down some of the strident points that he had annunciated two years prior. Without diluting the power of his message, the subtle changes he made reflected both a growing degree of professional maturity as well as a sense of diplomacy appropriate to his new position. He wisely decided that his first High Holiday sermons were not a forum to potentially antagonize any of his congregation, nor to come across like an angry father berating his children. This was nicely demonstrated near the end of his 1936 Rosh Hashanah sermon. After once more, as in 1934, asking the congregation, "What are we going to do about it?," he added a paragraph before launching into his two answers (that we must disarm and must sacrifice for peace). In 1936, he diplomatically added, "First of all, let it be clearly understood by all of us that there is no simple answer to that question. There is neither a simple nor a single way of stopping human sacrifice. But there are certain things we *must* do, certain steps we *must* take even before we attempt anything else. These things are not panaceas, which will in themselves end war. But they are essential beginnings; they are conditions without which the other steps are fruitless."[27] Compared to the 1934 sermon, he came across to his audience as a teacher who was lecturing and educating, not scolding.

Even more revealing was the 1936 version of his Yom Kippur sermon. In it, he once again told the story of Tom Mooney and how one of his congregants assumed that, since he was talking about Mooney, he too must be a communist. This time he wrote, "It happens that I definitely am not!"[28] In addition, in this version he added more statistics about poverty and more examples to illustrate his points. While remaining a powerful teaching experience in social justice, Gittelsohn made a key modification near the end of his talk. The controversial line—"The creed we must adopt is simple: First, the needs of all; second the luxury of a few. Only after *every man* has what he *needs* can *any man* have what he *wants*!"—was omitted and was never spoken by Central Synagogue's new rabbi.

———•———

On November 18, 1936, Gittelsohn delivered the first of his peace group discussions since his ordination. Speaking at the local chapter of the National Conference of Jewish Women, he presented his talk "If Women Wanted Peace." In his presentation he reiterated the main points from the fifth book of *The Jew Looks at War and Peace*. He would be a frequently invited guest speaker, covering the topics from his first book over the next two years. His notes indicate at least four more speaking engagements that included the Long Island Regional Sisterhood Boards in Jamaica, Queens, on September 29, 1937; the United Order of True Sisters on November 22, 1937; and the Kew-Forest Welfare League on January 11, 1938.

# Chapter Six

# Speaking Out for Peace

In the October 1, 1936, issue of *Foreign Affairs*, former Secretary of War Newton D. Baker published an article entitled "Why We Went to War." Baker, an able administrator with no military experience, served in Pres. Woodrow Wilson's cabinet during the World War, where he had a reputation of having pacifist tendencies. In his *Foreign Affairs* analysis of America's reasons for entering the war, Baker stated that industry and commerce had nothing to do with our decisions. Instead, he explained that our entry into the conflict could be explained purely by idealism. In December of 1936, Roland Gittelsohn would use Baker's article as a basis for one of his first sermons on foreign affairs that he would deliver to the Central Synagogue.

In a sermon entitled "How Can We Stay Out of the Next War?" Gittelsohn would touch on many themes that he would continue to embellish on up until America's entry into the Second World War. Government betrayal, business profit motives, pro-war propaganda, and the need to be educated on all these topics would appear repeatedly in his sermons over the coming years. What would also become obvious was his distaste for Woodrow Wilson and his growing disenchantment with Franklin D. Roosevelt. Beginning his sermon by mocking Wilson for getting re-elected on the campaign slogan "He kept us out of war," and noting that war seemed likely in Europe in the near future, he posed to his congregation: How can we stay out of the next war?

Gittelsohn acknowledged that it wasn't an easy question to answer, but to begin to attempt to answer the question, they must understand why the United States became involved in the last war. "I'm ashamed to say," he announced, "that there are still some people who believe that we entered the World War in order to make the world safe for democracy or to end all war,

91

or for some other silly fiction or fable."[1] It was at this point that he referred to Newton Baker's analysis, published less than two months prior, which idealistically supported the concept that the United States entered the war "to make the world safe for democracy." Totally deriding Baker's conclusion as fantasy, he countered Baker's assertion by bringing up the previously mentioned cable from United States Ambassador to Great Britain Walter Hines Page to President Wilson dated March 5, 1917. As previously noted, it was in this message that Page said to Wilson, "Perhaps our going to war is the only way in which our present preeminent trade position can be maintained . . ."[2] Asking from the pulpit if any of the congregants lost loved ones and friends in the last war, or if they had been affected by the total carnage wreaked by the conflict, he sarcastically noted that he was sure that they were comforted by the fact that the losses helped maintain America's "preeminent trade position." In a complete rebuttal to Baker's position, Gittelsohn declared, ". . . it seems to me that this very fact, a frank, honest recognition of the meanness, the baseness, the downright contemptible greed that led us into the war,—it seems to me that right here is our first step in preserving peace."[3]

As a second step, Gittelsohn proposed that they create a well-formulated plan of just what they could expect if war broke out. This was no time, he maintained, for the typical American approach to critical situations, in which citizens tended to adopt a "wait and see" attitude. This was the approach of certain United States senators who Gittelsohn claimed adopted the "wait and see" approach, thinking they could then legislate America's way out of a crisis. Throughout history, he noted that this approach never worked. Referring to the World War, he pointed out, "It didn't work 20 years ago either. Then too we decided to 'wait and see.' But 'wait and see' really means 'wait and drift,' and again we drifted into calamity."[4] Using the analogies of giving vaccines to prevent diseases and buying life insurance before one is too old to make it financially feasible, Gittelsohn asked, "Why can't we apply the common sense of health and insurance to the problems of war? After the war has started is *not* the time for us to chart our course. That's not a time for calm, cool thinking. That's a time of prejudice and pressure and passion! That's a time of hypocrisy and hysterics! And that's why a policy of 'wait and see' is doomed to failure."[5] In summarizing the second requirement to keep us out of war, he reiterated that we must clearly define what we mean by war and that we must have a pre-announced, well thought-out policy when the war starts. Passionately declaring that the country could not afford a policy of "wait and see," he advocated, "In time of peace, prepare for peace!"[6]

Gittelsohn next laid out the final requirement for America to escape the coming war. Stated simply, the country must be willing to pay the price for peace. And that price, he acknowledged, was very high—much higher than the "price" set by the neutrality bill that had been passed two days prior by the United States Senate. Among the provisions of the bill that would eventually develop into the Neutrality Act of 1937 was a prohibition on the exporting of munitions to nations named belligerents by the president or Congress by concurrent resolution. To Gittelsohn, this price was not high enough. "I believe that in order to stand even a ghost of a chance to stay out of the next war we must renounce all trade with all belligerents. We must sell nothing to anyone engaged in the war. We must make no exceptions whatsoever."[7] In answer to anticipated protests that this course was a costly way of avoiding war, he totally agreed that it was "*very* costly indeed." He then cited unnamed authorities who estimated that this ending of all sales to all belligerent parties would cost the United States one billion dollars a year.

As his congregation began to digest this staggering figure, Gittelsohn reassured them that the math involved in his proposed policy actually indicated a massive savings. Citing the work of economist J. M. Clark of Columbia University, he explained that the four years of the World War had cost the United States over ninety billion dollars cash. And this didn't take into consideration human life and suffering, he quickly pointed out. Combining his preplanning proposal for the next war with his "willing to pay the cost of peace" proposal, he summarized his thinking thusly: "$90,000,000,000 in four years! Now suppose someone had offered us a new kind of insurance in 1914, an anti-war insurance. Suppose the premium we were asked to pay had been $4,000,000,000 in order to avoid the loss of $90,000,000,000. Would you be willing to pay that cost? That is the cost of peace."[8]

To further illustrate the price of *not* paying the cost of peace, Gittelsohn proceeded to read accounts of atrocities reported from the ongoing civil war in Spain. After describing young children being killed in an air attack in Madrid, he exhorted his audience, "Mothers and fathers, is it worth one billion dollars a year to save your children from that? . . . If it isn't, then let's forget about peace . . . for me, the whole billion dollars that American business would lose isn't worth the life of one single child! Therefore I for one am ready to pay the price for peace."[9]

Gittelsohn ended his sermon by pointing out that the question with which he began really wasn't so hard to answer after all. The difficult thing was not the stating of an answer, but rather following it. How to stay out of the next war? Not by half-hearted congressional action or by waiting for something to happen and then reacting. The United States could stay out of the next war ". . . by understanding to begin with why we were trapped twenty years ago. Then by setting our course now while there is yet time . . . and finally, my friends, we can stay out of war only if we become willing to pay for peace."[10]

In December of 1936, an international peace conference took place in Buenos Aires, Argentina, that captured the attention of Roland Gittelsohn and compelled him so much that he spoke about it in a sermon to the Central Synagogue on January 15, 1937. The Inter-American Conference for the Maintenance of Peace was held from December 1 through December 23, 1936. Representing the United States was Secretary of State Cordell Hull. Gittelsohn's sermon entitled "Extemporaneous Lecture On: The Inter-American Peace Conference; Achievement or Illusion?" would be the next in a series of sermons to report on international events impacting the avoidance of war and to provide his congregation further insight into his analysis of these events and their meaning.

The conference was attended by 175 delegates representing twenty-one American nations. In the twenty-four days that the conference was in session, there was action taken on 67 of the 115 projects and proposals made. Gittelsohn reported to the congregation that there were three spheres of accomplishment: political, economic, and cultural.[11]

The political accomplishments were threefold. First was obligatory consultation of all parties when peace was endangered. Second was a restatement of the Monroe Doctrine that in essence condemned intervention from outside of the Americas. Gittelsohn's notes indicate "threat vs. 1 = vs. all."[12] Lastly, the conference mandated a common neutral stand in regard to war between any two conference members. In enumerating the economic results, Gittelsohn's notes reflect a degree of skepticism; before listing the results, he wrote, "much ado, talking, pious promises."[13] Reductions in tariffs and equal trade agreements were decided upon as the main consensus reached by the delegates. For cultural results, he noted the exchange of textbooks along with radio and art exchanges.

However, warned Gittelsohn, the Treaty of Versailles also appeared to have tangible results, and, as the deteriorating situation in Europe indicated, the results were ineffective. He posed this fact to the congregation and asked why this was the case. Proceeding to answer his own question, he explained that it was the essential spirit of the Versailles conference, its lack of honest intention and peaceful purpose, that was responsible for its unsuccessful results. What, then, he asked, was the essential spirit of the recently completed Buenos Aires conference? Was it any better than at Versailles?

His answer was unequivocally in support of the intentions of the conference attendees. The essential spirit of the conference, according to Gittelsohn, was the spirit of protest against growing fascism. The essential spirit was one of respect for international law and obligations (although he acknowledged that some of the delegates were discouraged with what they felt were empty promises). Overall, he was impressed with the sincerity of the proceedings and the potential for success. "This is the reason that I hail the conference," he proclaimed.[14]

In summation, Gittelsohn acknowledged that the conference's achievements were, indeed, only potential; they were just signposts of what could lie ahead for cooperating nations. It was up to all members of the conference to determine if they would achieve their goals or if it would all be just another illusion of achievement. To accomplish their goals, the member nations would have to bind together politically and economically, and teach each other culturally. "I pray," he concluded, "that 1938 will find us well on the road."[15]

---

Within the first year of the synagogue's existence, its membership rapidly grew and the board of directors realized that they would need the large capacity that the Masonic Hall Lodge offered for Friday night, holiday, and other religious services, as well as for the monthly meetings of the Women's Organization. Accordingly, they signed a long-term lease, assuring their access to the lodge while they formulated a long range growth plan.[16] A week after the temple's first High Holiday services, the first annual congregational meeting was held on October 5. It was the first opportunity for the congregants to hear reports from the temple's officers and committees, as well as the time they would elect officers and trustees. On February 12, 1937, Rabbi Gittelsohn conducted the first anniversary service. He oversaw the synagogue school classes that were conducted at the Cleveland Avenue School in Freeport, and during that time, the school's enrollment steadily rose. On May 16, 1937, the first confirmation exercises for nine students were held, with Rabbi Gittelsohn conducting the service. Very quickly, adult study groups, Hebrew study groups, and open forums to discuss national and international problems were initiated to meet the needs and interests of the membership.[17] All of these activities were well-suited for the energetic young rabbi whose overriding interest in activism and world affairs was dominated by his passion for pacifism.

The first year of the Central Synagogue's existence proved to be a successful time of increasing enrollment and the initiation of many key programs. Fundraising was going extremely well, and to a large degree the increased growth and bright future potential that was being realized could be attributed to the enthusiastic efforts of their new rabbi. But synagogue membership was not the only thing that was growing in the life of Rabbi Gittelsohn that year. In early 1937, Roland and Ruth Gittelsohn learned that she was pregnant with their first child, due in the fall.

In a sermon entitled "Is There a Road Back?," delivered later in 1937, Gittelsohn told the congregation of a panel discussion on peace that had been held six months prior in a New York City church. There were three panelists, two who upheld the militaristic view and one who argued the cause of peace. The former were newly-commissioned officers in the Army Reserve; the latter was an older man who also arrived in uniform, but it was an old, faded American Expeditionary Forces (AEF) uniform that he had worn when he fought in the World War. While the young officers could speak glibly and theoretically about war, it was the older man—the veteran of the previous war—who, as Gittelsohn emphasized, was for peace because he knew war.

At this point, Gittelsohn acknowledged the presence of many members of the American Legion who were guests of the synagogue that night. "You members of the Legion are the colleagues of that speaker who defended peace in a worn-out uniform of the AEF. You know war because you lived it. And therefore you're better able—or at least you should be better able—to understand why war must be avoided."[18] Pointing out that the audience contained Jews and Christians, veterans and non-veterans, and acknowledging the variety of beliefs among them all, he declared it was safe to say that there were two things that they all had in common, that bound them together. "First: all of us hate war; and secondly: all of us want peace. I think as a matter of fact that I might even go farther than that and say that all of us are devoted to peace, yes, devoted passionately to peace. And especially at this moment all of us are asking the same question: 'Is there a road back? Is there a road that leads from war to peace?'"[19]

Wanting peace and hating war isn't enough, he argued. Gittelsohn used the examples of medical plagues to drive home his point. He pointed out that hating the diseases wasn't enough. It took much hard work to defeat them—man had to pay the cost in order to accomplish that goal. And that, according to Gittelsohn, was the problem—we haven't been willing to pay the cost of peace.

> We want someone to give us peace as a gift. We pray for peace, and then we confidently sit back as if we expected God to lean down out of heaven and pat us lovingly on the back and say to us: "Here my children, you've been good today. So I'm going to give you peace." But let's not fool ourselves, my friends. Peace isn't that easy to get. Peace isn't the product of a wish-bone. Peace is one of the hardest things humanity has ever sought! Peace has a price on it! Do you know when you and I will finally attain peace? Only when we're willing to meet that price![20]

Noting that there were no discounts in the price of peace, he proposed to the congregation that they look at the costs and if they would be willing to pay those costs to attain peace.

The first of those costs no doubt seemed radical to the congregation. He declared: ". . . each nation, in order to achieve harmony, must be willing to sacrifice some small part of its own sovereignty."[21] In all likelihood, however, Gittelsohn was referring to the League of Nations, an organization that the United States never joined, in his statement. He immediately took pains to assure the audience that he did not want to be misunderstood, that his love of the United States and patriotism in defense of America, the land that delivered freedom and opportunity to his family, was second to none. This suggestion of his applied to all nations, not just the United States. "Peace of any kind means a partnership, doesn't it?" he asked.[22] Just as each of the thirteen colonies had to yield a little of its sovereignty when forming our country, so too, must all nations do the same in the quest for true peace. Only then will that goal be achievable.

The next cost to pay in the quest for world peace was the willingness to give up temporary profits of war. Once again, Gittelsohn railed against the armament industry and its influence, which he perceived as pro-war. To illustrate the madness that he sensed, he pointed out that in 1932 both warring countries of China and Japan were buying their weapons from the same arms manufacturer in England. One day the representatives from each government happened to arrive at the British firm at the same time and spent the day comparing their munitions purchases and the prices that each were paying. The two "then issued to the company a joint ultimatum for lower prices. A fine business, isn't it?" he asked with disgust.[23]

Gittelsohn then went on to the third cost to be paid to achieve peace in the world. "The third cost of peace is that we must once and for all get rid of an old idea that most of us still have, the idea that any worth-while purpose can be accomplished through violence or through war. . . . Today war is nothing more than mass murder; today war is nothing but organized butchery; today war is nothing but suicide, — senseless, shameless suicide!"[24] Appealing to the veterans of the World War in the audience, he pointed out that they all had clear aims when they went to war and that they fought the war to end all wars and to establish peace. Yet, the world was now closer to war than it ever was. "You wanted to save the world for democracy, didn't you? But look what's happened to that democracy!"[25] Dictatorship and fascism were now on the rise. "You won a war," he points out to the veterans, "but that victory didn't accomplish either of your purposes."[26]

Gittelsohn ended his sermon by asking: is there a road back? Unequivocally, he stated that there is, but that the road wasn't simple or easy. We have to stop pretending or trying to bargain our way out of the dilemma, he declared. We have to stop trying to buy world peace on the cheap. "Let's face the facts and face them honestly without pretense. Are we willing to pay the price of peace?"[27] He, Roland Gittelsohn, was willing to pay the price, no matter how high. He begged his audience to stand with him so that together they may be willing to pay the cost of peace.

# Chapter Seven

# Some of My Best Friends Are Jews

In early 1937, Gittelsohn delivered a vehemently angry sermon in which he addressed communism and the Soviet Union in a discussion entitled "Some of My Best Friends Are Jews." The source of Gittelsohn's wrath was a book published in December of 1937 by screenwriter and journalist Robert Gessner that was also entitled *Some of My Best Friends Are Jews*. Gessner had previously written a book entitled *Massacre* describing the plight of American Indians. (In 1934, the book had been adapted into a Hollywood screenplay and produced as a film of the same name.) Gessner, who was Jewish, was also a socialist with communist sympathies.

Born and raised in the Midwest, Gessner had received very little in the way of a Jewish education, nor was he particularly aware of the plight of Jews around the world. With the rise of Nazism in Europe and the acceleration of anti-Semitism in Poland, Gessner decided to travel abroad, searching for the stimulus for anti-Semitism and also the antidote for it. He attempted to answer several questions: How do we account for the Jews' "differentness"? Are Jews hated because they are not assimilable? To attempt to answer these questions, Gessner traveled to England, France, Germany, Poland, Palestine, the Soviet Union, and back to the United States on a quest to learn the possible answers.

In his travels, Gessner discovered prejudice of certain classes of Jews against others—almost a caste system in several of the countries he visited, even in Palestine. According to Gessner, this was a result of the exploitive nature of capitalistic societies that promote anti-Semitism whether they call themselves democracies or not. Class interests create prejudice, and class interests mislead and sell out the victims of prejudice. Gessner noted that the world was a madhouse of national imperialisms that were destructive to human happiness, whether it was in the style of the obvious offenders such as Nazi Germany or the more subtle kind practiced by the Zionists. The shining example of an antidote offered by Gessner was the new society in the Soviet Union, which offered ample proof that prejudice could be eradicated.[1]

Reviews of Gessner's book were generally favorable and his evidence, documented with photographs, was praised as irrefutable. The communist journal *New Masses* highly praised the book. A strongly positive review in the *Saturday Review* noted: "If anti-Semitism is a concomitant of a class society, then we can expect to find it absent from a classless society. He went to the Soviet republics for his answer, and he found it. He found the Jew a happy and respected citizen of Moscow, and creator of an autonomous province in Birobidjan." The reviewer concluded: "Mr. Gessner's study of his problem is consistently inductive, and if he emerges with a classless society as the only cure for anti-Semitism it is because the discoverable facts seem to him to point irresistibly in that direction."[2] In a short review of *Some of My Best Friends Are Jews* published by *Kirkus Reviews*, the reviewer's condescending air concerning Jews is patently obvious when he states that the book is "a valuable contribution to the rapidly increasing list of books about the Jewish problem. Extraordinarily dispassionate, objective, recognizing the faults of the jews [sic] and their contribution to the causes of their persecution . . ."[3]

Roland Gittelsohn had quite a different view of the merits of Gessner's work. To say he hated it was an understatement. It is ironic that one of the first public statements on communism and the Soviet Union from a man who in later years would be accused of being a communist would be an extremely caustic condemnation of both communism and the Soviet Union. In addition, his sermon would serve as a bitter attack on Robert Gessner and what Gittelsohn considered Gessner's total lack of qualifications to write a book on the "Jewish Problem." He began his sermon by noting that there was one subject where both education on a topic and experience were not required in order to be considered a subject matter expert. "There is one subject on which one can well be both foolish and ignorant, and still write with the expert voice of authority, and that subject, I am sorry to say, is the field of Jewish problems and Jewish life . . . if you're not quite sure you know anything but you'd like to write a book anyway, write about the Jews. . . . The world will accept you as an authority in a field you know nothing about."[4] Thus did Gittelsohn introduce his congregation to Robert Gessner.

Having just read Gessner's book, Gittelsohn was enraged by what he considered the factual errors it contained, as well as by the fact that he considered Gessner totally unqualified to write such a book. "Mr. Robert Gessner knows about as much of Jewish life as I do of Einstein's relativity," he maintained. "The difference is that I'm not posing as an expert or writing a book about Einstein."[5] To back up his statement, Gittelsohn proceeded to inform his audience of Gessner's background. Gessner, he pointed out, grew up in a small Midwestern town with very few Jews. He had received no Jewish education, and until he was five years old he didn't know that he was a Jew. The first time he was called a Jew he went crying home to his mother, saying he didn't want to be a Jew. Gittelsohn expressed his suspicion that Gessner was a self-hating Jew and then informed his audience that Gessner revealed in his book that until 1932 he didn't know there was such a thing as a Jewish problem.[6]

Continuing on in a sarcastic vein, Gittelsohn noted that Gessner did read a few books on Jewish history when he finally woke up, although Gittelsohn doubted that the man had remembered much of what he had read. Sarcastically, he mocked Gessner's new quest: "So Sir Galahad Gessner mounted his steed and set forth for the Holy Grail, a solution for the Jewish problem." After his worldwide journey, Gessner "returned and found his solution in Union Square."[7] Admitting that Gessner was a good writer who spoke with the voice of authority, Gittelsohn was then quick to liken the voice to that of a ventriloquist. At this point, he informed the congregation that he was going to expose Gessner's faulty methods and conclusions in order to show how he "became an expert in Jewish life in three easy lessons."[8]

In his book, Gessner admits that he left New York for his journey about as ignorant about the Jewish problem as the average gentile. It was here that Gittelsohn claimed that Gessner's expert status was largely built on faulty data. He produced statistics and data to refute several of the claims that Gessner had stated as fact. It was enough, claimed Gittelsohn, "to show how far we can trust the conclusions of a man who builds upon a foundation of misstatements and of lies."[9]

In the next phase of his criticism, Gittelsohn expressed strong doubts about Gessner's objectivity. Gessner claimed that he left on his journey without any idea of a solution and that only his impartial study of the facts that he learned led him to the answer: communism. Here, Gittelsohn's disdain of the man was on full display. "Mr. Gessner leaves N.Y. prejudiced and he returns prejudiced," claimed Gittelsohn. "He leaves with a solution and returns with the same solution. He leaves as a confirmed Communist and he returns as a confirmed Communist." Gittelsohn continued on with this caustic criticism of both Gessner and communism.

> See how simple it all is. See how simple it is for one who is ignorant, for one who is prejudiced, for one who knows nothing, to solve the problems which have plagued and perplexed our greatest and wisest minds for years. You simply decide in advance that Communism is the only answer to the Jewish problem, then you go on a cruise to find Communism, and when you think you have it you stick in your thumb, you pull out a plum, and you say: "See what a good boy am I; see how I've solved the Jewish problem." Simple indeed.[10]

Gittelsohn listed two examples of Gessner's lack of objectivity. When he was in Palestine, Gessner was dismayed with the general signs of militarism throughout Palestine and to see that many Jews had hidden arms to defend themselves in case of need. Yet in his descriptions of Russia, ". . . where the greatest military machine in history is being built,"[11] he doesn't mention seeing a weapon once in over sixty-one pages of text. While Gessner decried the transfer agreement whereby German Jews immigrating to Palestine could take part of their capital with them in the form of gold, he "conveniently" forgot to mention in his book that Russia was one of Hitler's best customers and that the Communist Party had never proclaimed a German boycott. "His solution of the Jewish problem," according to Gittelsohn, "is one part ignorance dissolved in two parts prejudice, and swallowed with a gulp."[12]

Turning to Gessner's proposed solution, Gittelsohn then unleashed his vitriol against the present-day Soviet Union. First and foremost in his criticisms, he pointed out that anti-Semitism had not vanished from the Soviet Union, not by a long shot. Acknowledging that the tsarist pogroms had vanished and the Soviet Union gave at least lip service to making anti-Semitism a punishable crime, Gittelsohn presented evidence offered by knowledgeable Jews and gentiles alike who were sympathetic to the Soviet Union that anti-Semitism was still rampant in that country. Concerning the Jewish settlement of Birobidjan described by Gessner as a classless model for Jewish happiness, and touted by the author as a settlement that offered hope to the Jews of Germany and Poland, Gittelsohn expressed skepticism. Noting that there were over six million European Jews who needed immediate help, Gittelsohn asked the congregation, "Do you know how many Jews were admitted to Birobidjan in the first three months of 1937? Exactly 469!"[13] This did not represent much of a panacea in his mind.

Lastly, there were other facts about Russia that did not sit well with Gessner's conclusions. Noting that it was still illegal to be a Zionist and to teach Hebrew publicly in Russia, Gittelsohn acknowledged that while there was hope for the individual Jew under the Soviet regime, "there [was] no hope whatsoever for Judaism or Jewish group life."[14] To support this conclusion, he offered a quote from Pierre Van Paasen, a distinguished Christian commentator who was sympathetic to communism, who had concluded: "I am at present completely disillusioned on the subject of the future of Judaism in Russia under the present regime. Russian Israel is being slowly driven to extinction."[15]

Gittelsohn finished his sermon with a final swipe at both Robert Gessner and the Soviet Union. He related a popular contemporary anecdote about a communist organizer who noted that people would share many things when the communist revolution comes to America. The communist saw a wagon full of strawberries and shouted, "Comrades, comes the revolution and we'll all eat strawberries like that!" A meek fellow at the back of the crowd chimed in, "But comrade, I don't like strawberries; they give me a rash." "Never mind," replied the speaker, "come the revolution, you'll eat strawberries, you'll like them, and you won't get a rash!"

"My friends," concluded Gittelsohn, "Russia's revolution hasn't eliminated anybody's strawberry rash. And in spite of Robert Gessner, Russia's revolution hasn't solved the problem of the Jew."[16]

# Chapter Eight

# Outspoken Foreign Policy Critic

In 1935, during the first session of the 74th Congress, Representative Louis Ludlow (D-Indiana) submitted a proposed amendment to the United States Constitution that reflected the strong isolationist sentiment prevalent in the country. His proposal, which became known as the Ludlow Amendment, was straightforward; it proposed a constitutional amendment that called for a national referendum on any attempt by the congress to declare war, except in cases where the United States had been attacked first. Ludlow's reasoning struck a chord with many idealistic Americans, especially those who had learned the "lessons" of the World War. The amendment's premise was an exercise in true democracy: those Americans who may be called once again to fight and possibly die in a war should have a direct vote in deciding if the country should go to war.

The Ludlow Amendment was actually a new iteration of the 1914 proposal of a national referendum on any declaration of war; the concept was supported by such notable politicians as three-time presidential candidate William Jennings Bryan.[1] Although Ludlow brought up his proposed amendment in Congress several times between 1935 and 1937 to no avail, it was in fact a popular idea to the American public. A Gallup survey done in September 1935 showed that seventy-five percent of Americans supported the amendment; the approval rate was seventy-one percent in 1936 and seventy-three percent in 1937.[2] Still, the legislation languished in the House Judiciary Committee, unable to get the support needed to vote on a discharge petition that would allow its release and permit debate on the floor of the House of Representatives.

In late 1937, an event took place halfway around the world that would reinvigorate congressional action on the Ludlow Amendment and provide inspiration and encouragement to the amendment's strong supporters nationwide, including Rabbi Roland Gittelsohn. They would all soon be disappointed and angry, and the source of their anger would be Pres. Franklin D. Roosevelt.

————•————

The USS *Panay* was an American gunboat on the Yangzte River in China, part of the US Asiatic Fleet. Its mission was to patrol the river and protect American interests and property in China. After Japan invaded the Chinese mainland in the summer of 1937, the mission of the American patrol boats became increasingly perilous as Japanese forces closed in on the city of Nanking. The *Panay* became involved in evacuating Americans from the city. On the morning of December 12, 1937, Japanese airplanes attacked the *Panay* along with three Standard Oil tankers. The *Panay* was sunk, three sailors were killed, and forty-three sailors and civilians were wounded. In addition, the three tankers with many civilian passengers were sunk.

Film was taken of the attack and rushed to Washington for personal screening by President Roosevelt and Secretary of the Navy Claude Swanson. In viewing the film, it became obvious that the hour-long attack was deliberate, despite the Japanese government's claim that their pilots never saw the American flag that the ship was flying.[3] Secretary Swanson demanded an immediate declaration of war against Japan, and Roosevelt discussed the options of economic or military retaliation against Japan with the rest of his cabinet and military commanders.

Two days after the sinking of the *Panay*, US Ambassador to Japan Joseph Grew cabled Secretary of State Cordell Hull, informing him that,

> [w]hile it is clear, in the light of the above circumstances, that the present incident was entirely due to a mistake, the Japanese government regrets most profoundly that it has caused damages to the United States man-of-war and ships and casualties among those on board, and desires to present hereby sincere apologies. The Japanese government will make indemnifications for all of the losses and will deal appropriately with those responsible for the incident.[4]

The Japanese government promptly admitted full responsibility for the *Panay's* sinking but claimed it was unintentional. Japan claimed its pilots did not see the ship's flag, although a US Navy court of inquiry later determined that the *Panay's* flag was clearly visible.[5] Roosevelt astutely observed that there was no outcry from the American public for retaliation against Japan and quickly quashed any suggestions of military action. A formal apology from the Japanese was delivered in Washington, DC, on Christmas Eve. The Japanese government paid an indemnity of over two million dollars to the United States in April of 1938 to close out the *Panay* incident.

However, on the same day that Ambassador Grew's cable arrived in Washington, Congress again resumed debate on the Ludlow Amendment. The strong isolationist sentiment around the country compelled its representatives to once again attempt to enact the legislation. With Europe and Asia both deteriorating into chaos and America once again in danger of being embroiled in these overseas conflicts, there was renewed interest in the proposed constitutional amendment. By the end of December there was enough congressional support, including the signatures of nearly half of the Democrats in the House, for a House vote on a discharge petition designed to permit debate on the proposed constitutional amendment.[6] The proposed congressional action was exactly what President Roosevelt did not want as he assessed the global situation. He sensed that the amendment would possibly make it to the floor of the House, and he was determined to stop such interference with his handling of foreign policy.

On January 6, 1938, Roosevelt wrote to Speaker of the House William Bankhead (D-Alabama) concerning his views on the Ludlow Amendment. Bankhead had written the president to get his thoughts on the subject, and Roosevelt was blunt with him. "In response to your request for an expression of my views respecting the proposed resolution calling for a referendum vote as a prerequisite for a declaration of war, I must frankly state that I consider that the proposed amendment would be impractical in its application and incompatible with our representative form of government."[7] Pointing out that the Founding Fathers agreed that the representative form of government was the only practical means of government, Roosevelt was certain that the proposed constitutional amendment would cripple any president in his conduct of foreign relations and encourage other nations to violate American rights with impunity. He diplomatically closed his letter by stating, "I fully realize that the sponsors of this proposal sincerely believe that it would be helpful in keeping the United States out of war. I am convinced it would have the opposite effect."[8]

On January 10, 1938, the House of Representatives voted on a discharge petition that would allow debate on the Ludlow Amendment to take place on the floor of the House. With the help of lobbying by Roosevelt's cabinet members, the discharge petition was defeated by a vote of 209 to 188. This was the closest that the amendment ever came to release from the House Judiciary Committee. Around the country, many of the amendment's supporters were livid over the failure to get the legislation out of committee, and many were angry with the man who seemed to be responsible for the outcome in Congress—Pres. Franklin D. Roosevelt.

———— • ————

Two months before the *Panay* incident, a joyous event that blessed the Central Synagogue community occurred on Long Island. On October 8, 1937, Ruth Gittelsohn gave birth to the young couple's first child, a healthy baby boy named David Benjamin Gittelsohn. Roland was rabbi to a new and growing synagogue, he was becoming an acknowledged authority on world affairs, and now he was a father. Certainly his life was complete and fulfilling. However, the world was becoming a more unstable place. Anti-Semitism was on the rise, Adolf Hitler was slowly absorbing much of Europe into the sphere of Nazi Germany, and Japan's aggressive moves in Asia were a constant threat to peace. Peace was Gittelsohn's passion, and he passionately believed in the need for the Ludlow Amendment. The *Panay* incident and the resultant defeat of the Ludlow Amendment in Congress would compel the young rabbi to deliver two scathing sermons on the subject shortly after the congressional vote on January 10, 1938.

———— • ————

Although he had been Central Synagogue's rabbi for only a year and a half, Roland Gittelsohn's social beliefs were already freely expressed in his sermons. He meant for his sermons to be thought-provoking and intentionally would insert examples of current secular social injustices and current world issues in his sermons to make his religious points. In his autobiography, he would embellish on his intentions when he lectured:

> This is the difference between a sermon and a lecture: the purpose of the latter is to convey information: of the former, to motivate changes of attitude and behavior. I am always more than mildly annoyed when, after I have preached my heart out, a congregant says, "I enjoyed your sermon." The aim of preaching is not to provide enjoyment. It would be a far better compliment to say, "Your sermon made me feel uncomfortable," or "I'm going to do something about that."[9]

Approximately two weeks after Congress's vote on the Ludlow Amendment, Gittelsohn delivered a sermon that was so livid and so impassioned that he had to break it up into two weekly services. His topic was the defeat of the Ludlow Amendment, and the title was "Why Was The American People Betrayed?" In his introduction, he freely admitted that he was extremely angry and had had to work hard to control his temper when thinking about the subject. As he explained to the congregation,

> Neither is my recent anger due to any sense of surprise that the Ludlow Bill was defeated,—not at all. The surprising thing is that it was ever even voted on! The surprising thing is that with all the pressure of propaganda against it, it lost only by eleven [sic] votes! I'm not angry because of that. I'm angry because in my humble but positive opinion, you and I have been betrayed. I'm angry because frankly it seems to me that we have been cheated. I'm angry because someone has succeeded in pulling the proverbial wool over our eyes and has at least convinced some of us that black is white and yes is no.[10]

The proceedings in their entirety, according to Gittelsohn, were a hoax. He couldn't recall another time in recent years where so much pressure was exerted in an "unholy" effort to sway congressional voting. He was specifically referring to President Roosevelt's letter to Speaker Bankhead and Bankhead's arm-twisting efforts to get members to vote against the amendment. (Gittelsohn went so far

as to accuse Bankhead of abandoning the concept of impartiality.)
Further infuriating Gittelsohn was the fact that only twenty minutes
of debate was permitted before the vote to allow the discharge
petition was taken. Why were these actions taken that betrayed the
American public, he rhetorically asked? In an effort to be fair, he
suggested they analyze the five main reasons argued by opponents
of the amendment.

The first argument was that the bill was a hasty measure and
was carelessly slapped together, a claim that Gittelsohn called "a
damnable lie."[11] He pointed out that the proposed amendment had
been presented to Congress as far back as 1935 and cited a poll
taken by the American Institute of Public Opinion that indicated
seventy percent of the American people polled supported
it. Further supporting his position, he pointed out that the
amendment's supporters included such distinguished statesmen
as former Secretary of State Henry L. Stimson and former Secretary
of State Frank Kellogg. Kellogg had near-deity status among ardent
pacifists for his co-authoring of the Kellogg-Briand Pact of 1928,
a multinational treaty that outlawed war as a means of settling
international disputes.

The second reason cited as contributing to the Ludlow
Amendment's failure concerned the recent *Panay* incident.
Opponents, according to Gittelsohn, claimed that the bill was
introduced in an effort to embarrass the United States government
in its handling of the recent crises. This was utter nonsense, he
said. First off, the bill was first introduced in 1935, long before
there was any such crisis. Secondly, even if the January 10 vote had
been for approval, it would have only been to release the bill to
be considered on the floor for the entire House to vote on. Had it
successfully passed a vote of two-thirds in the House and then the
Senate, it next would have to be voted on favorably by three-fourths
of the states in order to amend the Constitution. The earliest that
the entire process could have been completed would be in 1940.

The third reason why the Ludlow Amendment was opposed
was because it was said that it would hamper our government in its
handling of foreign affairs. "Well," pondered Gittelsohn, "that all
depends on what you mean by foreign affairs. If by foreign affairs
you mean bluffing, then maybe they were right, perhaps it is true
that the Ludlow Bill *would* be a bit hard on international bluffing."[12]

Noting that bluffing works much better in poker than in diplomacy, he pointed out that bluffing hadn't stopped Germany, Italy, or Japan yet and was unlikely to do so in the future. With his anger rising, he continued his argument, stating, "Or if by foreign affairs you mean sending American soldiers a few thousand miles away to die on foreign soil, if by foreign affairs you mean sending the flag after the dollar and human life after the flag, if by foreign affairs you mean protecting American investments at the cost of disaster and destruction and death, — then the answer is yes: the Ludlow Bill *will* hamper that type of foreign affairs. It *should* hamper that kind."[13] However, if what was meant was that human life is more precious than foreign investments, Gittelsohn assured his congregation that this type of foreign policy would never be hindered by the Ludlow Bill.

The fourth argument that Gittelsohn presented was that the bill's opponents claimed its adoption would make the United States vulnerable to foreign attack. Quickly, he pointed out that in the case of a foreign attack on our country the Ludlow Bill would not apply and a national referendum would not be called for. In a somewhat startling statistic, he claimed that Samuel MacGowen, the former paymaster general of the Navy, had shown that a nationwide referendum could be held if necessary in two to three days and claimed that no government spokesman had challenged that assertion.[14]

The last objection was also the one that Gittelsohn claimed was the most dangerous. Opponents, he said, felt that the people can't be trusted in important matters of war and peace. Angrily, Gittelsohn retorted, "I'd like to know where else the people have more *right* to be trusted. I want to know where else the people have more *need* to be trusted. To me this strikes at the very heart of democracy. And I think it is time for us to understand that there isn't such thing as half-a-democracy; democracy is like chastity:—either you have it or you don't,—there is no half-way point!"[15] What's the use of democracy, he rhetorically asked, if we can't be trusted to have a say in the big matters such as the issue of war and peace? Using the January 10 vote as a metaphor for the concept of whether we had a democracy or not, he cynically pointed out that while 209 representatives said no, 188 said yes.

Gittelsohn looked out on the congregation and posed a question to those 209 representatives and to anyone in the audience who agreed with them. If we couldn't trust the people to make decisions about war and peace—the people who would pay for the war and support the war and die in the war—then who on earth could we trust? The president? No, said Gittelsohn, "not if I have anything to say about it! I wouldn't be willing to trust any one man with that decision."[16] Pointing out that Woodrow Wilson claimed to want peace but led us into war in 1917, so too, was he afraid that Franklin D. Roosevelt would potentially do exactly the same thing.

He expressed the same lack of trust in the Congress to be given the decision-making authority in the matter of entering war, despite the fact that the United States Constitution grants Congress alone the authority to declare war. Here, his fury against the Congress was unbridled, and he vented his anger to his congregation. True, the people may be foolish and ignorant, but ". . . it's just as true of Congress! They too are foolish; they too are ignorant; and they too can be swayed. Plus one other thing: they can be bought. It's a whole lot easier to bribe 530 men than it is millions of men. It is much simpler, and incidentally, much cheaper for the makers of armaments or the investors of money to buy Congress than to buy the nation."[17]

But Gittelsohn was not done with his stinging criticism of Congress. In a statement that is eerily predictive of the Gulf of Tonkin Resolution engineered by Pres. Lyndon Johnson in 1964, Gittelsohn declared:

> Some day. . . we are going to wake up to the fact that in spite of our constitutional theory, Congress doesn't have any more to say about declaring war today than we do. When it comes to war any President at any time can make any Congress sit up on its hind legs and eat out of his hand. Just look what happened only 2 weeks ago. The President spoke, and presto! 55 Congressmen who had just signed the petition of discharge changed their minds. That's how much Congress has to say about it."[18]

According to Gittelsohn, it had always been that way. As he explained to his audience, on over sixty occasions a president had sent American troops on foreign missions without asking Congress and without Congress objecting.

No, concluded Gittelsohn, he could not trust the president or the congress in the matter of war and peace. "It isn't the President or the Congress or the traders who do the fighting. When it comes to war in which the *people* must suffer and the *people* must pay and the *people* must die, I say the people should be trusted."[19] Begging his congregation's indulgence, he apologized for not be able to finish his topic in one sermon and invited them to return the following week to actually address the question, "Why was the American people betrayed?"

A week later he returned to the pulpit to finish his thoughts on the defeat of the Ludlow Amendment and the betrayal of the American people. He began by quickly recapping the arguments that he presented the previous week, which he claimed the amendment bill's opponents used in engineering the bill's defeat. He then turned to answer the question posed by the sermon's title and no doubt surprised the congregation by announcing: "Well, my friends, frankly I think that at this particular moment and for some time to come, that is almost an unanswerable question. I think right now the best that any of us can do is guess. . . . So tonight I tell you at the start that our question cannot really be answered."[20]

The congregation could not have been surprised, though, when their rabbi immediately continued by revealing that there were three causes of the bill's defeat. "The first is that our government today has no such thing as a consistent foreign policy," he began. To illustrate this point, he once again turned to the May 16, 1933, speech by President Roosevelt and the president's statement that "The only way to disarm is to disarm. The way to prevent invasion is to make it impossible . . ."[21] Contrasting this to Roosevelt's buildup of the United States Navy as reported only nine months later by *Time* magazine, Gittelsohn pointed out to the congregation, "And that was 4 years ago. Since then we've gone insane, utterly and completely insane in our spending for war."[22]

The second reason he gave the audience was more startling if not shocking. The only thing consistent at all with any foreign policy that we may be pursuing, he claimed, was that the United States "is definitely and deliberately preparing not for defense and not for protection but for foreign war on foreign soil!"[23] To back up this statement, he urged the congregation to read two recent books that addressed United States military policy and strategy. "Read these books," he urged, "I beg of you. See what they say. And remember that not once has any other authority been able to challenge or disprove them."[24] The books—*We Can Defend Ourselves*, by Major General Johnson Hagood, and *The Tragic Fallacy*, by Maurice Hallgren—offered five premises on which the United States should base its military and defense posture.

When viewed retrospectively through the lens of presentism, the five arguments appear stunningly naïve. But it should be recalled that in the 1930s these views had wide acceptance. The authors' first premise was that the United States held a natural advantage enjoyed by no other world powers—namely, the geographic isolation afforded by large oceans on either side. As Gittelsohn quipped, our most reliable defenses were "Captain Atlantic" and "Corporal Pacific." Next, the authors claimed that for the present time and indefinitely into the future, no nation on earth would have any reason to attack us. Japan, for example, had its hands full with its current foreign endeavors and wouldn't for any logical reason want a conflict with the United States. While Gittelsohn didn't mention Nazi Germany, no doubt the same reasoning entered the authors' thoughts.

As their third premise, the authors cited the logistical improbability of any nation attempting to attack the United States. Noting our logistical difficulties in preparing for our entry into the World War that was fought halfway around the world, it would surely represent an equal if not more difficult logistical challenge to any potential attackers of America. Tied in with this was the fourth premise: the innate military unfeasibility of a foreign nation attacking American shores. "There isn't a bombing plane invented that could carry its full load of bombs from across the seas to our shore," Gittelsohn explained. "Furthermore, any nation foolish enough to attack us would need a fleet consisting of more than all the ships of all the world's fleets combined! To land an army of only 300,000 men on our shores—and that would be a small army to invade this country—to land 300,000 men on our shores would require a fleet of 580 ships, not counting escorts."[25] The last premise touted our strong natural defense position resulting from the previously described factors. Easily, explained Gittelsohn, we could defend ourselves with no more than half our present fleet. Hence, he concluded, our defense program was clearly not intended for defense of the American homeland but was, in fact, ". . . clearly and definitely and crudely a program of aggression on foreign soil."[26]

Together, these five summarized arguments from Hagood's and Hallgren's books supported Gittelsohn's second theory on why the Ludlow Amendment was opposed and defeated (that the United States was on the offensive, not the defensive). From there, Gittelsohn launched into his analysis of the *Panay* incident. Excoriating the media coverage of the event, he informed the congregation of the false hysteria that he perceived had been generated. "And the next day as a climax our papers were filled with lurid descriptions and screaming ads: the truth about Japan! And what was the truth? What did the pictures actually show? Nothing! For all practical purposes, nothing! And perhaps just because they really showed nothing the commentator certainly did his best to arouse our basest emotions of false patriotism and make us want to grab a gun and defend ourselves half-way around the world."[27] In Gittelsohn's opinion, all of the news coverage of the *Panay* incident had one purpose: to arouse the American public for war. The Ludlow Bill would have clearly been an obstacle in the government's conduct of foreign war and hence, to Gittelsohn, this was the second reason for the bill's defeat.

To explain the third and most important reason he offered for the Ludlow Bill's defeat, Roland Gittelsohn delivered a stinging rebuke on American society in general. As the congregation listened intently to their rabbi, he made no excuses for his thoughts.

> I'm purposely phrasing it just about as crudely and bluntly as I can to see if I can't jolt at least some of you out of a smug and dangerous complacency. I think the Ludlow Bill was defeated because as a group American citizens and especially American parents are suckers! That's a harsh accusation, isn't it? But harsh or not, it is true! We don't deserve peace. We haven't worked for peace. We don't sacrifice or lift a finger for peace. . . Rabbis and peace leaders can talk their throats out, and still the average American parent does nothing.[28]

The United States could have done something on behalf of the Ludlow Bill, he explained. How many in the congregation had written to their congressman, he asked? He answered with a stinging assertion that hardly anyone in the audience had done so. It should have been done, he insisted, for our children. "For God's sake," he implored; "what's wrong with us? We failed. And because we failed, we deserved to be betrayed." He closed by offering his solemn hope and prayer that they all may have learned something "from our tragic failure."[29]

# Chapter Nine

# Popular Front

Even as world events such as the *Panay* incident were fanning Roland Gittelsohn's pacifist passions, the anti-war movement as a whole was evolving and was beginning to fragment. By 1937 its emphasis was gradually ebbing away from pure pacifism and an endorsement of American isolationism to one of multinational collaboration against the threats posed by fascist regimes. Occurring almost simultaneously with the sinking of the *Panay*, and exactly when Gittelsohn was preaching that America had been betrayed, the anti-war movement would alter its course dramatically. As early as 1935, it was the activities of the communist radicals that began to shift the movement's goals away from isolationism and towards a collective security arrangement on behalf of a Popular Front against fascism. Influenced by the Seventh World Congress of the Communist International in August of 1935, the efforts of the communist students within the NSL were now intended to shift the movement's foreign policy away from neutrality and focused on the endorsement of collective efforts among the United States, the Soviet Union, and other anti-fascist states to prevent military aggression by Germany, Italy, and Japan.[1]

By late 1935, there was a grassroots movement within the socialist League for Industrial Democracy to push for amalgamation with the National Student League. In October of 1935, the executive boards of both organizations recommended their merger into a new organization, the American Student Union (ASU). Their initial convention was scheduled to be held in Columbus, Ohio, on December 29, 1935. The convention was attended by over four hundred students. After stormy debates, the union was approved and the new organization subsequently held its first meeting.

In establishing a platform for the new organization, designing a domestic agenda proved easy. It was basically a repetition of the previously stated domestic aims of both organizations, although to broaden its appeal to mainstream students they specifically avoided Marxist rhetoric.[2] It was the approval of a united foreign policy plank that proved extremely difficult for the two factions. The tension centered on the Oxford Pledge and the question of United States neutrality. Since the Seventh World Congress, Socialist students had real concerns about the communist-dominated NSL's commitment to the original anti-interventionist principles of the anti-war movement; they feared that NSLers would abandon those principles and support United States intervention in overseas wars in support of the Popular Front against fascism.[3] At the December 29 meeting, the issue was addressed head on by the League for Industrial Democracy (LID) faction.

A resolution proposed by socialist Hal Draper attempted to paint the communist block into a corner by asking them to address specific hypothetical situations. For instance: would the new ASU support the United States entering a war in which they were allied with the Soviet Union? The former NSLers refused to be drawn into the trap, relying on their previously stated support of the Oxford Pledge, not bothering to restate their views that they really only opposed "imperialistic" wars, not wars against fascism that they would support in concert with the Soviet Union. In the end, Draper's amendment was defeated and the new ASU ended its founding convention with the appearance of harmony among all of the factions. In fact, its governing structure was dominated by former NSLers.

The event that did the most to accelerate the emphasis of the anti-war coalitions as typified by the radical student peace movement was the Spanish Civil War. In July of 1936, military generals of the Spanish Republican Army, fearing the collapse of Spain into anarchy, staged a coup d'état in Spanish Morocco. The rebellion quickly spread throughout Spain, precipitating a civil war. The elected government, with its supporting factions of the communists, anarchists, and various other left-wing groups, became known as the Loyalists or Republicans, whereas the rebelling military along with other elements became known as the Nationalists. The Nationalists, led by Gen. Francisco Franco, soon had the support of the governments of Nazi Germany and fascist Italy. The Loyalists had strong support from the Soviet Union. International Brigades, consisting of volunteers from many countries, including the United States, traveled to Spain to fight for the Loyalists. It was in Spain that many historians note that a "dress rehearsal" for the Second World War took place between 1936 and 1939.

The Spanish Civil War served as the wake-up call for a generation of student activists who had been lost in isolationist slumber.[4] During the early 1930s, most students, Roland Gittelsohn included, assumed that the United States could be the vanguard in preserving peace by adhering to a policy of strict neutrality. In many ways, advocates of strict neutrality assumed that it was purely economic factors and profit motives that drove American entrance into world conflicts. Even as they uneasily read about the developing situations in Europe and the Far East, adherents of the Oxford Pledge and organizations such as the War Resisters (which Gittelsohn was a member of) clung to the advocacy of strict isolationism and American neutrality. The civil war in Spain would be the pivot point that would discredit United States neutrality in the eyes of many students, providing communist ASUers with many allies in their drive to convert the student movement from isolationism to collective security and anti-fascist interventionism.[5]

Nearly three thousand Americans volunteered to go to Spain and fight for the Loyalists as members of the Abraham Lincoln Battalion. The majority of the volunteers were members of the American Communist Party and over five hundred were students. Over seven hundred Americans would die fighting for the Loyalists as part of the battalion.

The *Panay* incident of December 1937 was merely the last of a series of world events that year that worked to push the American anti-war movement away from isolationism and towards a Popular Front against fascism. In April of 1937, a thoroughly disgusted world observed the Nationalist forces destroy the Spanish city of Guernica, an event soon to be immortalized in Pablo Picasso's memorable painting. In July of 1937, Japanese military forces engaged in a battle with Chinese forces at the Marco Polo Bridge near Beijing that served as a pretext for a full-scale Japanese invasion of the Chinese mainland. On October 5, 1937, Pres. Franklin D. Roosevelt gave a speech that would indicate his shifting view away from isolationism and toward one suggesting a course of American interventionism on the world scene.

Speaking to a large crowd in Chicago and on broadcast radio, Roosevelt began by lamenting the current state of world events.

> The high aspirations expressed in the Briand-Kellogg Peace pact [*sic*] and the hopes for peace thus raised have of late given way to a haunting fear of calamity . . . Without a declaration of war and without warning or justification of any kind, civilians, including vast numbers of women and children, are being ruthlessly murdered with bombs from the air. In times of so-called peace, ships are being attacked and sunk by submarines without cause or notice.
>
> Let no one imagine that America will escape, that America may expect mercy, that this Western hemisphere will not be attacked and will continue tranquilly and peacefully to carry on the ethics and arts of civilization . . . The peace, freedom, and the security of ninety per cent of the world are being jeopardized by the remaining ten per cent who are threatening a breakdown of all international law . . . The moral consciousness of the world . . . must be aroused to the cardinal necessity of honoring the sanctity of treaties, of respecting the rights and liberties of others and of putting an end to acts of international aggression.[6]

Roosevelt next compared the actions that the world must take to the actions taken by the health community when combating the spread of disease to prevent epidemics. "When an epidemic of physical disease starts to spread, the community approves and joins in a quarantine of the patients in order to protect the health of the community against the spread of the disease."[7] He concluded by declaring: "War is a contagion, whether it be declared or undeclared. It can engulf states remote from the original scene of the hostilities. We are determined to keep out of war, yet we cannot insure ourselves against the disastrous effect of war and the dangers of involvement. We are adopting such measures as will minimize our risk of involvement, but we cannot have complete protection in a world of disorder in which confidence and security have broken down."[8]

With his Quarantine Speech, Roosevelt's remarks signaled an abandonment of isolationism and espousal of collective security and a preparedness to face down aggressors, peacefully if possible but by force if necessary.[9] While angering isolationists like Roland Gittelsohn, it provided strong support to leaders in the ASU who were attempting to transform the ASU officially into a pro-collective security organization—a move that would alienate the student movement's Trotskyist Young People's Socialist League (YPSL), and pacifist minorities, while retaining the support from liberals, who constituted a majority of the national student body.[10] They made their move two months after FDR's speech.

At their national convention held at Vassar College in December 1937, both factions came prepared to do battle over the pro- or anti-collective security stance that should become the ASU's official position. The key issue emerging for the fight to come was the Oxford Pledge. The topic was a tremendous source of friction in both the pre-convention preparatory meetings as well as the convention itself, which was held over the Christmas break. Although seemingly allowing equal debate on the subject, the pro-collective security advocates (who were largely members of the communist faction) had used manipulative tactics to achieve their goal. One pro-collective security activist later gloated over the disingenuous behavior of the communist students in pushing their agenda. "The story is that the YCL [Young Communists League] pulled in a lot of delegates who never even registered to vote on it. Anyway, the whole thing is very sweet," she boasted.[11]

Prior to the final vote being taken, the YPSL were permitted to have the Socialist Party's most eloquent spokesman, Norman Thomas, address the convention. "Any involvement by Washington in these conflicts would only serve the interests of American imperialism and militarism," he warned. "We are not anxious to join the collective suicide club as proponents of collective action by governments would have us do."[12] Despite Thomas' impassioned arguments, most of the delegates were unimpressed. By a lopsided vote of 282 to 108, the convention resolved to drop the Oxford Pledge from the ASU platform and to endorse collective security.

The ASU proceeded to pass resolutions calling for the naming of aggressors on the international scene as well as the boycotting of such aggressors as Japan. As an interesting symbol of perceived support for their new position, the ASU embraced the new positions outlined by President Roosevelt in his Quarantine Speech, although Roosevelt would not soon follow up his speech with any concrete action. ASU president Joseph Lash requested and received from Roosevelt a letter of welcome to the delegates of the convention that was highly publicized by the ASU. While now promoting a national policy of collective security, the ASU still clung to policies that opposed United States preparations for war, including the "skyrocketing military budget" and mandatory ROTC, positions the organization held since its founding.[13]

In 1938, the still-sizable dissenting faction of the ASU that vigorously supported the Oxford Pledge—the YPSL, the Trotskyists, and the pacifists—broke away from the ASU. Forming their own organization called the Youth Committee for the Oxford Pledge (YCOP) (soon to be renamed the Youth Committee Against War, YCAW), they attempted to compete with the ASU for the hearts and minds of the American student population as well as the youth of America. They proceeded to organize a separate student strike for 1938 in competition to the annual strike called by the ASU. In the end, the ASU was able to draw the lion's share of student interest. They out-organized the YCAW and effectively used Roosevelt and the Quarantine Speech to appeal to the majority of liberal students who were admirers of the president.

The final defeat for the YCAW occurred in August of 1938 at the second World Youth Congress (WYC) held in New York City and Poughkeepsie. The ASU's goal was to translate the success of its student strike against war into a demonstration of solidarity among students internationally. Attracting more than five hundred delegates from fifty three nations, the culmination of the WYC meeting was the adoption of a strong collective security statement, the Vassar Peace Pact, which enraged the YCAW and proved to be a fatal blow to it and its isolationist allies. The pact codified the delegates' pledge "to bring to bear . . . upon our respective authorities to take the necessary concerted action to prevent aggression and bring it to an end, to give effective assistance to the victims of . . . aggression and to refrain from participating in any aggression whether in the form of essential war material or other financial assistance."[14]

The outcome of the WYC added greatly to the sense of progress and momentum of student activists promoting collective security on campus. Ulterior motives of the ASU's communist leadership were no less important as a driving force away from isolationism and towards collective security. Demonstrating their dogmatic loyalty, as well as their spectacular naïvete, ASU's communist student leaders regarded the USSR as a leftist utopia, a worker's paradise. A Popular Front security, they believed, was essential for the protection of the Soviet Union against its fascist enemies.[15]

The same month that the ASU rejected the Oxford Pledge and endorsed a Popular Front concept, the USS *Panay* was bombed by Japanese warplanes. Also in that same month, the Ludlow Bill was re-introduced into the House Judiciary Committee in the United States House of Representatives only to go down to defeat a few weeks later. It was in this setting that Rabbi Roland Gittelsohn, staunch pacifist and War Resisters League member, delivered his two-part sermon "Why Was the American People Betrayed." In 1938, the student anti-war movement began to fragment, and the new emphasis became one of collective security. The ASU and its Popular Front platform had become dominant. In spite of the changing anti-war movement that, to a degree, was passing him by, and despite the deteriorating world situation, Gittelsohn remained committed to total pacifism and would continue to speak out against war in the upcoming years.

But the ASU's importance and dominance would come to a crashing halt a year later when Adolf Hitler, widely known to be a rabid anti-communist, signed a non-aggression pact with the Soviet Union. The West was stunned by the hypocrisy of Joseph Stalin and the Molotov-Ribbentrop Pact, signed on August 23, 1939. Here, American peace advocates were in many instances working for a Popular Front solely for the protection of the Soviet Union from fascist Nazi Germany, and now Stalin signed a non-aggression pact with the devil incarnate. The non-communist members of the ASU abruptly abandoned the organization. The ASU, which would meet for the last time in 1941, would be exposed for the communist front organization that it largely was.

Roland Gittelsohn was never a member of the ASU but was instead a War Resisters League member and a pacifist. As such, he opposed the precepts espoused by President Roosevelt in his Quarantine Speech and frequently commented on what he considered the hypocrisy of the president, who seemed to talk out of both sides of his mouth when it came to armaments and national defense. Gittelsohn would continue to speak out against war, promote isolationism, and argue against the economic incentives that he believed threatened to entangle us in another overseas war. And he would continue to restate the lessons of the World War in many fiery sermons. War, he believed, must be avoided at all costs.

But by May of 1940, even he would begin to have doubts.

## Chapter Ten

# "The Next War for Democracy Will Kill Democracy"

In 1938, Europe continued to fall under the domination of Nazi Germany. On March 12, 1938, the *Anschluss*, or annexation of Austria into Germany, took place. For years Germany had been pressuring the Austrian government to submit to annexation, and there was a sizable part of the Austrian population that favored the action. Austrian chancellor Kurt Schushnigg attempted to resist Germany, but bowing to pressure from both German and Austrian Nazis, he scheduled a national referendum to vote on the issue. In spite of the chancellor's intentions and hopes that Austria would remain independent, the Nazi Party in Austria engineered a coup d'état on March 11; the following day, Hitler annexed Austria.

The actions of Nazi Germany against Austria infuriated many Americans, especially those who, like Roland Gittelsohn, loathed fascism. He would address his congregation less than three weeks later, on April 1, and deliver a stinging denunciation of fascism and war. His ardent opposition to war would not be a surprise. However, his emphasis on the dangers of fascism would be directed not toward Germany but rather to the threat of fascism that he perceived arising in the United States. The bulk of his wrath would be aimed at legislation pending in the United States Congress.

In a sermon entitled "Should We Fight for Democracy?" Gittelsohn began by admitting that he, as a pacifist, was going through a period of discouragement. To him, mankind's short memory was frustrating; he noted that it had only been nineteen years since the end of the World War, when the country had vowed never again to fall into the abyss of war. Yet, he exclaimed, had we kept that vow, the congregation would have no need for a sermon with a title that asks if we should fight for democracy. He told of conversations he had with two members of the congregation after the announcement of the Nazi annexation of Austria. Knowing that the rabbi was a pacifist, one congregant asked him whether "recent events and especially the rape of Austria hadn't changed [his] opinions. He said that he, too, hated war; he too loved peace and wanted peace. But then he added what to [Gittelsohn was] a tragic conclusion. He said: 'Rabbi, we live today in a world of force. Force must be met with force. The only way to stop fascism is with war. The only way to stop Hitler is to smash him. Much as I love peace and much as I want peace, I wouldn't hesitate to enlist tomorrow in a war against fascism.'"[1] Less than a day later, a woman from the congregation who had a son nearly of draft age told her rabbi, "I would gladly sacrifice my son in a war against Hitler and for democracy."[2]

Gittelsohn explained that he wanted these conversations to be the background for the evening's sermon as, in a sense, he would be speaking to these two people through the entire audience as they pondered the question posed by the sermon's title. It seemed to him that there were certain things these two people had forgotten—as most of the audience likely had forgotten also—and it would be his role to remind them of these things. He would be speaking plainly and bluntly, especially to those who would be ready to take up arms.

Reminding the audience that it wasn't the first time that many were ready to take up arms in a fight for democracy, he quoted an eloquent statement that claimed, among other things, that right is more precious than peace. Were these the words of the two previously mentioned congregants? No, Gittelsohn informed them. They were "not the words of 1938; they come from 1917; and they're the words of President Woodrow Wilson, spoken 21 years ago tomorrow, when he asked Congress to declare war."[3] He advised those who would be willing to go to war for democracy to read those words over and over and remember what they resulted in for Americans in 1917 and 1918.

In the next part of his sermon, Gittelsohn vented his frustrations, passions, and absolute hatred of fascism. In preparing for this address, he had often asked himself, "What's the use? If history hasn't taught people anything how can I?" With bitter cynicism, he exclaimed, "We fought to save the world, to make the world safe for democracy, didn't we? What we did in the name of democracy sounds like a funeral dirge."[4] After listing the horrendous cost of blood and treasure, he demanded: "Well, where is the democracy that these 10 million boys died for? Answer me, where is it?"[5] He asked his congregation how he could he make them see, how he could impress these things on them. "If I thought it would do any good, believe me, I'd get down on my knees this very moment and plead with you: let's be sensible. Let's not be stupid! Let's not be fools! We tried it once and we failed. Let's at least be willing to learn that can't defend democracy by war!"[6]

Democracy, he informed them, could no more be created by war than love could. Democracy is the opposite of war. To illustrate the preposterous idea that war would result in democracy, he used the following example: a doctor believes that he can prevent the spread of scarlet fever by infecting the population with typhoid. It's true that the scarlet fever would be wiped out, but the Pyrrhic victory would, of course, result in the death of the population, not preserve it. "That's the only way war will wipe out fascism;—if it destroys the last living remnant of humanity and civilization, then perhaps the monkeys who remain will have more sense than to be fascists."[7]

"We've forgotten that fascism was itself created by war and thrives on war," Gittelsohn continued. "After all, what is fascism if it isn't an extension of the psychology of war? . . . You can't teach men for 4 years how best to kill and then suddenly to think human life is sacred. You can't tell men for 4 years that everyone must obey an absolute leader and then suddenly expect them to recognize individual freedom . . . We must understand that war and fascism are like the two sides of a coin; you can't have one without the other. . . . The last war created fascism, and the next war isn't going to end it." He then indulged in a grim prophecy for his congregation: ". . . the next war for democracy will make fascism supreme. The next war for democracy will kill democracy. Remember that! It will stifle it and strangle it and choke it! After the next war, democracy will be something to read about in books."[8]

It was at this point that Gittelsohn stated that on the day the United States entered its next war for democracy, America would automatically become fascist. What was the basis for such a seemingly outrageous assertion? The answer lay in legislation then being proposed in Congress. The Sheppard-May Bill, a wartime industrial mobilization bill introduced in both houses on January 6, 1937, represented to Roland Gittelsohn as big of a threat domestically as Nazi aggression did overseas. The House's version—the May Bill (HR 9604), which was sponsored by Military Affairs Committee chairman Andrew J. May—was then under debate in the House. To Gittelsohn and others, it represented nothing less than an executive-branch power grab by President Roosevelt, one that would make him a dictator.

The expressed purpose of the May Bill was to take the profits out of war. It had many supporters, such as the American Legion, the Secretaries of War and the Navy, and influential presidential advisor Bernard Baruch. Gittelsohn insisted that the bill did not remove the profits from war, and he was actually correct. The flawed legislation, described by critic Sen. Gerald Nye of North Dakota as a "very peculiar kind of bargain" that "offers something for every shade of believer in what ought to be done in time of war,"[9] actually offered pious hopes of eliminating excessive war profits and offered no concrete means of achieving such elimination.[10] To Gittelsohn and like-minded others this was bad enough, but it wasn't the provision of the bill that outraged him the most. Gittelsohn noted that under the expanded powers of the president proposed by the law, the president "could draft every man in America within the age limit for fighting."[11] In addition, he pointed out to the congregation that the president would be allowed to freeze wages and fix prices. Senator Nye described the legislation thusly: "In general, the bill provides for an undisguised dictatorship to be set up under the executive."[12] In the Minority Report of the Military Affairs Committee, minority dissent to the bill was expressed by Texas representative Maury Maverick, who denounced the bill as taking absolutely no profits out of war and giving to the president "gigantic, impartial, dictatorial power of the most extreme kind."[13]

"Well, how do you like that?" Gittelsohn asked his audience. "Is that fascism or isn't it? Of course it is! You know it is!" he thundered. "Then remember that when the next war for democracy begins, that's what you and I are apt to have in this land."[14] Did this all mean that he was an isolationist, he rhetorically asked? No, he explained, not at all. "I am an isolationist only in this sense: isolation from everything that leads to war; cooperation with everything that makes for peace." He believed in the need to defend democracy, but not through war. "I don't propose to defend democracy by killing it. We can defend democracy by preserving it and protecting it at home, not by passing the May Bill."[15] Gittelsohn's solutions to defend democracy included economic cooperation with other nations, boycotts of all belligerent nations, and other means of non-violent defense.

Before ending his sermon with an illustrative story from ancient history, Gittelsohn looked down on his congregation and explained that time constraints prohibited him from going into more details on his theories for the preservation of democracy. He did, however, issue a dire warning: "But of one thing I'm sure and of that one I would convince you if it is humanely possible. And that is that we should not, we cannot, we dare not, we must not fight war for democracy. War will be the end of democracy."[16]

The United States Congress never did pass the Sheppard-May Bill. Instead, it passed the Act of May 17, 1938, which amended the Vinson-Trammel Act of 1934—legislation that dealt with navy shipbuilding—in an effort to regulate shipbuilder excess profits.

# Chapter Eleven

# Opposing "Boss" Hague

By the spring of 1938, Mayor Frank Hague was in the twenty-first year of his thirty year reign as the "boss" of Jersey City, New Jersey. His total domination of Jersey City politics was highlighted by corruption, voter fraud, and political cronyism. His tolerance for dissent was nonexistent and his willingness and ruthless ability to crush his political opponents was legendary. So brazen was his ability to corrupt the political process that in 1937 Jersey City had 160,050 registered voters but only 147,000 people who were of the legal voting age.[1] Among the many enemies perceived by this Democratic Party boss was organized labor. A particular target for Hague's wrath was the newly formed labor union, the Congress of Industrial Organizations.

Originally named the Committee for Industrial Organization, the group was founded by John L. Lewis in 1935 as a union representing unskilled industrial workers. It was originally part of the American Federation of Labor (AFL), but within a year conflicts between the parent organization and its focus on craft unionism and the Lewis organization's emphasis on unskilled labor made the partnership untenable. In 1936 the membership of the Committee for Industrial Organization was expelled from the AFL. Lewis's union, representing such workers as miners and steelworkers, reorganized itself as the Congress of Industrial Organizations (CIO) in 1938.

The Soviet Union had already ordered the dissolution of its American labor union, the Trade Union Unity League, in 1934 and ordered its members to join the AFL. The Communist leaders now saw the newly formed CIO as a better opportunity to advance its agenda and ordered its members to withdraw from the AFL and to join the CIO, where they would rapidly achieve disproportionate influence.[2] This made it even easier for Hague, who equated the labor movement with anti-American communism, to oppose the CIO (or any labor movement that he didn't agree with). In a February 1938 *Life* magazine profile of Hague that documented, among other things, his battle with the CIO, Hague was quoted as saying, "All the forces arrayed against me is [*sic*] animated by the Communists!"[3] Destruction of the CIO became a priority for the "Boss."

In 1938, the Jewish population of Jersey City was approximately twenty-eight thousand. A schism had developed among the Jews of the city in regard to their mayor, and their opinions on Hague depended on whether one was a recipient of the mayor's largesse or whether one opposed his tyrannical methods and his obvious corruption. In the spring of that year, the schism erupted into open warfare, and the source of the widening conflict was an activist rabbi named Benjamin Plotkin. Rabbi Plotkin of Temple Emanu-El crossed the line laid down by boss Hague in his pursuit of free speech for all Americans and would quickly pay the price. The resulting chaos would also have a divisive effect on the Jews of Jersey City.

The trouble erupted when Rabbi Plotkin appeared in court as a character witness for a bitter opponent of Mayor Hague. On May 2, almost immediately after Plotkin had appeared in court, a committee representing Temple Emanu-El received an eviction notice from the synagogue's landlord—they had leased space to conduct their religious services from the Jewish Community Centre of Jersey City. The congregation was ordered to be out of the building by June 30. The eviction came as a result of the action of the community center's president, Judge Morris Barison. Barison, himself a Jew, considered himself a friend of Hague and was also the head of the Jersey City division of the American Jewish Congress. The treasurer of the Centre was Louis Jacobs, a member of the Hague-controlled Board of Education. Neither Barison nor Jacobs would comment on the record, but Barison did tell a reporter from the Jewish Telegraphic Agency that he was behind the eviction move "one million per cent." It was one of the Centre's board members who issued the public statement on behalf of the Centre that claimed that Rabbi Plotkin had been ordered to leave "because the Jewish people of the city believe he [had] double-crossed them and held them up to scorn and ridicule among their neighbors."[4]

Roland Gittelsohn did not know Rabbi Plotkin, had never seen him or heard him speak. However, the situation had captured his interest and he was following it closely in the press. He mentioned it briefly in synagogue earlier in May when he reported that on May 7 several Jews in Jersey City were beaten by Hague's henchmen. He informed his congregation that day that the tactics of Frank Hague were fascist; that Jersey City fascism meant anti-Semitism and, hence, they must oppose it.[5] Two weeks later he would have much more to say about Frank Hague, Benjamin Plotkin, and the overall situation in Jersey City.

The press revealed the deep-seated differences in the philosophy of how Jewish affairs in the city should be conducted. While the schism appeared to the public to have begun with the eviction of Temple Emanu-El, its roots could largely be traced back to the previous year's campaign by the CIO to organize in New Jersey and to Rabbi Plotkin's staunch support of the CIO. The court appearance by the rabbi served as the convenient excuse for the Hague machine to attempt to administer payback to him. Much of the conflict erupted over Plotkin's support of the CIO and his avid free speech stance. Plotkin and his allies had become an anathema to Hague, who was committed to the AFL as he had the leaders of that organization in his pocket. CIO organizers arriving in Jersey City were harassed by the police and thugs hired by Hague, had their attempts to distribute literature stifled, and found all meeting halls closed to them. The CIO leadership teamed with the American Civil Liberties Union in an all-out fight to establish free speech, free assemblage, and the right to collective bargaining.[6] Hague countered all efforts of outsiders to influence the inner workings of Jersey City by labeling all involved with the CIO and its efforts as communists and "Red agitators."

With the eviction of Temple Emanu-El, the press portrayed the philosophical divide in the Jewish community as one that pitted the "get-along-go-along" Jews such as Judge Barison, who prospered as Hague allies, against the civil-libertarian-minded activists like Rabbi Plotkin. As mentioned earlier, the faction represented by Barison considered the Plotkin activists an embarrassment that caused them to be ridiculed and scorned by their Christian fellow citizens of Jersey City. The attitude of the faction represented by Plotkin could be described thusly: Mayor Hague was a dictator and fascist-minded, and his brand of fascism bred anti-Semitism. Jews could only be free where free speech and civil liberties were protected, and hence Jews must proactively oppose all efforts to curtail civil liberties. All Jews should oppose the efforts of Hague to deny free speech to the CIO and to political groups that opposed him. Jewish leaders who supported Hague were traitors to the Jewish people.[7]

In contrast, the position of the faction represented by Barison could be described in the following manner: There was no anti-Semitism, as such, in Jersey City, but Jewish leaders who opposed Hague, supported the CIO, or in other ways would "make trouble" aroused this "conservative" community against them, and thereby harmed the Jews. They were traitors to the Jewish people.[8] Their very actions had created anti-Semites.

In late May, Roland Gittelsohn addressed the situation in Jersey City in a sermon entitled "A Rabbi is Dispossessed." In addition to containing his usual oratorical flare, the powerful sermon is significant as it not only clearly outlined his passionate beliefs on the civil rights of man and social responsibility but also clearly annunciated Gittelsohn's personal philosophy on religion as well as the roles and responsibilities of religion. In this sermon, he brilliantly outlined the clear linkage of religion as a part of everyday life and not as an isolated phenomenon to be kept inside of a place of worship.

After beginning by noting that this was the third time he had mentioned the chaos in Jersey City, Gittelsohn reiterated the fact that Rabbi Benjamin Plotkin had appeared in court in support of a political opponent of Frank Hague, whom he referred to as "Czar Frankie I." Like their own Central Synagogue of Nassau County, Temple Emanu-El did not own their own building, and immediately after Plotkin's court appearance the synagogue received an eviction notice. Gittelsohn then began with a challenge to his audience, asking them if they were wondering if Plotkin was acting within his rights by speaking against Hague.

I suppose that the way in which you laymen would probably ask that question would be whether a rabbi has the right to do what you call "mixing in politics." That's a queer and convenient phrase which covers a multitude of sins. Whenever a minister or a rabbi takes a practical stand which certain of his members don't like, they accuse him of "mixing in politics." And very often those who use that phrase have a very strange notion of what constitutes religion. Usually they think of religion as something which is confined to Temples and Synagogues and Churches. It's a thing, for them, which exists in a separate compartment, off by itself, and it has nothing to do with other compartments, nothing to do with business or economics or politics. Therefore these people speak so often of religion "mixing" in politics or "meddling" in business.[9]

Having set the philosophical underpinnings of his thoughts in place for his congregation to absorb, he continued and proceeded to drive home his point powerfully. The first lesson that critics of Rabbi Plotkin had to learn was that there was no such thing as religion "meddling" with other spheres of life. "Religion isn't a separate compartment of life," he announced firmly, "it's a spirit which suffuses the whole of life. Religion isn't supposed to be a convenience and an escape! It's supposed to be a hardship, an inspiration, a challenge!"[10] Likening religion to a searchlight that must shine into business, politics, private affairs, wars, and everything and anything where human beings have or should have ideals, Gittelsohn drove home his point by telling them that he didn't know a lesson that a rabbi needed to teach his congregation more than that: "The lesson that wherever one man oppresses another, that's where there's a place and a need for religion. Wherever one group persecutes or takes advantage of another, that's the place for religion. Wherever freedom is denied, wherever righteousness is betrayed, wherever truth and justice are crushed, —I don't care if it is in business or politics or anything else—that's the place for religion. A religion that doesn't 'mix' or 'meddle' in every sphere of life isn't worth the name of religion!"[11]

This concept was not a new one that he had just formulated, Gittelsohn informed his congregation. It was simply a reiteration of the views of the greatest religious leaders of all time. In a somewhat humorous and sarcastic comparison, he noted, "[T]he trouble with us is that we love dead prophets, but we hate living ones, and it happens that Benjamin Plotkin, in his own humble way, is a living prophet."[12] With this preamble, Gittelsohn related three anecdotes from the Old Testament that illustrated his point. Using the stories of Elijah's opposition to King Ahab, Nathan's stand against King David's transgression, and Amos' stance against the greed of wealthy citizens, he masterfully illustrated his point, concluding, "How's that for religion meddling in business? That, my friends, was more than 2,600 years ago."[13]

Informing the congregation that he didn't personally know Rabbi Plotkin and had never met him, Gittelsohn assured them that he admired him, saluted him, and honored him. As one who truly followed the examples of Elijah, Nathan, and Amos, Plotkin had set a shining example of true religion in action. "And I pray to God that if the occasion should arise, I may have the courage to do the same thing. That's real religion!" he assured his audience.[14] The exact antithesis of Plotkin was the rabbi who sat on the platform with Frank Hague during a pro-Hague rally. That rabbi ought to be ashamed of himself, Gittelsohn declared. "That rabbi has taken the meaning of true religion and he has twisted it, he has sabotaged it and corrupted it and perverted it."[15]

With the time remaining, Gittelsohn shifted his attention to the delicate situation posed by the journalist who documented the apparent rift in the Jersey City Jewish community. This local rift surely served as a metaphor for the greater question that confronted the entire Jewish community throughout the United States. Gittelsohn was not in the least bit skittish in considering whether a Jew didn't harm his fellow Jews by taking a stand like Benjamin Plotkin in situations such as the one in Jersey City. It is here that the essence of Roland Gittelsohn's core beliefs clearly come across to the reader just as his words must have stirred his listeners back in 1938. To him there was right and there was wrong—there was no middle ground. To him, the consequences of not supporting "right" were the same as supporting "wrong." "First of all," he began, "I personally don't believe that the actions of a man like Plotkin will cause us anywhere near the amount of harm which some people think that it will. Let's not forget that if a Gentile wants to believe that if we Jews are Communists and radicals, he's going to believe it even if every Jew in America grows wings and joins the Liberty League. I personally believe that if we Jews fight courageously and openly for justice and righteousness, we will gain the love and respect and esteem of all intelligent Gentiles, and the other kind won't like us no matter what we do."[16]

Gittelsohn continued on, elucidating his personal beliefs on right and wrong—and the consequences of always pursuing "right." His summary of the topic is both stirring and inspiring, reflecting not only the power of his intellect, but the strength of his heart.

> This isn't an easy thing to say, and it's still a harder thing to do, but we Jews have always stood for something, and if we mean to continue standing for something, then we've got to do it even if it *does* bring us suffering and harm. If our supreme goal in life is to avoid conflict and opposition, then let's be jellyfish; no one ever opposes a jellyfish. But if we want to be true to ourselves, if we want to remain a people of teachers and prophets,—then we've got to stand for justice, justice always, justice constantly, justice eternally,—even if it does mean temporary discomfort and harm.[17]

Gittelsohn concluded his thoughts on the subject with words that would, in many ways, come to epitomize his life: "A great modern leader of the Jewish religion said this, and I humbly repeat his words: 'It is better to be hated for our significance than to be tolerated for our insignificance.'"[18]

Herein lay the challenge before them: "If Frank Hague succeeds and his fascism spreads, then we Jews are gone, finished, through! We *must* fight him! Instead of opposing that rabbi, if we know what's good for us, we'll fight with him and by him and for him, before it's too late."[19] To any in the congregation who may have perceived that the actions of the Hague machine were purely anti-union and had nothing to with hatred of Jews, Gittelsohn quoted on-scene reporting by correspondent Donald B. Robinson: "Don't talk to me about the possibility of fascism in these United States," Robinson said. "I saw fascism, Nazism, anything you want to call it, in all its bestiality. I heard the cry I've expected but dreaded hearing in this country: 'Kill the Jew bastard!'"[20] Later in his report Robinson commented, "We reporters were sick, but what could we do? Cowards, of course, all of us."[21]

Finally, Gittelsohn concluded his sermon by summing up his feelings toward Benjamin Plotkin by saying: "I defend him because I know that any religion worth having isn't afraid to tackle injustice whether it's political or economic or whatever it is. I defend him because I know we Jews have always stood for something beautiful and lofty and noble, for something of which every decent and intelligent human being can be proud, and I want my people to continue that way. . . . We have a prophet in our midst, my friends, a descendent of Elijah and Amos. Too many prophets have been crucified and stoned. Let's not make that mistake!"[22]

Here, in a powerful sermon given in May of 1938, Roland Gittelsohn presented the distillation of his interpretation of the meaning of true religion and its nexus with the real world. One cannot truly understand him or his sense of the intertwined relationship of religion, personal freedom, and social justice without reading this sermon. The courage that he would often display throughout his life when supporting controversial and unpopular positions never shone brighter.

Frank Hague would continue his battle against political opposition and especially against the CIO by using city ordinances to ban their meetings and to stop the distribution of their literature. Both district courts and circuit courts would rule against Hague, and he appealed his position up to the United States Supreme Court. In 1939 in the case of *Hague v. Committee for Industrial Organization*, the Supreme Court ruled against Hague's ban on the meetings, declaring that the ordinances violated the First Amendment right to freedom of assembly. The ordinances were immediately voided.

Chapter Twelve

# "On Three Things Does the Whole World Depend"

Domestically, the United States struggled to recover from the depression. Factions having strong isolationist sentiments clashed with others who were warning of the dangers of Nazi aggression, while the anti-war movement was being co-opted to support a Popular Front. As conflict continued in the United States, troubles escalated on the world stage. Next in Adolf Hitler's sights was Czechoslovakia. Hitler used the three million ethnic Germans living in the Czech portion of the country known as Sudetenland as the basis for his demands on Czechoslovakian president Eduard Benes. Though he agitated for Sudetenland's autonomy, Hitler used the "Sudeten Crisis" as a pretext to launch the first phase of his plan to conquer Europe, then Russia, and ultimately the United States.[1] As the crisis deepened, Great Britain and France made it clear they didn't intend to go to war over Sudetenland. Hitler planned to stage "atrocities" against ethnic Germans in Sudetenland as his excuse for ordering his armies into the country. It was the active efforts of Prime Minister Neville Chamberlain of Great Britain that ultimately ended the crisis.

Chamberlain had proactively agitated for a peace conference and had agreed to meet Hitler and negotiate without President Benes even being present at the sessions. Stepping back from his initial demand that Czechoslovakia be overrun by the German war machine and incorporated into Nazi Germany, Hitler at the last minute changed his demand to the annexation of the Sudetenland. On behalf of England and France, Chamberlain agreed to give in to Hitler, feeling that it would be Hitler's last territorial request. The Munich Agreement, a classic example of appeasement of an aggressor country, was signed on September 29, 1938. The next day, Neville Chamberlain returned to England and announced to ecstatic crowds that the agreement had attained "peace for our time."

Less than five months later, Hitler would overrun the rest of Czechoslovakia, and less than five months after that the Second World War would begin.

---

On October 1, 1938, Roland Gittelsohn would deliver one of the most significant sermons of his career. Although it would, on first glance, appear to be another in a series of stinging commentaries on the world situation and the continual slide of the world into a state of war, it touched on several issues affecting war and peace and not only those concerning Nazi Germany, a country whose policies and leadership Gittelsohn totally despised. For the first time, his notes for the sermon reveal his thoughts on the worsening plight of Jews in Palestine and the deteriorating relations between Jews and Arabs in the British Mandate. Lastly, in his speech he outlined the three key concepts on which the world depended, based on the two-thousand-year-old writings of an ancient rabbi. For Gittelsohn, the significance and relevance of these three points would only grow over the years. Ultimately, at the end of World War II, he would come back to these three concepts in his realization of why pacifism was ultimately doomed to fail before World War II.

Roland Gittelsohn's notes indicate the title for the sermon simply as "Shabbos Shuvah, 5699—1938." Shabbos Shuvah is the Sabbath that falls in between Rosh Hashanah and Yom Kippur. Outside of Yom Kippur, it is the holiest Sabbath of the whole Jewish year. As Gittelsohn explained to his congregation, Shabbos Shuvah is correctly translated into "the Sabbath of Returning." "I don't think there ever was a time before in human history when the real, literal meaning of this day was needed so desperately," he declared.[2] And that, he explained, is because Americans like to move forward and not return or look back. Why look back when mankind has accomplished so much? Perhaps it is because of this feeling, he suggested, that Shabbos Shuvah has diminished in importance in the lives of modern Jews. "Most of us no longer look upon it as a vital and essential part of the High Holidays. And yet," he stated, "the sad thing is that it is precisely and exactly the Jews of this century, those who want it least, who need it most."[3]

In spite of mankind's accomplishments, Gittelsohn assured the congregation that they indeed had lost something from the past, something that they "most definitely and assuredly *do* need to return. . . . And on this Shabbos Shuvia, this Sabbath of Returning, we need to return to that something."⁴ That something was the teachings of a rabbi who had lived nineteen hundred years ago. Rabbi Simeon ben Gamliel, who lived just before the destruction of the Temple in Jerusalem, spoke words of simplicity and eloquence that would remain with Gittelsohn his entire lifetime. "Al sh'loshaw d'vawrim haw-clawn ka-yawm, he said; on three things does the whole world depend; al haw-emes, v'al ha-din, v'al ha-shawlom; on truth, on justice, and on peace."⁵ At first glance, he related to the congregation that there doesn't seem to be anything profound or spectacular about this simple statement. That is, he pointed out, unless you mean the eternal eloquence of great and abiding and permanent truth. Once again, he repeated: on three things the whole world depends: on truth, on justice, and on peace. In his sermon, Gittelsohn evaluated the volatile world situation through this framework.

First, he considered truth. The young rabbi's cynicism of international politics came to the forefront in his discussion of truth. Nations, he said, do not believe in the truth—they have perverted, twisted, and rejected truth and in its place have substituted expediency. For his prime example he cited the ongoing war in Spain. It is a ridiculous myth that there is a civil war going on in Spain, he maintained. "There are at this moment close to 100,000 German and Italian troops in Spain; that isn't civil war. There are in Spain today over 800 military planes, flown by the forces of Franco but manufactured in Germany or Italy; that isn't civil war. Long months before the war started there were as many as 36 newspapers published in Spain, but paid for by the Nazis; that isn't civil war." After pointing out that Mussolini was financing the war efforts of General Franco, Gittelsohn explained with exasperation that "these facts are not secrets! You know them, I know them, all the governments and nations know them. And yet they insist on denying truth."⁶

In further embellishing on the distortion of the truth in the case of the ongoing war in Spain, Gittelsohn turned his audience's attention to the Non-Intervention Agreement that had been signed in August of 1936, followed by the establishment of the

Non-Intervention Committee that first met the following month. Originally an idea of the British and the French, its members also included Fascist Italy and Nazi Germany. In all, twenty-four nations were represented on the committee. Its expressed purpose was to keep the rest of the world neutral in regard to the Spanish Civil War and to prevent the flow of war materials into Spain. Consistently, Germany, Italy, and the Soviet Union violated the agreement and sent war materials to the opposing sides, as the Fascists and the Communists used the war in Spain as their proxy war.

Gittelsohn vociferously protested the hypocrisy of the committee's actions to his congregation. His demonstration of the twisting of words by the warring powers predated the writings of George Orwell by a decade, but Gittelsohn epitomized the sentiment of the author's classic 1949 novel *1984*: "War is peace, love is hate." To the passionate young rabbi, the committee's very existence was the ultimate lie. "That's enough to make the very corpse of truth turn over in its grave," he lectured. "Non-intervention! We might just as well call Germany the land of the free and the home of the brave; it would be just as close to the truth. If anything in the world has caused intervention it's the committee on non-intervention . . . it's the very committee which was formed to prevent it."[7]

As his congregation was digesting this fact, Gittelsohn then added more fuel to fire that he was fanning over the bastardization of truth. The Non-Intervention Committee announced a few weeks prior that it would have to suspend its operations due to lack of funding. "Do you know who came to its financial rescue to the tune of 36,000 pounds in valuable and precious foreign exchange?" he thundered. "Our newspapers didn't tell us about that. The government of Germany. Just imagine that! The government of Germany rescuing the committee on non-intervention!"[8] Anticipating many surprised expressions on his congregant's faces, he explained that the Nazis were smart enough all along to know that the whole thing was a big smoke screen, a convenient bluff to help the very thing it presumed to prevent.[9]

England and France were also complicit, he charged. They too, were smart enough to see through the smoke screen, but they willfully turned a blind eye to real workings of the committee. With disgust, he added: "That's how much they're concerned with the truth." To summarize his analysis of the first of the concepts of Rabbi Simeon ben Gamliel, Gittelsohn concluded by saying, "If, then, the first pillar on which the world stands is truth, it shouldn't surprise us in the least that today that world seems to be a bit wobbly and unsteady and weak."[10]

Gittelsohn next moved on to the second of the pillars elucidated by the ancient rabbi and noted that it was not much sturdier than the first one he had just finished discussing. For his analysis of the true meaning of justice in the world, he chose to make his primary teaching point by using the Arab-Jewish conflict that was ongoing in Palestine. It is the first time that the subject appears in the notes of his early sermons and serves to emphasize his passionate belief in Zionism, a conviction strongly influenced by the teachings of his father, Reuben.

The creation of Palestine resulted from the Allied victory in World War I. Prior to the end of the war, British Foreign Minister Arthur Balfour issued a policy statement in a letter to Lord Rothschild that came to be known as the Balfour Declaration. This short letter, dated November 2, 1917, expressed "sympathy with Jewish Zionist aspirations," proclaiming "His Majesty's Government views with favour the establishment in Palestine of a national home for the Jewish people."[11] In February of 1920, the Supreme Council of the Principal Allied Powers—consisting of Great Britain, France, Italy, and Japan—met in London, where they prepared a peace treaty that divided up the territories acquired from the defeated Ottoman Empire. It was at this London conference where they defined the borders of Palestine (within its ancient limits of Dan to Beersheba) and declared it to be under British Mandate. More precisely, the conference participants described the borders of Palestine to include those areas of the Promised Land that had been conquered, settled, and ruled by the Twelve Tribes of Israel and their descendants in both the First and Second Temple periods. At that time no mention was made of a Jewish homeland.[12]

The Supreme Council of the Principal Allied Powers reconvened in April at San Remo, Italy, where after heated debates between the British and the French representatives, they decided on April 24, 1920, to approve the Balfour Declaration, effectively converting the statement of policy by the British government into a legal, binding document. Thus, until that date, Britain's promise was not legally binding. As a direct consequence of this decision, Britain committed herself to establish—or more precisely, to reconstitute—the Jewish National Home in Palestine for an ancient nation, most of whose members then lived outside Palestine. Only for that specific objective was a mandate then conferred upon it the following day, April 25, 1920.[13] This document, formally known as the San Remo Resolution on Palestine, was incorporated into the total minutes of the San Remo Peace Conference that were approved also on April 25, 1920. Initially administered by the British military, as per the San Remo Resolution, Great Britain replaced its military occupation government with a civilian administration for Palestine, led by High Commissioner Herbert Samuel on July 1, 1920.

Several other key documents further clarified the status of Palestine. The Mandates System, conceived by South African statesman Jan Smuts, proposed that the colonies and territories liberated by the victorious Allies from the Ottoman Empire and Germany not be annexed but instead be created as new states under the Mandates System to be administered by Mandatories or trustees chosen from among the Allied Powers.[14] The Mandates System became endorsed as part of the Treaty of Versailles. Great Britain, already designated as a mandatory for Palestine by the San Remo Resolution, would again be designated at the Mandatory for Palestine, a status confirmed by the Council of the League of Nations on July 24, 1922. The Franco-British Boundary Convention that concluded in Paris on December 23, 1920, provided formal recognition under international law to the Jewish legal rights and title of sovereignty over most of what had constituted the historical Land of Israel.[15]

The migration, or *aliyah,* of Jews to Eretz Yisrael, the land of Israel, took place in several phases in the modern era. The third *aliyah* began shortly after the end of World War I, bringing over forty thousand Jewish immigrants to the newly created British Mandate of Palestine. Coming mainly from Russia and excited over the prospect of a homeland, they brought with them tradition, determination, and ingenuity. By the time the League of Nations formally confirmed British Mandatory status to Palestine, the Jewish immigrants were already beginning to transform the barren desert into a flowering and progressive modern oasis. And while the Balfour Declaration clearly stated that in establishing the Jewish homeland it was "clearly understood that nothing shall be done which may prejudice the civil and religious rights of existing non-Jewish communities in Palestine," the presence of the industrious Jews who were buying the land and improving and modernizing areas of the region was greatly resented by the native Arab population.

Stormy relations between the Jews and the Arabs became a way of life in the British Mandate of Palestine. A series of anti-Jewish riots broke out, the first major one in August of 1929. In Jerusalem, on August 15, a scheduled march by several hundred Jews to the Wailing Wall aroused Arab anger. While it was a peaceful demonstration and the Jews carried no weapons, rumors quickly spread that they had attacked local Arabs, as well as insulted the prophet Muhammad. After a counter demonstration at the Wailing Wall the following day organized by the Supreme Muslim Council, the situation spiraled out of control as rioting broke out throughout the region. The native Arab population of the town of Hebron was incited to riot, and crowds of Arabs attacked the Jewish residents. In the end, sixty-seven Jews were killed at Hebron, along with nine Arabs. Of note, 435 Jewish survivors were hidden by twenty-eight Arab families, who risked their lives in doing so. In the end, an investigation of the riots was conducted by a commission of inquiry led by Sir Walter Shaw. The Shaw Commission, as it was known, found as the fundamental cause of the riots, "with which in our opinion disturbances either would not have occurred or would not have been little more than a local riot, is the Arab feeling of animosity and hostility towards the Jews consequent upon the disappointment of their political and national aspirations and fear for their economic future."[16]

In April of 1936 violence again flared, precipitating the Arab Revolt. It began with an Arab attack on a convoy of trucks that resulted in two deaths. Within days, the Jews sought their revenge and retaliated with series of attacks on the Arab population; rioting soon broke out in several cities. Six prominent Arab leaders promptly overcame their factional differences and formed the Arab High Command. The group's leader was the Grand Mufti of Jerusalem, Haj Amin al-Husseini, a viciously anti-Semitic Muslim cleric and Nazi sympathizer. The Arab High Command called for a general strike that crippled the country and also called for a tax boycott. In addition, they issued three demands to the British: 1) put an end to Jewish immigration in Palestine, 2) cease further land sales to Jews, and 3) create a national Arab government for the region. Soon Arab gangs, armed and financed by Fascist Italy and possibly by Nazi Germany, were roving the countryside, both murdering and plundering.[17] The initial Jewish response was one largely of restraint. They did not want to become part of the problem, preferring the British to handle the situation.

The British response to the Arab Revolt was initially tepid. The British, sensing that a war was looming in the near future and realizing that they would depend on Arab oil for their war aims, were hesitant to further erode any potential goodwill between them and the Arabs. The general strike was called off in October 1936 when the British agreed to send a high government official to investigate the situation in Palestine. The Arab High Commission called for an end to the strike and curtailment of violence while the Palestine Royal Commission—also known as the Peel Commission since it was led by Lord William Peel—did its work. The Commission arrived in Palestine in November 1936.

The Peel Commission completed its investigation and published its results in July of 1937. Their findings were not encouraging. The irreconcilable differences between the Jews and the Arabs portended a very bleak future for the Mandate. They specifically noted that "their cultural and social life, their ways of thought and conduct, are as incompatible as their national aspirations."[18] The Arab desire for independence coupled with their hatred and fear of a Jewish national homeland were the underlying causes of the riots and the strike. The solution recommended by the Peel Commission was to partition Palestine into separate Jewish and Arab states. The Arab leaders rejected the partition plan outright. However, the Zionist Congress, an international Jewish policy-making body dedicated to the creation of a Jewish homeland in Palestine, accepted it with qualifications—against the wishes of a substantial minority.[19]

The second phase of the Arab Revolt began in the fall of 1937. On September 26, Lewis Andrews, the British District Commissioner for Galilee, was murdered by Arab gunmen. This time the British acted with force. Within a week, arrest warrants were issued for the members of the Arab High Commission, but Haj Amin al-Husseini was able to flee the country and escape to Iraq along with other members of the Arab High Commission. Throughout 1937 and into 1938, Arab violence was met increasingly by the British military that was determined to suppress it. It was in this context that Roland Gittelsohn addressed his congregation on October 1, 1938, and used his disgust with the ongoing Arab riots as his teaching point concerning the second of Rabbi ben Gamliel's pillars on which the world depended—that of justice.

There hadn't been any justice in international politics for a long time, Gittelsohn declared. So long, in fact, that he doubted that any of them could remember what it looked like. Look only to Palestine, he offered, for the prime example of the twisted form of justice that exists in the world today. "We Jews go to Palestine and in 20 years we create a garden out of a desert," he said. "We build cities and schools and a university and hospitals. We give the whole world an example of social justice in action, of how employers and employees can live together without exploiting each other, of how the good of the many can be placed before the profit of the few. We lift up the Arab in peace from his pile of dung and refuse and filth. We clean him and cure him and serve him. We teach him again how to live like a human being. All this we do in twenty years; and then what happens? The world watches while two gangsters light up a fire of terrorism against us, and the world pretends to be blind, and the world does nothing. That's justice!" he raged. "It isn't the kind of justice Simeon ben Gamliel meant, but it's the only kind that nations today seem to know."[20] While it is not entirely clear who the two gangsters are who Gittelsohn referred to, one is almost certainly Grand Mufti Haj Amin al-Husseini.

Gittelsohn mentioned two other examples of the sad state of modern justice to emphasize his point. He asked his audience, what kind of justice did the Spanish Republic receive? The justice of Francisco Franco! It was the same kind of justice that Czechoslovakia had just received at Munich. "Perhaps it's a good thing that Simeon ben Gamliel isn't here to see what a mockery the nations have made of the truth and the justice he loved," the rabbi somberly reflected.[21]

Simeon ben Gamliel also loved peace—the third pillar on which the world depended. The point that Gittelsohn wanted to drive home to his audience was that it wasn't an accident that ben Gamliel placed peace immediately after justice and truth. It was intended to be the last of the three pillars. In modern times, he noted, man has tried every possible method of achieving peace. There is only one method they haven't tried — "that's the method of righteousness; that's the method of ethics and morals. It's the only method that we haven't tried and it's the only method that will work. . . . It's strange that . . . we haven't learned that yet when Simeon ben Gamliel knew it 1,900 years ago. That's why he spoke of truth and of justice and then of peace. Once we enthrone truth and once we establish justice, we won't have to worry about peace."[22] This, then, is what Rabbi Roland Gittelsohn called for on this Shabbos Shuvah, this Sabbath of Returning: a real return to ancient truths as exemplified by the world's necessary pillars described nearly two thousand years before by Simeon ben Gamliel.

It was the three pillars described by that ancient rabbi that Roland Gittelsohn would once again turn to in 1945 at the end of World War II when he would reflect on the failure of pacifism in preventing the most horrendous war that mankind has ever known.

Occurring almost simultaneously with the delivery of his Shabbos Shuvah sermon, another massacre took place in Palestine. In the city of Tiberias, seventy armed Arabs attacked the Jewish quarter of the city. According to the British Mandate report, "it was systematically organized and savagely executed. Of the 19 Jews killed, including women and children, all save four were stabbed to death."[23] Due to the coincident timing of the massacre, it is not known whether Gittelsohn actually knew of the incident as he delivered his sermon, but it is seems unlikely. He was well aware, however, at the time of his sermon of the events transpiring in Munich that he briefly touched upon in his section on justice. He would have much more to say on the subject in the very near future.

# Chapter Thirteen

# Munich

On September 30, 1938, Prime Minister Neville Chamberlain returned to England with the Munich Agreement in his hand to the deafening cheers of adoring citizens. Invited to come immediately to Buckingham Palace to personally report to King George VI, it took him an hour and a half to make the nine-mile journey due to the massive crowds. Afterward, he returned to 10 Downing Street, where he addressed the large throng of people in the street from a window upstairs on the first floor. Recalling the words that Benjamin Disraeli spoke on his return from the Congress of Berlin in 1878, he told the crowd, "My good friends, this is the second time there has come back from Germany to Downing Street peace with honor. I believe it is peace for our time. Now I recommend you go home and sleep quietly in your beds."[1] Chamberlain received overwhelming support from the British press and had great support in the House of Commons during the October 3 debates on the Agreement. One notable exception to the tide of support was Winston Churchill, who proclaimed, "England has been offered a choice between war and shame. She has chosen shame, and will get war."[2]

On October 1, 1938, German troops marched into the Sudetenland. Four days later, Eduard Benes resigned as president of Czechoslovakia and would go into exile in Great Britain. In the United States, public opinion was largely supportive of the Munich Agreement, with fifty-nine percent of those polled expressing the opinion that England and France did the right thing in giving in to Germany instead of going to war.[3] Among the still-sizable minority of Americans who opposed the agreement was Roland Gittelsohn. It would take him several weeks before he could speak in public about Munich, and he broke his silence on Friday, October 21. Being so opinionated on the evil that he believed the agreement represented, it would again take him two sermons to cover his thoughts.

He began his sermon "Peace with Honor or Dishonor without Peace: Which is It?" by explaining that he thought the results of the conference were self-evident and that he initially didn't see any point in discussing it. But then he realized that there was likely much confusion over Munich; that people looked at the result and didn't know whether to laugh or cry. And that was his purpose that evening, to clear up any confusion. The suddenness of the agreement that seemed to prevent war was an intoxicant, but now "it's the morning after," and "the drunk is ended."[4] It was time to forget about laughing and crying and it was time to sober up and look at what really happened in Munich and what the likely results would be.

The first question that Gittelsohn believed they all should consider was this: how much did Hitler actually accomplish in Munich? Was there really a genuine negotiation? "Was it a case of legitimate bargaining, or was it one of barbaric, brutal brow-beating? This is the first question we've got to ask."[5] With disgust, he informed the congregation that the answer to this question was easy. "Because the plain, unpleasant, shameful truth is this: that Hitler was handed free of charge everything . . . the only difference is that instead of gobbling down his dinner in one gulp, the vulture was persuaded to eat a little slower and finish his prey on October 10 instead of October 1. That was the phenomenal diplomatic success for which the world has been applauding Chamberlain!" Hitler had been handed 23 percent of the territory and 23 percent of the population of Czechoslovakia without any strings or reciprocal obligations. "That's Chamberlain's idea of compromise! . . . That's what Hitler got at Munich and that's why the answer to our first question tonight is unfortunately so easy."[6]

The second question posed by Gittelsohn was not so easy, but it was even more important—just how much was compromised by this unprecedented sacrifice of land, materials, and population? To answer this question, he started down a course that suggested his thoughts were not that different than the British prime minister's; however, he was merely setting his congregation up to jolt them with his main point. "All of us are agreed, I think," he began, "that the betrayal of Czechoslovakia was one of the most colossal pieces of injustice in all human history. But we're also agreed that modern warfare is even worse, that it's tragic and senseless and shameless and useless." In his very next sentence, Gittelsohn likely stunned his audience when he proceeded to mimic Neville Chamberlain, a man he detested, by declaring: "And I think most of us would be willing, if necessary, in spite of ourselves and in spite of our ideals, to give up the Czechs and forget about justice if at least that would mean the prospect of a lasting peace." If the congregation was initially confused by what seemed to be an agreement in principle between the minds of Gittelsohn and Neville Chamberlain, he quickly disabused them of that idea.

"But let me assure you, my friends," he countered, ". . . that the results of Munich do *not* mean a prospect of peace. We aren't closer to peace today than we were 4 weeks ago; we're farther from peace. We've rejected peace; we've sabotaged peace; we killed and crushed and murdered peace. Or I should say, Mr. Chamberlain and those whom he leads and those who lead him,—I should say that they have killed and murdered and crushed peace."[7]

What was the source of Gittelsohn's certainty that Munich represented a betrayal of Czechoslovakia and just the latest in a series of lies propagated by Adolf Hitler? How could he have been so certain that war hadn't been averted by the Munich Agreement and instead just the opposite had been achieved by it? The answer is simple: he had read Hitler's book, *Mein Kampf.* "Over 10 years ago," Gittelsohn informed the audience, "in his self-written Bible, *Mein Kampf,* Hitler announced to the whole world that he would use any kind of chicanery or deceit to achieve his ends. He said so openly and publicly. So far that's the only promise he *has* kept."[8] He further embellished his point regarding Hitler's treachery by quoting the Nazi leader himself from *Mein Kampf:* "The very enormity of a lie contributes to its success. The masses of the people easily succumb to it, as they cannot believe it is possible that anyone should have the shameless audacity to invent such things. Even if the clearest proof of its falsehood be forthcoming, something of the lie will nevertheless stick."[9] With disgust, Gittelsohn stated, "And this is the man Chamberlain would believe! That's the philosophy he would trust! That's the basis of his hope for peace!"[10]

He went on to note that the blueprint for Hitler's actions in Europe—the rearming of the Rhineland, the annexation of Austria, the probable expansion into Czechoslovakia—were all clearly laid out in *Mein Kampf*. All laid out for the world to see, without any secrecy or subtlety. Noting that most diplomats were hesitant to announce their plans even so much as twenty-four hours in advance, Gittelsohn angrily pointed out that Hitler had announced his ten years in advance. "He gave the whole world a blueprint of exactly what he intended to do if he ever attained power. And since he has come to power, he hasn't departed from that blueprint one single iota. He's done everything he intended, and he's done it the way he intended, and he's done it exactly when he intended."[11]

In an ominous tone, Gittelsohn went on to explain that for Hitler, Czechoslovakia was not the end; rather it was a necessary means to an end. Tying together the situation developing in Europe with the intentions elucidated by Hitler in *Mein Kampf*, he provided an analysis that was precise, to the point, and highly accurate. It is almost striking that a clergyman—a dedicated and committed pacifist—would come up with an analysis that was so prescient one would almost conclude it had been written by planners at either the State Department or the War Department. "As a matter of cold, hard fact," he explained,

> Hitler couldn't stop with Czechoslovakia even if he wanted to. Hitler's trouble to begin with is the fact that he has too many mouths to feed and not enough food to fill them. Austria and Czechoslovakia won't help him. Austria and Czechoslovakia gave him more mouths to feed. He took them for one reason only. Because they weren't an end. Because after them come the oil fields of Rumania [*sic*]. And after that come the rich grain fields of the Ukraine. And after that comes an about-face and the absolute, resolute crushing of France. This isn't idle prediction or prophecy. This is a plain, honest, literal reading of *Mein Kampf*, by which Hitler has been guided in the past and from which he hasn't any intention of departing in the future.[12]

Mocking Neville Chamberlain, Gittelsohn bemoaned that if only Chamberlain had read Hitler's book (or had the intelligence to believe it) he too would know that that the only place where Germany could acquire both the resources and the *Lebensraum*, or living space, that it needed "—and I quote the book literally now—is 'from Russia and her border-states.'"[13] Apparently Joseph Stalin was too busy purging his own military to also note that part of

*Mein Kampf,* an omission that Russia would pay dearly for when Germany invaded Russia in 1941, despite the fact that the two nations had a non-aggression treaty between them.

Gittelsohn next outlined the events that had occurred in the three weeks since the Munich Agreement had been signed. Not only had England immediately launched "the biggest race for armaments in all British history," but Mussolini had begun openly expressing threats against Hungary. Japan, in its campaign against China, had imposed a naval blockade that threatened to starve out the population of Hong Kong, despite its previous promises to England that it wouldn't touch the British Crown colony. If Munich meant peace, he asked, why had Germany and Poland just launched a massive publicity campaign against Lithuania that strongly suggested another aggressive move, similar to the actions against Austria and Czechoslovakia? "That's how Czechoslovakia appeased him. That's how sated and filled and content he is. Only 3 short weeks have passed, and so far are we from peace that already Herr Hitler has begun the next step in his uncanny and rotten progress," declared Gittelsohn with disgust.[14]

As he came to the end of his sermon, he assured the congregation that he and others were not surprised at all with the outcome of the Munich Agreement. They may have been discouraged, but they were not surprised at all to read the previous day the summary of Munich written by Pulitzer Prize-winning columnist Frederick Birchall. Writing in the *New York Times,* Birchall stated, "The new development indicates that any who believed that Czechoslovakia's downfall would end the land-grabbing and substitute peace in Eastern Europe were incurable optimists. . . . The Eastern European pot still boils. If it does not boil over again within a year, Europe will be lucky."[15] As his time drew to a close, Gittelsohn informed his audience that he would continue this discussion at a future date, when they would examine "whether Neville Chamberlain was really as stupid as he thus far seems or whether he was perhaps strangely not so stupid. And then it remains also to ask what possible alternatives there were, and whether a different stand on the part of England and France would have plunged Europe and the world into war."[16]

In closing, he promised his congregation that he would conclude his discussion of Munich at a future date. If the congregation thought they had witnessed their rabbi at his angriest that evening, they were dead wrong.

———•———

Two weeks later on Friday, November 4, Roland Gittelsohn resumed his highly charged analysis of Munich with the second part of his sermon, entitled "Peace with Honor or Dishonor without Peace: Which is It?" He began by relating to the congregation that after he finished the first part of his analysis of Munich, one of the members of the synagogue came up to him and thanked him, as he was delighted that he was not the only one who was bitter and angry over the actions of Neville Chamberlain. Although he was tempted to assure that member that he hadn't seen anything close to real anger from his rabbi, Gittelsohn now admitted to the audience: "[I] felt like reassuring him that my feelings and emotions of two weeks ago—bitter as they may have sounded and excited as they may have been—were like the peaceful cooing of a dove compared to the things I have left unsaid for tonight." He explained the reason for his fury in advance, claiming, "Two weeks ago I was simply reporting facts. Tonight I intend to dig down deep beneath those facts. Tonight my purpose is to discover the hidden motives behind those facts, and needless to say, there's much more about which to be bitter and angry in a discussion of motives than there is in a simple and straightforward reporting of facts."[17]

Briefly reviewing his points from his previous sermon, he recalled to the audience that the Munich Agreement was as ineffective as the Treaty of Versailles. Hitler completely dominated the proceedings in Munich, gave nothing, and took everything. Using the analogy of throwing oil on a fire, Gittelsohn declared that feeding victims to dictators like Hitler could not, in the wildest stretch of the imagination, lead to peace. Using this summary of his previous lecture and asserting that it was factual and accurate, he now moved on to the next logical question: why did Chamberlain do what he did?

Was Chamberlain simply a stupid old fool or just a tired, weary old man betrayed by his colleagues? After putting those choices out on the table, Gittelsohn quickly asserted that he was, in fact, neither. Rather, the British prime minister was something more dangerous. Before proceeding with his line of thought, he gave a word of caution to the audience. "Perhaps right at this point I ought to speak just a brief word of explanation. I might as well warn you that in the next few minutes I intend to say some extremely harsh things about the Prime Minister of England. And I want you to know that I do so intentionally. I do so with malice aforethought. I do so because I'm firmly and profoundly convinced that some extremely harsh things about the prime minister need to be said."[18] After explaining that he was critiquing not only Chamberlain's action at Munich but also his entire record since assuming the office of prime minister, Gittelsohn then proceeded to answer the question that he posed about the man.

"My answer," he told the congregation, "is that Neville Chamberlain was neither an innocent fool nor a helpless victim. He was a deliberate and scheming deceiver. He was a malicious and conscious betrayer. He was a cunning and conniving and vicious pretender!"[19] The whole business at Munich was a deceitful subterfuge, a cleverly manipulated smokescreen, according to Gittelsohn. For the rest of his sermon, he would rail against Chamberlain and the motives for his actions and then provide an analysis of why Hitler could have been stopped at Munich without the precipitation of war. His explanations for the former were highly biased by Gittelsohn's largely anti-capitalist sentiments concerning the causes of war and were very questionable, as was his description of the political nature of Neville Chamberlain, which appeared to be highly influenced by his hatred of the man. His analysis of the latter, as compared to his excellent analysis of Hitler's war plans provided in his first sermon, is simplistic and largely inaccurate.

The primary reason why Chamberlain betrayed Eduard Benes and the Czechoslovakian people was, according to Gittelsohn, "because Benes didn't mean enough in dollars and cents to the financial overlords of England for whom Chamberlain is both a representative and a puppet."[20] It was a question of practical economics—Czechoslovakia simply wasn't worth it. "I submit to you that as a true explanation of what happened at Munich this simple mathematical fact which most of you haven't heard is worth more than all the cheap eloquence that you have heard."[21] But this wasn't the only motive of the controlling financial overlords of England, explained Gittelsohn. Chamberlain was willing to sacrifice Benes "because the controlling financial oligarchy of England isn't afraid of fascism. It deliberately and consciously wants fascism." Explaining that the controlling industrialists of England were witnessing "some of their absolute and intense stranglehold on the welfare and happiness of the masses beginning to slip away" and "the inevitable and inescapable dawn of a new society and a new day," he assured his audience that these industrialists didn't like these trends that they saw. According to Gittelsohn, they were quite ready to set up some form of fascism to protect their selfish rights.

The above explanations are highly exaggerated and largely untrue, but they are actually quite representative of leftist ideology in interpreting the results of Munich. Gittelsohn's sermon that evening actually pre-dated several prominent anti-Chamberlain interpretations that also delved into the "financial oligarchy" explanations of Chamberlain's actions. Written in 1939 by British MP Simon Haxey, *England's Money Lords: Tory M.P.* almost looks like it was largely based on Gittelsohn's assessment of Munich that he presented in his two sermons. In it, Haxey bitterly excoriated the Conservatives, stating that while they are in power "the class of the major employers of this country direct the nation's destinies. This class uses Parliament as a weapon to facilitate the pursuit of profit and as a means to fortify its power and authority."[22] What are we to think of the promises of Conservative leaders to defend against fascism when they can't even exclude fascists from among their members of Parliament, he asked. Haxey assessed the virulent anti-Communist sentiments in the Chamberlain government as the reason behind Britain's rejection of the Soviet Union as a potential ally, deducing that they preferred the rise of Nazi power to that of the specter of Moscow.[23] Mirroring a strong sentiment expressed by Gittelsohn in his sermon, Haxey concluded that the reason for the Conservative sympathy for fascism was that "they believe that unless fascism succeeds in Europe, the privileged position of Britain's wealthy governing class may be irretrievably lost. Their policy of retreat before fascism is the instinctive act of self-preservation of a wealthy oligarchy."[24]

It is accurate to state that the upper class of Great Britain was more accepting of Hitler and fascism; some were even outright admirers of Hitler. This was exemplified by the so-called "Cliveden Set," an aristocratic social group anchored around Cliveden, Lady

Astor's Buckinghamshire estate. The group supported the appeasement of Hitler and friendly relations with Nazi Germany. From 1932
through 1940, the British Fascist Union, led by Sir Oswald Mose-
ley, gained some notoriety on the British political scene, but it was
never a major force in British political life. Yet it was not economic
protectionism that guided Neville Chamberlain at Munich. While
he can be faulted for many things, such as not being more proactive
early on in attempting to force a more robust alliance with France
and other European states to act as a deterrent to Hitler and for his
overly simplistic assessment of Hitler's ambitions, Chamberlain's
actions at Munich had little to do with protecting the pockets of
England's industrialists. The memories of the carnage of the First
World War were still vivid in the minds of many Englishmen, and
Chamberlain was no exception. They would do virtually anything
to avoid another war, and the prime minister chose appeasement of
Hitler in his sincere attempt to prevent global conflict. It is highly
dubious that the "industrial overlords" had anything to do with
Chamberlain's actions at Munich. Gittelsohn was much more ac-
curate when he noted the British aristocracy's greater loathing of
Russia and communism than its distaste for fascism.

Gittelsohn next went on to accuse Chamberlain of being a fascist
himself. "I know that a few of you . . . will think that I've gone too
far in openly and categorically accusing Mr. Chamberlain of himself
being a fascist and being dominated and controlled by fascists," he
told his congregation. To prove his point, he quoted the German
novelist and social critic Thomas Mann, who said, "I am firmly
convinced that Mr. Chamberlain is a fascist and that he knew the
true state of affairs. There is no use in sparing words. There is a
growing party in England which leans strongly toward fascism
not perhaps because it believes in it, but because it fears Russia."[25]
Mann was wise enough to accuse Chamberlain of being a fascist,
Gittelsohn claimed, because he knew Munich wasn't just an isolated
event. Closing the frontier of France to Spain, the whole policy of
non-intervention and the "Anglo-Italian conspiracy" against Spain
were all aspects of Chamberlain's true fascist ideology.

Gittelsohn cited the two semi-official visits made by Chamberlain's sister-in-law, Ivy Chamberlain, "one to that great democrat,
Mussolini, and the other to his humanitarian colleague, Franco,"[26]
as more proof of Chamberlain's political leanings. As a further

indication of the treachery of the prime minister, he noted Chamberlain's manipulation of the press in England, claiming that "in the 50 weeks since November 19, 1937" — the day that Lord Halifax, representing Prime Minister Chamberlain, arrived in Berlin to begin negotiations with Hitler — "not one single cartoon offensive to either Hitler or Mussolini has been printed in any English newspaper." Another example of the media control exercised by Chamberlain was the inability of British novelist Phyllis Bottome to get her scathing criticism of the Chamberlain government printed in any British paper, even when she offered to do it at her own expense.[27]

Gittelsohn's assertions concerning Chamberlain's manipulation of the press are entirely accurate. Only on rare occasions would the thoroughly compliant media not parrot the party line in support of the prime minister and his agenda. As Chamberlain's premiership progressed, he became increasingly aggressive towards the journalists and openly manipulative, refusing, for example, to answer off-the-cuff questions and insisting that any questions should be submitted four hours in advance if the journalist was to expect a reply.[28] Richard Cockett best described the relationship of Neville Chamberlain and the press when he wrote in 1989: "If a democracy can be defined as a healthy, continuing clash of opinion, then the Chamberlain government, through its close control of the press, certainly succeeded in subverting democracy during the years 1937 to 1940."[29]

Neville Chamberlain's name will be forever linked in history with appeasement; and while he displayed many flaws in his foreign policy dealings with Adolf Hitler, Gittelsohn's assertion that Chamberlain, too, was a fascist in league with Hitler is patently absurd. He took over a government that was paralyzed with the memories of the World War and had tremendously cut back its military. The Spanish Civil War was raging and the fear of Bolshevism was great in the minds of many in Europe. It was his fear of another war and his naïve belief that he could trust Hitler to be satisfied with the acquisition of the Sudetenland that was the driving motive behind Chamberlain's actions. While it is true that Chamberlain's policies also served some of the goals and desires of fascist sympathizers in Great Britain, this no more proves he was a fascist than Gittelsohn's own leftist sympathies prove that he was a communist. Chamberlain can be accused of being a mediocre prime minister at a time when his country truly needed greatness. He can and should be accused of being an appeaser who clearly did not understand Adolf Hitler. But Gittelsohn was wrong when he stated emphatically that the man was a fascist.

To begin the second part of his sermon, Gittelsohn told his audience that many of them had already asked him the question he was going to answer next. "You want to know how I, a confirmed and extreme and radical pacifist, can condemn the Conference at Munich if the only alternative was war. My answer to that is that I still condemn it and I am still a pacifist, because the only alternative wasn't war."[30] He immediately followed with his explanation in a discussion that was largely wrong and stunning for its misguided analysis, especially when one considers his superb analysis of Hitler's vision in *Mein Kampf* that he delivered only two weeks before. Claiming that Hitler was bluffing, he explained thusly: "Hitler could have been stopped and he could have been stopped with peace. I for one am more convinced that if England and France had refused to betray Czechoslovakia, Adolf Hitler would not have gone to war."

After announcing that stunning conclusion, one that would be proven wrong within nine months, Gittelsohn provided three basic reasons to explain why Hitler would have not gone to war over Czechoslovakia. The first involved an analysis done by Dr. Edward Sampson of Princeton, who concluded that "Germany is by no means ready to undertake a protracted war, and indeed has probably not gathered sufficient supplies to support her full manpower in a short war against a major power." So, according to Gittelsohn, there wouldn't have been a war "because Hitler couldn't fight one."[31] Sampson's analysis was written at a time when concepts such as blitzkrieg were unknown, as were the even greater depths of perfidy that Hitler would sink to in order to achieve his goals, such as attacking the Soviet Union after negotiating a non-aggression pact with them.

The second reason that Gittelsohn offered as to why Hitler would not have gone to war was that he would be very reluctant if not actually afraid to do so. To support this argument, Gittelsohn claimed that Hitler wasn't "as big a dumbbell as the world sometimes pretends he is" and that Hitler had to have noted how none of the rulers who got their countries into the World War were still in power at the war's end. The rabbi also cited the revolt of the coal miners in Upper Silesia the previous July; when rumors surfaced that war had broken out, a melee erupted that required thousands of secret police to put down. Gittelsohn was sure that these types of incidents would make Hitler think twice about initiating a war. Yet as he explained this, he also noted that it took the importation of over five thousand secret police to put down the rebellion. As he amply displayed in 1934 in the Night of the Long Knives incident, where he liquidated all potential opposition within his own Nazi party, Hitler was not reluctant at all to brutally crush dissent. It is highly unlikely that Hitler was in the least bit worried about dissent or about using ruthless force to crush it.

The third reason given by Gittelsohn was that everything Hitler had achieved he did through bluster and bluff. "And yet they know that every time someone had the courage and the gumption to say stop, immediately and unhesitatingly Hitler stopped! And that happened not just once, but at least three different times."[32]

The examples Gittelsohn proceeded to give are not only weak but also inaccurate. The logic of his first example is difficult to accept as indicating anything other than Hitler's duplicitous and manipulative nature, discounting any theories that he may display weakness and a tendency to back down when confronted. Referring to Hitler's abortive coup d'etat in Munich in 1923, known as the Beer Hall Putsch, Gittelsohn pointed out that Hitler had proclaimed that if the putsch failed, he would kill himself. Hitler, of course, did not kill himself after the putsch was put down. He was tried, convicted, and sentenced to five years imprisonment in Landsberg Prison, where he served only nine months. Gittelsohn used the fact that Hitler hadn't committed suicide as proof that he was bluffing and would back down when confronted, as if dishonesty and lies were something new in Hitler's repertoire. One must logically weigh the adversity produced by Hitler's theoretical, "promised" suicide against the reality of his decision to live and, while in prison, write the manifesto for his world plan—*Mein Kampf*—and go on to wreak havoc on the world. In this example, Hitler's "bluffing" and backing down led to the bloodiest war in world history.

For his next example, Gittelsohn listed Hitler's actions when dealing with the dictator of Poland, Marshal Jozef Pilsudski. The nation of Poland had been established by the Treaty of Versailles in

1919, which also created a "Polish Corridor" extending northward to prevent Poland from being landlocked. The free city of Danzig at the northern end of the corridor was to provide a port for Poland. This corridor separated Germany from East Prussia and was a constant source of friction between Poland and Germany. When the Nazis rose to power, "reuniting Germans in the Polish Corridor" with Germany became one of their bellicose aims, as they threatened to take the corridor from Poland. Gittelsohn told his congregation that a prime example of Hitler's bluffing had occurred "a few years ago when Hitler decided to march in and reclaim the Polish Corridor. But he wasn't dealing then with a toy dictator like Chamberlain, he was dealing with a real dictator. And when the late Marshall [*sic*] Pilsudski gave Hitler his choice of signing a ten year pact of non-aggression and renouncing the Corridor, or else fighting, Hitler didn't fight. He signed and he renounced. His bluff had been called and he quit!"[33]

Gittelsohn's interpretation of the situation is questionable. It is undeniable that there was no love lost between Hitler and Pilsudski. However, most historians report that driven by his fear and distrust of the Nazis, Pilsudski approached France with a proposal that their two nations invade Germany with the purpose of overthrowing Hitler and the Nazis. The French rejected the plan out of hand. Scholars have cited France's refusal of Pilsudski's proposal as one of the reasons for Poland's signing of the German-Polish Non-Aggression Pact in January 1934. There is no evidence that Pilsudski threatened Hitler as Gittelsohn suggested, or that he was eager to go to war with Germany. Hitler's plan of rapprochement with Poland bought him time to re-arm Germany, which was a much stronger nation militarily at the time of the Munich conference than it was in January 1934. Hitler's word on a treaty, even if it had been forced as Gittelsohn suggested, was as worthless in 1934 as it was less than a year after Gittelsohn's sermon when Germany invaded the Polish Corridor, precipitating the Second World War.

For his third example illustrating the tendency of Hitler to bluff and back down when confronted, Gittelsohn chose a more convincing case to argue his point. He described the assassination of Austrian dictator Engelbert Dollfuss in July of 1934 by Austrian Nazis and noted: "That was supposed to be a signal for Hitler to march in then and there, just as he actually did three and a half years later. But at that time Mussolini had other ideas. So he mobilized his Italian troops at the Brenner Pass on the border between Italy and Austria, and he told Hitler without equivocation and without pussyfooting and without any dramatic plane flights, that when the first German soldier set foot on Austrian soil, Mussolini would march. Needless to say, the first German soldier didn't set foot on Austrian soil, and Mussolini didn't have to march."[34] In this example, Gittelsohn is correct. Hitler was surprised by Mussolini's reaction, and despite many Nazi-provoked riots in Austria following Dollfuss' murder, he did not want to risk intervention at that time.

Again, the power of Nazi Germany in 1934 was not nearly what it was at the time of the Munich conference. Mussolini would soon embroil Italy with a war in Ethiopia as well as provide support for Franco in the Spanish Civil War. By 1937, Mussolini would come under the spell of Adolf Hitler and ally with him. The following year, by annexing Austria without consulting Mussolini, the increasingly powerful Hitler had relegated him to junior partner status. While Gittelsohn's third example did actually show Hitler backing down, this 1934 incident was largely irrelevant to the realities of 1938.

Gittelsohn ended his sermon by decrying Chamberlain's actions at Munich, stating, "Whenever Hitler's bluff has been called in the past, without a single exception he has surrendered. That bluff could have been called again."[35] He provided a somberly accurate prediction when he stated that what happened at Munich was simply a prologue for a more tragic drama, the end of which was nowhere in sight. Quoting Eduard Benes, he cautioned, "I do not wish to criticize, nor must you expect from me a single word of recrimination. History will be our judge."[36]

In the first part of his discussion of Munich, Roland Gittelsohn provided an excellent analysis of the long-range plan that Adolph Hitler outlined in *Mein Kampf*. In the second part, he revealed a total misunderstanding of the true nature of evil that drove Hitler. His incorrect belief that Hitler was all bluff and no action when confronted was even further compounded by his almost bizarre belief that Hitler could have been stopped with peace. Hitler could not have been stopped by peace at Munich. He had decided in early May of 1938 to attack Czechoslovakia to both strengthen

Germany's strategic position in central Europe as well as to use ethnic Germans in that country to enlarge his armies for the next war.[37] It was to be the first in a planned series of wars he intended to fight. At the last moment he had changed his mind and decided to settle at the Munich conference for what others thought of as a German triumph. Hitler, though, came to consider it the worst mistake of his career.[38] He would come to feel that he had been cheated out of his war at Munich and he had no intention of being cheated again.

Hitler would clearly outline his plans for phased wars in his unpublished sequel to *Mein Kampf*, written in 1928.[39] As noted above, a war to destroy Czechoslovakia and secure the German position in central Europe would be the first war. Next, he would attack the western powers—England and France. After the conquering of these countries, he would next turn his sights on the Soviet Union. Conquering the Soviet Union would provide the food and the "living space" that the enlarging Germany would need. Lastly, he would ultimately have to destroy the United States of America. When Chamberlain appeased Hitler at Munich, "cheating" him out of the war he desired, Hitler turned his sights on Poland in order to secure his eastern border as a reason to initiate his first war. Manufactured incidents against ethnic Germans in the Polish Corridor would provide Hitler the context to invade.

Adolf Hitler was not bluffing. He could not have been stopped with peace. The only thing that could have stopped him was the very thing that did stop him—the total destruction of Nazi Germany. After 1938, Hitler was able to avoid being cheated out of the wars that he had planned and wanted badly. The result was that Hitler's "Reich to last a thousand years" was destroyed after twelve years in another world war.

# Chapter Fourteen

# A World on the Brink

In late 1938 and early 1939, events occurring in the troubled British Mandate of Palestine would further serve to anger Roland Gittelsohn and increase his hatred of Neville Chamberlain and his distaste for England in general. In November of 1938, the British government issued its "Policy Statement Against Partition" in regard to Palestine, effectively reversing its position on partition as recommended by the Peel Commission. Citing the seeming inability of both sides to accept partition, the British government called on representatives from both Palestinian Arabs and the Jewish Agency to meet in London and attempt to work out their differences. Should the meetings not produce any agreement within a reasonable time frame, it was the British government's intention to examine the problem and to propose a policy that they intended to pursue.[1]

The London conferences met in February and March with the Arab delegates attending only on the condition that they would have no direct negotiation with the Jews, forcing the British government representatives to hold separate meetings with the two groups. After two months the meetings ended without the Palestinian Jews and Arabs being able to resolve any differences. On May 17, 1939, the British government issued its new policy statement known as the White Paper. The paper formally dismissed the idea of partition and called for an independent Palestinian State, stating that "It should be a state in which the two peoples in Palestine, Arabs and Jews, share authority in government in such a way that the essential interests of each are secured."[2] Starting with this highly unrealistic goal given the history of the region since the formation of Palestine, the White Paper went on to basically provide support for the Arab position.

The White Paper represented nothing less than the betrayal of the San Remo Resolution, as well as the spirit and stated intentions of the Mandate for Palestine. It called for a limitation on Jewish immigration to Palestine, limiting it to a maximum rate of fifteen thousand a year for the next five years, and after that it would cease completely unless the Arabs would accept more Jewish immigrants. The White Paper also put restrictions and certain outright prohibitions on the further purchase of land by Jews.[3] The Jews of Palestine, as well as Jews and Zionists worldwide, were outraged by the new policy. Interestingly, the Arabs also rejected the White Paper, demanding that Palestine become an Arab state immediately and that Jewish immigration to Palestine be abruptly ended. In addition, they demanded that the status of every Jew who immigrated since 1918 be reviewed.[4]

A Jewish general strike was called on May 18 to protest the new policies. On July 13, the Mandate authorities announced the suspension of all Jewish immigration to Palestine until March 1940, citing an alleged increase in illegal immigrants arriving.[5]

Shortly after the White Paper went into effect, Gittelsohn erupted in anger over both the new policy and England itself in an undated sermon from that time frame. As usual, he was preaching against our country getting involved with the deepening morass overseas. The sermon, entitled "America and the Next War," contained the usual elements of his sermons. It was heavily laced with economic motives that promoted war as well as the hypocrisy of going to war to preserve democracy when history had indicated that if anything, these idealistic wars ruined democracy. He strongly warned his congregants to be wary of the barrage of propaganda that they were all being subject to about fighting for democracy. It was in this context that he brought up the developments in the Middle East.

"Well before we fall again for that kind of tommyrot," he warned his audience, "let's at least stop kidding ourselves about what we'd be fighting for. Let's stop mouthing a lot of cheap phrases about defending a noble cause with the great democracies of England and France. Great democracies indeed! What's democratic about an England which betrays every sacred promise it ever made? What's democratic about Munich? What's democratic about an England which right at this moment is seeking to break the hearts and crush the last hope of a Jewish people which is hated and hunted and desperate? I do not love England! I hate England! I will not fight for England!"[6]

Further showing his contempt for the British, Gittelsohn made a comparison of England to Germany, "as despicable as it is," claiming, "At least Hitler's Germany never pretended to be our friend or the friend of democracy. At least Hitler's Germany never embraced us so that it could knife us. At least Germany never made us a sacred promise in the highest tribunal of mankind, and then, when we needed the fulfillment of that promise most, held it to be meaningless and cheap."[7]

On the morning of March 15, 1939, Hitler summoned elderly and frail Czechoslovakian President Emil Hacha to Berlin and warned him that Germany was about to invade his country. Suffering a heart attack during the meeting, Hacha capitulated to Hitler's demands and German troops entered the country to minimal resistance. The betrayal of Czechoslovakia that began at Munich only six months prior was now complete. The reaction to Germany's latest aggression was swift; the British were especially infuriated by Hitler's actions. Lord Halifax warned the German ambassador to Great Britain thusly: "I can understand Herr Hitler's taste for bloodless victories, but one of these days he will find himself up against something that will not be bloodless."[8]

Neville Chamberlain's initial public statement was tepid at best, claiming that England was not bound to protect Czechoslovakia. The resultant outrage from the press, which Chamberlain appeared to control only months prior, caused him to have an apparent change of heart when he spoke in Birmingham on March 17. Explaining that he had never denied that the terms which he secured at Munich were not those that he would have desired, he proceeded to ask rhetorically, what was the alternative? After the events two days earlier in Czechoslovakia, Chamberlain told his audience that they must ask: "Is this the last attack upon a small State, or is it to be followed by others? Is this, in fact, a step in the direction of an attempt to dominate the world by force?" Stating that there was hardly anything that he wouldn't sacrifice for peace, he noted, ". . . There is one thing that I must except, and that is the liberty that we have enjoyed for hundreds of years and which we will never surrender."

Closing his speech, Chamberlain made his position clear and sent a message to Adolf Hitler. "No greater mistake could be made than to suppose that, because it believes war to be a senseless and cruel thing, this nation . . . will not take part to the utmost of its power in resisting such a challenge. . . . I have not merely the support, the sympathy, the confidence of my fellow countrymen and countrywomen, but . . . the approval of the whole British Empire and of all other nations who value peace, indeed, but who value freedom even more."[9]

On March 31, both England and France gave military guarantees to Poland, Romania, Greece, and Turkey and also inaugurated political and military talks with the Soviets.[10] England was now committed to the protection of Poland, the object of Hitler's next planned war. On May 22, Germany and Italy signed a military alliance, the Pact of Steel, pledging to fight alongside each other in the event of war. Europe was on a collision course, headed for a war planned and desired by Adolf Hitler.

---

Hitler next set his sights on Poland. But first he had business he needed to conduct with the Soviet Union: Hitler needed to keep the Soviets out of any potential war with Germany. His master plan called for him to wage war against England and France after destroying Poland. To accomplish this, he needed his eastern front quiet and sought a non-aggression pact with Stalin, despite his known hatred of communism and all things associated with it. In secret, Hitler sent his foreign minister Joachim von Ribbentrop to Moscow to negotiate with his Soviet counterpart, Vyacheslav Molotov. In early August, they negotiated an economic deal known as the Ribbentrop-Molotov Pact and commenced to negotiate a political alliance. The two ministers explained to each other the reasons for their foreign policy hostility in the recent years, finding common ground in the anti-capitalist sentiment of the other's country.[11]

While the negotiations were ongoing, Stalin was also negotiating with representatives from England and France over a possible military alliance against Germany. Stalin cut off these negotiations and proceeded to sign a non-aggression pact with Nazi Germany. Included in the pact was a secret protocol carving up Europe into spheres of influence for both Germany and the Soviet Union. Poland was to be immediately cut roughly in half, the western part going to Germany, the eastern part to the Soviet Union. The entire Ribbentrop-Molotov Pact was signed on August 23, 1939. The following day a stunned and upset world awoke to the news of the new alliance between these seemingly incompatible partners. The citizens of Poland were upset, as they knew what Hitler, his eastern front cleared by the treaty, was planning for them in the very near future. Pres. Franklin D. Roosevelt wrote to Hitler, urging him to "refrain from any positive act of hostility for a reasonable and stipulated period."[12] Hitler ignored the request.

As previously mentioned, the news of an alliance between Nazi Germany and the Soviet Union spelled the death knell for the largely communist-dominated student anti-war movement in the United States. Many lost faith in the Communist Party, viewing the Ribbentrop-Molotov Pact as a sellout of principles to Adolf Hitler, and many wanted no part of this apparent abandonment of anti-fascism.[13] Their naïve, idealized picture of the Soviet Union as a "worker's paradise" was forever destroyed as Joseph Stalin partnered with Hitler, the very embodiment of the fascist evil that they opposed so vehemently. For pacifists such as Roland Gittelsohn, the pact was another indication of the world descending into chaos. While many felt war was inevitable now, they felt it was still their duty to push for American non-involvement in war developing in Europe. Unlike 1917, they were determined to keep America out of the conflict.

———•———

On August 26, 1939, Roland Gittelsohn traveled into Manhattan to the Central Synagogue of New York City. He was invited to speak on the weekly radio program *Message of Israel*. The program had been founded in October 1934 by the Central Synagogue's rabbi, Jonah B. Wise. Wise—the son of the founder of Reform Judaism, Rabbi Isaac Mayer Wise—broadcast his Sunday programs on WJZ in New York City. Only two days had passed since the world learned of the Ribbentrop-Molotov Pact, and that night, as Gittelsohn recorded his message, his sadness at the inevitability of war was plain to all. There was one message that he wished to drive home to all of the program's listeners: the United States must stay out of the coming war.

He began by quoting the German poet Heinrich Heine, who said that we human beings learn nothing from history except that we learn nothing from history.[14] Were Heine alive today, Gittelsohn assured the audience, he would repeat that conclusion with emphasis and conviction. "Today," Gittelsohn continued, "you and I have the doubtful privilege of standing upon the darkest threshold in the past twenty-five years of human history. Almost at any moment the continents of Europe and Asia may be plunged once again into the burning inferno of mass murder . . . even Frederick Birchall wrote this week from Europe that the question is no longer asked *if* war will come; the only question now is, *when* will it come?"[15]

At this point, Gittelsohn delved into his reason for the address, why he insisted on speaking on such and unpleasant topic. He did so for one reason and with one hope: "that at least we may manage to use what may be our last free moment of peace to *think* and *talk* and *plan* sanity. We need that sanity! We live in a world which is about to burst into the passion of insanity! Let us at least in this land stay sane."[16] Therein was the crux of his message—the United States must not be drawn into the evolving war. We had to resist and not act as we did in 1917.

When the war erupted in Europe, he warned, the United States would once again be subjected to "an absolute avalanche of poisonous propaganda" that had, in fact, already begun. To support this contention, Gittelsohn pointed out the article in the current issue of *Harper's* by American journalist Frank C. Hanighen in which he stated that both the French and British newspapers were "constantly and deliberately giving their readers the impression that as soon as the hostilities commence, the United States too will be fighting."[17] Once the war actually began, Gittelsohn cautioned, the propaganda would only be much more intense—the worst and most vicious that any modern people will ever be subjected to. And the propaganda would not be easy to resist.

It will be difficult to resist, the rabbi cautioned, because

other nations are going to talk our language, the language of ideals. You may be positive that they will not speak a single word about investments, about profits or about secret treaties. They'll do the self-same thing they did in 1914 and 15 and 16. They'll talk eloquently and glibly about a war for ideals. They'll talk about the truth. They'll talk about justice. They'll talk about honor and decency and most of all about democracy. And they'll create some new kind of fancy slogan to convince us again that we've got to help make the world safe for democracy.[18]

He pleaded to the audience to know that while the nefarious "they" spoke to us in the language of ideals, we had to be prepared to be thinking in the language of facts. As in prior speeches and sermons, Gittelsohn then recited statistics profiling the killed, wounded, widowed, and orphaned from the last war. "All for democracy!!" he exclaimed. "Well, then, where is that democracy now? Where is that democracy at this moment? Where is the democracy that we paid for and bled for and died for? You know the answer as well as I, and the propagandizing countries of Europe know it too. With the sacred exception of our own United States, that democracy has almost vanished from the face of this miserable earth."[19]

He next returned to a familiar theme—that the last war didn't save democracy and the next one won't either. We must remember, he said, that war can't save democracy, that it is the opposite of democracy. Launching into a point that was perhaps more appropriate for a philosophical debate in a classroom, Gittelsohn continued, saying, "Surely if democracy means anything, it means an infinite respect for the dignity and worth of each individual life. How, in the name of common sense, can war, which destroys life, teach us to respect life? Democracy means the discussion and solution of human problems by calm, unprejudiced thinking. How on earth can war, which solves problems by the hatred and passion of bullets, teach us that? Democracy means the protection of each man's right to think and speak as he wishes. How in the world can war, which destroys liberty, help us to preserve liberty?"[20] To illustrate his point, he referred to the discussion that President Woodrow Wilson had with journalist Frank Cobb on April 5, 1917, when Wilson somberly told Cobb that in reconstructing civilization after the war had ended there wouldn't be any peace standards to work with, only war standards.[21]

In addition to pleading with his audience to resist the onslaught of war propaganda that was inevitable and to give up any illusions that wars ever produce or defend democracy, he recommended one more thing. "This time, instead of hoping, foolishly and vainly, to make the world safe for democracy, let's stay home and make democracy safe for the world. Let's use the money and energy and life we might have wasted in the war to solve the problem of ten million unemployed," he urged, without possibly being able to know at the time that it would, in fact, be the war that would end the Great Depression and restore full employment to the country.[22] Foreshadowing the policies of future presidents Lyndon Johnson and Barack Obama by decades, he said, "Let's mobilize an army against poverty. Let's fight for a decent distribution of our country's vast and abundant wealth."[23] These are the wars we should fight, right here at home, he insisted. To drive home his point Gittelsohn ended his radio address with the conclusion that "this is the war we must fight! And this is the only war that can ever save democracy. Therefore it's the only war which America has any right to enter."[24]

# Chapter Fifteen

# The War Begins

Adolph Hitler had already made his decision in regard to Poland months before the Molotov-Ribbentrop Pact. On April 3, 1939, he issued a war directive marked "Most Secret" and had it hand delivered to his most senior commanders. Outlining the upcoming attack on Poland, named Operation White, Hitler instructed his military leaders: "Since the situation on Germany's eastern front has become intolerable, and all political possibilities of a peaceful settlement have been exhausted, I have decided upon a solution by force."[1] The attack would begin on September 1.

The pretext for the German invasion of Poland would be a series of staged provocations conducted by the Schutzstaffel (SS) depicting atrocities allegedly committed by Poles against ethnic Germans in Poland. The overall campaign, named Operation Himmler, culminated on August 31, when members of the SS wearing Polish army uniforms attacked various border villages, committed acts of terrorism, and left behind dead bodies in Polish military uniforms. The bodies were actually those of concentration camp victims who were killed in order to add to the ruse. The week before, Hitler had informed his generals of the plan, stating, "I will provide a propagandistic *casus belli*. Its credibility doesn't matter. The victor will not be asked if he told the truth."[2] The following day, Hitler invaded Poland.

The day of the invasion, Neville Chamberlain contacted both the Germans and the Poles, attempting to get the parties to cease any hostilities and come to the negotiating table. The Poles immediately replied in agreement with England's proposal. Germany never responded to Chamberlain's request. On September 2, the British government consulted with France in order to consolidate their response to Hitler's aggression. Accordingly, on September 3, 1939, Prime Minister Chamberlain addressed the House of Commons.

He informed them that he had sent their ambassador in Berlin instructions that he was to deliver to Hitler that morning. The instructions included the vow that "the United Kingdom would, without hesitation, fulfill its obligation to Poland." Noting the lack of response to Chamberlain's prior request, the ambassador informed Hitler that unless England received satisfactory assurances from Germany in that regard by 11 a.m. that morning, "a state of war [would] exist between the two countries at that time." Not having heard a reply by the deadline, Chamberlain informed Germany that a state of war did then exist between their two countries and that the French government would be pursuing an identical course in alliance with Great Britain.[3] In a little under twenty-one years, the world was again at war.

---

For the next several months, although war had been declared in Europe, there was no combat on the ground. The seemingly "peaceful" version of war between Germany and the British-French allies led to a phase of the Second World War that would be referred to as the "Phony War." While the antagonists postured on the ground, real warfare broke out in Finland on November 30, 1939, when the Soviet Union invaded the country. The West roundly condemned the Soviet Union for this action, which led to its expulsion from the League of Nations. Although the Soviet Union prevailed in the conflict, they did not accomplish their goal of total conquest of Finland due to the rousingly strong defense by the Finns of their homeland. As a result of the Moscow Peace Treaty, signed in March of 1940, Finland ceded 11 percent of its territory and 30 percent of its economic assets to the Soviet Union.[4] The Soviet losses were high and, accordingly, its international reputation suffered.[5]

The Phony War ended on April 9, 1940, when the Germans, using blitzkrieg tactics, attacked Denmark and Norway. Less than two months later the Nazis occupied both countries. The Low Countries—the Netherlands, Belgium, and Luxembourg—desired to remain neutral in the war and resisted efforts by the British and French to entice them to ally with them. On May 10, the Germans occupied Luxembourg and attacked Belgium and Holland. As the

British and French fought their way north attempting to assist the Belgians, a massive armor attack by the XIX German Army Corps, assisted by the Luftwaffe, fought its way to the English Channel. By May 20, they had cut off the British Expeditionary Force (BEF) along with a large number of French and Belgian troops. Isolated in an ever-tightening noose, the BEF fell back to the port of Dunkirk.

In what was referred to as the "Miracle of Dunkirk," nearly three hundred forty thousand British, French, and Belgian troops were rescued by a makeshift flotilla and transported across the English Channel to England between May 27 and June 4. The German high command had halted the German ground offensive and instead relied on the Luftwaffe to destroy the BEF. In spite of this strategy that allowed a large number of allied soldiers to escape, it was a devastating defeat for the Allies, regardless of the spin put on the evacuation. The German blitzkrieg tactics had mauled their armies with speed and precision. Later that month, France surrendered to the Nazis. Europe was effectively under Nazi control.

Back in the United States, Roland Gittelsohn was closely watching the developments from the war in Europe. Dunkirk would prove to be a watershed moment for him. For the first time he would begin to feel doubts about his absolute pacifism. In his memoirs he would later confirm that it was the result of the Battle of Dunkirk that first caused him to realize that there was something worse than war itself—that perhaps there really was something worth fighting for.

---

Things were going well for both Rabbi Gittelsohn and his new congregation by the fall of 1939. Temple membership had continued to grow steadily and their rabbi had established several adult study groups, Hebrew study groups, and open forums to discuss national and international problems. He proved to be a lively and highly knowledgeable facilitator of these various discussions. He was highly regarded by the congregation, who became accustomed to the detailed sermons on social responsibility and pacifism that he would frequently deliver. In spite of the deteriorating and distressing situation in Europe, coupled with his fear that the United States would once again be dragged into a

European conflict, Gittelsohn's professional life and his personal life were sources of great pride and satisfaction.

In the fall of 1939, the Synagogue School began Saturday classes in the Wilson School with 160 pupils. A Kol Nidre appeal was made to raise a sufficient sum for the purchase of property for a permanent home. Later, in 1940, a suitable site was found on DeMott Avenue; the purchase contract was consummated on November 7, 1940.[6] Shortly after the land purchase, a joyous occasion blessed Roland and Ruth Gittelsohn. They had learned the previous winter that Ruth was once again pregnant. On November 24, 1940, Ruth gave birth to their daughter, Judith Gittelsohn.

## Chapter Sixteen

# The Riddle of Russia

On June 22, 1941, Hitler ordered the commencement of Operation Barbarossa — the invasion of the Soviet Union. In the largest military operation in history, 121 German Divisions attacked along a two-thousand-mile front. In blitzkrieg fashion, the German war machine advanced rapidly against the poorly prepared Russian forces. By September, Hitler ordered the offensive for the capture of Moscow, which began in October. A successful counterattack led by Marshal Zhukov was eventually able to prevent the German capture of the Russian capital. By mid-September, Leningrad was cut off and would remain under siege for over two years. A combination of the onset of the dreaded Russian winter, increasingly long German supply lines, and stubborn Russian resistance allowed the Soviet Union to hang on despite its seemingly primitive social structure and its loss of much of its military leadership due to Stalin's purges of the late 1930s.

The United States Naval Base at Pearl Harbor was attacked on December 7, 1941. The next day, the United States declared war on Japan, and Adolph Hitler would immediately declare war on the United States. Less than six weeks later on January 23, 1942, Roland Gittelsohn addressed his congregation in a sermon that discussed the situation in Russia. Entitled "The Riddle of Russia," it was a discussion that highlighted Gittelsohn's highly knowledgeable grasp of the war situation and also again publically expressed his personal political convictions against communism. This discussion is also notable for its laudatory comments concerning Russia and for Gittelsohn's final conclusions on the correct road ahead in regard to our relationship with the Soviet Union. Most striking is the unusually dispassionate and, at times, almost cruelly objective tone that the rabbi's analysis conveyed.

Gittelsohn began his discussion by stating up front that there was no such thing as an objective opinion when it came to Russia:

people were either one hundred percent for or one hundred percent against Russia. The same kind of people will look at the same facts with the same eyes and yet reach diametrically opposed conclusions regarding the country, its politics, and its leaders. Having begun to lay the framework for his discussion, Gittelsohn informed the audience that his sermon was going to be very pro-Russian. "I will speak tonight almost entirely in favor of Russia, but I want it to be clearly understood, specific enough even for Dies," he told the congregation, referring to anti-communist crusading Democratic congressman Martin Dies Jr. "I am not a communist, a son, shadow, or fellow-traveler of one," Gittelsohn continued. "No one who believes in religion in general, Judaism in particular, and Zionism especially, can be a communist. I do believe in all three of these things, so I can't be a communist."[1]

Having stated his beliefs, he felt he needed to clarify his opinions on Russia even further. "I also believe in human dignity and the value of a human person. Russia is still a dictatorship and I don't like dictatorships no matter what color, and not even if it happens to be on my side and is saving me from destruction. . . . So long as it is true, I must as a matter of permanent principle be opposed to what goes by the name of communism in Russia today."[2]

After his preamble, Gittelsohn framed his discussion around two questions to consider regarding Russia, as well as his attempts to answer them with facts. To begin, he posed the following to his audience: Why did Russia sign the Molotov-Ribbentrop Pact in 1939? Undoubtedly, stated Gittelsohn, this provided Hitler his "green light" to proceed with the invasion of Poland. Also, he stated unequivocally, history would judge Russia harshly for this action. But Gittelsohn next proposed another reason for Russia's action that certainly must have surprised some of his congregation: Russia had no choice in the matter.

"In our proper and understandable eagerness to condemn them," he urged, "let us not forget that for twenty years Russia was the only major nation in the world that took the idea of collective security seriously."[3] Reminding his listeners that the Soviet Union was the first nation to sign the Kellogg-Briand Pact outlawing war in 1928 and that it was the first nation to call for complete and absolute world disarmament, Gittelsohn reasoned that they did these things "not because they were ethnically superior to other nations, but only because they were intelligent enough to realize that war was the worst thing for her own self national interests."[4] Here, to a degree, Gittelsohn seems to be wearing blinders with his interpretation of the events. He conveniently overlooked the Soviet invasion of Finland in 1940. Still other damning facts about the Soviet Union were widely suppressed, so Gittelsohn could not possibly have known of them. (This was the case, for example, with the true extent of Stalin's political purges of his enemies or the severe famine of 1932, an event that was also denied by "useful idiot" *New York Times* reporter Walter Duranty.)

If Russia was devoted to collective security against fascism, why did it enter into the pact that provided a "brief honeymoon" with Germany? Gittelsohn promptly answered his own question: because she was forced to; because England and France and, to a lesser degree, the United States, "gave her no alternative whatsoever." Here, he was more accurate with his answer. He pointed out that the influential powers of England and France were more afraid of Russia than they were of Adolf Hitler: "We do know that right while England and France were presumably negotiating in Moscow in August of 1939 for an ironclad pact with Russia, they were at the same time conspiring with Hitler against Russia. Russia knew that."[5] Gittelsohn cited a September 11, 1938, conversation between Soviet diplomat Maxim Litvinov and French Foreign Minister Georges Bonnet where Litvinov assured him that Russia would come to the aid of Czechoslovakia militarily if invaded by Germany. This intention was stymied by the Romanian refusal to allow Russian troops transit through their nation.

Further support of Gittelsohn's contentions on this point were unearthed when the Russian Foreign Intelligence Service, the SVR, declassified archival material related to the Munich Agreement in 2008. In Memo #8604 sent by Russian intelligence in Prague to Moscow several days before the agreement was signed, it was stated, "On September 19, British Ambassador Newton and French ambassador De Lacroix conveyed to Milan Hodza [Czechoslovak prime minister in 1935-1938] the following on behalf of Chamberlain and Daladier, respectfully: 'Guided by the lofty principles of preserving peace in Europe, they consider it necessary for Germany to incorporate the Sudeten region. A system of mutual aid pacts with other countries should be cancelled.

Instead, all of Czechoslovakia's neighbors, plus France and Britain will guarantee the inviolability of its frontiers.'"[6] By their actions, France and England destroyed any existing elements of collective security against Nazi aggression. The Western policymakers did this behind the back of the Soviet Union, which had mutual aid agreements with Czechoslovakia and France.[7]

Further declassified documents revealed the details of correspondence between European embassies and their foreign services. The Finnish ambassador in London noted that France would not be able to render any effective military aid if Hitler invaded Czechoslovakia. The SVR press officer Sergei Ivanov noted that the Soviet Union was ready to render such support to Czechoslovakia, but because of the heavy pressure from London and Paris, Prague did not dare address Moscow with such a request. He went on to state, "As early as November 1938, diplomatic missions of a number of countries reported to their departments that Britain and France would not prevent Germany's eastward expansion." Most damning are the comments recorded by the Finnish ambassador to London G. A. Grippenberg to his Foreign Ministry on November 25, 1938, in which he related a conversation he had with a British government official who assured him that Britain and France would not interfere in Germany's eastward expansion. "Britain's position is a follows: let's wait until Germany and the U.S.S.R. get involved in a big conflict," stated Grippenberg.[8]

The Soviet Union did attempt to set up a system for resisting Nazi Germany, and as a result both Britain and France sent their military missions to Moscow for negotiations. According to SVR veteran and archivist Major General Lev Sotskov, in the event an anti-Hitler agreement between the three countries could be worked out, the U.S.S.R. was ready to employ 120 infantry divisions, 16 cavalry divisions, 5,000 tanks, and as many aircraft.[9] The negotiations failed to produce an agreement when it became obvious that it really didn't fit into the agenda of England and France. The documents released in 2008 make it abundantly clear that both Britain and France realized their position was driving the U.S.S.R. into a corner and that Moscow would have to come to terms with the Germans.[10]

In light of the documentation that has surfaced since Gittelsohn first spoke these words in 1942, his contention that Russia had no choice and was forced by circumstances to sign the pact with

Germany seems validated by history. To further emphasize his point that the pact was a "marriage of convenience" and that Russia knew it was only a temporary arrangement, he cited reports of Russian troop movements heading westward, away from their traditional enemy Japan, in anticipation of a probable future conflict with Germany.

Gittelsohn had another question to pose to his congregation. But before doing so, he cautioned that though the evidence he had just provided was factual, "it doesn't mean Russia should get credit for finally turning Germany. Remember, it was Germany that turned against Russia in June of 1941. If Germany hadn't made its most serious mistake of the war by doing that, Russia would still be playing the game of 1939 to 1941, which was the Slavic interpretation of the old game of Munich."[11]

Gittelsohn then continued on to his second discussion point: how was Russia able to offer such remarkable and sustained resistance when most US Army experts predicted in June of 1941 that Russia couldn't hold out for more than three to six weeks? He provided four reasons for Russia's staunch defense against invasion of the German war machine. His discussion once again showcased this vast knowledge of world affairs in general and of Russia in particular. He began with reason number one, a simple idea: Russia is Russia. It was the largest country in the world, and its vast size alone made it almost unconquerable by an invading force. To sum up this first factor, Gittelsohn quoted German President Paul von Hindenburg, who said, "I could get to Moscow, perhaps farther — but Russia is so vast she would swallow the largest army. Russia has no heart at which to strike."[12]

The second reason Gittelsohn provided to explain Russia's surprising resistance was similar to the first: Russians are Russians. With this, Gittelsohn spoke namely to the morale of the Russian people. He explained that as a result of the political purges and show trials in Russia that had been going on for years and that did get reported in the American press, most Americans assumed that at the first sign of war, the morale of the Russian people would be shattered. There was a problem with this assumption, he explained — people were judging the situation in Russia by American standards when they should have been judging it by Russian standards. "They were forgetting that as little as the average

Russian had in 1941, it was a million-fold more than they had before 1918."[13] While the examples that he cited, such as positive reports by Soviet sycophant reporter Walter Duranty, are just anecdotes, the fact does remain that the Russian people were fighting for their lives and for the survival of their Motherland against a hated invader. Their motivation was largely genuine. After the war and the fall of the Soviet Union, reports would emerge documenting more sinister motivators of the Russian fighting man's "morale." During the Battle of Moscow, to prevent his soldiers from deserting the front line around the capital, Stalin ordered special "blocking detachments" to shoot all deserters. The Soviet leadership also instructed Soviet partisans operating in the countryside to kill anyone whom they believed was disloyal.[14]

Gittelsohn next cited the astounding industrial growth of post-Revolutionary Russia as the third reason for Russia's surprisingly strong resistance against the German invasion. He backed up his argument with statistics on coal, oil, and steel production, comparing the 1913 production numbers with those of 1938 and 1940. The stark contrast between those years was impressive to note. The abundance of natural resources in the Soviet Union was harnessed into its rapid industrialization plans such that in the 1930s the Soviet Union's industrial output was second only to the United States.

Gittelsohn then turned to the fourth and final answer to his question regarding Russia's staunch resistance against the Germans. At first glance, his reason seems extremely cold and startling. It would appear to be incongruous that a man such as Roland Gittelsohn, a believer in the rights of man, freedom of speech, and the right of dissent could both write and then speak these thoughts as he did that night. Upon closer examination, though, what he was doing was stating cold, hard facts. He was also stating the truth. "Russia succeeded in doing what no other nation on earth could do," he said. "She got rid of the German fifth column before the war started."[15] Undoubtedly some members of the congregation were stunned to hear him state this, but he went on to embellish and analyze what Russia had done in a factual, unvarnished manner. He described what Russia had to do in order to eliminate this internal threat by declaring unequivocally that "The price she paid was shocking; it was the coldest and most brutal wholesale attack on human values and human life that civilization has ever seen."[16] What he was refer-ring to, of course, was the long series of purges that had taken place since the Russian Revolution and that had accelerated in the 1930s under the dictatorship of Joseph Stalin. This ongoing brutal cam-paign, in Gittelsohn's words, had virtually "bled Russia to death."

To provide evidence to support his contention, he again turned to the words of Walter Duranty. Even this admirer of the Soviet Union, who continually turned a blind eye to the horrors of the Soviet regime, would estimate that 60 to 70 percent of the leaders of Russia in the military, economic, and industrial fields were either exiled or executed during the Stalinist purges.[17] In a very matter-of-fact manner, Gittelsohn reported on Duranty's terrible accounting data of the Stalinist purges: "For every guilty man liquidated, unquestionably as many as ten innocents were dispensed with. But the fact remains that with all the shocking and calloused brutality, the fifth column in Russia was definitely eliminated."[18] Gittelsohn ended this section by again quoting Duranty, who reported a comment from a Frenchman who told him "but don't forget, mon ami, that in Russia they shot the fifth columnists, and in France they made them cabinet ministers."[19]

Having provided detailed answers to the two questions he had posed concerning the "riddle" of Russia's past and present, Gittelsohn proposed that the congregation look towards the future and consider two more questions. First he asked them to consider this: Could Russia continue to hold in its struggle against Nazi Germany? That depends, he offered. Russia could not win the war alone, continuing to fight Germany and Japan, attempting to defend Singapore, etc. It could, Gittelsohn explained, continue to hold Hitler on his Eastern front, tying him down in a two-front war. "The rest of the job," he said, "we'll have to do, together with England and the other United Nations."[20]

The other question when considering the future was twofold: Will Russia let us down? Will they back out at the first opportunity and fall in league with Germany again? The answer, Gittelsohn once again offered, was that it depends on us.

The only chance I see Russia letting us down at this stage of the game is if we give the impression, as we did in 1939, that we would use Russia for our own present purposes and then betray Russia as soon as those purposes were satisfied. Anyone who says or even thinks we ought to take all the help Russia can give, but offer in return only enough to keep the Nazis from winning but not enough to enable Russia to win—and there are such people!—or anyone who begins to suggest that we should help Russia now with subversive intentions of betraying her later, is inviting Russia to let us down.[21]

This analysis by Gittelsohn preceded the start of the vast Lend-Lease support provided to the Soviet Union by the United States by five months. During the course of the war, the second front, so desperately needed by Stalin, would be launched by the Allies at Normandy on June 6, 1944. By the end of the war, the United States would have provided Russia with eleven billion dollars in aid, consisting of over 400,000 jeeps and trucks, 12,000 armored vehicles (including 7,000 tanks), 11,400 aircraft, and 1.75 million tons of food.[22]

Gittelsohn reminded his audience that thus far Russia had absorbed at least half of the suffering of the war and had done approximately 90 percent of the effective fighting. To him, it seemed very presumptuous for the British and Americans to continue to talk about what the English-speaking peoples were going to do to Hitler and even more presumptuous for them to express public fears about Russia letting us down.[23]

Drawing near the end of his sermon, Roland Gittelsohn offered the courses of action that he felt should be taken in regard to Russia. First, England and the United States should accept Russia as a full and indispensable ally. Despite his previously stated distaste for Russian communism, he recommended that Russia had the same right to keep communism as we did to maintain capitalism. Anticipating a world where the allies would ultimately prevail over the Nazis and where a new world organization would work to prevent future war, Gittelsohn insisted that we must "say now and continue to say that Russia shall have a chief voice in preparing the peace and administering the world that shall survive the peace."[24] History had given us a chance to atone for Munich, he insisted, and we have already paid a staggering price for that mistake. "But we have been given one more chance," he explained. "Now that we have solved the riddle of Russia, our job is to take the chance which history has given us."[25]

# Chapter Seventeen

# Private Life

By the end of the summer of 1942, the United States had launched its first offensive in the campaign in the Pacific. After being thwarted in the Coral Sea and then at Midway, the Japanese war machine turned its sites on the Solomon Islands. After first occupying Tulagi, they then began construction of an airfield on nearby Guadalcanal. Realizing that a Japanese bomber base there could interrupt vital lines of communication between the United States and Australia, the United States chose to take the airfield, landing the First Marine Division at Guadalcanal on August 7, 1942. It was the beginning of a series of battles that comprised the campaign for Guadalcanal, culminating with the Japanese defeat and withdrawal by February 1943.

Back on Long Island, Roland Gittelsohn followed the events of the war with increasing interest. His professional life was fulfilling and the Central Synagogue of Nassau County continued to grow. In addition, he was very contented with his home life. At the Gittelsohn household at 88 Lewis Place in Hempstead, Long Island, he and Ruth had two growing, healthy children: David, now nearly five years old, and Judy, now nearly two years old. There was a restlessness that was growing within him, however — a new sense of mission and calling that he was having an increasingly difficult time ignoring. That new perceived mission would become public less than two months later.

Up to this point, we have the written words left by Gittelsohn to draw our impressions of him, as well as accounts written *about* him. The picture of him that results from all of this is of an extremely intelligent, stern, and serious young man — a man who appeared to relish debate and was often confrontational and uncompromising in his views. In his most passionate sermons he almost comes across as an angry, bitter individual. One is tempted to consider if this is really an accurate description of Roland Gittelsohn. What was the man really like? Was he that way at home with his family? What type of a husband and father was he?

The descriptions of their father provided by son David and daughter Judy put a human face on Gittelsohn that paints quite a different picture of him. Looking back to their earliest memories of him, both David and Judy remember their father as a strong, highly intelligent, and opinionated man. They also describe him as being a completely different personality at home. Judy would refer to his "multifaceted" personality in this regard.[1] He displayed a great sense of humor, and even as young children David and Judy felt that he was a fun person to be around. Judy recalled how he enjoyed going to his rabbinical conferences every year because, among other things, he would always arrive home with a fresh supply of jokes to share.

In the Gittelsohn household, he was the disciplinarian; their mother, Ruth, was more of the quiet, artistic soul. Both Roland and Ruth Gittelsohn were very sociable and were wonderful hosts who loved to entertain. Judy would describe how her parents would go out to a party every New Year's Eve; but before they did, their dad would always bring home Chinese food and the four of them would a have a "traditional" New Year's Eve dinner before the adults left for their party. At least once a year, the family would travel in to New York City to go to a Broadway show and dine in the city.

Although he was not athletic, Roland would regularly take his children roller skating in nearby Jones Beach. One of the rituals that began after he returned from the war was the annual deep-sea fishing trip for members of the synagogue. This was strictly a "dads and kids affair," no moms were allowed. All of the participants from the temple looked forward to this yearly treat, especially Rabbi Gittelsohn. With laughter, both David and Ruth recalled that on all the fishing trips that they went on, they never once saw their father ever touch a rod or a reel. He would always bring a book and read, while all the time taking part in the discussions and enjoying himself very much.

Their home life was always centered on their father's schedule. He would be home promptly every night for a 6 p.m. dinner and possibly have a cocktail before the family ate. It was very common for him to have to return to the temple on business or to meet with members of his congregation in the evenings. He didn't have a lot of time to be with the family during the school year, but the summers were different. Gittelsohn would take a large part of the summer off and, starting when Judy was seven or eight years old, the Gittelsohns would rent a cottage in New Hampshire and spend the summers there. The family of four followed a daily routine in the summer: Mornings were reserved as quiet time for Roland to write and also read. (Judy described her father as a meticulous student and also a voracious reader.) The rest of the day was family time. These were very happy days for the Gittelsohns.

When asked about his father's skill as a public speaker, David's answer was unequivocal. He described his father as a spellbinding speaker, a "golden-tongued" orator.[2] This is, of course, consistent with the many descriptions of Roland Gittelsohn's oratorical skills. One can easily sense how the power of his sermons must have been made even more striking by the delivery style of such a dynamic public speaker as him. David described his father as a natural debater and proudly recounted the many awards that he had attained both in high school and in college at Western Reserve University. David also recollected that his father would rehearse his sermons at home to perfect their timing. As a matter of ritual for each sermon, once he approached the pulpit of the temple to begin his sermon, he would always remove his wristwatch and place it next to his notes so he could keep exactly on schedule.

Both children recalled that, despite his superb debating skills and his vast fund of knowledge, Roland was perfectly capable of admitting when he was wrong. To illustrate this very point, daughter-in-law Donna Gittelsohn related a humorous anecdote involving a "debate" between her father-in-law and herself over correct grammar. During a visit to her dentist, Donna mentioned that she was nauseous; her dentist corrected her grammar, saying that the correct term was "nauseated." When she mentioned the grammar debate to Roland, he informed her, "You were wrong. The correct term is 'nauseated.'" After Donna cited Webster's Dictionary and bolstered her case, he replied, "Webster's! What do they know?"

Several days later, Donna contacted a friend who worked in the English department at Harvard University and mentioned the disagreement. After a few days her friend called her back and announced, "It's the consensus of the English department that you were correct." A very pleased Donna Gittelsohn could not wait to inform her father-in-law later that week when she and David joined Roland and Ruth for dinner at a Boston restaurant. She knew that Roland Gittelsohn relished debate and also admired people who stood up for their beliefs. Proudly, she informed him that it was the opinion of the Harvard University English department that she was right and he was wrong. Gittelsohn smiled at her and said, "You have to tell me this, when I'm paying the bill?"[3]

After he returned to Hawaii from Iwo Jima, Roland Gittelsohn sent his family a letter that included a photograph of him with a mustache. Never having had a mustache before, and always the true believer in democracy, he asked his family to vote if he should keep it. Judy voted yes, but both Ruth and David voted no. Democracy prevailed in the Gittelsohn family, and Roland dutifully shaved his mustache off. He did, however, mail the clippings to Judy, the one member of the family who appreciated his hirsute appearance, however brief it was.

From the accounts of his children, Roland Gittelsohn was an attentive and loving father whose home persona did indeed differ from the stern, sometimes strident lecturer that he may have appeared to be from the pulpit. In his 1988 autobiography, Gittelsohn would talk about his family and the effect that being the community's rabbi may have had on the children. "A rabbi's children must often pay a price for his success," he noted. "In this respect they are like the children of any person in public life. The community expects them to be perfect; other parents demanded more of them than from their own sons and daughters."[4] Looking back on his own busy life, he commented on the effect that his long hours away may have had on David and Judy. "They suffer too—as do the sons and daughters of all busy professionals and executives—from their parents' busyness."[5]

Chapter Eighteen

# A Vision of the Common Man at War and a Surprise

Throughout the 1930s, some of the harshest criticisms of President Roosevelt's New Deal appeared in the pages of the *Saturday Evening Post*. A staunchly conservative magazine that espoused an isolationist point of view over the developing conflicts in Europe and Asia, it attracted old guard journalists and editorialists such as Garet Garrett who regularly attacked FDR and his policies. The October 10, 1942, issue contained an editorial entitled "Neo-liberal Illusion: That Collectivism is Liberty." While the actual author of the editorial was not known, for the purposes of his sermon Gittelsohn would attribute the editorial to the recently hired editor, Ben Hibbs. Although the magazine had been expressing similar views for years, the United States was now engaged in a two-front war; the article's message, as well as its timing, especially enraged Roland Gittelsohn. After reading it several times, he decided to devote a sermon to addressing the editorial and its message. He had so much to say on the matter that he delivered the sermon in two parts, on October 23 and on October 30, 1942. The title was "Saturday Evening Post Americanism."

He began by stating his position on the article up front and unequivocally. The editorial with the "quasi-scholarly title . . . contained just as much outrageous and impossible nonsense as anything we've seen on page one in a long time," he said.[1] Hibbs proposed a vision of Americanism "which some of us had hoped was dead long ago, but which apparently is still very much alive and with which we'll have to reckon if this war is to end in anything other than the ghastliest and costliest joke in history."[2] This opinion should not be surprising to any of them, he noted, as the *Saturday Evening Post* had always embraced a strange concept of Americanism and had remained rabidly isolationist right up to the attack on Pearl Harbor, almost to the point of appearing to be "Nazi sympathizers." The magazine had fired their previous editor after a series of controversial articles that expressed a view of Americanism that appeared to be both fascist and anti-Semitic and for which the magazine also issued a public apology; after the incident, they had hired Ben Hibbs, who seemed to adopt a less strident approach. With the publication of the October 10 editorial, the "paint wore off and the leopards' spots became visible again," Gittelsohn declared, calling the editorial unblushingly fascist.[3]

Uncertain if many in the congregation had read the editorial, Gittelsohn continued by reviewing the key points made by Hibbs. According to the editor, the United States was considering abandoning individual responsibility and going back to earning its living in packs, in what he referred to as the "total state." This was due more to the First World War than to the current one and the resultant economic imbalance that swept through Europe and eventually reached the shores of our country in the form of the Great Depression. The result, he claimed, was "a horde of economic cure-alls, each one of which marked a step backward toward the old, old situation of the strong state and the weak citizen."[4] Natural forces were not allowed to cure the economic body; instead the patient was loaded with artificial "stimulants" and "sedatives" in the form of debt, subsidy, and federal handouts. The progress of civilization, claimed Hibbs, "had been measured by the people able to leave the pack and care for themselves without the leader doing their thinking for them."[5] The natural progression of history was an evolution away from the group or "pack" to the individual. The war had accelerated the reversal of this process by putting in place military controls that were identical to those needed to socialize industry.

Hibbs noted with dismay that our national character had changed. To him, this was largely due to the wave of immigration coming to the United States since the turn of the century. "Too many of the nineteen million immigrants who have come to our shores since 1900 did not come seeking freedom," he astonishingly deduced. "They came to share a ready-made prosperity. Ignorant of basic American ideals, they are easy prey for demagogues, and no one knows exactly what changes this new blood has made in America."[6] In Hibbs' analysis, there were two types of people in the country: the talented economic geniuses, and the semi-talented or untalented people who were the parasites of society. There appears to be no other group of people between these two extremes. The relationship between the two groups was cyclic in nature. "When no one has anything, the talented, capable individuals are encouraged to exercise their economic genius, to invent, to dream, to initiate new enterprise and to create work for those incapable of creating their own," Hibbs claimed. "The result is a rich reward to the talented and a very substantial reward to the semi-talented or untalented individuals clinging to the kite tail of genius."[7]

Hibbs explained that technological advancement made the individual less and less capable of directing his own work. Hence, someone else must direct it. According to the editor, there were only two agencies capable of doing this: private enterprisers using free labor, and the government using Hitler's type of labor. "We must choose between freedom and state control. Those who say that the people can collectively direct their own industrial efforts are either liars or fools."[8] Allowing the gifted minority to use their own money and allowing them to compete with one another for public patronage provided a benefit to society that it should not take for granted.

Displaying his elitist version of charitable thought, Hibbs turned to the plight of the "untalented." "There is no way, in the long run, of rewarding an individual beyond his fair value to society, and the brutal truth is that there always has been, and always will be, a certain proportion of any population unable to contribute enough to society to warrant more than a minimum humane living standard. They cannot be allowed to starve, and the only way to make up the deficit between what they need and what they earn is to take it away from those able to produce more than they need." And herein lies the crux of the problem:

> And, though it is human nature to help the unfortunate, it is also human nature to restrict charity to bare living standards. If the state persists in subsidizing and pampering the relatively useless citizen at the expense of the useful citizen, one of two things will happen: Either the useful citizen will rise up in his wrath and overthrow the state, or lacking the power to overthrow the state, he will lose his initiative and sink toward the level of the group which he is being made to support.[9]

Having set the stage by summarizing the editorial's content,

Gittelsohn launched into his scathing analysis of Hibbs' views. Belittling Hibbs' "two-class" American society, he described the editor's view of Americanism as "Let the rich get richer—then they'll have all the more money with which to give charity to the poor, out of whose sweat and labor they got rich in the first place." But remember, Gittelsohn sarcastically cautioned his audience, "not to give too generously to the poor—this may be bad for them. Just give them enough to keep them alive."[10] Although Hibbs never outright said it, his total rejection of government involvement in any aspect of business clearly indicated his preference that the New Deal be rescinded before it destroyed the American way of life. Gittelsohn indicated his strong support of FDR's New Deal, an interesting endorsement from a man who was a frequent critic of the president's policies. Hibbs did clearly claim that state-owned enterprises were never efficient, a statement that Gittelsohn called "obvious rubbish."

Having indicated to the congregation that he believed he had just presented an accurate summary and portrayal of Ben Hibbs' view of Americanism, Gittelsohn announced, "Now then, I object violently to this *Saturday Evening Post* Americanism for half a dozen reasons. I'd like to express and explain only the first two of them tonight and then necessarily leave the others for next week."[11] His first objection was succinct—he believed that the editorial's explanation of Americanism was ". . . a perverted and deliberate distortion of human history. When Ben Hibbs tells me that the course of human history has been to minimize the importance of the group and to increase the absolute economic independence of the individual, I'm curious to know in what school or from what books did Mr. Hibbs study his history. Oddly enough, every scholar from whom I've ever studied history interpreted the course of human events the very opposite way."[12] He was taught, as he presumed most of his congregation was taught, that human beings began as individualists and that only gradually did they at last begin to learn the meaning of cooperation in groups. Hibbs was trying to reverse the whole meaning of human affairs.

There were no two ways to look at this, Gittelsohn stressed. History was a one-way street; it doesn't move in two directions at once. Either history was moving from the group to the individual, or vice versa. "If Hibbs is right, then both Isaiah and Amos were wrong. They envisioned a human society of growing justice and righteousness in which men would more and more cooperate with each other rather than compete versus each other. If Hibbs is right, both Judaism and Christianity are dead wrong." In an elegant explanation, Gittelsohn informed his congregation: "Judaism and Christianity alike both insist that the wealth of this world is a loan made by God to humans, to be managed by humans, always and everlastingly for humans. So take your pick—Ben Hibbs or religion—we can't have both because they are mutually exclusive."[13]

To further embellish his point, Gittelsohn turned to America's founders. "If Ben Hibbs is right, our American pioneer fathers were wrong." They were not "rugged individualists," he informed his audience. "They were rugged alright, but they were rugged cooperatively, not individualists. Helping their fellow pioneers was the American way. They cleared the forests, conquered the land, built their homes and harvested their crops together." Gittelsohn concluded this first reason for his violent disagreement with Hibbs by stating: "Read as I have the accounts of the founding of any one of the new settlements in pioneer America, friends, and you'll see how true it is that this nation more than any other in history was founded on the cooperative efforts of men and women acting together in groups for the good of all."[14]

Gittelsohn next turned to his second objection to the vision of Americanism presented by the *Saturday Evening Post*. It was Hibbs' "outrageous libel against one-fifth of the American population." The editor's comments on immigrants coming to America—who Hibbs claimed were motivated by a desire for "ready-made" prosperity—infuriated Gittelsohn. His fury was fanned by the memories of his father's and grandfather's experiences in tsarist Russia and their arrival in America, where they proceeded to become hard-working and respected figures in the community. Gittelsohn considered the twenty-seven million immigrants to the United States over the prior sixty years as he declared: "As a son of one of those immigrants, I deeply and bitterly resent Mr. Hibbs saying that those twenty-seven million as a class came here for ulterior motives or that they're ignorant of basic American ideals, or that they're less loyal to American democracy than the *Saturday Evening Post*." Citing well-known immigrants such as Albert

Einstein, Thomas Mann, Arturo Toscanini, and Robert Wagner, the rabbi stated unequivocally: "I'll take their understanding of American democracy and ideals 1,000 times over before Ben Hibbs' misunderstanding."[15]

After relating an anecdote about immigrants in his home state of Ohio, Gittelsohn felt no further need to belabor his point. "You and I are entitled to whatever interpretation of American democracy we want. For my part, I'll pass up the mud and silt of the *Saturday Evening Post*, if you don't mind; I'd rather trust our twenty-seven million immigrants and their children than I would Ben Hibbs to cherish and preserve Americanism, and his gratuitous insult to twenty percent of our population is my second reason for rejecting his specious ersatz Americanism."[16] With that, he was out of time and he asked his congregation for permission to continue his analysis the following week.

---

On October 30, Gittelsohn resumed his critical analysis of Ben Hibbs' editorial. After a brief summary of the previous week's discussion, he continued on with the third reason that he so violently objected to the *Saturday Evening Post*'s vision of Americanism. It must have startled his congregation to hear him exclaim "I resent the *Saturday Evening Post*'s Americanism because it's a libelous and unfounded insult to American businessmen and industrialists." He no doubt smiled when he told them, "I suppose that some of you think it is strange that I of all people should be defending businessmen and industrialists. Don't let it floor you—stranger things than that will happen before this war is over," he assured them.[17] His congregation had no idea how true and how close to home his statement would prove to be.

To drive home his point, Gittelsohn repeated Hibbs' statement concerning the two courses of action for the "useful citizens" if the state persisted in subsidizing the "useless citizens": either the overthrow of the state or the loss of his incentive to work toward profit generation and hence loss of benefit to the state. Gittelsohn was totally appalled by the brazen statement of Hibbs, comparing it to both the situation in fascist Spain and also a little child who can't get his way and will not play anymore.

Ladies and gentlemen, if I were a businessman or an industrialist with a conscience, I think this scandalous, petulant, threatening, lying accusation would make me see just about every shade of red in the spectrum. There are so many ways of proving that by and large this cheap, dishonest statement isn't true of American businessmen that it's really difficult to select only a few of them for present purposes. As a matter of fact, every American industrial leader who recognizes that even from its own selfish point of view our capitalism needs rather drastic overhauling, is himself an effective answer to Ben Hibbs.[18]

Gittelsohn further surprised his audience by stating that Wendell Willkie, the Republican presidential candidate in the 1940 election, provided a pretty good answer to rebut Hibbs' slander of American business. Claiming that Willkie had the right to speak for large segments of the American business community if anyone had, Gittelsohn reminded the congregation that he had opposed Willkie in the past election and remained delighted that he was defeated, but he was nonetheless pleased that Willkie had learned more in defeat than he possibly could have in victory. He jokingly asked the audience not to construe his upcoming compliment as an endorsement for the man in 1944. The reason for Gittelsohn's praise of Willkie was a radio broadcast that Willkie had done four nights before, on October 26.

Willkie had recently returned from a trip abroad where he visited the Middle East, Russia, and China, traveling as a free citizen and not as a representative of the government. In his speech entitled "Deliver the Materials of War- Define Our Peace Aims," Willkie noted that "the people of every land, whether industrialized or not, admire the aspirations and accomplishments of American labor, which they have heard about, and which they long to emulate. Also, they are impressed by American business and industry."[19] With great admiration, Gittelsohn quoted Willkie when he said, "People like our works, I found, not only because they help to make life easier and richer, but also because we have shown that American business enterprise, unlike that of most other industrial nations, does not necessarily lead to political control or imperialism."[20] He looked out on his congregation and asked, "Does this sound like Ben Hibbs and the *Saturday Evening Post*? Does it sound like American businessmen closing up shop or overthrowing the state because they can't have their way?"[21]

Gittelsohn then proceeded with an even more startling example of Hibbs' slander of American business: a statement provided by Col. Lewis Sanders, a witness called to testify to the Senate Military Affairs Committee. Sanders, the chief of the re-employment division of the Selective Service System, was an industrial engineer between the wars and had been employed by some of the largest corporations in the United States. Gittelsohn pointed out that Sanders had never belonged to a labor union and would hardly have been expected to be very sympathetic to the concerns of labor.

The week before, in testimony before Congress, Sanders stated, "I believe that eighty percent of our labor trouble has its basic origin in management, and I speak as one whose background is primarily of management."[22] Gittelsohn was adamant that his point in presenting Sander's testimony not be misunderstood. He was "merely trying to indicate that there are large numbers of American businesses and industries who like Colonel Sanders, and far from the stupid reactionary-ism of the *Post*, have accepted labor, have learned to live with the regulations and restrictions of the New Deal, and who don't intend to revolt or stop production!"[23] Hence, according to Gittelsohn, the *Saturday Evening Post* had no right to speak for the business community of America; nonetheless, they did have the perfect right to speak for the extreme fringe—the "Fritz Thyssens of America," he called them, referring to Nazi industrialist Fritz Thyssen. These were the types that would rather beat Roosevelt than Hitler, he claimed. Thank God, he explained, that our "Thyssens" were neither representative of American business nor all-powerful, as they had been pretty much repudiated by their fellow businessmen.

Having concluded his defense of the American businessman, Gittelsohn went on to the next reason for his opposition to Hibbs' editorial. Here his passion was obvious, as he claimed that in attacking the common man, the *Saturday Evening Post*'s take on Americanism in fact attacked both religion and democracy. "Take it from me," he assured the congregation, "you who have not read the article yet, if you haven't seen this, you don't know what naked, disgusting contempt for the common man is. Compared to Ben Hibbs, Marie Antoinette was a lover of the masses and Czar Nicholas II was a union leader."[24]

Gittelsohn claimed he had to read the article four or five times as he could not believe Hibbs' vile descriptions and choice of language in describing most Americans. Hibbs referred to the wealthy members of society as "those talented members of society," "those talented, capable individuals," "the gifted citizen[s]," and "the useful citizen[s]." In contrast, Gittelsohn pointed out, "the following classics of invective are reserved for all those who aren't wealthy, for those twelve or thirteen million people who were unemployed in 1933, for the majority of our population who still live at less than a minimum level of decent health; 'the untalented,' 'the relatively useless citizen[s],' who Hibbs later refers to as simply 'the useless citizen[s],' and finally 'the semi-talented or untalented individual, clinging to the kite tail of genius.'"[25]

To put these descriptions into perspective, Gittelsohn offered biting interpretations of Hibbs' logic. "That means that Charles Steinmetz"—the immigrant from Germany who discovered alternating current and thus started the harnessing of electricity in America—"who died with $300 to his name was a semi-talented individual clinging to the kite tail of Tommy Manville"—the multimillionaire playboy who's main lifetime accomplishment would be to get married thirteen times—"whose chief distinction in life is that his father was born before him. That's really rich."[26] The same would apply to Lillian Wald, a woman born into wealth who became a nurse and then dedicated herself to helping the poor and founding the Henry Street Settlement. Obviously, she had become a "relatively useless citizen," Gittelsohn noted sarcastically.

It was at this point that Gittelsohn plunged straight to the heart of his argument, the crux of his violent disagreement with Ben Hibbs' version of Americanism. His next words would serve not only to clarify and drive home his point but would also define who Rabbi Roland Gittelsohn truly was, what he believed, and why he loved America. It wasn't just a matter of quibbling or debate, he explained. "This goes to the very essence and heart of democracy—because democracy is a much simpler thing than most of our political theorists make of it. Democracy is nothing more nor less than love of, and abiding faith in, the common man. That's all—it's as simple as all that." He then defined the simplicity of his definition with everyday examples: "If you believe in treating your maid (assuming you have one) and your gardener and the waitress who serves you in the restaurant as human beings equal in dignity and rights to yours, then you believe in democracy."[27] Using the words of Thomas Jefferson and Theodore Roosevelt to support his love of the common man and his own vision of Americanism, Gittelsohn then asked his congregation to compare and contrast this with the Americanism espoused by the *Saturday Evening Post*. Compare the words of Jefferson and Roosevelt with those of Hibbs, he urged, and you'll easily reach your own conclusions.

Realizing that the end of his allotted time was drawing near, Gittelsohn quickly moved on to his third objection to Hibbs' article. He declared passionately, "I submit to you that this editorial is an unconscionable and not too thickly disguised effort to sabotage our war effort." Gittelsohn explained that he had heard a speech two weeks prior by senate majority leader Alben Barkley in which Barkley claimed that there were "three groups of Americans today who wanted us to win the war, but a) without Russia, b) without England, and c) without Roosevelt. I wish it were funny," he added.[28] The *Saturday Evening Post* wanted to win the war, explained Gittelsohn; they didn't want Roosevelt or the New Deal to win it. And the publication, he said, is "willing, if necessary, to keep Roosevelt from winning it by risking the nation's losing it."[29]

If any of the congregation doubted his analysis of the *Post*'s intentions, he invited them to look back with him over each of the four major points made by Ben Hibbs and evaluate what their only possible effects on the war effort could be. First, if the direction of history is away from the cooperative group and toward the wealthy and successful individual, as Hibbs stated, why would groups of people fight as a team under those circumstances? "That great blessing we can have without a war," Gittelsohn noted. Next, if the thirty million immigrants and their sons were no good, why are they fighting as many of them were, and why were they willing to die in defense of their country? If American industrialists would only produce to their maximal capability if they received unlimited profits, then why would labor sacrifice any of its rights? Under this scenario, how could America possibly obtain the equipment without which it would be impossible to win the war? Lastly, and most strikingly, Gittelsohn asked, "If the common man is useless and to be spat upon, then what on earth is he fighting for? Is the *Post* really so infantile as to suppose that the common man will fight heroically for the right of Tommy Manville to get richer? Or," he darkly suggested, "does the *Saturday Evening Post* know full well that this kind of talk is apt to discourage the common man from fighting altogether and thereby lose us the war; and thereby put an end to the New Deal; and thereby bring in Hitler with whom the *Saturday Evening Post* perhaps stupidly believes it could do business better than it can with Roosevelt?"[30]

In light of all the evidence, Gittelsohn pronounced that whatever Ben Hibbs and his backers were, they were not infantile and naïve. "Their words as published here," he claimed, "are calculated to hinder, not to help out striving for military victory." In closing, he told the congregation that he knew they probably initially wondered why he had dedicated two sermons to the "ridiculous editorial" and that he hoped they now realized why he had. Gittelsohn thus ended with his final salvo against the Americanism envisioned by the *Saturday Evening Post*, stating, "It's because this is the last desperate death rattle of an economy that's doomed. Because this is the last disgusting lunge of those who are determined not to permit this war to be the people's war, nor to let it usher in the century of the common man."[31]

---

Gittelsohn's battle with the *Saturday Evening Post*'s vision of Americanism is both interesting and instructive on many accounts. While he made Ben Hibbs the object of his wrath, in all likelihood the editorial was written by Garet Garrett, who served as the editorial writer-in-chief at the *Post* from 1940 until 1942, when he left the magazine's employ. The tone and arguments presented in the piece are clearly reflective of Garrett's ideology. The iconic Garrett, who so strongly opposed American entry into the war, then volunteered for military service at the age of sixty-four. Hibbs, on the other hand, served as editor of the periodical from 1942 until 1962, when he left to become the editor of *Reader's Digest*. Ironically, Hibbs has been described by the Kansas Historical Society as an unassuming, humble man who consciously kept in touch with the common man.[32]

The elitist business community described in the editorial never really existed. In January of 1942, by executive order, FDR established the War Production Board to regulate the production of materials and consumption of fuels during the war. Industry in the United States worked hand in hand with the government to develop unprecedented industrial power in the war-time economy. Labor and business worked cooperatively to support the American war effort. The American public in general dutifully submitted to price controls and gasoline rationing to support the war effort. Business titans such as Henry Kaiser and Andrew Higgins responded not with the resentment that the editorial predicted, but with drive, innovation, and genius to contribute greatly to the American war goals. The self-centered, "my way or the highway" reaction predicted by the *Post*'s Americanism never materialized.

Gittelsohn's definition and description of democracy say much about the man. His lifelong focus on "democracy" would continue to define him. And there was one fact in his analysis that stands out: that the war would, in fact, become a war of the common man. When World War II broke out in September of 1939, the United States had the eighteenth largest military in the world, behind such countries as Belgium and Poland. After Pearl Harbor, thousands of Americans flooded our enlistment centers on a regular basis. By the war's end, there were twelve million Americans in uniform. It was a military made up of ordinary Americans, not professionals. They were citizen soldiers. They wanted to be throwing baseballs, not hand grenades, shooting .22s at rabbits, not M-1s at other young men. But when the test came, when freedom had to be fought for or abandoned, they fought.[33] These were the common men whom Gittelsohn empathized with and admired so much.

The *Post*'s use of the term "useless citizens" was most offensive to Gittelsohn, and for good reason. It was disturbingly close to the Nazi description of mentally handicapped citizens under the authority of the Third Reich. They were referred to as "useless eaters" whose very existence was a burden to the German people and who hence needed to be sterilized, lest they propagate more burdens for the German citizenry to support.

Gittelsohn's use of examples such as Albert Einstein and Charles Steinmetz to counter the *Post*'s anti-immigrant stance was brilliant. His sense of outrage over the slanderous statement implying that immigrants weren't seeking freedom but were instead coming to America as part of a virtual "get rich quick" scheme is well justified. Gittelsohn correctly pointed out the high percentage of the immigrant population currently serving in the military. He needed only to reflect upon the contributions of his immigrant father and grandfather to find powerful ammunition to counter the ridiculous claims of the *Post*.

Reading over his sermons refuting the *Saturday Evening Post*, one can discern some subtle evolution in Gittelsohn's thinking and overall views. True, he would always remain a civil libertarian devoted to the rights of the common man and to justice and fairness for all. His basic support of labor in issues where labor and management conflicted would also remain unchanged. Now, however, his focus on Franklin D. Roosevelt had shifted away from what he had perceived and highly criticized as FDR's efforts to entangle us into war; instead, Gittelsohn had come to support the president's New Deal policies. The rabbi appeared to no longer view Hitler and his European hegemony as something that the United States could or necessarily *should* avoid, as evidenced by his support of Russia in their war against the Nazis. And most interestingly, he now could speak in positive terms about American businessmen and industrialists while still retaining a distaste for certain forms of capitalism when they stressed excessive profits over the good of the working man. His core principles were immutable and would remain unchanged until the day he died, but some of his perceptions were changing and evolving.

———•———

As mentioned above, in his October 30 sermon, Gittelsohn jokingly warned his congregation after he told them he was about to come to the defense of American businesses, "Don't let it floor you; stranger things than that will happen before this war is over." That month, he indicated just how strange things had gotten. He announced that he was taking a leave of absence as rabbi to the Central Synagogue of Nassau County. Then he dropped a bombshell—his reason for the leave of absence.

He was joining the United States Navy.

Part II

# Warrior

*O Lord! Thou knowest how busy I must be this day:*
*If I forget Thee, do not Thou forget me.*
—Sir Jacob Ashley at the Battle of Edge Hill, 1642


*Praise the Lord and pass the ammunition.*
—From the song "Praise the Lord and Pass the
Ammunition," inspired by the actions of Chaplain
William McGuire at Pearl Harbor on December 7, 1941

# Chapter Nineteen

# Becoming a Chaplain

Like virtually all Americans, Roland Gittelsohn's life was forever changed that first Sunday in December 1941. On the afternoon of December 7, the Gittelsohn family was driving on the Long Island Expressway not far from Hempstead, where they lived. Gittelsohn was absorbed in the sounds of the New York Philharmonic Orchestra when suddenly the music stopped. Annoyed at the interruption, he began fiddling with the volume and station knobs, suspecting that the radio station transmitting equipment had died. Hearing the voices of announcers from the station reassured him that this was not the case. For a brief moment, his annoyance began to build when suddenly the announcer on the radio urgently spoke: "Ladies and gentlemen, we interrupt this program to bring you a late news bulletin. Japanese planes have attacked the United States Naval Base at Pearl Harbor . . ."

At that moment, Rabbi Roland Gittelsohn was about to begin confronting the greatest challenge to his convictions that he would ever face. The main thought that went through his mind over and over that day was "I don't believe it!"[1] As details of the attack on our naval base in Hawaii emerged throughout the day, Gittelsohn could only protest to himself, "I don't believe it!" Here was a man who was an ardent pacifist his entire life, a rabbi who had delivered a sermon to his congregation in the recent past where he opined, "If we do nothing else, we must stay out of this war . . . It shouldn't be necessary to convince you that I hate Hitler and want desperately to see him defeated. You will know how I want America to stay out of this war if I tell you from the bottom of my heart that, much as I want Hitler to lose, I want us to stay out of the war even if he seems to be winning."[2] Here was a man who in the 1930s was a member of the War Resisters League and had signed the Oxford Pledge. Here was a man to whom the concept of total pacifism was uncompromising and crystal clear. And now, on December 7, 1941, it was as if his lifelong belief in the avoidance of war at all costs was suddenly caught in the collision between classroom theories and cruel reality; one where his long-held views on pacifism, when weighed against the outright aggression against his country by Japan, suddenly didn't seem quite as clear cut. The choices were no longer as simple as "war is bad, peace is good." Evil, in the form of the Japanese attack on our soil, had made his conceptual argument less focused, and at the same time it had now crystalized into a more basic black and white issue: that of good versus evil, the struggle of the United States and her allies versus the evil and threats of the fascism and fanaticism of the Axis powers. We were now involved.

At the end of the war, Gittelsohn would determine that there were three basic reasons for his initial astonishment and disbelief in regard to the attack on Pearl Harbor.[3] The first of his reasons was overconfidence. Since his high school debating days, he had opposed every naval appropriation bill and was convinced that the United States—and especially the United States Navy, as a result of this unnecessary spending—had built an impregnable military force. No one nation would be mad enough to attack so great a military as ours. As a pragmatic man, he also refused to believe that the Japanese were any more warlike than Americans. It would infuriate him when people would insist otherwise. Leave the Japanese alone, he had reasoned, and they will leave us alone. Lastly, and most importantly, he was a pacifist, or as he described himself, a complete, convinced, literal, unreasonable, dogmatic, unchangeable pacifist![4] He had even told friends that he was prepared to spend the next war in prison. He had argued with his father that submission to the worst evil was better than resisting it by force.[5]

In reality, Roland Gittelsohn's previously unshakable belief in pacifism had already begun to waiver over a year before the Japanese attack on American soil. By his own admission, he began to question his own views in the spring of 1940 as he was following the events of the war in Europe. In May of that year, the British Expeditionary Forces were driven back to the coast by the forces of Nazi Germany. From May 27 through June 4, over 338,000 British soldiers were evacuated from the French port of Dunkirk, along with nearly 140,000 French, Polish, and Belgian troops. An armada of

861 vessels (of which 243 were sunk by the Germans) was involved in the evacuation.[6] On June 22, 1940, France surrendered to Germany. The world was stunned—Nazi Germany now controlled all of Europe. Reading about the evacuation at Dunkirk, Roland Gittelsohn was shaken. The four months following the evacuation proved to be very difficult for him, as he kept weighing the choices that now seemed to be facing him.[7] For the first time, he began to have his doubts over his rock-solid, uncompromising views on war and peace. The lines between the theory of pacifism at all costs and the reality of the evil that was on the march in Europe and the Far East were starting to blur for him.

World War II would have similar effects on the belief systems of other longtime, committed pacifist Reform rabbis. Approximately two miles away in nearby Lynbrook, Long Island, Rabbi Harold Saperstein of Temple Emanuel was undergoing a crisis of conscience similar to Roland Gittelsohn. Born in exactly the same year, he too had been a lifelong and staunch pacifist. He admired Gittelsohn for the strength and clarity of his sermons, and his own sermons were as passionate about the cause of pacifism as were his neighbor's. By October of 1940, Saperstein's doubts were becoming evident when in his Rosh Hashanah sermon he stated, "And yet I have come to realize that some things are worse than war, and some things more important than peace. And so as I pray for peace, I find myself fearing a peace on Hitler's terms, a peace of submission to the forces of barbarism."[8]

On December 10, 1941, three days after the attack on Pearl Harbor, Harold Saperstein received a letter from the influential Rabbi Stephen Wise. In it, Wise implored him, "Would you be willing to take a leave of absence from your congregation for the duration of the emergency in order to serve as a Chaplain in the U.S. Army? . . . I realize that this might entail a great sacrifice on your part, but nothing short of the greatest sacrifice on the part of us all will carry us through to victory."[9] On June 23, 1943, Saperstein said farewell to his congregation and left for the Army Chaplain School at Harvard University.

Even more representative of the crisis of conscience experienced by many Reform rabbis was that of Judah Magnes. After the entry of the United States into the First World War in 1917, Magnes, already an outspoken pacifist, became one of the country's most vociferous critics of the war. Joining with other prominent pacifists such as Norman Thomas, he became the first chairman of the pacifist political organization, the People's Council of America for Democracy and Peace.

After emigrating to Palestine in 1922, Rabbi Magnes became chancellor and then president of the Hebrew University in Jerusalem. In a speech he delivered to the student body to begin the academic year on October 29, 1939, the lifelong, committed pacifist revealed that he reluctantly supported the war against Germany. He informed the audience, "Although the war confronts each one of us with a difficult spiritual problem, yet I shall ask you to bear with me if I discuss the problem of those radical pacifists and conscientious objectors, of whom I was one during the last war, and who now regard it as their duty to give their support to this war."[10] Comparing Hitler to the devil who used the power of persecution against Jews and other minorities, Magnes ruefully posed a question to his students: "Peace at almost any price is better than war. But what is that price? For myself, I would answer in a word: that the devil be bereft of the power of persecuting."[11] With reluctance, he concluded that the only way to deal with the devil was to support the war that would be waged by the Western powers to destroy him.

Roland Gittelsohn would look back at the end of World War II in an unpublished book and recall his pre-war feelings on the military. In a surprisingly candid admission, he revealed the somewhat naïve thinking that was more suitable to a debating society than to a confrontation of the realities of a world moving almost inevitably toward another world war. "In the old days we pacifists used to base part of our unalterable opposition to war on the fact that it and democracy were incompatible. Over and over again, we insisted that a military machine had to be a dictatorship, could not be democratic."[12] His views on the military would undergo a sobering revision after the onset of the Second World War.

While Gittelsohn searched his soul for answers, his journey from anti-war rabbi to military chaplain was also being shaped by the thoughts of his best friend, Rabbi Jacob P. Rudin of Great Neck, New York. Like Gittelsohn himself, Rabbi Rudin had been an ardent and outspoken pacifist while the chaos in Europe evolved in the 1930s. He and Gittelsohn had many discussions over their future courses of action. Ever since the attack on Pearl Harbor, the two men met frequently to discuss what paths of action they should take and what God intended for them to do. Rudin struggled over the proper course to follow, and by the beginning of the summer of 1942, he had made his decision. He sought a commission as a chaplain in the United States Naval Reserve.

The two rabbis, despite being the best of friends, had fundamentally different approaches to their dilemma. By Gittelsohn's own admission, Rudin had a much keener insight into the issue than he did.[13] In the month following the attack on Pearl Harbor, Jack Rudin felt the issue was both immediate and intensely personal. It was a decision that he felt he needed to make at once and without equivocation. Immediate personal action was called for, and Rudin intended to respond in that manner. On the other hand, Gittelsohn approached the whole situation as a matter of theory, one to be analyzed in a detached, impersonal manner. The situation had to be studied from all angles, and all facets needed to be examined and evaluated. In his theoretical approach a decision would have to be made, although not necessarily in the immediate future.

For several months, Gittelsohn struggled with the pros and cons of following his best friend's example and going into the military. Rudin had undoubtedly influenced him, and by the fall of 1942, he had come to the conclusion that he, too, must join the military. "This was where I had come in," he would later declare.[14] Certainly, one of the key factors influencing his decision to join the military came from his studies of Jewish scripture and thought. He knew that Jewish tradition describes two kinds of war: *milchemet chovah*, compulsory or obligatory war, and *milchemet r'shut*, optional war.[15] Every Jew is obligated to participate in the first. Unlike the teachings of Quakers and Mennonites, for instance, Jewish tradition did not force absolute pacifism upon its adherents. Tradition had franchised each Jew to decide whether for him a given military conflict is a compulsory war or an optional war. Clearly, the war against Hitler and the Axis powers—where nothing less than the survival of the Jewish people was at stake— was a *michemet chovah*. This was a "just war" that Gittelsohn could reconcile with his previously strident views on pacifism.

It was this common thread that ran through the minds of these rabbis who were formerly avowed pacifists. The rise of Nazism and the Holocaust made it crystal clear: the war was a fight for the survival of the Jewish people. This understanding imbued Jewish religious military personnel with a determination to serve in the armed forces that was not generally expressed by their Christian counterparts.[16]

During those difficult times of reflection and introspection after the Pearl Harbor attack, Roland Gittelsohn's decision-making was also influenced by several trains of thought that would lead him away from pacifism and towards military service. His religion was the source of his first two lines of reasoning.

As a Jew, and especially as a rabbi, he was immensely proud of the part that his people played not only in this war, but in every struggle in American history.[17] Reflecting back on these previous conflicts, he proudly noted that in World War I, Jews represented about three percent of the nation's population but supplied close to five percent of the men in the armed forces. He also reflected on how much gratitude his family owed to America, the nation that received his father and grandfather with open arms when they fled from the oppression and vicious anti-Semitism of tsarist Russia. Didn't he, Rabbi Roland Gittelsohn, owe a debt to the United States? What better way to pay that debt than with military service in support of American troops?

A second major reason influencing Gittelsohn's ultimate decision was the rise of Adolf Hitler and Nazism. Although the total nature of Hitler's Ultimate Solution for the Jewish people was not completely known at that time, certainly enough was known of the actions of the Nazi regime by the United States and its allies to realize that Jews in Europe, and ultimately Jewry worldwide, were in true peril. Every day, as Gittelsohn would read in the Jewish Telegraphic Agency of a new bloodbath or similar atrocity, he would ask himself the question, "And what are you doing about all this? . . . [Will] I play a part that is immediate and direct, or be a good cheerleader on the sidelines? Which will it be?"[18]

His next thought was a common motivation for clergymen of all faiths in their desire to join the military. He knew that young men and women who were often indifferent to religion in the past would feel the need for religion and its comfort for the first time in their lives during the war. This fact was borne out by virtually every chaplain already serving in the military. The effects on servicemen's lives, their spouses, children, and parents were overwhelming, and many, perhaps for the first time, turned in their time of need to the synagogue or church. There simply weren't enough chaplains on active duty to deal with the ever-increasing number of military men and their families. To Gittelsohn, religion was "on the spot," and he stated unequivocally, "If religion has nothing to offer our soldiers and sailors now in their moment of greatest need, they will have nothing to offer religion, indeed, no use at all for religion when the war is over."[19]

His final motivation was intensely personal. To him, his decision would be a test of his own faith, of whether he was willing to live what he preached. He had preached that it wasn't material comfort or ease that mattered most in life; it was the moral and spiritual values that were most important. That it was better to die for a good purpose than to live for no purpose. That sacrifice for the common good was often necessary. Did he truly believe in these concepts, or was he really saying "Do as I say, not as I do"?

Gittelsohn went on to answer his own question, quoting Jewish sages of centuries past when they said, "Lo ha-midrash iker, elo ha-ma-aseh": "Not study (or theory) is the essential thing, but action!" He, Roland Gittelsohn, had to practice what he preached or he would never able to say these things again.[20]

His country was in peril. Now he saw it was his duty to contribute to saving that very country that had given refuge to his immigrant father and grandparents, that had given him his many freedoms, including the freedom to dissent with policies he disagreed with. He would now seek to join the "undemocratic" military that he had, for years, looked on with disdain. By this very action, he was providing answers to the timeless questions posed over two thousand years before by the Hebrew philosopher Hillel when he asked: "If I am not for myself, who will be for me? If I am only for myself, what am I? And if not now, when?"

Reflecting back in his late seventies, he would write, "What made me, after the most excruciating moral dilemma of my life, renounce my pacifism and apply for a military commission? Several things. Hitler's nefarious ambition to exterminate the entire Jewish people had become transparent. I couldn't possibly accede to so ugly and evil a price for my pacifism. Young men whom I had taught and confirmed were being drafted. I had no right to hide behind my rabbinic exemption or to leave them away from home and in combat bereft of religious leadership. Finally, I felt a heavy sense of responsibility to my colleagues."[21]

By the fall of 1942, with the total support of Ruth, his wife, he made his decision. He would seek a commission to become a chaplain in the United States Naval Reserve, just as his good friend Jack Rudin had. His path was now clear and his conscience was clear.

In October of 1942, Rabbi Roland Gittelsohn announced to his congregation his plan to enter military service the following spring. The radio broadcast of December 7, 1941, had crystalized the seeds of doubt that had been planted the previous year by the evacuation of Dunkirk. "Dunkirk had found me a pacifist, — disturbed but still convinced. Pearl Harbor had jolted the last of my uncomfortable pacifism. By the beginning of 1943 my conscience had completed the cycle, had compelled me to apply for the right to wear the uniform of a chaplain in the Navy."[22]

Gittelsohn was embarking on a path that few rabbis had ever tread before. The records of the Navy Chaplain Corps reveal that only two rabbis served in the United States Navy prior to December 7, 1941.[23] He certainly met the newly formulated entry qualifications developed by the Navy Chaplain Corps. The criteria required that all applicant clergymen be male, United States citizens between the ages of twenty-one and forty-five years old, be regularly ordained, and duly accredited by and in good standing with some religious denomination or organization that held an apportionment of chaplain appointments in accordance with the needs of the service. Applicants must be graduates of both a four year college and a three year theological seminary. Although the United States Army also required that applicants have an additional three years' experience in post-seminary studies as an active clergyman, the Navy had no such requirement.[24] As a rabbinical candidate for a Navy commission, Gittelsohn also had to obtain an endorsement from the National Jewish Welfare Board.

After he received his endorsement, he had to successfully complete written examinations administered by the Chaplain Corps. He accomplished this task and was next found to be within the physical fitness standards for commissioning. Having successfully jumped through all of the hurdles required of him, Roland Gittelsohn was ready to answer Hillel's question, "If not now, when?"

He had come full circle. The fire-breathing pacifist of the pre-Dunkirk days was now accepted for entry into the in the United States Naval Reserve. He was commissioned as a lieutenant (junior grade) in the Chaplain Corps on May 12, 1943, the day before his thirty-third birthday. That summer, Lieutenant Junior Grade Roland B. Gittelsohn, Chaplain Corps, United States Naval Reserve, reported for his initial military training in Williamsburg, Virginia.

———•———

Prior to World War II, clergymen joining the military received no formal military training. They were apprenticed to experienced military chaplains and learned by shadowing them and watching them perform their religious duties in the military environment. After the onset of the war, both the Army and the Navy acknowledged not only the need for a much greater number of chaplains on active duty to minister to the soldiers, sailors, and airmen but also the need for a more formalized training curriculum for their incoming clergymen if they were going to be an effective asset to the troops. The Army re-established a chaplain school in Indiana in January of 1942. (That summer, it was moved to Harvard University.) In February of 1942, the United States Navy established the Naval Chaplains School (now called the Naval Chaplaincy School and Center, or NCSC) at Naval Station, Norfolk, Virginia. The purpose of the new school's mission was succinctly described in its mission statement:

> Crowd(ing) into two months the indoctrination that a chaplain would ordinarily acquire through long service. It will include lectures and reading courses on Navy Regulations and Procedure, Customs and Traditions, Etiquette, Naval History, Marine Corps History, Applied Psychology, Counselling [sic], a course in physical fitness, and actual practice among men of the area. Students will be made thoroughly acquainted with sociological program of the Naval Service, particularly as it concerns the work of the Navy Relief Society and the American Red Cross.[25]

In an effort to provide better and more spacious facilities, the school was moved about an hour's drive north of Norfolk to the campus of the College of William and Mary, in Williamsburg, Virginia. On February 22, 1943, the school was reopened in its new location and renamed the Naval Training School for Chaplains. The College of William and Mary, the second oldest college in the country, was then and remains now a beautiful collection of colonial-style buildings, located about an hour north of the home of the United States Atlantic Fleet in Norfolk, Virginia. Adjacent to the campus was the recently restored Colonial Williamsburg, an effort that had been spearheaded by the Rockefeller family. The school held classes in Marshall-Wythe Hall, then located near the center of the campus, as well as in Old Dominion Hall. Religious services were held in the Christopher Wren Chapel at the south end of the campus.

The new school was the work of Captain Clinton A. Neyman, a Baptist minister and career Navy chaplain. Neyman conceived the idea of the school, designed the curriculum, and served as the officer in charge until the summer of 1944. He staffed the school with about a dozen faculty members, all of whom had key background experience that made them eminently qualified for their roles as mentors to their students. In addition to being Navy chaplains themselves, they all had prior shipboard experience or overseas experience with the Navy. Most of them had combat experience.

The curriculum that Neyman designed was eight weeks long and had three main goals. The first and foremost was to train all of the students, who were already ordained clergymen and "hopelessly unmilitary civilians," and to transform them into naval officers. Next was to prepare them physically and get them into excellent physical shape. These chaplains would be going overseas with their men, going to sea with them, and ultimately living "in the field" with them. They had to be physically ready for the challenge. Lastly, the school would give them the tools of their future trade, the ones that they would require to attend to the special needs of military servicemen.

The course was unlike any that its students had ever attended. The experiences of Neyman and his fellow instructors would ensure that this was not just a collection of courses in theology. They would translate their naval experiences into a teaching program that would make it crystal clear to all the students what it meant to be a chaplain in America's fighting Navy. Given what these instructors had lived through, it could be no other way. Two of the instructor chaplains had each served on aircraft carriers that had been sunk by the Japanese in combat in the Pacific theater. Two of the first chaplains to ever serve with the United States Marines were also faculty members.

The training curriculum was divided into three phases. The first three weeks consisted of classroom lectures and training, as did the last three weeks. In between these two blocks of classroom work was a two-week field exercise at one of the naval installations in the region. During this time they would be working with Navy chaplains, acting in the capacity of an apprentice. There were two hours of field drills and physical exercises a day, as well as weekly swimming sessions.

A common theme was weaved throughout the training that the chaplains received. It was a concept new to them and crucial to their future success as Navy chaplains: for the first time in their lives, they would be ministering to men of other religions in addition to their own. They had to learn about all religions and their customs and rituals in order to serve the entire naval force. In training, they were constantly told: You are Navy chaplains first, denominational chaplains only secondly! Your job is to provide for the needs of all men of every faith![26]

Roland Gittelsohn reported to the school on June 21, a sweltering day that was typical for Tidewater, Virginia, summers. He was a member of Class 12-43, which consisted of fifty newly commissioned Navy chaplains. Gittelsohn was one of two rabbis in the class.

As part of their in-processing at Marshall-Wythe Hall, all of the student chaplains filled out a "Chaplains' Questionnaire." Part one of the form required the listing of "Civilian Data." In neat printed letters, Gittelsohn listed his name, place of birth, date of birth, and indicated that he was married to Ruth Freyer on September 25, 1932. He also listed his children: David, born October 8, 1937, and Judith, born November 24, 1940. Attached to the top of part one was his first formal photograph as a naval officer. This head-and-shoulders portrait showed him in his service dress blue uniform, his "cover" nattily angled on his head slightly to the right. He didn't appear at all like a fierce warrior or a Hollywood version of a naval officer. Rather, with his wire-rimmed glasses and scholarly expression, he appeared more like a college professor, a man of letters.

PHOTO

PART ONE: CIVILIAN DATA

NAME **GITTELSOHN,**     **Roland**     **Bertram**
    Last              First             Middle

PLACE OF BIRTH **Cleveland**     **Ohio**     **USA**
                City           State          Country

DATE OF BIRTH **May**     **13**     **1910**
                Month         Day          Year

If foreign born, DATE OF ENTRY INTO U.S. _____

          DATE U.S. CITIZENSHIP GRANTED _____

ARE YOU MARRIED? **Yes**

If married, WIFE'S MAIDEN NAME **Ruth Freyer**

         DATE OF MARRIAGE **Sep. 25, 1932**

NAMES AND BIRTHDATES OF CHILDREN:
         **David — Oct. 8, 1937**
         **Judith — Nov. 24, 1940**

*The first page of Roland Gittelsohn's US Navy file, 1943* (Courtesy American Jewish Historical Society, New York, NY)

Gittelsohn and his forty-nine classmates were immediately thrown into a new world that was both exciting and a bit bewildering to adjust to. Many graduates of the Naval Training School for Chaplains would later note that one of the first of the immersion techniques used by Neyman and his faculty was to teach them the new language that they would be communicating with when they entered the fleet.[27] They quickly learned that floors were "decks," walls were "bulkheads," stairs were "ladders," and beds were "racks." Sailors didn't eat meals prepared in the kitchen; they ate "chow cooked in the galley." As Gittelsohn accurately observed, "Sailors are very apt to lack the time or the inclination to translate a sermon as they listen."[28]

An anecdote serving to emphasize the importance of the new "language" that they were learning was mentioned in a *Time* magazine article about the Chaplain School, written while Roland Gittelsohn was in attendance there. In the June 21, 1943, issue, an article about the Williamsburg school, entitled "Religion: Seagoing Men of God," noted that a typical remark by an instructor in class had been, "The last Sunday you preached from your pulpit some nice lady came up and said, 'That was a wonderful message, Doctor.' The first Sunday you preach after you finish this school, some bluejacket may come up and say, 'Damn good sermon, padre.' You must realize that there is as much sincerity in one as in the other."[29]

The next orientation emphasis for the newly commissioned chaplains was to master naval customs and courtesies. All of the students were taught how to properly wear their new uniforms and how to identify the various ranks and corps of the Navy as well as those of the Marine Corps. They were taught how to salute and whom to salute. Naval protocol was drilled into them. Among these skills were the proper way to board and disembark a Navy ship. Gittelsohn would recall at the end of the war his first clumsy attempt at boarding a ship. To make the experience even more humiliating to him, it was a British aircraft carrier. After very self-consciously walking up the gangplank, he tripped at the top, falling into the arms of the bewildered British officer of the deck.[30] He and his fellow students would come to appreciate very quickly the skills that they were learning in Williamsburg. They all realized that unless they knew how to comport themselves like naval officers—

unless they knew how to be "one of them" among their troops—their usefulness to the men that they would be serving would be considerably diminished.

"Tools of the trade" was a critically important concept for the students to master. To completely minister to their men, the new military chaplains would have to attend to more than only spiritual needs. Chaplains would have to be familiar with real-world issues affecting Sailors, issues that would inspire them to turn to their chaplain for guidance when there was no one else to turn to. The chaplains would be taught about insurance, allotments, and family allowances. They would learn how to prepare a will or a power of attorney. They would be taught in detail about the policies and procedures of both the Navy Relief Society as well as the American Red Cross. The official handling of weddings and funeral services in the Navy, as well the proper procedures for burial at sea, were also topics that were taught. Often it was the chaplain who was in charge of the ship's library and newspaper, so management techniques were included in the curriculum as well. For Class 12-43, there was one lecture on the United States Marine Corps and its relationship to the United States Navy. Although Gittelsohn couldn't possibly have known it at the time, it was a subject that would soon have a profound impact on his life.

One aspect of the students' training that had a surprisingly beneficial effect on many of them was the physical fitness program. By the end of the first week, all of the chaplains were suffering from aching muscles that seemed to be worsened by even the slightest movement. There was much complaining and moaning by the majority of men who were not used to a vigorous exercise program, although many admitted that they really enjoyed being forced to exercise and to get into better physical condition. In addition to abandon-ship drills and survival swimming, there were the frequent long-distance runs over the two-and-a-half mile running trail near the campus. It was with much pride that Gittelsohn noted that, by actual testing, in his class there was a 35 percent improvement in strength and endurance by the week of their graduation.[31]

One of the most important aspects of the training curriculum was to teach the students about different religions. This was crucial if a Navy chaplain was to be able to minister to the needs of all Sailors and Marines, many of whom would be of a different religious denomination. They needed to learn how to comfort and sustain a dying Sailor or Marine of a faith different from their own, which was something they had never done before in their lives. In this particular aspect, the Naval Training School for Chaplains was highly successful. Every student who went through the course was unanimous in their appreciation of the interfaith training that they received in Williamsburg. As Gittelsohn wryly noted, "Nothing but a war could bring three hundred clergymen—Protestants, Catholics, and Jews—to live together intimately for a period of two months."[32] He estimated that in his seven years as a rabbi before joining the Navy, over 90 percent of his contact with clergymen had been with those of his own faith, namely rabbis. No doubt, he surmised, his Christian classmates had experienced something similar. He thought it not improbable that the majority of his fifty classmates had never spoken to a Jew for more than a fleeting second, face to face, before they had come to know him and his fellow rabbi in the class.

Gittelsohn's appreciation of the unique comparative religion "learning laboratory" offered by the Naval Training School for Chaplains was shared by virtually all of its graduates. Reverend Ross Trower offered a common opinion of the program in a 2003 interview for the University of North Carolina at Wilmington: "It was a marvelous experience. I know that there were probably two things, maybe three things that meant a great deal to many of us, perhaps all of us. First of all, we suddenly became involved with ministers, priests and rabbis of many persuasions, many traditions, a consequence that hardly any of us in those days and few of us even in these days experience in rubbing shoulders with other religious leaders of other faith groups. It was wonderful."[33]

*Time* magazine, writing at the time when Gittelsohn was in attendance of the school, also noted the beneficial impact of clergymen of different faiths living together and learning together. The article described a Protestant minister who at first wanted to quit because "there were Papists there." By the end of the course, though, his best friend was a Catholic priest. Another quoted graduate "wondered out loud how he [could] go back to strictly denominational ministering after the war."[34]

A facet of the chaplain training school that proved to be universally popular and highly successful was the assignment of roommates. This policy, adopted by the Navy when the school opened in Williamsburg, was the same as that espoused by the Army in February of 1942. Student chaplains would live with other students of different denominations. Gittelsohn noted that he had three roommates during his two 3-week stays in residence at the school. They were a Presbyterian, a Southern Baptist, and a Roman Catholic. Enthusiastically, Gittelsohn stated, "If they learned half as much about my faith as I learned of theirs, they will never regret an experience which to me is priceless. Every night before 'securing,' while they knelt for their bed-time prayers, I, in the same room, at the same moment, laid on my 'sack' reciting to myself the watchword of Judaism, 'Shema Yisroel, Adonoy Elohaynu, Adonoy Echod; Hear O Israel, the Lord our God, the Lord is One!' In what other land could that happen? Under what other circumstance *would* it happen?"[35]

All of the students heard lectures about faiths other than their own, given by the respective clergymen of that faith. For the first time in his life, Roland Gittelsohn attended both Catholic and Protestant masses in the form of a dry (or shortened) mass to learn about Christian doctrine, necessary for him to minister to Christians. In turn, his Christian colleagues saw a Torah and an Ark for the first time in their lives. In addition to holding Sabbath services each week in the Christopher Wren Chapel library, Gittelsohn and his fellow rabbi classmate would attend the daily Protestant devotions at 6:40 each morning. With pride, he noted that, during his entire stay at Williamsburg, one of the twelve members of each class who were invited to conduct these daily Protestant devotions was always a rabbi.

Gittelsohn wrote that words would be insufficient to capture the living thrill of what he and his classmates experienced together at Williamsburg. Describing it as just an honest effort to understand each other and an honest determination to help each other, he pondered, "Did we succeed?" To answer his own question, he turned with joy to the words of one of his roommates on the day they broke up: "I wouldn't hesitate to entrust the religious training of my Christian child to a rabbi like either of you in the class."[36]

By the end of their eight-week course, Roland Gittelsohn and his classmates were ready. They were now trained in the various aspects of the Navy and Marine Corps that they would need in order to be successful chaplains. They were in the best physical conditions of their lives. It was August of 1943, and their assignments were announced. A stunned LTJG Roland Gittelsohn learned that he was to become the first Jewish chaplain ever assigned to the United States Marine Corps.

# Chapter Twenty

# The First Rabbi

With the Nazi aggression expanding in Europe and Japan increasing its military goals in the Pacific, the United States was slowly awakening from its doldrums. Pres. Franklin D. Roosevelt had declared a limited national emergency on September 8, 1939, and nearly two years later, on May 27, 1941, he declared an unlimited national emergency. In July 1941, the end strength of the United States Marine Corps was 53,886. A year later, following the declaration of war and the national rush to volunteer for service, the Marine Corps strength had nearly tripled to 143,388.[1] To accommodate the training of these new Marine recruits, major training centers had to be enlarged on both coasts.

The Marine Corps looked to Camp Kearny, an old US Army base established in World War I in the Kearny Mesa section of northeast San Diego. In 1934 they acquired a portion of the base, and on June 14, 1940, they renamed it Camp Elliott in honor of Major General George F. Elliott, the tenth commandant of the Marine Corps. Through a series of the rapid acquisitions of adjacent lands, the base grew in size and ultimately reached 26,034 acres.

The Second Marine Division, commanded by Major General C. F. B. Price, was activated on February 1, 1941, at Camp Elliott. Its mission was to train individual replacements for combat duty, and in January 1942, the division assumed responsibility for all of the training on the base. In September 1942, Camp Elliott became the home of the Fleet Marine Force Training Center, West Coast, at which time there were more than ten thousand Marines in the San Diego area.

Looking back in 1988, Gittelsohn would humorously recall: "I applied for a commission in the Navy, explaining my preference facetiously by saying that my wife preferred me in blue, that I wanted to eat off a white tablecloth, that I didn't want to carry a knapsack

223

or dig foxholes. So I became a Marine Corps chaplain, wearing only khaki and green, never blue; there were no tablecloths of any color; I carried a knapsack and dug foxholes."[2]

After a cross-country drive, the Gittelsohn family arrived in San Diego in August of 1943. Gittelsohn formally reported in for duty at Marine Barracks, Camp Elliott on August 30, 1943. Prior to reporting for duty, Gittelsohn had read the physical requirements for the Marine Corps. He was barely five foot six inches tall, well above the US Navy's minimum height requirement of five foot two inches. The minimum height for acceptance into the United States Marine Corps, however, was five foot six inches. All medical assets and clergy serving with the Marines were US Navy personnel, as the Marine Corps was a department of the Navy. Therefore, as a chaplain, Gittelsohn had to meet Navy standards, but he feared that the Marines would reject him if he was measured below *their* minimum height requirement. Accordingly, on his intake paperwork for the Marines, he listed his height as five foot seven inches. The Marines never actually measured his height.[3]

Gittelsohn reported in as an assistant chaplain to the Fleet Marine Force, Pacific Fleet Chaplain, Captain William A. Maguire. Maguire was already a legend in the United States Navy. A Roman Catholic priest, he had joined the Navy in July 1917. In April of 1918, he received the Navy Cross for heroism for his efforts to rescue men from another ship that was on fire and laden with explosives. Maguire was present at the Japanese attack on Pearl Harbor, in a motorboat en route to the battleship USS *California* (BB-44) to conduct morning mass when the attack commenced. He made multiple efforts to rescue men in the water and also commandeered a Navy ferry to help transport more wounded Sailors to the hospital. The expression "praise the Lord and pass the ammunition" was widely attributed to him, although he insisted that he never said it.

Maguire had served as fleet chaplain, US Pacific Fleet from October of 1941 until May of 1942. He was appointed as chaplain for the Naval Training School at San Diego on June 13, 1942, and on July 22, 1943, he was appointed to the staff of the commanding general, Fleet Marine Force (FMF), Pacific Fleet. A little more than a month later, LTJG Gittelsohn reported to Maguire's staff as an assistant chaplain.

As the only Jewish chaplain on staff, Gittelsohn covered all of the half-dozen or so Marine installations in the San Diego region. He quickly learned that being a military chaplain entailed more than just administering to the spiritual needs of his Marines. It meant, to him, keeping up the morale of his men, which he defined in his writings as "the measure of determination to succeed in the purpose for which the individual is trained or for which the organization exists."[4] Gittelsohn considered the key to bolstering the morale of his men very basic: just be available to them. The young men, many of whom were teenagers and away from home for the first time in their lives, needed someone to talk to, a friend away from home. On many occasions, young Marines would seek him out without an obvious reason. Gittelsohn quickly realized that these young men often just needed a quiet place to feel at home with someone who they could talk to, vent to, and who would understand this need for companionship and council. There were very few people in their Marine Corps hierarchy to whom they could turn for this comfort, and their chaplain filled a needed role for them.

Gittelsohn loved having these young men come into his office just to shoot the breeze. Young Marines would turn to him and his fellow chaplains to discuss anything from marital problems to financial problems; and though these Marines may have only met the chaplain minutes before, their spirits were lifted just by having someone listen. Many came from broken or troubled homes and Gittelsohn would become a surrogate big brother or even father to them. To whom else could these men turn? As Gittelsohn noted, no one in the military setting other than the chaplain had the interest or the time for this task.[5] After describing numerous examples of his crucial role as the friend away from home in his unpublished memoir after the war, he stated definitely: "Don't, for a single second, underestimate the morale value of just having the chaplain around as an available friend at a time like that."[6]

Before long, Gittelsohn recognized that although the military services seemed to have adequate numbers of doctors and medical personnel to attend to the physical needs of servicemen, there appeared to be a shocking scarcity of trained psychiatrists available to servicemen. He astutely anticipated the need for increased psychiatric support for combat troops in all services, and he saw a role for military chaplains in helping to remedy this situation somewhat.

Gittelsohn realized that there was little he could do for advanced or complex psychiatric cases, other than to attempt to get these men to doctors who were qualified to treat them. Nonetheless, he did see a valuable opportunity for the chaplains to act almost as a counselor for milder cases of anxiety and stress that could be handled by a professional trained to listen and advise—as all chaplains were. Their training in Williamsburg had prepared these chaplains well for this sort of challenge. The nature of the Marine Corps population also contributed to the ability of Navy chaplains like Gittelsohn to succeed in this role. The Marines who came to Gittelsohn were almost all very young and very candid with him. As he described it, "When civilians come to their pastors for personal guidance there is usually a threshold of embarrassment and hesitance that must be crossed. When military men come to their chaplain, sometimes they won't even wait to sit down before plunging into their stories. Within three minutes they've told everything important in their lives, and by the end of five minutes nothing has been spared. In short, there is a forthright directness which makes it that much easier for chaplains to know their men, and therefore very much more probable that they can help them."[7]

In his notes, Gittelsohn described the invaluable aid that chaplains provide their men in dealing with emergencies at home. Often this involved the chaplain being proactive and getting involved with the Marine's chain of command in order to facilitate emergency leave. Many young Marines would look back with great appreciation of the efforts of the professorial-looking chaplain who acted as their advocate, stood up to a sometimes rigid chain of command, and helped them deal with intense family issues at home. To Roland Gittelsohn, this was all part of his overall duties as a Navy chaplain, one of his most important tasks in maintaining and improving the morale of his Marines.

A fascinating case that the rabbi dealt with during his tour at Camp Elliott involved a young Marine with a problem somewhat unusual for a man who had enlisted in the United States Marine

Corps. After the Marine revealed his problem to his chaplain—he was not certain he could kill another man, even in combat—Gittelsohn spent half a day counseling him. Here, the former pacifist acknowledged that there is such a thing as a human being who is almost constitutionally incapable of killing. Although he felt that the young man was probably one of these people, Gittelsohn, seeing no way for the man to transfer out of the Marine Corps, felt that his only alternative as a chaplain was to help him adjust to the unpleasant but inevitable future he would soon encounter. He told the young man, "Sometimes it is necessary to destroy, precisely in order to save! A forest fire can be stopped only by building a back-fire against it. The killing of millions tomorrow may at times be prevented only by the destruction of thousands today. Suppose, as an armed Marine, [you] were to kill a Jap who would later have murdered ten Americans. Had [you] saved ten lives any less clearly than by dressing the otherwise fatal wounds of ten Americans who had already been shot?"[8] The young man had never quite considered the situation from this point of view. With some satisfaction, Gittelsohn determined that he had, at least, provided the Marine a new perspective with which to consider his dilemma.

Like all military chaplains, Gittelsohn quickly learned that the "friend away from home" role often entailed counseling his Marines on marital and relationship issues, as well as on loose women and venereal diseases. He very much enjoyed getting involved when he felt he could help his young charges with the Marine Corps bureaucracy. Helping Sailors and Marines maintain a sense of individuality within the overall context of a massive military organization was particularly fulfilling for him, and he felt it was extremely important to spend the time to treat everyone as an individual. At the same time, Gittelsohn and his peers had to balance their compassion as chaplains and advocates with a suspicious eye able to spot potential malingerers trying to get out of duties. In short, they had to separate out real issues from minor ones. At Williamsburg, the student chaplains were warned about rare, crusty old sergeant-majors who looked upon the chaplains as soft marks. They would keep a pad of "sympathy chits" with them; if one of their men had personal problems, they would give him one that admitted the bearer to the "mythical order of the bleeding heart," entitling him to thirty minutes of the nearest chaplain's time.[9]

———•———

After entering the United States Navy, Roland Gittelsohn's commitment to civil rights and racial equality was undiminished. Although these views were espoused by very few chaplains in that era—at least in public—Gittelsohn made his opinions on the subjects known in both his words and actions. While stationed in San Diego, he actually rarely interacted with the other chaplains assigned to Headquarters, Fleet Marine Force, Pacific Fleet. In his subsequent assignment he and his family lived off base, and he commuted to his job at Camp Pendleton. There he reported directly to the senior chaplain, "to whom [he] was directly responsible." He later remembered how his contact with the other chaplains was "limited to very rare staff meetings and to those occasions when protocol required that [he] work through chaplains assigned to specific regiments."[10] He didn't realize it at the time, but in San Diego his views on racial equality, coupled with the anti-Semitic views of a number of his fellow Christian chaplains, were beginning to make him somewhat of an outcast among his peers.

One evening when he left Camp Elliott, he saw a young Marine standing at the gate, hoping to get a ride into town. Gittelsohn picked him up, along with several others. Sitting in the front next to him, the Marine spontaneously began spouting out remarks disparaging African Americans. Infuriated, Gittelsohn turned to him and said, "It's too bad I didn't know you felt that way before I picked you up. If I had, I probably would have let you stand there, and would have looked for a colored boy to occupy this seat instead! My advice to you, when you get into combat, is to make sure that if you're ever in a tight spot you don't allow a Negro Marine to save your life." He wryly noted that the young man probably stuck to taking the bus from that point on, figuring that bus drivers were not social crusaders.[11]

Although his progressive views on issues such as racial equality and the deleterious effects of profit-driven armament industries on world peace would begin to subtly isolate him from his fellow chaplains at Camp Elliott, in his wartime notes, Gittelsohn reveled in the interfaith efforts of his colleagues and himself. One night while standing the duty at Norfolk Naval Station during his off-site rotation at the Naval Training School for Chaplains, a young Catholic Sailor came to see him with an issue. The young man kept addressing Gittelsohn as "Father"; finally, Gittelsohn told him, "You don't have to call me 'Father,' I'm not a priest, but of course I'll be glad to help you if I can." To which the Marine's immediate response was, "O.K., Father!"[12]

Gittelsohn would cite two specific incidents during his tour at Camp Elliott to illustrate his sense of pride in the religious teamwork exhibited by all of the Navy chaplains in the area. Due to the large number of military installations that he had to cover as the sole Jewish chaplain in the San Diego area, he was only able to visit the Marine Corps base once a week. At one point in between these visits, a young Jewish boy needed to see the chaplain, and the chaplain on duty was Lieutenant Commander Walter Mahler, a Roman Catholic priest. The young man was probably away from home for the first time in his life—and this was realistically the first time he lived in a predominantly non-Jewish environment. In short, he was having trouble adjusting to his life in the Marine Corps. In particular, he felt pitifully exposed as a minority, and he "wore his Jewishness with uncomfortable awkwardness."[13] Under the circumstances, a Catholic priest could have deferred and told the boy to wait for an appointment to see Rabbi Gittelsohn. With pride, Gittelsohn noted, "He could have, and he might have, but he didn't. For that would have been neither the 'Navy way,' nor Walter Mahler's way."[14]

Displaying superb counseling skills, Mahler sat the young man down and patiently said to him, "Look here, my boy, don't ever let me catch you walking around this base ashamed of the fact that you're a Jew! As a Catholic priest, I get down on my knees every morning to pray to a Jew, Jesus. I hold a Jewish girl, Mary, to be one of the most sacred personalities of my faith. You just walk out of this office and hold your head as high as you know how. Being a Jew is something to be proud of, not something to hide!"[15]

Gittelsohn would later work with the young man and noted that he had acquired a new sense of self-respect, largely due to the initial counseling of a Navy chaplain who happened to be a Catholic priest. The young man also gained a degree of new knowledge of Christianity and its intimate relationship to Judaism. This, concluded Gittelsohn, was "the Navy way."

In the unpublished memoir of his wartime experiences,

Gittelsohn recorded with pride several stories that showcase "the Navy way" servicemen of all faiths accommodated their different religions while they all, as Americans, trained for their common crusade against the Axis powers. An article published through the Jewish Telegraphic Agency on December 24, 1943, explained that, throughout the Army and Navy, Jewish Sailors were requesting duty on Christmas so that their Christian colleagues could enjoy the holiday off. The article specifically mentions Roland Gittelsohn by name, citing him as a source of this news.[16] On Passover of 1944, Marine Corps cooks and messmen, none of them Jewish, worked for weeks to prepare a traditional Passover Seder for their Jewish colleagues. These same men also prepared the meal to break the fast after Yom Kippur and wouldn't allow the Jewish Marines to help clean up, stating, "This is your holiday."[17]

---

Gittelsohn's unpublished memoirs also include a description of the most unusual experience of his tour in San Diego. He recounted the frenetic activity every Sunday at the chapel of the Marine Corps base, which would conduct two Protestant services alternately with two Catholic services, followed by his Jewish service at 11 a.m. One service would have been barely concluded before the chapel would be set up for the next; and with surprising efficiency, it would be converted from a Christian sanctuary into a Jewish synagogue. It was while conducting a Sunday synagogue service that Gittelsohn noted from his pulpit a most unusual worshiper.

The young man, obviously a Catholic, crossed himself and kneeled in one of the rear rows. He recited his own prayers while Jewish worship proceeded in the chapel. Once his own worship was concluded, he remained in his seat, listening to a large part of the rest of the service with obvious interest. In a while, he stood, crossed himself again, and quietly left as the Jewish service continued. From his pulpit, Gittelsohn noted the same young man returning for four consecutive weeks.

It was not clear whether perhaps the man's military duties prevented him from attending Catholic services. What seemed obvious to Gittelsohn was that this young man could enter the chapel in the midst of a Jewish service and, without embarrassment or self-consciousness, worship God in his own way while all around him Jews were worshipping the same God in their way. Gittelsohn described the situation thusly: "What an inspiring example for civilian life in the world of tomorrow! Americans—worshiping together because they have learned to live and suffer and rejoice together . . . That boy was not less Catholic, nor were we less Jewish, because we worshipped—each in his own way—the same God at the same time in the same room. But he knew and respected our faith more than he did before, even as we increased our knowledge and respect for his. Thus do men at war learn to pray together."[18]

After moving three thousand miles from New York to San Diego, the Gittelsohns at first settled into housing at Camp Elliott. There, Roland and Ruth established important friendships, some of them with fellow chaplains and their families. While at the Naval Training School for Chaplains in Williamsburg, he had become friends with a Congregational-Christian minister named Herbert Van Meter. By coincidence, both Gittelsohn and Van Meter were assigned to Camp Elliott and would soon after that be assigned together again. Their personalities meshed perfectly, and soon after arriving at Camp Elliott, the Gittelsohns and the Van Meters became close friends and frequently dined together. Their friendship would endure even after the war; the two former Navy chaplains would remain close friends for thirty-seven years until Van Meter's death in 1982.

Gittelsohn wrote several times about 2nd Lieutenant Martin Weinberg. Weinberg was the first Jewish Marine Corps officer that he met after reporting to San Diego. The epitome of the gung-ho Marine, Weinberg was an extremely capable officer itching to be sent to the combat zone. Gittelsohn noted that Weinberg was one of the most unique individuals that he had ever met. The two men were immediately impressed with each other.

In the fall of 1943, Roland Gittelsohn presided over Weinberg's wedding to Miss Yetta Adler of San Diego. It was the first marriage he performed as a Navy chaplain, and, in his autobiography, he noted that it may have been "the first and perhaps the only marriage ceremony uniting two Jewish Marines."[19] Shortly after,

Ruth and Roland became close friends with Yetta and Martin. The Weinbergs attended Friday Services at Camp Elliott regularly, and when Martin was shipped out to the combat zone, Yetta continued her synagogue attendance, as well as her close friendship with the Gittelsohns.

Martin Weinberg corresponded as often as he could with Roland Gittelsohn. He shipped out with the Replacement Battalion of the Second Marine Division for Camp Tarawa on the island of Hawaii. There the Marines prepared for the invasion of Saipan and the rest of the Mariana Islands. Weinberg wrote to Gittelsohn, discussing his fears and doubts as he prepared to face battle for the first time. He missed Yetta and their friends, but he did take his greatest comfort from the Jewish services conducted on the island. Before leaving Hawaii, he wrote, "The meetings we have been able to have are a great source of relaxation, release of tension, and enjoyment for the boys. There is nothing equal to a Jewish atmosphere, and thank God, wherever we Jews are, we are able to gather, to create that atmosphere, to be content beyond words."[20]

Gittelsohn received only one negative letter from his friend. At Camp Tarawa, Weinberg encountered a small number of fellow Marine officers who resented him because he was a Jew. Though they did nothing overt, it became obvious to Weinberg that they wanted nothing to do with a United States Marine Corps officer with an obviously Jewish-sounding name like Weinberg. While this was just a small cadre of anti-Semites, it still bothered Weinberg, and he shared his disgust in his correspondence with his good friend back in San Diego.

In July of 1944, right after the Battle of Saipan, Yetta Weinberg received a telegram from General Alexander Vandergrift, commandant of the Marine Corps. It contained devastating news, regretfully informing her that her husband, 2nd Lt Martin Weinberg, was killed in action at Saipan. Gittelsohn would describe the telegram poignantly: "[It was] the most final and irrevocable thing I've ever held in my hand or seen with my eye [*sic*]."[21]

Yetta Weinberg was devastated by the death of her husband. She wrote to Gittelsohn, "My only thought and prayer is that Marty's death was not in vain. He held his ideals very high and was willing to die for them; should they ever be destroyed, I would lose all faith and trust in humanity."[22]

Gittelsohn was stunned and shaken by the death of a man he so admired and loved. He would reflect back with anger when thinking about the anti-Semitism that his friend, a dedicated Marine officer, had to endure from other Marines he went into combat with. The eloquent rabbi strove for words that could express this discordant expression of American ideals. He would write, "Whoever did not or would not welcome Martin Weinberg—no matter how high his rank, how numerous his medals—is an enemy of the United States, a faithless betrayer of her most cherished ideals. Whoever understands America—understands her and loves her—must also understand and love Marty Weinberg."[23]

As the spring of 1944 approached, Roland Gittelsohn neared the end of his tour at Headquarters, Fleet Marine Force, Pacific Fleet. He would reflect back on his tour at Camp Elliott with pride and took great satisfaction in knowing that he taken care of the Jewish Marines in the San Diego area and had helped all the Marines who had come to him for assistance. Truly, Gittelsohn had been their "friend away from home." In addition, his relationships with his fellow chaplains had been, by and large, satisfactory. In May, he received orders to report up the road to the newly formed Fifth Marine Division at the newly built Camp Pendleton.

Gittelsohn's personal notes would take on a darker, more somber tone after he reported to this new assignment. Although he would inadvertently achieve fame throughout the United States as a result of his new assignment, his tour would be tarnished by the increasing resentment of fellow chaplains towards his new job, increasing hostility towards his stance on social issues, and outright anti-Semitism. In addition, during his next tour, the former pacifist would take part in the bloodiest battle in the history of the United States Marine Corps. On May 23, 1944, Roland Gittelsohn reported to the Fifth Marine Division.

By mid-1944, the tide had clearly turned in the war in the Pacific. In December 1943, planning began on Operation Forager, the invasion of the Mariana Islands. The capture of Saipan, Guam, and Tinian would be critical to stage America's newly developed, long-range bomber for use against Japan. On June 15, the Second and Fourth Marine Divisions, along with the US Army's Twenty-Seventh Infantry Division, invaded Saipan. After fierce fighting, the island was secured on July 9. On July 21, Guam was invaded by the First Provisional Marine Brigade and the US Army's Seventy-Seventh Infantry Division. The island was secured by August 10. Lastly, the Second and Fourth Marine Divisions landed on Tinian on July 24 and secured the island by August 1. With the Marianas conquered and now in American hands, the United States had what it needed to begin the final phase of the war: air bases from which to stage the air assault on the Japanese mainland. With airfields on the newly captured islands, Japan was within flying range of America's newest and most advanced bomber, the B-29 Superfortress.

The B-29 was introduced into the United States Army Air Forces in 1944. The largest aircraft in the Air Forces inventory, it contained several revolutionary advances. It featured a pressurized cabin and had centralized fire control of its .50 caliber machine guns. Its mechanical systems were so advanced and complex that a new specialist had to be added to each air crew—the flight engineer. The B-29 was capable of flying long-range missions from the Mariana Islands to Japan—fifteen hundred miles away—and back. Each mission lasted approximately fourteen hours. The first B-29s reached their bases in the Marianas in October and began their long-range bombing missions to Japan in November 1944.

At first, the bombing results were disappointing. There was relatively little damage inflicted using daylight, high altitude bombing tactics, and conventional explosive ordnance. Soon, another factor came into play: B-29s were often damaged over targets by antiaircraft fire. These crippled planes would have to struggle over a fifteen-hundred-mile, seven hour return flight to their bases. Halfway between targets in Japan and the Mariana Islands was another island under Japanese control. Frequently, Japanese fighter planes were sent up from the island's airfields to intercept returning B-29s. In addition, the Japanese launched aircraft on bombing raids from the island's airfields against the American airfields on Guam, Saipan, and Tinian. The island's name was Iwo Jima.

Iwo Jima's primitive radar station worked well enough to give

Japanese fighter aircraft adequate time to take off and ambush Japan-bound formations of B-29s, resulting in significant losses to American aircraft. B-29s, crippled and barely able to stay airborne, much less engage in combat, had to face these Japanese interceptors who were waiting for them on the return flight to the Marianas. It became more and more apparent that securing Iwo Jima was necessary to avoid such casualties. In addition, if Iwo Jima was in American hands, the crippled bombers could land on its airfields, thereby eliminating the need to fly an additional 750 miles to their home bases.[24]

Iwo Jima was the largest of three small islands known as the Volcano Islands that had been under Japanese possession since the mid-nineteenth century. Iwo Jima was first visited by an English explorer named Gore, who called it "Sulphur Island" because it reeked of the vile-smelling mineral.[25] The eight-square-mile island, shaped like a pork chop, featured two beaches, one on its east shore and one on its west shore. It was five miles long, less than three miles wide at the north end, and a half-mile wide on the south end. The Japanese had two functional airfields and were in the process of constructing a third. The most prominent feature of the island was the inactive volcano Mount Suribachi, a 528-foot cliff on its southern tip. Anticipating that the Americans would need to take the island to continue their drive towards the Japanese mainland, Emperor Hirohito ordered an all-out build-up of the defenses on Iwo Jima.

By mid-1944, there was a disagreement in strategy to conquer Japan among the two top military leaders in the Pacific, General Douglas MacArthur and Admiral Chester Nimitz. MacArthur envisioned a three-part plan: First, the Philippines would be recaptured. Next, Okinawa and Formosa would be conquered, and from there a million-man American force would be assembled on the Chinese mainland. From the mainland, the invasion of the Japanese home islands would be launched. Nimitz, however, endorsed a different strategy: a direct seaborne assault led by the Marines to establish a beachhead on Kyushu, the southernmost of the Japanese home islands. Part of Nimitz's overall strategy was to invade and conquer Iwo Jima and eliminate the threat it posed to his plan.[26] In order for either plan to succeed, the United States would be required to have unchallenged control of the skies over Japan and the thousands of miles of ocean approaches to it. The American Joint Chiefs of Staff, regardless of which plan they would ultimately endorse, had promulgated an immediate strategy to completely pulverize the Japanese mainland's war-making capabilities with massive saturation bombing of its industrial centers and military installations. This job would fall to the hundreds of B-29s now stationed in the Marianas and would be greatly facilitated by invading and securing Iwo Jima. In coming to this conclusion, the Joint Chiefs also gave consideration to the length of the bombing missions, the Japanese fighter attacks on the B-29s, and the Japanese bombing raids originating from Iwo Jima. Another crucial factor was the much shorter distance to Japan (seven hundred miles), and if the United States had Iwo Jima in its possession, crippled B-29s returning from bombing raids would have a much shorter distance to fly to return to American airfields. Hence, in early July, General George C. Marshall, Chairman of the Joint Chiefs of Staff, ordered that Iwo Jima must be taken by American forces by mid-January 1945.

Chester Nimitz was able to convince the Chief of Naval Operations, Admiral Ernest King, to endorse his immediate strategy of invading Iwo Jima versus MacArthur's recommended invasion of Formosa. In his meeting with King at Treasure Island in San Francisco Bay, Nimitz presented his plan, which included the full endorsement of Army Lieutenant General Simon Bolivar Buckner, who was selected by MacArthur to command the United States Tenth Army in the Formosa invasion, and Lieutenant General Millard F. Harmon, the ranking Army Air Forces general in the Pacific. King arrived at the meeting with his mind set on endorsing MacArthur's proposed invasion of Formosa. In addition, he was planning on working to change General Marshall's mind about requiring the invasion of Iwo Jima.

In the five-hour meeting, Nimitz and his staff successfully argued their case and were able to change King's mind. Upon his return to Washington, King recommended to the Joint Chiefs that the proposed invasion of Formosa be scrapped. Instead, he argued, they should proceed with the assault on Iwo Jima as ordered by Marshall. The Joint Chiefs unanimously agreed with King's recommendation, and back in Hawaii Admiral Nimitz and his staff were given the green light to begin planning Operation Detachment: the amphibious invasion of Iwo Jima.

In September 1944, the planning for the invasion of Iwo Jima began in earnest. The logistics required for the assault were staggering. Seventy-three ships would transport the Marines, along with all of their combat supplies. Each ship would have rations for sixty days, 6,000 five-gallon cans of water, and gasoline for twenty-five days for all vehicles, as well as medical supplies, spare parts, and general supplies to last approximately thirty days. The weight for each Marine was 1,322 pounds.[27]

The Japanese knew the importance of Iwo Jima to the Americans' war plans. They had troops on the island since 1943 and had accelerated their efforts to fortify the island after the fall of the Marianas. Japanese military leaders knew that the fall of Iwo Jima would bring the Americans virtually to the next logical goal: the Japanese mainland. The island therefore needed to be defended at all costs. The man who Emperor Hirohito hand-picked to oversee the fortifications of Iwo Jima's defenses, as well as to lead the defense of the island against the anticipated American onslaught, was Lieutenant General Tadamichi Kuribayashi. Kuribayashi would oversee the around-the-clock grind involving soldiers and sailors and a battalion of Korean laborers, burrowing miles of tunnels and building hundreds of concrete gun emplacements, bunkers, and pillboxes at a frantic pace to make the island impregnable to invaders.[28]

Kuribayashi was a brilliant strategist who had served as deputy military attaché at the Japanese embassy in Washington, DC, in 1928. He was fluent in English and spent more than two years traveling around the United States. He was an admirer of America and Americans, and during his travels around the country he had written his family: "The United States is the last country in the world Japan should fight. Its industrial potential is huge and fabulous, and the people are energetic and versatile. One must never underestimate the Americans' fighting ability."[29] On June 19, 1944, Kuribayashi landed at the Chidori airfield on Iwo Jima to take command of the island's defense against the expected American amphibious invasion. The manner in which he constructed his defenses made shelling and bombing essentially useless. The positions were masterpieces of concealment and construction: walls of many of his underground defensive bunkers and tunnels were more than three feet of steel-reinforced concrete and impossible to spot from the natural terrain upheavals that camouflaged them.[30]

The top Marine commander in the Pacific was Lieutenant General Holland M. "Howlin' Mad" Smith. The brash, outspoken Marine had come under much criticism because of the large number of Marine casualties suffered during prior Pacific campaigns at Peleliu and, particularly, Tarawa, where 3,056 Marines were killed or wounded in the seventy-two hours of combat. There were loud cries for his dismissal from some family members of killed servicemen, several members of Congress, and several newspapers, especially those published by Robert R. McCormick and William Randolph Hearst. In their demand to have Smith removed, McCormick's *Chicago Tribune* had described Smith with such harsh terms as "Butcher . . . cold-blooded murderer . . . indiscriminant waster of human life."[31] Because of other issues, including Smith's age (sixty-two) and his medical condition (diabetes), it took the personal intervention of President Roosevelt himself to keep Smith on active duty and commanding his men overseas.[32]

In the initial planning phase, three Marine Corps divisions were selected for the amphibious invasion force that would comprise the Fifth Amphibious Corps under the command of Major General Harry "The Dutchman" Schmidt. This would be the largest force of Marines ever sent into combat. It would consist of the Third Marine Division, the Fourth Marine Division, and a recently formed division that had never as a unit been in combat before: the Fifth Marine Division.

---

On November 11, 1943, the Fifth Marine Division was activated. Although it was a brand new division to the Marine Corps, it was comprised of many veterans of prior Pacific campaigns, such as Tarawa and Peleliu. Its division Headquarters Battalion officially began functioning less than a month later, on December 1. In less than two weeks, two infantry regiments (the Twenty-Sixth and Twenty-Seventh Infantry Regiments) and one artillery regiment (the Thirteenth Artillery Regiment) were organized. The official activation date for the Fifth Marine Division was January 21, 1944. The acting division commander was Brigadier General Thomas A. Bourke. On February 4, Major General Keller E. Rockey became the commanding general of the division.

This new division was based at the recently developed Camp Pendleton, located on the California coast in San Diego County. In order to create the large West Coast training base, the Marine Corps acquired nearly 123,000 acres to construct the base in February 1942. Named after Major General Joseph Pendleton, it was dedicated by Pres. Franklin D. Roosevelt on September 25, 1942.

The urgency surrounding the creation of the Fifth Marine Division centered on the grim reality of the Pacific war. The staunch, fanatical resistance exhibited by the Japanese at Tarawa and Peleliu, coupled with the high Marine casualty rates, drove home the need to recruit and train large numbers of additional Marines and prepare them for combat.[33] It was at Camp Pendleton that the more than twenty thousand Marines of the Fifth Marine Division trained for months to acquire the combat skills that would be critical to fight a determined and well-entrenched foe in the Pacific campaigns to come.

When he reported in to the headquarters of the Fifth Marine Division in May of 1944, LTJG Gittelsohn met a man who was to have a profound effect on his military career. The division chaplain was a career Navy chaplain, Commander Warren C. Cuthriell. Cuthriell was a forty-four-year-old Baptist minister who immediately impressed Gittelsohn with his intellect and his sense of fairness. He informed the rabbi that he was the newest and also the last of seventeen chaplains that would be assigned to the division. It was then that Cuthriell delivered a stunning bit of news to Gittelsohn. Division policy dictated that that one Jewish chaplain in the division should have access to every regiment in the division. In order to accomplish this, the Jewish chaplain was automatically designated as assistant division chaplain and placed in Headquarters Battalion. Hence, on his first day after reporting to his new command, Roland Gittelsohn, the newest of the chaplains to report in, became the number two man in the chain of command of the Fifth Marine Division's chaplains. It was shortly after his appointment as assistant division chaplain that Gittelsohn would first detect signs of resentment from his fellow division chaplains.

Gittelsohn wrote very little about his four months at Camp Pendleton. He had minimal contact with the other chaplains in the division—excepting his immediate superior, Commander Cuthriell—unless he attended a rare chaplain staff meeting or if his job as assistant division chaplain otherwise required such interaction.[34] Gittelsohn and his family lived off-base, and most of the time he was able to leave the base and head home at 4 p.m. In addition to tending to the spiritual needs of all the men and conducting Jewish services on Friday nights, he continued with the other various chaplain duties that he performed while at Camp Elliott. The difference in this assignment was the scale of his job. He was now responsible for four infantry regimens consisting of approximately three thousand men each, fourteen battalions (Headquarters Battalion; Medical, Artillery, Tanks, Engineering Battalions; four Amphibious Tractor Battalions; and various other support Battalions) that included two Replacement Battalions of 2,650 Marines each. The scope of his responsibilities now included over twenty thousand Marines.

During the training phase, Roland Gittelsohn made another somewhat symbolic break from his strict pacifist roots. He requested a revolver and learned how to competently fire it. He would practice at the firing range on a regular basis and learned to strip the gun, clean it, and maintain it in working order. Technically, the Geneva Convention forbade doctors and chaplains from carrying weapons, but almost all did for self-defense. Gittelsohn did not want to take any chances with the Japanese. "I never had to fire it in combat," he wrote in his autobiography. "Would I have done so if directly attacked? I think so, but don't really know for sure. Thank God, the choice was never forced on me."[35]

---

At Camp Pendleton, the Marines participated daily in grueling physical activities, including forced marches in full combat gear and regular calisthenics that transformed many recent civilian recruits into physically hardened Marines. They learned to hone their combat skills with all forms of weaponry, including hand-to-hand combat. They mastered the techniques of climbing over the rails and down the sides of large transport ships and into small landing vehicles that would transport them to beaches on some yet-unknown Pacific islands.

They then built on their combat skills and learned what was required for amphibious assaults on enemy-held beaches. In July of 1944, the Fifth Marine Division staged a series of full-fledged mock amphibious assaults. The nine landing teams, each consisting of an infantry battalion with guns, armor, and other support elements, were taken by large transports for practice amphibious landings on San Clemente Island off the California coast. Once the second landing exercise was completed, the troops re-boarded the transports and headed for their final exercise—an assault on the California coast, "Pendleton Island."[36] During this planning and training phase for Operation Detachment, the Marines had no idea where they would be fighting. They only knew that they were preparing for amphibious assault on an island they were sure they never heard of. They also knew that the fighting would be savage.

## Chapter Twenty-One

# Fifth Marine Division

Meanwhile, at the three major planning meetings for Operation Detachment, Gen "Howlin' Mad" Smith was not happy. He didn't like Nimitz and in general felt that the Navy never gave enough pre-bombardment support to his Marines prior to their landings. Now this complaint again reared its head. "This will be the bloodiest fight in Marine Corps history," Smith announced. "We'll catch seven kinds of hell on the beaches, and that will be just the beginning." After a dramatic pause, he continued, "The fighting will be fierce and the casualties will be awful, but my Marines will take the damned island." Staring at Nimitz, he asked, "How much bombardment will we get before H-Hour?"[1]

General Smith had requested ten days of pre-invasion bombardment at the minimum. Nimitz, however, was under many constraints. The Iwo Jima invasion had to mesh with General MacArthur's Philippines campaign, and also preparations were underway for the anticipated Okinawa campaign that would follow shortly after Iwo Jima was secured. Nimitz's reply infuriated him. "Three days," he informed the Marine, was all the bombardment they could provide under the circumstances. In an effort to mollify Smith, Nimitz offered a fourth day of naval bombardment, but only if the weather was perfect. Nimitz again explained that their naval resources were stretched too thin to provide any more to Operation Detachment. In the end, Nimitz would request—and the Joint Chiefs would approve—a thirty day delay to the operation. Iwo Jima was now scheduled to be invaded on February 19, 1945.[2]

---

With the deployment overseas looming shortly, Gittelsohn wrote a letter to all the Jewish Marines of the Fifth Marine Division on August 8, 1944. After reminding them all of regular Friday night services, he instructed them to be sure that their dog tags were properly marked with an "H" or "J" to indicate their religion. Otherwise, if they became a casualty, fellow Marines would not be able to identify their faith and secure the Jewish chaplain. Gittelsohn promised the men he would visit them as frequently as possible and assured them that he could be reached through Headquarters Company, Headquarters Battalion. He also reminded them that the regimental Protestant and Catholic chaplains could help them in his absence.

After assuring them he would arrange for regular Friday night services once they reached their base in Hawaii, he noted with pride, "Attendance at our Jewish Services has been growing steadily. If you have not yet attended, please consider this a personal invitation. The more interest we show in our religion, the more respect we can expect from others, and, the more consideration we shall receive when the time comes to request special Jewish holiday privileges." He also noted, "My incomplete records show close to two hundred Jewish men in the Division as of this date; the probability is that we have a total of about three hundred." He ended the message with the following: "Don't hesitate to call on me for any assistance I can possibly give you. Until I see you again, good luck, and God bless you!" [3]

As the summer of 1944 was coming to an end, the knowledge that Roland would soon be going overseas and into combat began to wear into the soul of the Gittelsohn family. In one of his regular columns written for the *Nassau Daily Review* entitled "Somewhere in the Pacific," he described the stress of the upcoming deployment on all of the Marine families, using his own children to illustrate for those back home what it was like when their father was leaving for the war. At the time, David was seven years old and Judy was four years old.

Prior to leaving Camp Pendleton, he wrote:

Every visit to camp meant the visible presence of war and what it might do to their daddy. Almost daily there were other children's fathers leaving for overseas; soon they came to understand that one day it would be their daddy's turn. . . . Both children kept asking with alarming frequency, what I would do if, when I arrived overseas, I encountered a Jap who wanted to kill me. When they learned that I was to be shipped out by plane rather than ship, one of them said, "Boy, Dad, am I glad you're going to fly. Now I know you won't drown!"[4]

In his writings, Gittelsohn would lament the effect of his absence and the effect of the war on his family. "What can I do, dear David and darling Judy, to make up to you this terrible thing that life has done to you? You didn't ask for this war. You don't even understand it. . . . But you are among its most lamentable victims."[5] He also would reflect back towards the end of his life and conclude that the stress of the war very well could have been the genesis of the severe emotional crises that his wife, Ruth, would begin experiencing not long after the war.

---

Some of the elements of the Fifth Marine Division left in July for Guam to act as reserve forces for the Marianas campaign. It turned out they were not needed and instead reported to Camp Tarawa, the division training base near Hilo, on the island of Hawaii. Towards the end of the summer, the orders were issued: the Fifth Marine Division would board transport ships in San Diego and embark for Hawaii, where the division would train at Camp Tarawa. They would leave on September 19.

After the operational orders were issued, Gittelsohn had to send the family back to New York. They spent the afternoon together in Los Angeles before Ruth, David, and Judy boarded a train headed for the East Coast. He would describe these hours as the saddest he had ever known. When the moment came to kiss his father goodbye, David sat on the edge of his seat, "almost hypnotized, and as [his father] kissed them [David] whispered over and over again as if in a trance, 'Good luck, Daddy . . . good luck, Daddy . . . good luck, Daddy.' He must have said it at least a dozen times."[6] Gittelsohn was only partially successful in suppressing his tears. He spent several hours wandering around Los Angeles, had dinner and sat through a movie in an effort to take his mind off of the sobering thought that his family may never see him again. He was going to catch a midnight train for San Francisco and from there fly out to Hawaii.

He had to share a cab to the train station with three businessmen, as wartime conditions made the sharing of taxis mandatory. Stunned, he listened to the three businessmen begin to complain endlessly about all of the hardships being imposed on them by the war. Hotel rooms were almost impossible to get, service and food even at the best restaurants were abominable, etc. They seemed oblivious to the man in the uniform of a Navy lieutenant (the rank Gittelsohn was promoted to on September 1, 1944) sitting with them. Finally, Gittelsohn exploded. "I don't know who you guys are, but I want you to know how sorry I am over your troubles. I just kissed my wife and children good-bye, not knowing whether I'll ever see them again. Tomorrow I am being flown overseas, sooner or later into combat. But your plight really touches me; my heart bleeds for you."[7]

Stunned silence followed in the cab. Gittelsohn then refused their awkward invitation to be their guest for drinks while they all waited for their trains at the station.

---

In order to be with the majority of the men in the division, Gittelsohn did not fly over to Hawaii until more than half of them were already at Camp Tarawa. Upon his arrival, he was delighted to again see his good friend Herbert Van Meter, who was assigned as chaplain to the Twenty-Sixth Regiment. Van Meter pleasantly surprised his friend; knowing that Gittelsohn's arrival to Hawaii would be delayed—and concerned with the spiritual needs of the Jewish Marines—Van Meter began conducting regular Friday night Jewish services on the base. Van Meter was so skilled and knowledgeable about Judaism that the Jewish Marines began to call him Rabbi Van Meter.[8] He was one of the few Christian chaplains who liked and respected Roland Gittelsohn. This was partly attributable to Gittelsohn's outspoken personality and liberal, progressive views, and as well as his politics. Clearly, anti-Semitism also factored into other Christian chaplains' disapproval of the rabbi. Lastly, their continued resentment over his appointment as assistant division chaplain would continue to fester. In later years, Gittelsohn would recall, "Clearly, I was not very popular among the Christian chaplains."[9]

Shortly after reporting to Camp Tarawa, Gittelsohn was presented with a plum perk that came with his job. He and Warren Cuthriell, as members of the Headquarters Battalion, were assigned cabins for their living quarters while at the base. The other fifteen chaplains were billeted in tents. From that point on, Gittelsohn could sense increasing hostility towards him by his peers.

In addition, an increasingly obvious reason for their dislike of Gittelsohn was his unapologetic support of the black Marines in the Fifth Marine Division. As he would later note, he could tell that the blacks had "quickly learned that there were only two chaplains in the division who gave a damn about them, who would take their complaints about discrimination seriously, and do something to defend them."[10]

In his wartime notes, Gittelsohn wrote two entries under the title of "Negroes."[11] In each note, he took pains to document acts of discrimination and humiliation that he had both witnessed or had been told of. In the first entry from Camp Tarawa, he described the problems that the black Marines were having at USO-sponsored dances. Although there had been no overt words spoken, the blacks felt unwelcome at the dances and mentioned that there were problems getting girls to accompany them. In general, the blacks had nothing to do on their days off and would instead hang around the barracks, where they at least had some recreational gear. Gittelsohn noted that he spoke to "Chap. C.," presumably Commander Cuthriell, about trying to arrange for girls to come to the dances for the men.

In the same entry written at that time, he described an incident that took place on October 29, 1944, after one of the dances. In detail, he described how, after three of the blacks left the dance to return to their jobs as dishwashers back at the galley, they were harassed and provoked by two white Marines when one of the three arrived late. To prevent a brawl from occurring, their supervisor, a Colonel Shipply, promptly intervened and told them all to forget it, promising them that they'd get a fair break if "they'd behave and do their job." After Shipply left, "Major A." came on the scene and counseled the black Marine who had arrived late, telling the man, "[you have] those racial feelings in the back of your head and you think your people are being walked on, but you've got to get this out of your head—You're a Marine now."

The last entry in that section was dated October 31 and concerned a crack made by a Sergeant Morrison when he heard that two of the blacks were promoted to the rank of sergeant. "Why, if he goes back to South Carolina with those stripes, they'll shoot him."

In another note, one under the heading of "Negroes," Gittelsohn described an incident that occurred on Christmas Day 1944. At about midnight, two of the black Marines from the Twenty-Sixth Regiment came to see him and told him of an incident earlier that evening involving another black named Booth. After being given a bottle of whisky as a Christmas gift by one of the officers, Booth was accused of being drunk by Gunnery Sergeant "B.," who sent someone to get him, stating, "Tell Booth he'd better straighten up and come here, and stop staggering around . . . [he] better be walking straight!" Admitting that he (along with everyone else) had had a couple of drinks, but livid at the accusation of drunkenness, Booth pushed away Gunnery Sergeant B.'s hand when he grabbed him, exclaiming, "Get your God-damned hand off of me!" Noting that the "other Negroes rushed in to make sure that B. didn't do anything rash" and to restrain him, Gittelsohn went on to state that Gunnery Sergeant B. then ordered the MPs to take Booth to the hospital for a sobriety test. The test revealed he had alcohol in his system but was not drunk. He was released shortly after.

The name "Kelley" appears in Gittelsohn's wartime notes in this section. In his autobiography, written in 1988, he explained how he intervened on behalf of Jack Kelley Jr., a black Marine who has been thrown in the brig. Knowing Gittelsohn's passion on the subject, someone at Headquarters Company asked if he was aware of the situation and that the man was imprisoned at the instigation of a Southern warrant officer. Gittelsohn did investigate, convinced that Kelley's sole offense was insufficient subservience to a white man. Within a day, Kelley was released. With pride, Gittelsohn noted that after the war, Kelley became a shipyard worker, a dedicated family man, and that he, a rabbi, remained his chaplain to that day.[12]

Roland Gittelsohn's efforts on behalf of the black Marines of the Fifth Marine Division would do little to enhance his standing among most of the other chaplains. Being the only Jewish chaplain already had cast him as an outsider, and his outspoken views on racial equality and other social issues would continue to strengthen their impression of him as a left-leaning activist and possible communist. The discussion groups that he initiated after his arrival at Camp Tarawa proved to be a source of increasing friction between not only Gittelsohn and the other chaplains but also between him and the command structure of the division.

In the 1930s, Gittelsohn and his fellow pacifists had disdain for the military, as they felt that a large military organization couldn't possibly be "democratic." The rabbi had now come to embrace the leadership styles of those in the Marine Corps who he had once felt were unorthodox leaders. He had unbridled admiration for Lieutenant Colonel Evans Carlson, leader of the Second Marine Raider Battalion, more famously known as "Carlson's Raiders." From 1937 through 1938, Carlson had served as a military observer with the Chinese communist forces under Mao Tse Tung. It was there that he came to admire their organization, and he would use their egalitarian concepts when he formed the Second Marine Raider Battalion. Under Carlson, all of the men would embrace an egalitarian, team-building approach. Leadership would entail responsibility, not privilege, and Carlson included the novel concept of giving his men "ethical indoctrination" so that they would know what they were fighting for. Their exploits on the August 17, 1942, raid on Makin Island would be memorialized in the movie *Gung Ho*.

Another leader who Gittelsohn expressed great admiration for was Captain Leon Goldberg. Goldberg's exploits in the Eniwetok campaign were featured in the March 13, 1944, issue of *Life* magazine. Gittelsohn had the pleasure of meeting Goldberg in Hawaii after he returned from Eniwetok. He was both surprised and impressed to find Goldberg to be somewhat mild-mannered and almost timid-looking. Yet Goldberg had fearlessly led his men after the landings, and they unhesitatingly followed him into the fray. Goldberg called all of his men by their first name; they, in return, all called him "Goldy." Gittelsohn recorded his thoughts after meeting Goldberg: "Here was a group of men who knew that democracy was worth fighting for,—knew it because they were themselves living democracy then and there."[13]

It was the influence of Marine Corps leaders like Evans Carlson and Leon Goldberg that inspired Gittelsohn to begin his weekly evening discussion groups. His basic motivation was simple: In his opinion, the American military had done a great job teaching its soldiers, Sailors, and Marines how to fight. Yet it had done a poor job in teaching these men what they were fighting for. The main purpose of the groups was to answer the question "Why are we fighting?" If the men could truly answer that question, Gittelsohn felt that they would be more motivated and that their morale would be at its peak. The topics centered mostly on issues—social, ethical, political, moral—for which he believed the war was being waged.[14]

The discussion groups were open to all and averaged about fifteen participants per session. At first, due to the fact that these men had volunteered to participate in the groups, Gittelsohn thought that he would hear extraordinary thoughtfulness from the members about why the war was being fought. Much to his initial disappointment, however, he heard answers such as "To kill Japs before they kill me" and "It's my neck or theirs."[15] He felt that these goals were, of course, adequate for initial survival in combat, but he wanted his men to consider the long-range picture. He wanted them to see beyond this and to think forward towards a new world, the one that would be the result of their efforts. The combat skills and the necessary combat engagements were the means; a new, just world that emerged would be the end, the ultimate reason why they strove so hard to defeat the evil of the Axis powers.

In Gittelsohn's view, the inability to realize this end vision was America's greatest failure and potentially its most disastrous defeat. He decried the low level of political awareness in the military. In his view, the military in general had failed in this regard. He believed the Marines were probably the least politically aware since all servicemen in that branch—regardless of their ultimate specialty—were considered infantrymen. He felt it was not surprising that in an organization that had dedicated itself to sheer fighting skills, the big-picture goals for which they were fighting would sometimes be overlooked.[16]

Gittelsohn had no doubt that America's allies—the Russians, the Chinese, and the British—were more advanced than American fighting men were in their understanding of the goals for which they truly were fighting. Hence his creation of the discussion groups, from which he derived much satisfaction and through which he felt he was doing much to increase his men's awareness. Undoubtedly the inspiration for these discussion groups was truly the experience of Carlson's Raiders. Gittelsohn would refer to the Raiders many times in his notes about the groups.

The enthusiastic tone with which he wrote about the discussion groups and their purpose in his immediate post-war memoirs disappears in his reminiscences in his 1988 autobiography. The passage of time seemed to have erased the idealism with which he initially approached the groups during the war and replaced them with bitter memories. Upon reflection, the groups were an unintended source of pain and conflict for him.

In his autobiography, he revealed that he had, in fact, conducted two evening meetings a week, one on Monday nights, the other on Wednesday nights. The meetings were open to all who were interested. They proved to be a source of dissension and controversy, and Gittelsohn would reflect that he made two "cardinal sins." First, he invited black Marines to attend, and five or six regularly would attend. Secondly, he made the decision that all sides of important issues should be discussed as fairly as possible. His handling of both of his "sins" would do much to isolate him further from his peers and to mark him as a troublemaker in the eyes of his chain of command.

After Iwo Jima was secured and the Fifth Marine Division was able to return to Camp Tarawa, Gittelsohn resumed his twice-weekly discussion groups. Major General Thomas A. Bourke, who had replaced Gen Keller Rockey as the division commander on June 25, 1945, sent him a message via Division Chaplain Warren Cuthriell. General Bourke suggested that, since there were two weekly meetings, it perhaps would be a good idea to hold separate sessions for blacks and whites instead of mixing the races. Finding the suggestion extremely offensive, Gittelsohn responded back through his chain of command via Chaplain Cuthriell. In a response that bordered on disrespect to a superior officer, he stated, "'I promised faithfully never to interfere with the military leadership of the division, because I didn't consider myself to be an expert in that field; it would be greatly appreciated if the general would reciprocate when it came to my area of competence.' Dale Carnegie would not have approved."[17]

His efforts to present all sides of the various issues that were discussed also became a source of controversy within the division. As an example, to enhance the discussion of labor unions, he had written to various unions, requesting materials for the group. Among those from which he solicited information was the International Longshoreman's Union. At the time, the union was headed by Harry Bridges, an acknowledged Communist who had had been ordered deported by the attorney general of the United States. The issue was currently being decided by the Supreme Court. Gittelsohn would wryly note, "The fact that I also ordered pamphlets from the United States Chamber of Commerce and the National Association of Manufacturers was apparently considered irrelevant. I was a dangerous person to have around."[18]

In spite of the controversies generated by his discussion groups and the ill will that they engendered between him and his fellow chaplains, Roland Gittelsohn was convinced of their necessity. For him, answering the questions "Where do we go from here?" and "For what are we fighting?" was the key to the effort to build the morale of his Marines. He sincerely believed that his men should consider the type of world and society they wanted and envision an American way of life worthy of possibly sacrificing their lives for. In his own words, "The mere asking of questions, the churning of ideas, the stimulation of clear, honest thinking about goals, will be our most valuable aid in winning a war to obtain those goals."[19]

---

As the training for the upcoming invasion of "Island X" continued and intensified, it was perhaps inevitable that the festering resentment the other chaplains felt towards their outspoken assistant division chaplain would begin to be expressed more overtly. The subtle anti-Semitism that Gittelsohn had perceived up to this time also began to be expressed much more freely. The situation erupted in October of 1944 over printed religious materials that he had obtained for the regimental libraries.

Gittelsohn had learned of two pamphlets that he felt would be important materials for the libraries. One was published by the Anti-Defamation League of B'nai Brith and was a brief, effective compilation of questions and answers concerning popular misconceptions about Judaism and Jews. The other pamphlet, entitled "Fighting for America," was issued by the Jewish Welfare Board and detailed Jewish participation in the military history of the United States.

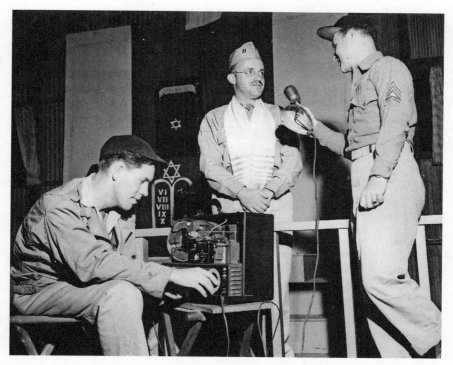

*Roland Gittelsohn (with his infamous moustache) doing radio broadcast from Hawaii, probably in 1944* (Courtesy United States Marine Corps)

At the time, there were about three hundred Jews in the Fifth Marine Division alone. Gittelsohn was no doubt attempting to dispel the negative stereotype that Jews were connivers who often tried to escape military service in World War I as well as in the current war. This was an all-too-common belief, especially in light of the fact that, until 1918, the Army Manual of Instructions for Medical Advisory Boards stated: "The foreign born, especially Jews, are more apt to malinger than the native born."[20] In reality, although Jews comprised only 3.3% of the United States population, they accounted for 4.23% of the United States armed forces during World War II.[21]

At a staff meeting for all of the division's chaplains, Gittelsohn brought copies of the two pamphlets and made them available to his colleagues so that they could be distributed to the regimental libraries. To his surprise, several of them refused to accept the material. One chaplain in particular made a scene in front of the entire group. Facing Gittelsohn, he angrily objected to both pamphlets. Claiming he had read both, he objected to the Jewish Welfare Board publication because it "made Jews out to be perfect patriots." Complaining about the Anti-Defamation League's publication, he stated unequivocally that the pamphlet was unacceptable because it stated that the Romans had crucified Jesus, while "anyone who knows anything at all knows that the Jews were guilty. If you want your Jewish boys to read this trash, give it to them yourself. I refuse to put it on the shelf for Christians to read!"[22]

On November 9, 1944, a particularly acrimonious exchange took place when Gittelsohn was confronted in a meeting with three of his division chaplains.[23] Present at the meeting with him that day were three Christian chaplains: Roman Catholic chaplain Fr. Paul F. Bradley, Rev. Glenn E. Baumann, an evangelical minister of the Reformed Church of America, and Roman Catholic chaplain Fr. John L. Ecker. Gittelsohn's notes written on that date described the venomous attacks delivered by his fellow chaplains.

Chaplain Baumann reiterated the complaint about the account of the crucifixion in one of the pamphlets. Why should he put this literature in his regimental library, he asked, when there weren't any Protestant or Catholic materials in the library? He then went on to complain about a prior chaplains' meeting that they all had sat through. With disdain, Baumann informed Gittelsohn that at that meeting's roundtable discussion he had listened to Gittelsohn talk for an hour about "the Negro problem," "a subject which wasn't important in the first place."

Chaplain Ecker proceeded to inform Gittelsohn the hatred many people felt towards Jews was most likely something that they brought on themselves. He noted that no child is born with prejudice, and then he posed the question of where it must come from. To Gittelsohn, he clearly implied that there was something wrong with the Jewish people that "naturally and automatically leads to prejudice."

It was Chaplain Bradley who was the most opinionated and outspoken at the meeting. Describing Bradley as the most popular priest in the division, Gittelsohn sat in stunned silence as he listened to his tirade. Gittelsohn, according to Bradley, was a poor chaplain because he spent too much time fighting anti-Semitism and not enough time teaching Judaism. As for the Jews in general, they controlled too much of the government. In Bradley's view, both Washington, DC, and New York City had gone too far in appeasing the Jews.

Bradley was just getting warmed up at this point. He began to ramble on with other assorted opinions about Jews in general. He began to lecture Gittelsohn on the Abraham Lincoln Battalion, the group of American volunteers who went to Spain in 1937 to fight in the Spanish Civil War on the side of the Spanish Republican forces against Franco's Nationalist forces. Many of these volunteers were members of the Communist Party as well as other socialist organizations. The brigade, Bradley informed Gittelsohn, was made up mostly of Jews. (Actual estimates put the percentage of Jews in the battalion between 25 and 30 percent.) While in the same train of thought, Bradley expounded his thoughts on who he felt were lapsed Catholics. The Basques, he informed the other three chaplains, were actually renegade Catholics who had been excommunicated since the early 1900s. Former New York governor Charles Poletti, a former activist in the Roosevelt administration, was another "lapsed Catholic" and target of Bradley's ire.

In an interesting thread of reasoning, Bradley presented Gittelsohn with this idea: should the Russians close all houses of worship except for one Catholic church and one synagogue in Moscow, he said, it would not be equal discrimination since there were so many fewer Jews than Catholics there. The labor movement next became the subject of Bradley's lecture. He informed the rabbi that the CIO Political Action Committee, a labor organization formed in 1943 to support President Roosevelt's 1944 campaign, was a communist organization and that "the Jews control and run it."

Bradley continued on with his tirade, next expressing his admiration for two of the most controversial Catholic priests of the era. Fr. Charles Coughlin, the notorious "Radio Priest," was a rabid anti-Semite who had a huge following in the United States before the war; Fr. Edward L. Curran, author of *One Hundred Great Moments in Catholic History*, was known as Coughlin's spokesman in the East.[24] According to Bradley, Edward L. Curran was a man "whose veracity can't be doubted." He went on to describe Fr. Coughlin, the admirer of fascists and staunch advocate of the notorious forgery *The Protocols of the Elders of Zion*, as "the greatest Catholic priest in the world. I'd kiss the ground he walks on."

To end the confrontation, the two priests demanded to know why Gittelsohn, as one of only three hundred Jews in the division, had been appointed as assistant division chaplain when there were no Catholics serving in the division chaplain's office, despite their much greater numbers. Gittelsohn patiently tried to explain that his appointment had resulted from Fifth Division policy, but the priests weren't satisfied. Ignoring Gittelsohn's point, they went on to state that the assistant division chaplain of the Fourth Marine Division was a Catholic priest. One of the regimental chaplains in the Fourth Marine Division was Rabbi (Lieutenant) Leon W. Rosenberg, who had graduated from the Naval Training School for Chaplains two weeks after Gittelsohn.

The following morning, one of the Christian chaplains who was present when the other three confronted Gittelsohn came to his quarters to speak with him. Obviously embarrassed by the behavior of his colleagues, he looked his fellow Jewish chaplain in the eye and sincerely said, "I just wanted you to understand clearly and directly that far from all of us feel the way . . . does. If there's anything I can do, now or ever, to cooperate, I want to be called on."[25]

Less than two months later, they would all be departing for the invasion they had been training for. It had become obvious to Gittelsohn that he was greatly resented by his fellow chaplains for a number of reasons, and that anti-Semitism was a large factor in this resentment. Yet, in spite of all of the dissension in their ranks, the chaplains as a team would perform superbly in the upcoming Iwo Jima campaign, displaying courage and working together to minister to all of their Marines. The rancor would once again rear its head when the island was secured.

# Chapter Twenty-Two

# Invasion

Since June of 1944, aircraft launched from the Navy's aircraft carriers had bombed Iwo Jima daily. In addition, B-24 bombers from the Seventh Air Force flying out of Saipan would also bomb the island daily in preparation for the invasion that the Japanese defenders knew was ultimately coming. By the time of the amphibious landing, Iwo Jima would have suffered the most prolonged bombing campaign of any of the islands in the Pacific war.

That fall, the invasion plans were formulated. The senior Marine Corps officer ashore would be MajGen Harry "The Dutchman" Schmidt. He would be the commanding general of the Fifth Amphibious Corps, which consisted of the three component divisions. The Fourth Marine Division was commanded by Major General Clifton Cates, the Fifth Marine Division was commanded by Major General Keller Rockey, and the Third Marine Division was commanded by Major General Graves Erskine.

The Marines would land on the southeastern beaches at Iwo Jima. The beaches were divided into seven adjacent landing beaches, each five hundred yards wide. They were color-coded, starting with Green Beach near the base of Mount Suribachi. In sequence going eastward, the other beaches were called Red Beach 1, Red Beach 2, Yellow Beach 1, Yellow Beach 2, Blue Beach 1, and Blue Beach 2. The First and Second Battalions of the Twenty-Eighth Marine Regiment, Fifth Marine Division would land on Green Beach, the Second Battalion, Twenty-Seventh Marine Regiment, Fifth Marine Division would land on Red Beach 1, and the First Battalion of the Twenty-Seventh Marine Regiment, Fifth Marine Division would land on Red Beach 2. To the right, the Fourth Marine Division would make its landings on Yellow Beach 1, Yellow Beach 2, and Blue Beach 1. Originally, the Third Marine Division was to be held back as a floating reserve and would remain eighty miles out at sea. That would change on the first day of the battle when the extremely high casualty rates necessitated using elements of the Third Marine Division as part of the landing force.[1]

In addition to the experienced, battle-hardened Marines that comprised the three divisions, each division had replacement battalions of 2,650 men each. The vast majority of these replacements were green; most of the troops were fresh from boot camp and had little advanced combat training or were older men reporting from desk jobs back in the States. Over 250 were new second lieutenants who recently completed the platoon leader's school in Quantico, Virginia. These nearly eight thousand men facing a baptism of fire generated deep concern, from General Smith down to the platoon level.[2]

While the Fifth Marine Division trained on Hawaii, the Fourth Marine Division did its advanced training on the island of Maui, and the Third Marine Division trained on Guam. Every day, these Marines climbed steep slopes and staged frontal attacks against mock pillboxes and bunkers. The combat training conditions were realistic, featuring live machine gun and artillery fire and ordnance delivered from Marine aircraft to simulate combat conditions. Veterans of prior Pacific island campaigns sensed that this upcoming operation would be "a real man-killer, no pun intended," in the words of a gunnery sergeant who had fought at Guadalcanal. The ruggedness of the training, always very strenuous as another campaign neared, was the clue.[3] There was no liberty and no place to go even if there was liberty. For months, the Marines had been training for another amphibious invasion of an island somewhere in the Pacific. Had they known the name of the island they were training to invade, most of them would have shrugged their shoulders and admitted that they never heard of it. For a few weeks longer, the men of the Fifth Amphibious Corps would only know that they were training to invade "Island X."

On Christmas Eve, 1944, the men of the Fourth and Fifth Marine Divisions celebrated with huge Christmas dinners. On the following day, December 25, 1944, lead elements of the Fifth Marine Division boarded the attack transport *Athene* amid cheers and well-wishes of many local residents. Another farewell celebration was repeated two days later, on December 27, when the men of the Fourth Marine Division came down from Camp Maui and boarded their transport ships. The last units of the Fifth Marine Division pulled out of Hawaii on January 4. The men of the Third Marine Division on Guam, located fifteen hundred miles closer to Iwo Jima, wouldn't embark for another five weeks.[4]

The three Marine divisions would all rendezvous off of Saipan. Prior to leaving Hawaiian waters, the Fourth and Fifth Divisions made rehearsal landings on Maui and Kahoolawe. The landings were best described as "chaotic," but by the first week in January, all remaining elements of the Fourth and the Fifth Divisions had departed Hawaii. On February 14, the Fifth Amphibious Corps made a final dress rehearsal before leaving Saipan. Marines climbed down the cargo nets into their landing craft and made runs to the beaches. Again, realistic combat conditions utilizing live ordnance was the order of the day. Two days later, all of the ships had left Magicienne Bay, headed for Iwo Jima.

Meanwhile, the bombing campaign against Iwo Jima intensified. Starting with the December 8 raid, where 212 B-24s and fighter aircraft attacked the Chidori Airfield, Iwo Jima would be pounded daily from the skies and from frequent close-in naval shelling by US Navy ships often only a mile offshore. From their deeply fortified underground caves, bunkers, and tunnels, General Kuribayashi and his men waited for the Americans, who they knew were going to use Iwo Jima—if they conquered it—as a stepping-stone to invade their homeland. The orders were issued: when the Americans landed, General Kuribayashi's men would fight to the death with the command "No man must die until he has killed at least ten Americans."[5]

———•———

In the first week of January 1945, LT Roland Gittelsohn, assistant division chaplain of the Fifth Marine Division, departed Hawaii aboard the USS *Deuel* (APA-160), a Haskell-class attack transport ship. On the ship that would be their home for the next five weeks, all eighty officers lived in cramped quarters in a space equivalent to a five-room apartment. The average bunk had half the headroom of a Pullman lower.[6] Although he and his fellow officers were "hot . . . nervous, irritated, and lonely" in these living conditions, Gittelsohn also recalled that there was no quarreling and that everyone demonstrated the utmost respect for one another. Noting that "there was an unconscious consideration and kindness on the part of the men who knew that in all literal truth they were 'in the same boat,'" he proudly commented on the fact that "men facing the most uncomfortable present and the most frightening future of their lives were wonderfully human toward each other!"[7]

The deployment from Hawaii to Iwo Jima took forty days. After rendezvousing off Saipan in early February, 485 surface ships prepared for the six-hundred-mile journey to their destination. During the forty-day transit, the Marines learned the real name of "Island X" for the first time. They were informed that they would be landing at an island called Iwo Jima.

As the seventy-mile-long convoy headed north, the Marines noted the drop in evening temperatures. This was a distinct change for most veterans of the prior Pacific campaigns. The days remained warm enough for the men to sun themselves on the decks during daylight. To pass the time, they played cards, chess, and checkers and repeatedly checked their weapons and their ammunition. They talked about anything and everything—their families, women, and liberty experiences—and reviewed their training exercises and maps and studied the models of the island. In short, they discussed anything to escape the boredom of their time at sea, as well as to distract themselves from their anxiety over the coming battle, which they all knew would be horrific.[8]

On February 16, Rear Admiral William "Spike" Blandy's Task Force 54 arrived off the coast of Iwo Jima. Consisting initially of six battleships, five cruisers, and multiple destroyers, the ships commenced their bombardment of the island as planned by Admiral Nimitz and his staff. Poor weather and limited visibility that day necessitated an additional day of bombardment.

On the morning of February 17, the weather had cleared and Blandy's ships closed to within three thousand yards of the shore. Advancing toward the beach, Japanese spotters saw a flotilla of rocket-firing Landing Craft Infantry (LCI) ships closing in. General Kuribayashi was placed in a quandary: was this the invasion force? In fact, these smaller ships carried a crew of fifty Sailors and about 100 frogmen from the Navy's Underwater Demolition Team (UDT). Their mission was to check the beach for landing obstacles and to obtain soil samples for analysis.

Kuribayashi made one of the few serious errors of the defensive campaign and concluded that this was indeed the invasion landing force approaching. Immediately, all of the Japanese defensive sites opened fire. They wreaked havoc on the LCIs, but by doing so they revealed their positions to Task Force 54's gunners, who proceeded to decimate all exposed Japanese positions.[9]

Meanwhile, many of the frogmen made it to the beach, where they took their soil samples. They would be able to report that the bottom terrain at the beach line was firm and clear of obstructions, but the surf just a few yards from the shore was nearly six feet high. In a display of humor that can only be exhibited by men facing deadly combat, the frogmen planted a small sign on the beach that read "Welcome to Iwo Jima."[10]

That night, believing that he had repulsed the initial American landing attempt on Iwo Jima, General Kuribayashi radioed the Imperial Army headquarters in Tokyo that he had beaten back the Americans, but he knew that they would be back very soon. To boost the morale of the Japanese people, Radio Tokyo announced that evening: "On February 17 in the morning, enemy troops tried to land on the island of Iwo. The Japanese garrison at once attacked these troops and repelled them into the sea."[11]

Aboard the American warships gathered off the shore of Iwo Jima, the men of the invasion force listened to the Japanese broadcast with both surprise and, no doubt, joy over the misinterpretation of the day's events by the Japanese High Command. Aboard the *Deuel*, Gittelsohn recorded the day's events in his notes. "1-2 underwater demolition and recon. teams went in to within 100 yds. on ea. coast, under intense naval gunfire- spent 90 min. on each side- UDT men swim under w. spec. apparatus to destroy underwater obstacles & mines- Japs reported this as having repulsed 2 landing attempts this day!"[12] This was tempered by the other broadcast that many of the Americans also listened to that night. With uncanny accuracy, Tokyo Rose announced the names of the units that would be involved in the landings and which beaches they would land at. After naming many of the ships involved in the American armada, she went on to assure her listeners that although the Americans had required a huge number of ships to get them to the island, the survivors would later be able to be fit into a phone booth.[13]

By the morning of the 19th, D-Day, two more battleships and

three more cruisers had joined Task Force 54. On this fourth day of the bombardment, Blandy's battleships moved within a mile and a half of the beaches and were able to destroy over two-thirds of the exposed guns and blockhouses in their target areas near the beaches and strip away camouflage that revealed even more targets to Blandy's forces. The last three hours of the third bombardment day was effective, but there were still many targets that had been untouched.[14] The reality was that by the time of the bombardment, a veritable city of twenty-two thousand was functioning below the surface of Iwo Jima.[15] American intelligence had concluded that, due to the lack of potable water, there could only be about thirteen thousand Japanese troops there. Most of the Japanese forces and their weaponry were underground, undetectable by aerial reconnaissance.[16] Clearly, more pre-invasion bombardment would have helped eliminate detected targets on the island, but they were out of time. The landings were to take place as scheduled on the morning of February 19.

---

On February 18, the officers and men aboard the USS *Deuel* sat through their final briefings. Gittelsohn's wartime notes describe the multiple topics covered, including "size, relief-maps . . . geography, history, S.O.P, no. of enemy troops & units involved & their jobs, beach terraces . . . Jap emplacements, results of preliminary bombardments."[17] The officers were told to expect approximately seven hundred deaths per division. Based on that estimate, the Fifth Marine Division staff planned a cemetery that could hold nine hundred bodies. The grim reality would prove much worse than they could imagine. After thirty-five days of combat on Iwo Jima, 2,280 men were buried in the Fifth Marine Division Cemetery and several hundred others would be missing in action.[18]

That evening, Gittelsohn and the Protestant chaplain aboard the *Deuel* delivered a joint pre-invasion religious service over the 1MC, the ship's public address system. After the service, he was asked to speak to the men; Gittelsohn spoke from the heart. "Men," he said, "I'm going to be speaking in these next few minutes quite as much to myself as to you. We're in this thing together. The same fears and doubts and high hopes which fill your hearts tonight are in mine." He proceeded to remind them of the spiritual weapons that he and his follow chaplains could add to their physical arms and ammunition when they hit the beaches the following morning. He spoke of the love of their parents and wives who were with them all despite the many intervening miles. He reminded them of the pride they all felt, not only in the United States Marine Corps, but in themselves. "It's you and I who will win this campaign with our tanks and planes, not they with us . . . You may fire the shot that will break the enemy's back. You may, by your own example of courage give strength to fifty other men and they to five hundred more."

Lastly, he spoke of faith: faith in themselves, in each other, and in all who supported them. And of course, faith in God — "a Power that makes for righteousness and insures the triumph of righteousness."

He offered them no guarantees, only hope. Closing his message, he stated, "God bless you! May we win our objective with the least possible loss. May we carry through, each of us so that he never need be ashamed of himself. And may we return speedily to our dear ones to carry on with them in peace our struggle for the rights of common people everywhere. Amen."[19]

In both his wartime memoir, written in 1945, and in his autobiography, written in 1988, Gittelsohn recalled that weeks later, when ministering to the wounded after the battle in the division field hospital, many of his Marines, both Jewish and Christian, told him how much his words broadcast on February 18 meant to them and helped sustain them in the critical hours after they had been hit.[20]

After the broadcasts, both Gittelsohn and the Protestant chaplain were assigned cabins that night so they could conduct personal consultations with the men. Arriving at his cabin, Gittelsohn was at first puzzled by the long line of Marines waiting to meet with him. Certainly, he noted, there appeared to be many more Marines in line than those he had identified as being Jewish in the seven weeks they had been at sea since leaving Hawaii. In a very short while, the rabbi figured out what was going on. A number of those who waited impatiently in line to see him had already visited the Protestant chaplain, and still others were planning to see Gittelsohn first and the other chaplain next. The men of the Fifth Marine Division were "covering their bases" and taking no chances. The next day, these young men, both Christians and Jews, would be carrying crucifixes or crosses supplied by the Protestant chaplain, *mezuzot* given to them by Rabbi Gittelsohn, and pocket Bibles provided by both of them.[21]

That night, Gittelsohn tried to meet each man who had come to see him "where he was; this was not the time for theological instruction." He was ministering to the young men's needs, acting all at once as friend, mentor, father figure, and spiritual advisor. After all, he was an older man of thirty-four, and with his owlish, professorial look, he no doubt reminded his men of their high school teachers and college professors. He was a source of comfort and strength to his Marines, many of whom would not be alive less than a day later. Never before had these young men needed the assistance and guidance of a chaplain more than on the night of February 18, 1945; and, for many, this assistance and guidance would never be needed so badly again.

# Chapter Twenty-Three

# Heat of Battle

At 3:00 a.m. reveille sounded aboard all of the invasion force ships. Marines dressed, prepared their weapons and gear, and had their final breakfast. Daylight soon began to pierce the night sky, and through broken clouds, a clear, sunny day was emerging. At 6:30 a.m. the order was passed: "Land the landing force!" Aboard landing craft—the LSTs—amphibious tractors were manned, and on larger transport ships, Higgins boats were lowered into the water as cargo nets were slung over the sides. In short order, Marines began descending the netting and began loading the landing craft.

Next, the last shore bombardment commenced. Beginning at 6:40 a.m., the battleships and cruisers unleashed a final torrent of heavy shelling on the beach that continued until 8:05 a.m. Next it was the turn of the carrier-based aircraft. Seventy-two Navy Corsairs, Hellcat fighters, and Dauntless bombers began bombing and strafing runs on the island's beaches. This final murderous bombing assault on the landing beaches served to reassure the Marines as they watched from their ships and landing craft. They felt certain that there could be no one near the beaches who could possibly survive such an onslaught.

At 8:30 a.m. sixty-eight amphibious tractors (amtracs) crossed the Line of Departure four thousand yards from the shore and began their half-hour run to the beaches. Crewed by three men, the first wave of amtracs carried no assault troops. Their job was to hit the beach, destroy any enemy positions they found, and to fight their way fifty yards inland to set up a defense perimeter for the landing force. Five minutes after they crossed the Line of Departure, the final naval bombardment commenced. In total, eight thousand more shells landed on the beaches in less than a half hour in the final push to clear the beaches just before the amtracs went ashore.[1]

The bombardment ended, and the first wave of amtracs landed on the beach and performed their assigned task. Following closely after were six more waves of amtracs carrying Marine assault troops, landing at five-minute intervals. Each wave would have 1,360 men. Hundreds of Higgins boats followed in succeeding waves, landing Marines to consolidate and expand their beachhead. Four regiments formed the spearhead of the attack: the Twenty-Third and the Twenty-Fifth Regiments of the Fourth Marine Division landing on the right (on Yellow 1, Yellow 2, and Blue 1 landing beaches), and the Twenty-Seventh and Twenty-Eighth Regiments of the Fifth Marine Division landing on the left (on Green, Red 1 and Red 2 landing beaches).[2]

At 9:02 a.m. the first amtracs hit the beaches, two minutes behind the planned H-Hour. At 9:05 a.m., the first troop-carrying amtracs came ashore at the beaches. Hell on earth was about to begin.

———•———

Like virtually all of his shipmates, LT Roland Gittelsohn slept poorly if at all the night of February 18. During the day, he had learned that he would not be going ashore for at least two days. The USS *Deuel* had been designated as a casualty-receiving ship; once the Marine combat troops departed on D-Day, it would then be used as a hospital ship. The command element of the division felt Gittelsohn would be more valuable ministering to the casualties that would be brought back to the ship. At that point, he would be the only chaplain on board.

At 3 a.m., when reveille sounded, he got out of his rack and got dressed. After eating breakfast with his Marines, he went topside with the men and spent the morning walking back and forth on the deck, talking with and encouraging them as they were preparing to go over the side. While watching the Marines climb down the cargo net—something they had done many times and had become quite proficient at—it struck him that this time it really was different. This was no longer a rehearsal. And many of them would not be returning to the ship from the island they were about to invade.

He would later recall two young Marines to whom he spoke at length that morning. Although Gittelsohn was unable to recall details of his discussion with the first Marine, two months after the battle the young man wrote to him from the naval hospital where he was recovering from his combat wounds. He thanked Gittelsohn profusely and doubted whether he would have "made it" without the chaplain's words.[3]

The second man was a young pharmacist's mate who was terrified to go into combat. He was red-eyed from the lack of sleep and was trembling with anxiety when they spoke on the morning of the 19th. "What could I possibly say?" Gittelsohn wrote in retrospect. "Only that I understood his fear and shared it, that there would have been something abnormal about both of us if we felt other than we did. Whatever my words, he managed somehow to do what he had to and forty-eight hours later, when my turn came, I did the same."[4]

For the first three horrible days that he was ashore, Gittelsohn had no contact with the pharmacist's mate. But on the fourth day, he saw the young man's name on the list of men that he would be burying that day in the Fifth Marine Division cemetery. Later, after talking to the Marine's colleagues, Gittelsohn was able to piece together what had happened. In the midst of a savage Japanese counterattack, the young man had taken refuge in a shell hole. From about thirty yards away, he heard the moans of a wounded Marine crying for help. He selflessly set out to render medical aid to his wounded brother in arms, despite the carnage all around him. As he reached the wounded Marine, a Japanese shell exploded nearby. The shrapnel killed the brave man who only less than a week before had shared his deep fears with his chaplain.

On the morning of D-Day, Gittelsohn spotted a young major who he knew from the Twenty-Sixth Regiment. The major, a young officer of about thirty years of age, was, like Gittelsohn, a redhead. Gittelsohn saw him in a landing craft next to the *Deuel*, ready to embark to the rendezvous point just before H-Hour. The two men waved to each other as the boat headed away with the other landing craft. Gittelsohn would next see the major five weeks later on Iwo Jima. His hair had turned completely white.[5]

It wasn't long after the last of the combat troops had left the ship that the first casualties began arriving on the *Deuel*. For the former pacifist, the scene was horrifying.

Torn flesh . . . broken bones . . . shattered minds; every man demanded and deserved immediate attention. Neither the doctors nor I, the only chaplain still on board, knew where to turn first. I, who had always felt faint at the sight of blood, who would still turn pale if blood flowed in my presence now, stood by an improvised surgical table, holding a young casualty's hand while hunks of shrapnel were being dug out of his knee. The boy's face was pale with pain; his teeth had punctured his lips with blood; his fingernails dug into my palm so deeply that marks were still visible hours later. But each time I inquired about the pain, his grim answer was the same, "Okay, padre!"[6]

It was the beginning of thirty-five days of death and destruction that Gittelsohn, along with his fellow Marines, would become intimately familiar with. It was also the beginning of a five-week demonstration of courage, valor, and love for one's comrades-in-arms that would profoundly affect their chaplain. Admiral Nimitz would later summarize the heroism of the United States Marines at Iwo Jima with a short phrase that is now carved into the pedestal of the US Marine Corps War Memorial in Washington, DC: "Uncommon valor was a common virtue." Gittelsohn's wartime notes and reminiscences would contain numerous instances of individual acts of heroism, and his admiration and love for these men was obvious.

His anecdote about Hospital Corpsman Joshua Rosenfeld is one of many such stories documented by the chaplain. On the first day of the campaign, Joshua saw one of his buddies blown back by a mortar shell explosion. Rushing to his aid, Rosenfeld saw that three of the Marine's fingers had been blown off. Temporarily stopping the bleeding with pressure dressings, the corpsman knew that he needed to get his patient back for surgery. Yet the injured Marine was unable to walk, and mortar shells continued to rain down around them. Having no other options, he picked the injured Marine up on his shoulder and turned toward the beach. Carrying him several hundred yards to an aid station where he could receive care from one of the surgeons, he dropped off his injured patient and then returned to his duties. For his heroism, he was recommended for a Bronze Star.

Gittelsohn later learned of the incident and confronted Rosenfeld, a young man he had become friendly with, and complimented him on his heroic deed. Rosenfeld looked at him "as if [Gittelsohn] spoke a language he didn't understand, and said: 'Heroism? What else could I have done?'"[7]

As the Marines rushed off their amtracs, they confronted an unexpected obstacle. The surveillance maps of the beaches used for planning the landings were derived from aerial reconnaissance photographs taken in July 1944.[8] The maps accurately documented that about thirty yards from the surf the terrain sloped upward in a series of three terraces, each about eight feet high and sixteen feet apart.[9] The first terrace off the beaches varied from four to nine feet high. The materials also indicated that the beaches were volcanic sand. However, the Marines quickly learned that these were not typical, sandy beaches. Instead, they were landing on fine, black volcanic ash. With each step, their feet would sink to calf depth in the ash. This also made traction for the amtracs much more difficult, if not impossible.

The volcanic ash, combined with the steeply angled terraces off of the beaches, made departure off the beachhead much more difficult than anticipated. Even Gittelsohn would comment on this in his wartime notes under the title "Mistakes Discovered": "Sand wouldn't hold vehicles, many more caves than expected, more underground protection from naval gunfire, no scrub typhus, 1100 civilians evacuated in Nov., grades up from beaches much steeper, over 20,000 Japs instead of 14,000."[10] However, remaining on the beach was not an option, and the Marines would have to get organized and proceed on with their mission.

The Fourth Marine Division landing on the Yellow and Blue Beaches and the Twenty-Seventh Regiment of the Fifth Marine Division landing on the Red Beaches were tasked to go forward and take the nearby Chidori airfield, then designated as Airfield Number One. From there, the Marines would swing right and methodically take the other two airfields and push to the far end of Iwo Jima, killing all Japanese forces who resisted. Confident that the Japanese knew Iwo Jima was the last major obstacle to unlimited American bombing of their homeland, the Marines didn't anticipate taking many prisoners. In the end, of the more than twenty-two thousand Japanese troops on Iwo Jima, only 1,083 would be taken prisoner and survive the battle.

On the far-left side of the landing beaches, First and Second

Battalions of the Twenty-Eighth Regiment, Fifth Marine Division had a different D-Day mission. After landing on Green Beach, the two thousand men of the Twenty-Eighth Regiment, commanded by Colonel Harry "The Horse" Liversedge, would advance forward, cut across the neck of the island to the western shore, and cut off Mount Suribachi from the rest of the island. Next, they would swing to the left to scale and conquer Mount Suribachi, code-named "Hot Rocks" by the mission planners.

But first they all had to get off the beaches. Tanks, artillery, and amtracs were getting bogged down in the volcanic ash. More and more troops were landing, but the beach was getting too crowded to land more equipment. Offshore, more boats carrying troops and heavy equipment began circling, waiting for the beaches to clear. Bulldozers were landed to attempt to carve a path for the tanks. Meanwhile, the troops were getting organized and forming into fighting units. Luckily, the resistance was very light, with only scattered small-arms fire. The Marines began to believe that maybe the naval bombardment had broken the Japanese defenses.

They were wrong. This was all part of Kuribayashi's plan to lure the enemy ashore and then, from the hidden and underground machine-gun fire and artillery, unleash massive firepower and destroy them. Kuribayashi had waited until the beaches were jammed with immobile tanks and trucks. By 10 a.m., there were 6,200 Marines ashore on the small three-thousand-yard beachhead. The hidden Japanese forces then opened fire, reigning death upon the Marines. The volcanic ash made it impossible to dig foxholes for protection. The trapped tanks and artillery pieces became prime targets for Japanese gunners. Initially unable to clear the clogged beaches, unable to land more gear, and unable to evacuate casualties, the situation appeared grim by afternoon.

But Kuribayashi had waited too long to spring his trap, and there were over six thousand Americans ashore—proud, well-trained, disciplined, and determined United States Marines. While they had but few tanks and some artillery, they had their tradition and their belief. The Japanese were about to learn something about the Marines that Roland Gittelsohn already knew: They had something of everything needed to fight and survive for the time being. And they had faith that help would soon come; faith that, because they were Marines, they would pull through and win again.[11]

By late afternoon the Marine infantrymen had cleared the beaches and advanced against the murderous Japanese counterattacks. The original D-Day objective had been to secure the southern half of the island, including Mount Suribachi and the two operational airfields. But the savage Japanese defenses, coupled with the onerous landing-beach conditions, had made this impossible. The Americans had pushed across the southern neck of Iwo Jima and isolated Mount Suribachi. In addition, they had reached the southern edge of the primary airfield. By 7:00 p.m., it was dark and the Marines dug in the best they could as they fought off the chill of a cold night. They were hyper-vigilant, expecting banzai attacks throughout the night, consistent with Japanese tactics in the past. This was not to be—General Kuribayashi had other plans for the Marines. Shelling of Marine positions continued throughout the night. Very few Marines got much sleep with shells exploding all around them. Offshore, naval gunfire provided by US Navy battleships and gunboats pounded suspected Japanese positions, adding to the constant noise. On the beaches, shore parties worked nonstop unloading gear and supplies while bulldozers continued to carve out roadways for tanks and artillery. Casualties piled up on the beaches, awaiting transport to hospital ships and transport ships with medical facilities.

As dawn broke the following morning, Gen Holland Smith met with reporters aboard the USS *Eldorado*. After expressing surprise that there had been no banzai attacks during the night, he paid a compliment to General Kuribayashi. "I don't know who he is, but the Jap general running the show is one smart bastard."[12] He also realized that the large number of casualties would require that he land elements of the Third Marine Division.

In Washington, DC, Pres. Franklin D. Roosevelt was briefed at the White House on the results of D-Day of the Iwo Jima Campaign. At the end of the briefing he was given the grim news: 2,312 Marines had died that day. Author Jim Bishop reported, "It was the first time in the war, through good news and bad, that anyone had seen the President gasp in horror."[13]

# Chapter Twenty-Four

# Uncommon Valor

For the first two days of the Iwo Jima campaign, Roland Gittelsohn remained on board the *Deuel*, ministering to the wounded and dying. He, like all the crewmembers, was astonished and sickened by the amount of casualties they received. Yet every one of them did their jobs, and none faltered. A sadly typical experience was that of Lieutenant Commander J. H. McCauley, a Navy surgeon aboard one of the attack transports that became a casualty receiving ship once the Marines went ashore. Their ship had expected to handle twenty casualties at most on D-Day. They ended up handling seventy-four.[1]

Gittelsohn would theorize how the doctors, corpsmen, and chaplains could do their jobs day in and day out and not seem to let it affect them. He would refer to it as "combat anesthesia" and compared notes with other Iwo Jima veterans to see if his experience was similar to theirs in this respect. Not surprisingly, it was. "We felt at the time almost as if we were doped," he wrote.[2] He explained it to his sister in a letter he wrote from Hawaii after the battle. In a letter to her brother, she commented on his behavior, to which he replied:

> You know, it's strange reading that you think I was strong on Iwo. Somehow I don't impress me that way at all. The feeling one has in combat is hard to describe. All I know is that no one was weaker or more utterly frightened than I on the way up to Iwo, and now in recollection I wonder whether I was really able to go through the things the papers say I did. During our actual days on the island no one had time or energy to ask questions or to analyze whether he is weak or strong. It was almost like being under the influence of anesthesia: you had a job to do, so you did it. It was as simple as that. You didn't dare sit or stand in one place too long because you didn't want a sniper to get a "bead" on you. So you kept rushing around,

I suspect quite as much to get away from yourself as to avoid the snipers. Now in retrospect some of the things I had very little trouble living through bother me now more than they did then. But whatever you do, don't credit me with being strong in combat; no one but a fool is. The rest of us just acted like a bunch of marionettes whose strings were being skillfully manipulated.[3]

On February 21, Gittelsohn went ashore to Iwo Jima. Embarking on a landing craft, their arrival on the beach was delayed by wreckage blocking their original landing site. The sea was choppy on the half-hour run to the shore, and the chaplain felt slightly seasick. As they approached the beach, he noted that they were lucky they weren't greeted with mortar fire; but as soon as they hit the beach, sniper fire buzzed all around them. Gittelsohn's notes indicate that he landed on the beach with a Marine named Sanders and Dr. Daniel McCarthy, the Twenty-Eighth Regimental Surgeon. A half-hour after they landed, both were killed by enemy fire. McCarthy was hit by an enemy shell near the beach as he was heading over to help identify the body of a hospital corpsman.[4] Soon after, the Twenty-Eighth Regimental Chaplain, Fr. Paul Bradley, wrote to McCarthy's uncle and namesake, Fr. Daniel McCarthy of Savannah, Georgia, offering his condolences to the young surgeon's family.[5]

His first night on Iwo Jima, Gittelsohn was settled in a foxhole just off the beach. Mortar fire continued around him throughout the night, as it would his entire first week ashore. That first night, he witnessed combat on the beach that he would write about in his wartime notes as well as in his autobiography. On the beach, he watched shore parties unload much-needed supplies and equipment from a Landing Ship Tank (LST). About fifty yards away from the LST were a hundred drums of gasoline and ammunition that had been offloaded from other ships and were awaiting transport inland. Gittelsohn and his colleagues watched with horror as deadly accurate gunfire suddenly began raining down on the LST. The source of the Japanese shell's accuracy became apparent to them—they were able to see Japanese forward observers with binoculars on a partially sunken barge near the beach who were directing fire on the LST. The accuracy of the Japanese gunners was impressive. Eleven straight salvos hit the LST directly. To the Americans' astonishment and gratitude, none of the shells hit any of the drums nearby. Gittelsohn acknowledged his appreciation for the gunner's accuracy, stating, "Jap F. O.'s so accurate 11 consec. shots hit the LST, with none over on drums- hit there would have wiped out whole left flank of the beach."[6]

Gittelsohn would later ask several of the men who had offloaded the LST how they felt on that nerve-wracking night. "Felt? They didn't have time to feel," he noted. They had a mission to accomplish and "in their crowded, benumbed consciousness at that moment there was room for nothing else." Later, when Gittelsohn would discuss with them the close call they had experienced, he noted that their faces were perceptibly pale when they realized the full measure of what they had been through almost unwittingly. This, he would explain, was another instance of "combat anesthesia."[7]

---

Like all chaplains who see combat, Roland Gittelsohn's mission was to minister to the needs of his fellow warriors, to be with them during their time in battle and encourage, counsel, and support them. As he learned very quickly, the chaplain's job was also to be with his wounded men, visiting them and comforting them in battalion aid stations and field hospitals. And the toughest task of all—to be with his men, preparing them to meet their God, as they lay dying in his presence. All of the chaplains with the Marines at Iwo Jima performed these tasks exceedingly well. Having their chaplains at the front lines right alongside of them provided an immeasurable boost to all of the Marines' morale. As Gittelsohn recorded in his notes: "Gratitude of men on seeing them either at hosp. or in front lines- Talked of latter weeks afterward-"[8]

For the remainder of his time on Iwo Jima, Gittelsohn, like all of the Marines, was faced with the possibility of his own death. In several instances, his life would be spared by intervals that could be measured in inches or minutes. Once ashore, all of the Marines had to dig foxholes to sleep in, and their chaplains were not exempt from this duty. The rabbi learned to sleep as best as he could with intermittent to constant shelling taking place throughout the night. One morning he awakened to a stunning surprise. Less than a foot from the edge of his foxhole lay a foot-long piece of shrapnel. Had it landed only a few inches closer, it probably would have killed him.[9]

At Iwo Jima, there were no rear areas. Every single inch was a front line, a lesson that Gittelsohn learned very quickly. On several occasions, it seemed that fate intervened to spare his life. On the beach one morning he noted, "I once stood talking to a Marine not more than ten yards away; a sniper's bullet struck him and instantly killed him."[10] He recognized a similar situation in his wartime notes: "W. O. Stelburg killed by mortar on beach where we were before and after." In the same note, he documented that on his tenth day ashore, "boy hit by mortar 15' from us on hill."[11] Towards the end of his life, he would reflect on the thirty-five days of combat on Iwo Jima and succinctly distill his thoughts thusly: "How a single one of us left Iwo alive is a miracle."[12]

During the first two days of combat on Iwo Jima, most of the dead Marines were left where they fell. Not only was there no place to bury them but the Marines on the beachhead were also facing continual machine gun, small arms, and mortar fire from the determined Japanese defenders. These unburied dead raised serious health—as well as morale—issues. The organizers of the invasion had factored this into in the overall battle plan. Late in the afternoon of D-Day plus one, the Graves Registration Officer of the Fourth Marine Division and his team landed on Yellow Beach to begin the gruesome but necessary task of burying the dead as soon as possible. The following morning, D-Day plus two, their counterparts from the Fifth Marine Division landed on Red Beach.[13]

The cemetery for the Fifth Division was located furthest west, close to the base of Mount Suribachi. The Third and Fourth Division cemeteries were located side by side near the north-south runway of Airfield Number One, now designated as Motoyama Number One. All three cemeteries were studded with land mines that had to be defused or detonated before the burials could actually begin. Additionally, cemetery workers had the constant threat of small-arm and mortar fire when they established the burial grounds.[14]

Roland Gittelsohn spent much of his time ashore on Iwo Jima in the Fifth Marine Division Cemetery. It proved to be harrowing work. It was not possible to know the religion of every man buried because sometimes all they had to bury was a burlap sack containing fragments of bones and flesh; in many instances this was all that remained of a young United States Marine. Accordingly, it was division policy to have a Catholic, a Protestant, and a Jewish chaplain on hand. Gittelsohn, of course, was the only Jewish chaplain in the Fifth Marine Division.[15]

In writing about his work in the Fifth Marine Division Cemetery, Gittelsohn repeatedly reflected on two thoughts. The first was the day-to-day horror of working in the cemetery and having to bury young men who only a few days before were living, dedicated Americans with bright, hopeful futures. The other was the fortitude, courage, and inner strength that all of the Marines who worked in the cemetery displayed every day. Just as he would think about the doctors and corpsmen, he would remember the men who worked with him at the cemetery and wonder, "Where did they get the strength?"

The Fifth Marine Division assigned fifty black Marines and twenty-five white Marines to duty at the cemetery. This became their full-time job for almost a month. They worked all day, every day for the duration of the battle, performing such grim tasks as trying to identify body parts and going through the pockets of their dead fellow Marines. Not infrequently, they would discover the body of a friend, often burned, maimed, and mutilated. Lastly, they had the solemn duty of digging the graves and burying their fallen comrades. Gittelsohn spent two to three hours a day at the cemetery, and his experiences there profoundly affected his emotions. "I found as a chaplain that my two or three hours a day in the cemetery taxed more than the last ounce of my endurance and strength."[16]

The sheer number of casualties required that the internments be a mass and somewhat impersonal affair. Bulldozers cut long trenches in the ground—eight feet deep and thirty yards long—as graves. The shrouds were green GI blankets or ponchos. Cemetery workers placed the bodies in the ground in accordance with Marine Corps regulations: "Three feet from center line of body to center line of body, fifty bodies in a row, three feet between rows." Each grave was listed on a master location chart with the dead man's name, rank, serial number, and unit. Pre-manufactured crosses and grave markers had been brought with the graves registration personnel.[17]

Gittelsohn paid glowing tribute to the men of the cemetery detail. To him, they were heroes in very sense of the word. Describing their performance on Iwo Jima, he wrote, "No task from tip to tip

of Iwo Jima called for greater or nobler courage." Feeling that it
took a special kind of bravery to be able to accomplish what they
had to do, he summarized his feelings for these men by writing,
"Courage? I bow before it humbly."[18]

Perhaps Gittelsohn best summarized the spectrum of the
stressful duties that the workers at the cemetery experienced day
in and day out when he wrote in one of his wartime notes: "At
cem., hand, piece of foot & 12" of torso for identification- Going
thru pockets, fingerprinting & dental exam of corpses- bodies burnt,
bloated stumps- looking at shrouds impersonally until realizing
someone's son!"[19]

In his unpublished wartime memoir, he reminisced in a similar
vein when he wrote: "It was only later, — in your foxhole at night, —
on a ship returning to rest camp, — that a sudden wave of nausea
came over you with the dread realization: 'My God! These were not
empty shrouds or quarters of beef! Yesterday these were the sons of
mothers and the husbands of wives!'"[20]

On the morning of February 23, Gittelsohn was standing in a
mass grave at the division cemetery, tending to the grim routines
that his duty there required. At 10:31 a.m. he happened to look
up towards Mount Suribachi when he saw a group of Marines on
the summit hoisting a small American flag on a thin pipe. He was
witnessing the planting of the first flag on Mount Suribachi. In
his later years he would write, "Never since have I witnessed an
American flag fluttering in the wind without reliving that scene."[21]

On the morning of February 22, the Fifth Marines waited for the
weather to clear. Rain made the volcanic ash a slogging mess, and
again tanks and heavy equipment began to back up on the beach.
In addition to dealing with enemy fire and horrendous weather
conditions, the Marines almost became casualties of friendly fire
when Navy carrier-based aircraft arrived and began bombing
Mount Suribachi. Assuming that the planes mistook them for
Japanese troops, they frantically radioed back to have the planes
stop the bombing of their positions. Fortunately, the planes were
alerted and broke off, avoiding Marine casualties on the ground.
There was one near catastrophe that Gittelsohn commented on

later that day: "During fight for 1 ridge, elements of 28th got on it- One plane, not knowing they were there, attacked- 1 dropped 500 lb bomb on it- Dud, didn't go off."[22]

Even though the tanks and heavy equipment remained bogged down on the beach, the Marines continued to assault up the sides of Suribachi, taking out foxhole after foxhole, pillbox after pillbox. By 6:30 p.m., they stopped for the evening. Three Marine battalions surrounded the sides of the volcano. The Japanese defenders were also greatly hampered by the poor weather and the greatly reduced visibility. The Americans clearly had a foothold on the volcano and the Japanese knew it. That night, in a very unusual action for the Japanese military, one hundred fifty Japanese soldiers, about one half of the remaining force, attempted to flee the volcano fortress and link up with their fellow defenders on the northern part of Iwo Jima. They were acting on the orders of Colonel Kanehiko Atsuchi. All but about twenty of these men were cut to ribbons by the Marines as they attempted to escape.[23]

The Marines also had a plan. Earlier that afternoon, Col Harry Liversedge received orders from Holland Smith: the next day, Suribachi must be taken. He then went to pay a visit to the Second Battalion headquarters and sought out the battalion commander, Lieutenant Colonel Chandler Johnson. Johnson was a short, cigar-chomping, aggressive warrior who was all Marine. Liversedge had short and succinct orders for his battalion commander: "Tomorrow we climb."[24]

Offshore aboard the USS *Auburn*, Gen Holland Smith tallied up the casualty reports. Once again the figures were grim. By the end of the third day of the invasion, 4,574 men were killed and wounded. In its push eastward to take the airstrips, the Fourth Marine Division had lost 2,517 men. The Fifth Marine Division, in its drive to take Mount Suribachi, had suffered 2,057 casualties.[25]

The following morning, February 23rd, Lieutenant Colonel Johnson was up before dawn, briefing his company commanders. Their objective, he informed them, was to be on top of the volcano by sundown. At 8:00 a.m., he sent for 1st Lieutenant Harold Schrier, leader of the Third Platoon, Easy Company, Second Battalion, Fifth Marine Division. The Third Platoon would be the lead element of the assault. Just before the forty-man platoon embarked, Johnson turned to his adjutant and asked him to hand him something from his map case. "Take the platoon up the hill," Johnson instructed Schrier, "and when you get to the top, put this up."[26]

Johnson handed him a small American flag, measuring fifty-four by twenty-eight inches, that the battalion adjutant had brought ashore from the USS *Missoula*.

Already, scouts from two different companies were on the steep sides of Suribachi looking for the best path to the summit. The men were surprised by the lack of Japanese resistance, as well as the good footing as they ascended the mountain. It took them forty minutes to reach the top and they encountered no Japanese troops. It was 9:40 a.m. They rapidly descended back down to the Third Platoon to make their report.

Upon being briefed by the scouts, Schrier and his men collected their supplies. They stocked up on ammunition, hand grenades, and demolition charges and fueled their flamethrowers. Once geared up, Platoon Sergeant Ernest "Boots" Thomas turned to the men and barked out, "Patrol, up the hill! Come on, let's move out!" In addition to their forty-man patrol, they also took a radioman and two stretcher teams. Also added to the team was Staff Sergeant Louis R. Lowery, a photographer for *Leatherneck* magazine.[27]

They departed single file, ascending the slopes. Every few minutes, the men would have to stop to catch their breath as the angle of the sloping paths increased. All the while, Marines on the beaches and offshore followed their progress with binoculars. As the men passed the entrances to caves, they would toss grenades in to kill any possible Japanese troops inside. At all times, the platoon was expecting an attack by the Japanese defenders, an attack that never occurred.

At 10 a.m., the platoon reached the rim of the volcano. Not one shot had been fired against them. Peering down into the crater, Schrier noted unmanned machine guns, several destroyed rocket launchers, a number of mortar pits, and five artillery pieces.[28] Several of the artillery pieces were fused together by the heat of American bombing. "Where the hell are the Nips?" Schrier wondered as he signaled for his men to follow.

Upon arriving on the crest, Sergeant Thomas ordered his men to find a pole to attach the flag to. It was at that moment when several Japanese soldiers flung grenades from camouflaged cave openings. The Marines answered their attack with a barrage of fire and hurled grenades back at the cave. The skirmish quickly ended. While it was ensuing, two of the Marines had found a seven-foot length of pipe from a rainwater cistern and attached Colonel Johnson's flag to it. Lou Lowery captured the moment on camera as the Marines posted it in the ground. It was 10:31 a.m., the very moment when Roland Gittelsohn, standing in a mass grave in the cemetery, raised his eyes and looked up at Mount Suribachi.

Just as Lowery snapped the shutter, several Japanese soldiers leapt out of hiding at them and were cut down by the Marines. Japanese grenades flew out of more camouflaged cave entrances, and the Marines answered with heavy fire, finally burning out the caves with flamethrowers. This encounter, too, was over quickly.

On Green Beach, Gen Holland Smith watched the flag being planted on Suribachi while standing alongside a very important guest, Secretary of the Navy James Forrestal. "Holland, this means a Marine Corps for another five hundred years," Forrestal said. Smith nodded his head with pride, tears clouding his eyes.[29]

Watching from his command post, Chandler Johnson turned to his assistant operations officer, Lieutenant Ted Tuttle, and said, "Some sonuvabitch is gonna want that flag but he's not going to get it. That's our flag. Better find another one and get it up there and bring ours back." Tuttle was sent to the beach to find another flag.[30]

Lt Tuttle returned in a short while, out of breath from his climb back to the command post. He had gone aboard LST 779 and was able to obtain the ship's rarely used ceremonial flag. This flag was much bigger, measuring eight feet by four feet and eight inches. As Tuttle burst into the command post, three men were about to depart for the summit. Thirty-three year old Joe Rosenthal was a longtime photographer for the Associated Press who came ashore every day and took a multitude of photographs of the Marines in combat. Also with Rosenthal were Marine photographers Sergeant William Genaust, a motion picture cameraman, and Private Robert Campbell. Tuttle handed the flag to Johnson, who in turn handed it to nineteen-year-old Private First Class Rene Gagnon and told him, "When you get to the top, you tell Schrier to put this flag up, and I want him to save the small flag for me."[31] Gagnon, accompanied by the three photographers, immediately left and began the climb up to the top.

It was around noon when Gagnon reached the mountain's summit. After Gagnon handed the flag to Sergeant Michael Strank and conveyed Johnson's message to him, Strank in turn explained to Lieutenant Schrier, "Colonel Johnson wants this big flag run up high so every son of a bitch on this whole cruddy island can see it!"[32] Nearby, Private First Class Ira Hayes and Private First Class Franklin Sousley were dragging a heavy iron pipe toward them. Schrier ordered that the new flag should be raised simultaneously as the old flag was lowered. Strank attached the new flag to the heavy pole and he, Hayes, Sousley, Gagnon, Pharmacist's Mate Second Class John Bradley, and Corporal Harlon Block planted the new flagpole into the ground. Nearby, Sgt Bill Genaust was filming the flag raising and Joe Rosenthal snapped the shutter of his Speed Graphic camera. Rosenthal's photograph of the second flag raising was a masterpiece that would win the 1945 Pulitzer Prize and become the official symbol of the Seventh War Bond Drive. It has also become one of the most famous photographs of all time.

———•———

By D-Day plus five, the Americans had pushed northward from Suribachi and were on the outskirts of the second Japanese airfield, not that far from the original D-Day objective. It was at that time that the situation on the beaches finally improved. The combined efforts of the Marines, the Seabees, and all the support troops resulted in the gradual clearing of the beaches, which allowed more gear and more fighting men to come ashore. The adverse topographical conditions and the determined Japanese defenses had made the situation nearly untenable. In addition, the beach had to be adequately cleared of mines before the equipment could move off of the beach. Gittelsohn noted, "1,000 mines collected on 1 beach up to airfield #1."[33] Much of the credit in sorting out the chaos on the beach and coordinating the landing force logistics in any Marine amphibious invasion must go to the men in charge of the process—Navy beachmasters. In this case, the beachmasters deserved particular recognition, for the situation at Iwo Jima was different from previous Pacific campaigns.

In prior amphibious landings, the shore parties remained off-shore until the beachhead perimeter had been secured—usually a few hours after H-Hour—and the attack had started to move inland.[34] This was not the procedure for Iwo Jima. Nimitz's planners were thinking ahead to the future landings on the Japanese homelands and wanted to test out new techniques. The beachmasters went ashore in the assault waves with the Marines. By noon of D-Day, seventy-seven beachmasters were ashore on the landing beaches, beginning their critical work. To coordinate the landings at the seven color-coded beaches, gasoline-powered generators, amplifiers, and loudspeakers were dragged through the surf and set up in and around sand-bagged shell holes so that the beachmasters could direct the landing craft traffic.[35]

One of the Navy beachmasters that Gittelsohn observed on the beaches those first few days was Captain Carl E. Anderson, a very forceful individual with a strong Swedish accent. He had a loud voice that bellowed constantly over the loudspeakers, which added to his mystique of being a man who never slept. In a very short

*Gittelsohn conducting the first Jewish service on Iwo Jima, February 1945* (Courtesy United States Marine Corps)

time, Anderson's beach workforce became depleted, and raw replacements were sent in to work under his command. These men had never seen combat before and most were right out of basic training. Many were cooks, bakers, musicians, and clerks, sent into the deathtrap of the beaches of Iwo Jima, where twenty of Anderson's beachmasters would be killed or wounded before the battle ended. Yet, under Anderson's direction, they got the job done.

In Gittelsohn's wartime notes, he took the time to record an incident he observed on the beach shortly after he himself landed. It occurred on Yellow 1 Beach on approximately D-Day plus four. That night, the Japanese launched an intense mortar attack on the beach; the men, including Gittelsohn, leapt into shell holes and whatever foxholes they could fashion in the black ash of the beach. With machine gun fire piercing the air, the men could hear Anderson yelling over the loudspeaker, "Dig a hole! Dig a hole!" After a while, the mortar fire dropped off and Carl Anderson took charge again. It was time to get back to work.

Much to his surprise and disgust, Anderson couldn't get his men to move out of their foxholes. They were simply too scared to come out and resume unloading the supplies arriving on the beach. Spewing profanity, Anderson screamed at them, begging them to come out and resume work. Even after he threatened to put them on report, the men remained too scared to emerge from their foxholes. "All right," he yelled, "stay in your holes. Try me. See if I don't put you on report!" It was to no avail.

Gittelsohn concluded his note by revealing the ultimate leadership skills of CAPT Carl Anderson: He "finally sneered into mike: 'And you guys call yourselves Marines!'—Every last man came out."[36]

# Chapter Twenty-Five

# Coping with Hell on Earth

As the casualties mounted on Iwo Jima, stateside, Gen Holland Smith and ADM Chester Nimitz came under continued criticism, a cry that only increased the furor over the heavy Marine casualties that began with the landings at Peleliu and Tarawa. Back home there was a movement by prominent media persons to have Gen Douglas MacArthur named as overall United States commander in the Pacific. Highly critical of Smith and Nimitz was *Chicago Tribune* publisher Robert R. McCormick, who decried what he felt was the needless and tragic waste of Marine lives. However, the most vociferous opponent of Smith, and the strongest supporter of MacArthur, was the powerful head of Hearst Publications, William Randolph Hearst.

The February 27 edition of Heart's flagship newspaper, the *San Francisco Examiner*, featured a front page editorial with a heavy black border. It was personally written by Hearst, who explained that, while the Marines would ultimately conquer Iwo Jima, "there is awesome evidence in the situation that the attacking American forces are paying heavily for the island, perhaps too heavily." He continued in his attack by saying, "It is the same thing that happened at Tarawa and Saipan. If it continues the American forces are in danger of being worn out before they ever reach the really critical Japanese areas."[1]

The next day, Hearst published another editorial heavily criticizing Smith and Nimitz and strongly supporting MacArthur. The accolades, which featured key words in capital letters, included "GENERAL MacARTHUR is our best strategist" and "HE SAVES LIVES OF OUR OWN MEN." He concluded his editorial by stating, "Why do we not use him more, and indeed, why do we not give him the supreme command in the Pacific war, and utilize to the utmost his rare military genius of winning important battles without excessive loss of precious American lives?"[2]

Controversy over mounting Marine casualties at Iwo Jima continued to spread throughout the United States as the editorials were printed nationwide by Hearst's many newspapers. The evening that the first editorial appeared, over a hundred enraged United States Marines stormed into the editorial offices of the *San Francisco Examiner*, demanding to speak to the controversial newsman. Hearst, who was ensconced in his palatial estate in San Simeon, declined to speak to them. The San Francisco Police Department, as well as the Navy shore patrol, was called in to disperse the Marines.

On Iwo Jima, most of the Marines were engaged in deadly combat and were largely unaware of the firestorm that was brewing back home. A few months after the battle, Gittelsohn would record his feelings concerning what his Marine and Navy colleagues had accomplished at Iwo Jima, and he would not disguise his contempt for Hearst. He wrote with admiration of his fellow warriors and with equal disdain towards their critics: "Let anyone who doubts that stand as three of us did a few days after Mt. Suribachi had been secured, on top of Iwo Jima's southern-tip volcano, and look down on the sea lanes through which we approached and the ugly black beaches where we made our landings. From there, believe me, the wonder is not that we suffered such grievous losses, but that we succeeded in taking the island at all! In the face of what American marines and sailors accomplished against the impossible odds of Iwo, the cheap prattle of a William Randolph Hearst about unnecessary losses is nothing less than blasphemy." He would conclude that part of his memoirs by stating, "No one will ever again be able to use the words 'American' and 'impossible' in the same sentence to me . . . Along with a humble respect for the average American's courage, I carried back with me from Iwo an admittedly egotistical pride in the fact that for him, nothing is impossible!"[3]

---

The heavy casualty rate suffered by the Marines on Iwo Jima was a testimony to the defensive strategy employed by General Kuribayashi. His strategy was to allow the Americans to land on the beaches relatively unopposed, then to annihilate them there.

His troops were virtually invisible to the invading enemy, and their defensive positions were heavily fortified and relatively invulnerable to the daily heavy enemy bombardment. Perhaps most important of all was the Bushido code that Kuribayashi lived and breathed and no doubt further instilled into his troops. They all knew that surrender was not an option and that they must die defending the island if necessary.

Months before the invasion, General Kuribayashi had issued a proclamation to his men exhorting them to fight to the death. He called it "The Iwo Jima Courageous Battle Vows," and copies of this document were found by the Marines in destroyed bunkers, pillboxes, tunnels, and caves. It read:

> Above all else we shall dedicate ourselves and our entire strength to the defense of this island.
> We shall grasp bombs, charge the enemy tanks, and destroy them.
> We shall infiltrate into the midst of the enemy and annihilate them.
> With every salvo we will, without fail, kill the enemy.
> Each man will make it his duty to kill ten enemy before dying.
> Until we are destroyed to the last man, we shall harass the enemy by guerilla tactics.[4]

As the Marines drove northward and casualties mounted, Gittelsohn's work at the Fifth Marine Division Cemetery remained extremely busy. When he wasn't spending several hours a day there, he found himself splitting his time between visiting his Marines in forward combat areas and spending time with wounded Marines at the field and evacuation hospitals. The carnage he witnessed would stay with him forever. As he would recall towards the end of his life, "on the island itself, I saw enough blood to float a yacht."[5] The personal courage and the fortitude displayed by both the wounded Marines and their medical caregivers would astound him.

It struck Roland Gittelsohn that he never heard a wounded man cry during the five weeks of combat. To be sure, many men cried when their buddies were killed or when they visited the grave of a buddy at the cemetery. But like the young Marine that Gittelsohn assisted during surgery aboard the *Deuel* on D-Day, no wounded Marine cried for himself. "In five weeks of intensive combat, through many hundreds of contacts with men who were badly hurt, the only men I ever heard cry were those who were telling of a buddy who had been killed before their eyes, or those who themselves had cracked mentally under a strain too great to bear. Quentin Reynolds expressed more than the title of a book in his sentence: 'THE WOUNDED DON'T CRY.'"[6]

One afternoon, Gittelsohn remained at the Corps Evacuation Hospital tent for over three hours, waiting for one of his wounded Marines to regain consciousness. While he was there, he observed the duty corpsman performing his tasks. Gittelsohn was struck by the corpsman's youthful appearance, guessing that, since he had "no fuzz yet on his face or hair on his chest," he couldn't have been older than seventeen. Yet with the self-assurance of a man much older than he, the young corpsman would go from patient to patient, administering care to his wounded fellow Marines. The young man's poise and professionalism made a lasting impression on Gittelsohn. He would comment on the young man both in his wartime notes and in his autobiography written years later. "Where did this boy," he asked himself, "who should have been bending over school books, not broken bodies—where did he get such strength?"[7]

In a letter that he wrote to his congregants on March 17, 1945, Gittelsohn described the horrors of human destruction along with the incredible courage that he had witnessed on Iwo Jima. Towards the end of the letter, he described an example of this courage (one that he also mentioned in his wartime notes). Again, he was at one of the medical tents with wounded Marines when he simply observed a corpsman performing his patient care duties. With reverence, he described to his congregants in New York: "I know the courage and pride of a hospital corpsman who continued to administer whatever aid he could to the wounded even after both his legs had been blown off!"[8]

There was little respite from the violence and fighting even in a field hospital. One night during the third week on Iwo Jima, five Japanese soldiers entered one of the field hospitals. Spotted immediately, one was killed but four escaped. For the next few days tensions were high among the medical personnel. Finally, all the Japanese intruders were caught and killed. Gittelsohn also described an incident involving a wounded Japanese soldier who was brought to the division hospital. "1 Jap patient in Div Hosp tried to escape, shot up several Div. patients in Wards before killed."[9] In contrast to these anecdotes, Gittelsohn also recorded a note under the heading of "Dem(ocracy) vs. Fascism". Here he described an event that took place at one of the hospitals at 1:00 a.m. when he was visiting one of his men. There he witnessed a wounded Japanese soldier being treated by a Navy doctor and two corpsmen who were "pumping plasma & blood into Jap to save him."[10]

Like all of the Americans at Iwo Jima, Gittelsohn was profoundly affected by the deaths of close friends during the fighting. In both his unpublished memoirs and his autobiography, he recalled the death of a young Marine in the Fifth Marine Division that he had grown very close to. The man was named Don Fox, "a nice, decent kid," who was one of the division's photographers. One afternoon, Gittelsohn received word over the field phone that Fox had been hit by sniper fire in the head and was in the battalion aid station.

Gittelsohn grabbed a jeep and rushed to be with his friend. He searched for Fox at several aid stations but kept missing him as the wounded Marine was transported back to the beach. Gittelsohn finally caught up to his friend at the beach evacuation hospital. It was there that the neurosurgeon immediately told him that there was no hope—Don Fox would die shortly. The rabbi spent the next two hours with his dying friend in the hot, sweaty tent. Fox never regained consciousness.

Shortly afterward, Gittelsohn wrote, "His face will haunt me the rest of my life,—the face of a good, sweet boy,—his eyes so horribly blackened, his throat so gasping for breath, his life's blood so freely flowing onto the deck. There was nothing I could do for him except just sit there, pray, watch a fine young friend die. And very little I could do later for his grieving parents."[11] It was painful for him to acknowledge the desire to do so much for his friend and the ability to do so little. He somberly reflected, "A chaplain suffers that feeling of futility not infrequently."[12]

One night before blackout, Gittelsohn was in his foxhole when a piece of mail was delivered to him. The return address surprised him—it was from the wife of one of his fellow marines, a young man named Herman Podzeba. Podzeba had grown close to his chaplain and shared with him that his wife was pregnant with their first child. Because the Red Cross was unable to clear cables to men in active combat, she had written to Gittelsohn requesting that he deliver her husband the joyous news. She had just given birth to a baby girl. Gittelsohn would remember: "I felt happy to have such a mission. It was good, in the midst of carnage and death, to bear the blessed tidings of a new life."[13]

The following morning, Gittelsohn set out to find Podzeba to relay the news of his wife's letter. Podzeba had recently been transferred to a new unit, making him difficult to locate; but just before noon, Gittelsohn found him. He was at the cemetery—a corpse awaiting burial. He never found out about his little girl.[14]

---

On Iwo Jima, the Marines bore witness to the continued savagery of the Japanese soldiers. Their inhumane brutality towards Allied prisoners of war was already well known, as was their disregard for the Geneva Convention rules of warfare. Unlike in the European theater, Navy corpsmen on the battlefield quickly learned that the distinction of a red cross on their helmet or on their sleeve simply provided crosshairs for Japanese soldiers to target. Although technically noncombatants, all of the Navy corpsmen in the Pacific had been issued .45-caliber pistols for both self-protection and the protection of their patients. As they were also noncombatants, Navy chaplains were supposed to be unarmed. Most of them did, in fact, carry side arms.

On Iwo Jima, the Japanese soldiers had special instructions for dealing with Navy corpsmen. They were trained to recognize the corpsman and make him a priority target. The Japanese's logic was that if they could kill a corpsman, more Marines would be unattended, bleeding into the sand. Even better for them was to wound a corpsman. Since the Marines were very protective of their corpsmen, often three or four would rush to help them when injured, making them inviting targets.[15]

Even though they may not have had distinguishing markings on their uniforms, the Japanese were able to identify the corpsmen by their medical pouch, the Unit 3, and would specifically target them. Gittelsohn would observe this every day and recorded it with anger in his wartime notes: "Japs esp. shot at corpsmen & stretcher bearers, no doubt of this- So much so that many corpsmen swore to carry gear in future operations in gas mask case, not corpsmen's unit bag!"[16] Another Marine would record a similar note: "Jap snipers seemed to take a special delight in trying to kill Marines trying to recover bodies of Marines already dead."[17]

The atrocities committed by the Japanese at Iwo Jima left many of the battle's survivors with indelible images that they would never able to erase from their memories. For years, one of the six flag raisers on Mount Suribachi, Hospital Corpsman John Bradley, was unable to speak of his experiences at Iwo Jima. Towards the end of his life, he would finally share some of the repressed memories with his son, author James Bradley. One instance involved a friend of his from Milwaukee who was pinned down under intense Japanese fire. Bradley ran off to render aid to a wounded Marine, and when he returned his friend was gone.

"A few days later," recalled Bradley, "someone yelled that they had found him. They called me over because I was a corpsman. The Japanese pulled him underground and tortured him. His fingernails . . . his tongue . . . It was terrible. I've tried hard to forget all this.

"And then I visited his parents after the war and just lied to them. 'He didn't suffer at all,' I told them. 'He didn't feel a thing, didn't know what hit him,' I said. I just lied to them."[18]

After Bradley's death, James Bradley began researching his father's life and interviewed Cliff Langley, one of John Bradley's fellow corpsman at Iwo Jima. They discussed the discovery of the body of Bradley and Langley's good friend Ralph Ignatowski, or 'Iggy' as he was known. Langley grimly related that "both his arms were fractured. They just hung there like arms on a broken doll. He had been bayoneted repeatedly. The back of his head had been smashed in."[19]

But this was not the complete story. In 1974 James Bradley was living in Japan and invited his parents to come visit him there. James' brother Steve told him years later of their father's reaction. "He didn't say anything for a long while. Then he blurted out, 'Jim wants us to come visit him. They tortured my buddy. The Japanese stuffed his penis in his mouth. I'm not too interested in going to Japan.'"[20]

Gittelsohn was stunned by the horrors he had observed at Iwo Jima, and his wartime notes contain some cryptic references to these actions. A young Marine that he knew named Sokol was captured along with another Marine who Gittelsohn did not name in his note. The Marines recovered Sokol's buddy's body. It had been mutilated. His ears had been cut off and his bones were broken. In addition, his body was covered with cigarette or acid burns.[21]

He recorded his anger at finding watches and bracelets taken from dead Marines on the bodies of Japanese soldiers that they killed. He likewise revealed his revulsion in observing some of the Marines' actions in the heat of battle. "Horror of Marines stealing Jap teeth, ear-"[22]

In a somewhat ironic entry, Gittelsohn expressed his frustration with what was to him another form of barbarism that he personally loathed: capitalistic wartime profiteering. A battlefield discovery no doubt refueled his anger at wartime profit-making by large corporations, whom he felt would always serve to gain by pitting both sides of any conflict against each other. One day the Marines were inventorying captured Japanese weaponry. That evening he wrote a short note: "Captured Jap rifle ammo stamped WRA 42 (Winchester Repeating Arms, 1942)!- Jap field pieces bore stamp of Carnegie Steel!"[23]

He would vent his disgust and frustration in more detail at the end of the war. His anger is evident in his writing, the writing of a clergyman who has witnessed the horror of man's inhumanity and the seeming triumph of good over evil—only then to receive a slap in the face by sideline observers who invested money, not their lives, in the conflict. "It isn't easy," he wrote after the war, "after you've lived and watched that sort of thing for day after harrowing day, to remain calm and rational when you find 'Carnegie Steel' stamped on the metal of which Jap field pieces were made, or when you see Jap rifle ammunition marked WRA (apparently, Winchester Repeating Arms) 42! Some of us found it easier to control our sorrow on Iwo than it will be to harness our anger if ever again American corporations seek profit at the expense of American boys. We won't forget the kind of courage we bowed before in combat."[24]

For five weeks, the Americans were locked in savage combat with a Japanese foe determined to fight to the death. The level of casualties was horrific, far beyond what was predicted. Yet the Marines fought on, day after day. Alongside them, their Navy corpsmen and chaplains shared their burden in conditions that were unthinkable to most only a short time before. How could they cope with the death and destruction, watching their friends be wounded or die in front of their eyes? How could they go on day after day and do their jobs? In addition to "combat anesthesia," Gittelsohn theorized that a primary coping mechanism that enabled the men to carry on as they did was a not-so-secret weapon that he mentioned frequently in his wartime notes: humor.

He wrote of numerous events that would provide enough of a laugh or successfully force a smile on the men's faces. These stories and jokes provided a much-needed counterbalance to the horror to which they were subjected on a daily basis. One of these episodes occurred at a regimental command post when about a dozen Marines sat down to lunch of K rations and sardines. As the men cracked open their tins, they suddenly heard the unmistakable sinister sputter of a grenade less than a foot away from them. All twelve men, including Chaplain Roland Gittelsohn, dove to the ground to protect themselves the best they could. Knives, crackers, and mess gear went flying in every direction as the cry of "Incoming!" rang out. The men covered their heads and braced for the explosion. Seconds passed and there was none. As the men slowly began to lift their heads, they suddenly heard hysterical laughter coming from one member of their group, the chaplain's clerk. He proceeded to unravel the mystery of the "dud grenade."

The young Marine had grown tired of the culinary drabness that he and his colleagues were subjected to every day. So he hit on a novel idea to spice up the Marine Corps' cuisine—why not liven up the rations and improve the taste with grilled cheese? Putting the can of cheese on the fire to melt, he had forgotten only one thing: to pierce the tin can first with a few holes. When the heated can burst its seams, three unanticipated events occurred simultaneously: the hapless chef was sprayed with a thick coating of cheese, twelve men ranging in rank from private to lieutenant colonel moved faster than they ever had before, and to the American arsenal of secret weapons was added something new—the cheese grenade.[25]

Gittelsohn's good friend Chaplain Herb Van Meter had a grim task. He was in charge of the burial detail for his regiment, and each morning he would take a working party to the front lines and retrieve the bodies of dead Marines to be brought back for burial. As he related to Gittelsohn, one morning he and his men received the shock of their lives. They had moved one body only a few yards when the "corpse" sat bolt upright on the stretcher and demanded, "Hey, where the hell do you guys think you're taking me?" A Marine who was very much alive had laid down for a much-needed nap and wrapped a poncho around himself. To the weary work detail, any human form lying prone under a poncho with only two feet showing meant a "customer." Both the stretcher bearers and the "corpse that sat up and talked" would laugh heartily more than a few times in retelling the story afterward.[26]

On another occasion, one of the advancing Marine platoons overran a Japanese site and captured a number of military items, among them a bugle. At the time, Gittelsohn was nearby in a foxhole with his Marines. The men were still under heavy fire with the enemy surrounding them on three sides. All around, the air crackled with machine gun and carbine fire. Suddenly, from a nearby foxhole, the men could hear ringing out from the captured bugle the most improbable of all bugle calls, those for liberty and for movies![27]

Another humorous anecdote that Gittelsohn recorded involved a wager he made before he went ashore on Iwo Jima. It was well-known in the Fifth Marine Division that Chaplain Gittelsohn's favorite food was ice cream. In a moment of levity before heading for the beaches, he made a bet with the division chaplain, Warren Cuthriell, that he would manage to find ice cream even in combat. After four weeks on the island, he had not succeeded in finding any of his favorite food. Then, suddenly, he was struck with an inspired idea. A hospital ship was only a half-mile offshore. He contacted Cuthriell and quickly convinced him that there had to be Jewish casualties aboard.

Cuthriell agreed with his assistant, so with official authorization Gittelsohn commandeered a small landing craft and visited the Jewish men who were recuperating from serious wounds and brought them whatever comfort he could. However, before he headed back for shore, he visited the officer's wardroom. A short while later, he was able to hand-deliver a note to Warren Cuthriell from the wardroom's chief petty officer that attested to the fact that, after completing his visits, Gittelsohn had enjoyed a delicious dish of chocolate ice cream.[28]

One morning when he left the evacuation hospital on the beach, Gittelsohn observed several enlisted men with a captured

Japanese soldier, a rarity. The prisoner was a senior enlisted man, a sergeant major, who didn't appear to understand English. Obviously worried that he might have weapons on him or even a small explosive device, the Marines were trying to get him to take off his pants. For ten minutes, six Marine linguists tried every known dialect to get him to remove his pants but weren't able to convey their message to their prisoner. It seemed hopeless when a gruff Marine gunnery sergeant who spoke no Japanese walked up to the prisoner and loudly said in English, "Take off your God-damn pants!" The language barrier was apparently overcome, as Gittelsohn next wrote, "Off they came."[29]

Shortly after Mount Suribachi was taken, the Seabees bulldozed a narrow roadway up the side of the volcano. Almost immediately after completion, a hand-written sign appeared along the road, fifty yards up from the base of the hill. It read:

SURIBACHI HEIGHTS REALTY COMPANY
Ocean View
Cool Breezes
Free Fireworks Nightly![30]

Other chaplains also noticed the effective coping mechanism that humor provided in helping the Marines deal with the horror of combat on Iwo Jima. Navy lieutenant Louis H. Valbracht, a Lutheran minister serving as the Twenty-Seventh Regimental Chaplain, was also amazed at the humor exhibited by men who were about to face death. On the way in to the beach, he watched a young private hang over the side of the landing craft, looking at enemy shells exploding all around them. "Boy, what a place to go fishing," he said. "Look at those babies jump." Another young Marine cried out in mock hysteria: "Someone lied to me. The natives on this beach *ain't* friendly."[31]

Once his landing craft arrived on the beach, Valbracht, along with the rest of his boat mates, ran up the terraces off the beach. As he ran, he saw a corporal walking towards him from a previous landing wave, heading back to the beach. He had been hit by shrapnel that had torn his boot off, along with several of his toes. As he limped past the chaplain heading to an evacuation boat, he commented, "Short war, no?"[32]

Chapter Twenty-Six

# Endgame

The Fourth and Fifth Marine Divisions, joined by elements of the Third Marine Division, continued to fight their way northward throughout February and March. Their casualties mounted as they fought the well-entrenched, fanatical Japanese defenders. Cave by cave, pillbox by pillbox, and tunnel by tunnel, the Marines battled for every square foot of Iwo. During the entire time, the expected and dreaded nighttime banzai charges that the Japanese had utilized in all prior Pacific campaigns never materialized. The changed tactics employed by Kuribayashi, namely to attrite the American Marines from well-dug-in tunnels and caves, had proved devastatingly effective. On March 4, D-Day plus fourteen, the Marines had advanced only to the line that they were anticipated to reach on D-Day plus one. The casualties had been appalling: Col Harry Liversedge's Twenty-Eighth Regiment had suffered 1,952 casualties, nearly 60 percent of its landing force.[1]

In all three divisions, the high casualty rates necessitated the insertion of replacement troops. These troops were not like the experienced, battle-hardened Marines who had landed on the beaches on February 19. They were rear-echelon noncombatants— clerks, cooks, bakers, truck drivers, carpenters, mechanics, and musicians, anyone who could carry a rifle. Now, they had to be used to fill the ranks of front-line units.[2] Most of the green troops were 2nd lieutenants new to combat and men fresh from the States, not trained to the standard that they needed to be in the hell-like environment they were about to enter.[3] In his wartime notes, Gittelsohn also expressed his concerns regarding the replacements who, by necessity due to the high casualty rates, were thrown into combat. "Replacements very badly trained- High mortality. Some didn't know how to throw grenades or operate weapons they were put on."[4]

*Gittelsohn conducting Jewish service on Iwo Jima, March 2, 1945* (Courtesy United States Marine Corps)

Late that afternoon, Generals Cates, Erskine, and Rockey received orders from Fifth Amphibious Corps: "There will be no general attack tomorrow. Except for limited adjustment of positions, each division will utilize the day for rest, refitting, and reorganization in preparation for resumption of action on 6 March."[5] On the following day, assault plans were finalized for the three divisions. The Fifth Division would be on the left, fighting its way northward, past Motoyama Number Two and onto the west coast of the island, over the deadly Nishi ridge. The Third Division would fight its way up the center of the island, past Motoyama Number Three, which was under construction. They would link up with the Fifth Division at Kitano Point on the island's northernmost point. It was here that General Kuribayashi's headquarters was located. The Fourth Division would fight its way north up the east coast of the island, through defenses that were so heavily fortified that the Marines would refer to the area as the "Meat Grinder."

It would take the marines nearly three more weeks and many more casualties to secure Iwo Jima from the Japanese defenders, who were determined to fight to the death.

---

Just before noon on March 4, the B-29 Superfortress named *Dinah Might*, under the command of 1st Lieutenant Raymond Malo, dropped its bomb load over Japan at an altitude of thirty-five thousand feet. As the plane turned to begin its return leg to Saipan, the bombardier announced that they had a problem—their bomb bay doors were frozen open. Determined to avoid any potential Japanese fighter aircraft in their compromised condition, Malo elected to remain at that altitude, knowing that that their fuel consumption would be greatly increased as a result. After several hours of flying, the fuel in their main tanks was exhausted and Malo threw the switch that opened his reserve fuel tank. Unfortunately, it malfunctioned. *Dinah Might* had only several more minutes of flying time before it was totally out of fuel.

Malo's options were limited to three choices: bail out, ditch, or attempt to land on Iwo Jima, which they were approaching. The first two options were unpalatable, and *Dinah Might* radioed Motoyama Number One requesting permission to land. Although combat was raging less than two miles to the north, permission was granted. After two low level passes, *Dinah Might* landed on Motoyama's north-south runway. The Marines watched the B-29 land and observed with amusement as "one hatch opened and four or five men jumped and fell to their hands and knees. What a contrast! Here men were so glad to be on the island that they were kissing it. A mile or two north were three Marine divisions who thought the place was hell on earth, its ground not even good enough to spit on."[6]

*Dinah Might* was the first of nearly twenty-four hundred B-29s to land on Iwo Jima coming back from bombing runs over Japan, either disabled or running out of fuel. Approximately twenty-seven thousand airmen would be aboard these aircraft, extremely grateful for the airfields to land on. In addition, from March 3 through March 26, an average of 124 casualties a day were flown from Iwo Jima's airfields to the Marianas. In all, 2,449 casualties were flown from the island, and not one Marine died in transit.[7]

On March 14, D-Day plus twenty-three, heavy fighting continued in the northern sector of the island. However, this was the day that Admiral Nimitz had decided to proclaim that Iwo Jima was secured. A formal ceremony was begun at 9:30 a.m. On a patch of land two hundred yards north of Mount Suribachi, the Marine generals and the Navy admirals were assembled, along with an honor guard of twenty-four Marines, eight from each division. As the men stood at parade rest, Colonel David A. Stafford read the words that Admiral Nimitz had written declaring: "United States forces under my command have occupied this and the other Volcano Islands. All of the powers of the government of the Japanese Empire in these island so occupied are hereby suspended . . ."

The flag on Mount Suribachi was lowered as the color guard raised the American flag to the top of the newly installed flagpole at the ceremony site. As the generals and admirals saluted the stars and stripes, Iwo Jima officially became a United States territory. Nimitz would soon after come under criticism for the timing of this proclamation. "Who does the admiral think he's kidding?" asked one Marine upon hearing of the proclamation. "We're still getting killed!"[8] In fact, more than six thousand Marines would be killed in combat before the fighting actually ended nearly two weeks later.[9]

With the formal securing of Iwo Jima, planning began for the departure of the Fifth Amphibious Corps, despite the fighting that still raged. Originally, the planners had anticipated transferring the Fifth Marine Division to Saipan to prepare for the invasion of Okinawa, scheduled for April 1, 1945. However, the heavy casualties suffered by the division had greatly reduced the combat capacity of the unit, and they were not deemed ready for the invasion under the circumstances. They would instead be returning to Hawaii for rest and recuperation and to begin training again once they were fully augmented with replacements.

The date of departure was announced to be March 26. Looking at his calendar, Gittelsohn realized that the division's change in plans would impact the preparations that he had made for the Passover holidays, which were to begin the evening of March 28. They would now be at sea, bound for Hawaii, and the Passover Seders would be held at sea on the various transport ships. As per the original plans, Gittelsohn had arranged for all of the Passover supplies, including *matzot*, gefilte fish, wine, and *haggadot* to be sent to Saipan. Luckily, he mentioned his dilemma to his good friend, Chaplain Carl Elder.

Elder was an Army chaplain whom Gittelsohn had befriended on Iwo Jima and with whom he had grown very close. Chaplain Elder made it a point to round up all of the Jewish soldiers and bring them to Friday night Jewish religious services. He would attend the services with them in addition to conducting his own Christian services every Sunday. Elder epitomized the collegial interfaith mission of the military services that Gittelsohn had grown to enjoy so much at Williamsburg.

About four days later, Gittelsohn received a call on his field telephone and was surprised to hear Carl Elder's voice. "Roland? This is Carl. Get yourself over here to my area with a jeep or truck. I have half-a-ton of Passover gear for you and the other Jewish chaplains."[10] Elder had co-opted a cargo plane, flown six hundred miles to Saipan, and brought back all of the Passover supplies that Gittelsohn had arranged to be sent there. Gittelsohn had actually forgotten the conversation he had with his Christian colleague and was delighted and humbled by this act of kindness, an act that guaranteed the surviving Jewish Marines from Iwo Jima would be able to truly celebrate Passover Seders.[11]

Several years after the war, Carl Elder was in the New York area during Passover time. Roland Gittelsohn invited him to his synagogue to be the guest of honor at their Seder. During the Seder, he told the congregation of the selfless act of kindness that his fellow chaplain had performed on behalf of the Jewish Marines at Iwo Jima. When he finished relating the story, the entire congregation rose to their feet and gave Rev. Carl Elder a standing ovation.[12]

# Chapter Twenty-Seven

# The Purest Democracy

With Iwo Jima declared officially secured on March 14, planning began for the departure of the Marine combat troops and eventual replacement with Army occupation troops. One of the main preparatory items on the agenda for the entire Fifth Amphibious Corps was the dedication of the three division cemeteries. Responsibility for the planning for the dedication of the Fifth Marine Division Cemetery fell to the division chaplain, CDR Warren Cuthriell.

The original intention was for the three divisional cemetery dedications to be identical in format. There would first be a secular ceremony with the division commander as the speaker. This would be followed by a religious ceremony where the chaplains of the three major faiths would unite in a single religious memorial service. The dedication would culminate with one of the division's chaplains delivering the memorial sermon for their departed comrades in arms. After the common service, any group that desired could hold its own denominational service. It would seem logical for Cuthriell, as the senior chaplain, to be the chaplain to deliver the sermon at the combined memorial service. He, however, had different plans for the ceremony. Gen Keller Rockey, the Fifth Marine Division commander, would be the first speaker, but Cuthriell decided that the chaplain delivering the eulogy would be LT Roland Gittelsohn. He made the decision not only because Gittelsohn represented the smallest religious denomination of all the chaplains—a fact that appealed to Cuthriell's sense of democracy—but also because he was aware that Gittelsohn was an excellent speaker and preacher. To Cuthriell, having his assistant division chaplain as the speaker seemed to be an inspired choice. He did not anticipate the firestorm of outrage that his selection of Roland Gittelsohn would cause among many of the other Fifth Division chaplains.

Immediately after Cuthriell announced his plans, the firestorm erupted. Two of the Protestant chaplains went to see him and expressed their extreme displeasure with the proposed arrangements. They were highly offended that a rabbi would be the one to preach over the graves of men who were predominantly Christians. That argument highly offended Cuthriell, who countered that the right of a Jew to preach on such an occasion was precisely one of the ideals for which the war was being fought. As Gittelsohn would later note admiringly of Cuthriell, this counterargument had come from a Southern Baptist who had probably met no more than a dozen Jews in his life.[1] Cuthriell would not give in to his colleagues' demand; Roland Gittelsohn would remain the designated speaker for the combined memorial service.

Cuthriell believed that the problem would end after his confrontation with his fellow Protestant chaplains. He was wrong. Shortly after the first confrontation, the six Catholic chaplains of the Fifth Marine Division also came to see him, and they were livid. They expressed their unanimous and vociferous objection to any joint service, and most especially to one that would feature the sermon of a Jew. Cuthriell was stunned by their next threat: if the service was to proceed as Cuthriell planned, they all would refuse to participate and, more ominously, they would urge all of the Catholic Marines to boycott the ceremony.

By his own admission in his autobiography, Gittelsohn was not popular among many of the Christian chaplains. While Cuthriell may have not realized the extent of the animosity towards the rabbi, he almost certainly was unaware of the venomous confrontation between the Jewish chaplain and the three Catholic chaplains that took place the previous November while they were still in Hawaii. For days, Cuthriell did not share any of what was expressed to him at these meetings with Gittelsohn, who proceeded to work on the sermon that he was planning to deliver after General Rockey had concluded the secular service. During this time, Warren Cuthriell became progressively angrier at his fellow Christian chaplains.

After several days had passed and as the cemetery dedication planning had progressed, Cuthriell sent for Roland Gittelsohn. After inviting him to sit down, Cuthriell proceeded to reveal to his assistant division chaplain what had been transpiring since the initial planning for the ceremonies had begun. Gittelsohn listened in silence as Cuthriell revealed the dilemma facing him. While he wasn't happy about it, he could live with the protests of two of his fellow Protestant chaplains. However, the protest and possible boycott of the Catholic clergy and all of the Catholic Marines was a threat Cuthriell was having a difficult time ignoring.

Then, to Gittelsohn's utter amazement, Cuthriell announced to him that he had no intention to buckle to the demands. He was going to proceed as he originally planned.

After Cuthriell finished speaking, Gittelsohn absorbed all of the information that had been laid out before him. The pain of Cuthriell's dilemma was obvious to him. The utter discrimination and disrespect hurled at Gittelsohn by his fellow chaplains stung him deeply. Cuthriell was a man Gittelsohn respected, and he knew there would likely be career ramifications for him. The scandal that would erupt if Cuthriell held fast against his fellow Christian chaplains would likely stain his record and greatly dampen any potential for future promotions for this highly competent career naval officer. Gittelsohn felt he had no moral right to expose his friend to this kind of embarrassment. He thanked Cuthriell profusely for his efforts and withdrew his name from the combined service.[2]

In 1947, Gittelsohn wrote an article entitled "Brothers All?" that was published in *The Reconstructionist*. He recalled the hurt he felt when Cuthriell revealed to him the other chaplains' objections and proposed protests.[3] In the original, typewritten draft of the article, Gittelsohn hand-wrote two additional words in brackets. The passage then read:

> I do not remember anything in my life that made me so painfully heartsick. We had just come through nearly five weeks of miserable hell. Some of us [chaplains] had tried to serve men of all faiths and of no faith, without making denomination or affiliation a prerequisite for help. Protestants, Catholics, and Jews had lived together, fought together, died together, and now lay buried together. But we the living could not unite to pray together! My chief consolation at the moment was that another Jew besides myself [Jesus] would have been unacceptable as dedicator of the cemetery—even though these very men professed to teach in his name![4]

Warren Cuthriell no doubt appreciated the insistence by his

assistant that he be removed as the speaker for the combined memorial service. It was probably the only logical way to avoid an extremely awkward situation, not only for himself but also for the entire Fifth Division. However, he was still angry over the whole situation and made a decision that was his prerogative as division chaplain and overall planner of the ceremony. He announced that there would be no combined religious memorial service. After General Rockey's speech, each of the three denominations would have their own separate religious service in separate parts of the cemetery. Gittelsohn, meanwhile, had written a speech that he intended to deliver at the combined religious service. Now he would be speaking to considerably fewer marines, but there was little time to revise his talk. He decided that he would deliver the sermon he had already written despite the much smaller audience that would be in attendance for the Jewish memorial service.

On the morning of March 21, 1945, Marines started assembling at the three cemeteries for the formal dedications. That morning, the surviving remnants of the Fifth Marine Division stood as MajGen Keller Rockey spoke to them from the heart. "We are here today to dedicate the Fifth Marine Division Cemetery on Iwo Jima. Under these white crosses lie 1,876 officers and men who gave their lives in the capture of this island." Paying tribute to the fallen warriors under his command, he concluded his short speech by saying, "The finest tribute which we can pay these men who lie here is in dedicating ourselves to maintain in our organizations the high standards of courage and devotion which they have so nobly set."[5] Upon completion of this first part of the dedication ceremony, the men began to walk over to the different parts of the cemetery that were designated for the Protestant, Catholic, and Jewish memorial services.

Between forty and fifty Marines assembled in the corner of the cemetery that was designated for the Jewish service. Unbeknownst to Roland Gittelsohn, three of the Protestant chaplains from the Fifth Marine Division were in attendance among all the Jewish Marines. The three were so disgusted with the treatment accorded to Gittelsohn by their fellow Christian chaplains that they decided to boycott their own Protestant service and instead attend the Jewish service. Once all had assembled, LT Roland Gittelsohn began to speak:

"This is perhaps the grimmest, and surely the holiest task we have faced since D-Day. Here before us lie the bodies of comrades and friends. Men who until yesterday or last week laughed with us, joked with us, trained with us. Men who were on the same ships with us, and went over the sides with us as we prepared to hit the beaches of this island. Men who fought with us and feared with us. Somewhere in this plot of ground there may lie the man who could have discovered the cure for cancer. Under one of these Christian crosses, or beneath a Jewish Star of David, there may rest now a man who was destined to be a great prophet . . . to find the way, perhaps, for all to live in plenty, with poverty and hardship for none. Now they lie here silently in this sacred soil, and we gather to consecrate this earth in their memory.

"It is not easy to do so. Some of us have buried our closest friends here. We saw these men killed before our very eyes. Any one of us might have died in their places. Indeed, some of us are alive and breathing at this very moment only because men who lie here beneath us had the courage and strength to give their lives for ours. To speak in memory of such men as these is not easy. Of them, too, can it be said with utter truth: 'The world will little note nor long remember what we say here. It can never forget what they did here.'

"No, our poor power of speech can add nothing to what these men and the other dead of our division who are not here have already done. All that we even hope to do is follow their example. To show the same selfless courage in peace that they did in war. To swear that, by the grace of God and the stubborn strength and power of human will, their sons and ours shall never suffer these pains again. These men have done their job well. They have paid the ghastly price of freedom. If that freedom be once again lost, as it was after the last war, the unforgivable blame will be ours, not theirs. So it is we 'the living' who are here to be dedicated and consecrated.

"We dedicate ourselves, first, to live together in peace the way they fought and are buried in this war. Here lie men who loved America because their ancestors generations ago helped in her founding, and other men who loved her with equal passion because they themselves or their fathers escaped from oppression to her blessed shores. Here lie officers and men, Negroes and whites, rich

men and poor . . . together. Here are Protestants, Catholics and Jews
. . . together. Here no man prefers another because of his color. Here
there are no quotas of how many from each group are admitted
or allowed. Among these men there is no discrimination. No
prejudices. No hatred. Theirs is the highest and purest democracy.

"Any man among us 'the living' who fails to understand that
will thereby betray those who lie here dead. Whoever of us lifts his
hand in hate against a brother, or thinks himself superior to those
who happen to be in the minority, makes of this ceremony and of
the bloody sacrifices it commemorates, an empty, hollow mockery.
To this, then, as our solemn, sacred duty, do we the living now
dedicate ourselves: to the right of Protestants, Catholics, and Jews,
of white men and Negroes alike, to enjoy the democracy for which
all of them have here paid the price.

"To one thing more do we consecrate ourselves in memory
of those who sleep beneath these crosses and stars. We shall not
foolishly suppose, as did the last generation of America's fighting
men, that victory on the battlefield will automatically guarantee
the triumph of democracy at home. This war, with all its frightful
heartache and suffering, is but the beginning of our generation's
struggle for democracy. When the last battle has been won, there
will be those at home, as there were last time, who will want
us to turn our backs in selfish isolation on the rest of organized
humanity, and thus to sabotage the very peace for which we fight.
We promise you who lie here: we will not do that! We will join
hands with Britain, China, Russia—in peace, even as we have in
war, to build the kind of world for which you died.

"When the last shot has been fired, there will still be those whose
eyes are turned backward, not forward, who will be satisfied with
those wide extremes of poverty and wealth in which the seeds of
another war can breed. We promise you, our departed comrades:
this, too, we will not permit. This war has been fought by the
common man; its fruits of peace must be enjoyed by the common
man! We promise, by all that is sacred and holy, that your sons—
the sons of miners and millers, the sons of farmers and workers,
will inherit from your death the right to a living that is decent and
secure.

"When the final cross has been placed in the last cemetery, once
again there will be those to whom profit is more important than

peace, who will insist with the voice of sweet reasonableness and appeasement that it is better to trade with the enemies of mankind than, by crushing them, to lose their profit. To you who sleep here silently, we give you our promise: we will not listen! We will not forget that some of you were burnt with oil that came from American wells, that many of you were killed by shells fashioned from American steel. We promise that when once again men seek profit at your expense, we shall remember how you looked when we placed you reverently, lovingly, in the ground.

"Thus do we memorialize those who, having ceased living with us, now live within us. Thus do we consecrate ourselves, the living, to carry on the struggle they began. Too much blood has gone into this soil for us to let it lie barren. Too much pain and heartache have fertilized the earth on which we stand. We here solemnly swear: this shall not be in vain! Out of this, and from the

*Roland Gittelsohn delivering his famous sermon that would become known as "The Purest Democracy," Fifth Marine Division Cemetery, Iwo Jima, March 21, 1945* (Courtesy United States Marine Corps)

suffering and sorrow of those who mourn, this will come—we promise—the birth of a new freedom for the sons of men everywhere. AMEN."[6]

———•———

After the three chaplains finished their respective speeches, the men of all three Marine divisions walked again among the graves, visiting their departed fellow Marines, perhaps for the last time. As always in the cemeteries, tears flowed freely from the eyes of men—many of them teenagers—who had witnessed death and destruction that would live with them for the rest of their lives. At the Fifth Division cemetery, the three Protestant chaplains were simply enamored by the eloquence of Roland Gittelsohn's words and the heartfelt message that he had delivered just minutes before. They had boycotted their own Protestant service out of principle, but the sermon that they had just heard transcended religious differences. It was a message for all Marines regardless of faith, a message for all Americans. One of the three chaplains had a plan.

After the ceremony, he sought out Gittelsohn and complimented him on his sermon. With gratitude, the rabbi told him that the speech they had just heard was the one he had intended to give at the combined service; he had not changed it for the smaller Jewish service. Stating he wanted to read it over, Gittelsohn's colleague asked to borrow the speech; feeling flattered and gratified, Gittelsohn gave him his copy so he could read it at his leisure. He didn't give it a second thought when his Protestant colleague left with the onion-skin sheets in his hand.

Walking over to the division headquarters, the chaplain sought out a mimeograph machine. Unbeknownst to Roland Gittelsohn, he proceeded to make several thousand copies of the speech. Feeling this was one of those rare speeches that one would be privileged to ever hear in one's lifetime, he distributed it to all of the men in his regiment. Many of the Marines, most of whom were not at the Jewish ceremony, read it and were also touched by the message that it conveyed—one of purpose, brotherhood, and "pure democracy." Most of them proceeded to mail their copy of the speech home to their families. Roland Gittelsohn was about to become a name known throughout America.

It was Gittelsohn's reminiscences of the moments in the cemetery that produced perhaps the most heart-wrenching memories of his experience at Iwo Jima, a burden that all of the living would take away from the island. Gittelsohn witnessed many sad moments when Marines just back from the advancing front lines would come to the cemetery and look for their buddies. The non-sectarian nature of the cemetery made a huge impression on him as he observed the behavior of the men visiting their fallen comrades in arms. Typical of this was the morning when he observed two Christian Marines praying over the grave of a Jewish buddy. They noticed the Jewish chaplain's insignia on his collar and asked him to pray with them.

On one of the last mornings on Iwo Jima, Gittelsohn saw one of the Jewish Marines, Sid Randall from Boston, crying over the grave of a Catholic buddy. Gittelsohn would next see Randall seven years later when he moved to Boston to assume the rabbinic leadership of Temple Israel in Boston. Randall was among his new congregants, and they remained close for years. In his autobiography Gittelsohn noted, "We seldom talk about our shared combat experience; Sid still finds it difficult to ventilate his pain."[7]

Before leaving Iwo Jima, he recorded, "1 [sic] of most touching things- before we left several hundred graves marked w carved stones by buddies- 1 inscription: 'Zeke- God bless you- Your childhood buddy.'"[8] He embellished on this in both his unpublished post-war memoir and in his autobiography. Many of the Marines had discovered that the sandstone on the north end of Iwo Jima could be smoothed and carved. The men began to carve headstones for the graves of their friends to supplement the identical white wooden crosses and stars. On the last evening that he was on Iwo Jima, Gittelsohn walked through the cemetery. That night, he observed three to four hundred of these spontaneously carved monuments, each carved by a man "who had already expended his last ounce of strength in combat but could not leave without a final tribute to someone he loved. No one bothered to inquire whether the faith of the carver matched that of the deceased."[9]

Describing this incident in his post-war memoir, he said, "I don't know when any single experience in my life has touched me so deeply."[10] He ended the chapter by describing his Marine colleagues in such a way that his love for them was evident. "Marines tough? Don't let them ever kid you! They're tough only when they face a bitter, ruthless enemy. But in their innermost heart of hearts they're soft. And decent. And profoundly, everlastingly good!"[11]

———•———

Early on the morning of March 26, the remaining Japanese on Iwo Jima were desperate. Kuribayashi knew he was defeated and the end was obvious, but the Japanese Bushido code demanded that they not surrender but instead die fighting in defense of the emperor. On that morning, in the predawn darkness, Kuribayashi finally unleashed a suicidal banzai attack. Unlike prior banzai attacks that were characterized by shouting, drunken Japanese soldiers attacking with bugles blaring, this final, desperate attack was different. It was a silent, well-organized raid that began at 5:15 a.m. near the second airfield, Motoyama Number Two.

About three hundred Americans were asleep in their tents when the Japanese attacked from three directions, slaughtering their unsuspecting enemy. These American troops were shore party personnel, aircrew, supply troops, Army antiaircraft gunners, and Seabees. However, when the brunt of the attack hit the Fifth Marine Division's Pioneer Battalion, the tide began to turn. By 8:00 a.m., it was over. Nearly sixty Americans were killed in the attack. Strewn around the battleground were 262 Japanese bodies.[12] In his own notes, Gittelsohn would record, "Banzai our last night on Iwo- 65 casualties, 197 Japs killed."[13]

Later that day, the men of the Fifth Marine Division boarded transport ships for the transit back to Hawaii. It had taken twenty-two transport ships to bring them to Iwo Jima. The survivors would fit into eight.[14] In all, nearly 6,800 Marines were buried on the island. Gittelsohn's notes indicate that they had buried 2,280 marines in the Fifth Marine Division Cemetery.[15] After thirty-five days of sustained combat, they were finally leaving the site of the bloodiest battle in US Marine Corps history.

Before getting underway, Gittelsohn had one more mission to perform. He was determined to deliver the Passover supplies to the other ships in the task force that had Jewish Marines and Sailors aboard. His friend Carl Elder had certainly gone above and beyond the bonds of true friendship by procuring 850 pounds of supplies from Saipan; and now, before the ships got underway, Gittelsohn was determined to deliver the Passover Seder supplies to about twenty ships while they were anchored a short distance offshore.

Gittelsohn and his sergeant commandeered a small landing craft and packed several cartons for each ship. On that sunny and windy day, they set out on their delivery mission and soon ran into difficulties that he would find very humorous in retrospect. Once he arrived at each ship, he had to climb a Jacob's ladder to board, grasping each rung of the ladder with one hand and carrying the carton under his other arm. By his own admission, Gittelsohn was not known for his "kinetic dexterity." On his final delivery of the morning, he was struggling up the Jacob's ladder when suddenly a gust of wind lifted the ladder—and the rabbi—several yards away from the side of the ship. The wind dangerously swayed him back and forth, then twisted him around so that he was caught between the ladder and the ship, facing out. With much struggle, he finally was able to untangle himself and get aboard to deliver his package. Although he realized at the time he very well could have been killed, ironically as they were preparing to depart the island, he recalled years later, "I wish I had a movie to establish just how I managed to deliver my package and save my skin."[16]

A short while later, he arrived back on his own transport ship. Soon after, they got underway, departing for Hawaii. It was over. Five weeks of hell had finally ended. During the entire campaign, Gittelsohn had not let the stress hinder him in performing his work. "We moved about as robots, automatically performing the motions that had been programmed into us," he had written of their actions on Iwo Jima.[17] He had lived through the horror and recorded much of what he saw in his private notes. Perhaps it was the "combat anesthesia" that had steeled him through the ordeal. Whatever the source of his strength, it suddenly left him on the day they departed from Iwo Jima. That night at dinnertime, he sat down in the officer's wardroom and as a mess steward placed a bowl of hot soup in front of him, he would recall, "I burst into the most uncontrollable explosion of tears in my whole life. Everything I had somehow managed to absorb for five weeks finally caught up with me."[18] Like many combat veterans, he would suffer from what is now known as post-traumatic stress disorder, albeit a mild case. In the weeks that followed his departure, he suffered two horrifying combat nightmares. As the years passed, he would explain that his wartime experiences had increasingly receded to the point where it was almost as if they were incidents he had read about in a book rather than something he had actually lived through.[19]

For a long time certain things he would experience reminded him of his time on Iwo Jima. Any unpleasant or earthy odor would bring to his mind the stench of the decaying bodies of his dead Marine comrades. While on Iwo Jima one morning, his clerk, Sergeant Julius Abramson, came back to their foxhole "as pale as a ghost." It took him a few minutes before he could describe what he had just seen when he walked by the hospital operating rooms a few minutes before. Outside of one of the ORs, Abramson saw two feet, cut off at the ankles, still clad in socks and shoes.[20] Gittelsohn apparently went to the OR immediately after hearing this, because in a cryptic note written during the campaign, he had written: "how pale 1 a.m.- had seen 2 feet, in shoes, outside O.R."[21] This gruesome sight stayed with him for the rest of his life, and he noted in his autobiography, "Yet for a long time, there were grotesque reminders. The sight of bare feet protruding from a blanket—even in the most benign of settings—evoked nightmarish memories of corpses lined up in neat rows, entirely covered except for their feet."[22]

Easter Sunday fell on the sixth day that the task force was underway for Hawaii. That morning, Gittelsohn stood on the fantail of the ship during Catholic mass. It was partly out of curiosity, but, after their experiences on Iwo Jima, he also felt the urge to share companionship and religious reinforcement with others. Memories of his fellowship with the other Christian clergymen students during his days at the chaplains school no doubt came to mind as he listened to the mass. To his astonishment, he heard the ship's Catholic chaplain, preaching on the theme of Resurrection, repeat several times as a litany, "Remember, men, it was the Jews who crucified our Lord! Remember . . . remember . . . remember . . ."[23] It was a harbinger of things that were to come when they arrived back in Hawaii.

Chapter Twenty-Eight

# Aftermath

The Fifth Marine Division arrived back in Hawaii in mid-April. The Marines all felt good to be ashore in a familiar, friendly, and safe environment once again. They knew that they would not be participating in the invasion of Okinawa, but their immediate futures were uncertain beyond that. For Roland Gittelsohn, it was a return to his familiar duties as assistant division chaplain. Along with his fellow Marines, it was a time of rest and recuperation, as well as a time of reflection. Back home in the United States, the American public was digesting the reports of the entire Iwo Jima campaign and the price paid in blood by the United States Marine Corps: 26,000 casualties, of which 6,800 were buried in the three cemeteries. In addition, the American public was learning of a sermon delivered by a Navy chaplain at the dedication of one of those cemeteries. All across the country, families were receiving letters from their Marine sons and brothers telling them they had survived and were okay. Thousands of these letters contained a copy of the speech given by Roland Gittelsohn, and the readers were struck by the power of his message. A copy of the sermon was sent to *Time* magazine, which published parts of the speech on April 30, 1945. In a short article entitled "Religion: The Purest Democracy," three excerpts were given after the short introduction: "When the 5th Marine Division cemetery was dedicated on bloody, windswept Iwo Jima, the sermon was delivered by the division's Jewish chaplain, Roland B. Gittelsohn."[1] The news of the powerful speech, which came to be known as "The Purest Democracy," spread like wildfire across the United States.

———•———

Back at the Fifth Marine Division headquarters on Hawaii, awards were issued for the members of the American invasion force that conquered Iwo Jima. As a combat veteran of the campaign, Gittelsohn earned the Asiatic-Pacific Campaign Medal. The Fifth Amphibious Corps was awarded a Presidential Unit Citation and all of its members were entitled to wear the accompanying ribbon. The Fifth Marine Division was awarded a Navy Unit Commendation. In addition to these three campaign ribbons, the former pacifist was also recognized for his individual contributions to the Iwo Jima campaign. That summer, LT Roland Gittelsohn was awarded a Navy Commendation Medal in recognition of his meritorious service with the United States Marine Corps at Iwo Jima.

---

Among the routines that Gittelsohn began back on Hawaii were the discussion groups held on Monday and Wednesday evenings. As before the Iwo Jima campaign, these meetings were again open to all Marines, including the black Marines. The discussion groups seemed once again to create friction between Gittelsohn and his fellow chaplains. Although he didn't know it at the time, there was also growing resentment of him by the Christian chaplains who had opposed Warren Cuthriell's original decision to have Gittelsohn speak at the proposed combined religious ceremony on Iwo Jima. Much of the renewed resentment seemed to coincide with the increasing acclaim that was being accorded to Gittelsohn as more and more Americans became aware of "The Purest Democracy."

As mentioned in chapter twenty-one, not long after Gittelsohn had re-established his discussions groups, he received a "suggestion" from the new Fifth Marine Division commanding general, MajGen Thomas Bourke, recommending the he hold separate discussion groups for the white Marines and the black Marines. Gittelsohn's previously described none-too-subtle and borderline disrespectful reply, conveyed via Warren Cuthriell, no doubt infuriated General Bourke. There would be consequences for the outspoken chaplain.

A short time later, while at the Headquarters Company, Gittelsohn was approached by a young lieutenant whom he casually knew. The lieutenant, a Christian, asked Gittelsohn if they could take a walk together. Gittelsohn was flattered and quickly agreed, suspecting there was a personal issue that the young man wanted to discuss. They walked off the camp limits, exchanging small talk and pleasantries, when suddenly the young Marine turned to him and asked: did Gittelsohn know that he was being investigated by G2, the intelligence arm of the division? As Gittelsohn stared at him dumbfounded, the lieutenant proceeded to tell him that all of his mail, both incoming and outgoing, was being read. After absorbing the disturbing news, Gittelsohn thanked his fellow officer, realizing the risk that the man had just taken. By jeopardizing an ongoing "intelligence" operation such as this in speaking to Gittelsohn, the young man was risking court-martial and other possible severe punishments. Walking back to the Headquarters Company, Gittelsohn decided his course of action—he would not change his behavior in any way. He would continue to write his letters as he always had, continue to expose the men in his discussion groups to contrasting ideas and points of view, and continue his outspoken ways.[2] It seemed to him that the right to free expression and exchange of points of view, as well as the concepts of equality of all men, were the very ideals that they had fought for and that many had died for. As he continued with his daily work, beneath the surface, investigative efforts concerning Gittelsohn continued.

***

After *Time* magazine published its article on "The Purest Democracy," the exposure the speech received skyrocketed. One American who was extremely impressed with the sermon was famed journalist Robert St. John. St. John, a noted author and world traveler, had a regular radio program on NBC. He would later become the first journalist to announce the end of World War II, seconds after the Japanese surrender. After reading Gittelsohn's speech, he was convinced that it truly evoked the American ethic and provided the explanation of "why we fight." To Robert St. John, Gittelsohn's speech needed to be heard by all Americans. On Memorial Day, May 31, 1945, he introduced the sermon to the nation when he broadcasted: "And now I want to do something unusual, but when I get through, I'm sure you'll understand why I've done it. I want to read to you a memorial address, delivered over the graves of some Fifth Marine Division dead, on the island of Iwo Jima, by Chaplain Roland Gittelsohn, of Rockville Center, Long Island, New York. . . . I think that the words I am about to read to you should be printed in every history book, that millions of copies of the address should be distributed across the land."[3]

St. John proceeded to read the speech, and the entire NBC listening audience nationwide was introduced to "The Purest Democracy." For many years afterward, St. John would include a reading of "The Purest Democracy" during his Memorial Day broadcasts.[4]

A competing radio network, CBS, also decided that the message Roland Gittelsohn delivered on Iwo Jima needed to receive the widest dissemination. Accordingly, the distinguished Hollywood actor Fredric March read the entire sermon on air for CBS's national audience. In addition, officials of the United States Army were impressed with the power of the speech. The Army arranged to have the speech released for short-wave broadcast to American troops stationed around the world.[5]

On Capitol Hill, several members of Congress had read the speech and were duly impressed with the power of its message. One member of Congress had the entire speech inserted into the Congressional Record. Over the next six decades, "The Purest Democracy" would be read on the floor of the House of Representatives and inserted in the Congressional Record on many occasions in tribute to the valor of the United States Marine Corps at Iwo Jima and to one of their chaplains, Rabbi Roland Gittelsohn.

———————

A few weeks after his reply to General Bourke concerning his discussion groups, Gittelsohn received Temporary Additional Duty (TAD) orders transferring him to serve as a staff chaplain at the headquarters of Fleet Marine Force, Pacific Fleet at Pearl Harbor while he awaited orders to return stateside. He was no longer supervising other chaplains as the assistant division chaplain, but he performed his duties with enthusiasm and remained an effective advocate for his men in the performance of his chaplain duties. During this time, Gittelsohn stumbled firsthand on evidence of the investigation being conducted of him by the Fifth Marine Division G2.

One Sunday morning when he was the duty chaplain, he returned to the duty office to find his service jacket on the desk with papers that the duty chaplain would normally work with. He was taken aback—normally his personnel file, along with all other similar personnel files, was kept secured under lock and key with access granted only to a limited few. Now he was staring at his own personnel file that was "strangely left among papers to which the duty chaplain always had access. That could have been an innocent mistake; I'm more inclined to think it was the deliberate act of my new senior chaplain, who wanted me to see the file."[6] Gittelsohn was now working for Captain Herbert Dumstrey, a career Navy chaplain who was a minister in the Reformed Church of America.

Included in the file were the results of the investigation of LT Roland Gittelsohn by the G2 of the Fifth Marine Division. The final endorsement was by MajGen Thomas Bourke, who wrote, "There is no evidence that LT Gittelsohn is an actual Communist, but he favors many of the causes supported by the Communists. It is requested that he be transferred out of the Division."[7]

Gittelsohn would recall in his 1988 autobiography his response to reading the endorsement, one that was highly consistent with the overall views he expressed in his January 23, 1942, sermon "The Riddle of Russia." "I was fragrantly guilty," he wrote. "At the time the Communists were our military allies, favored a victory over Japan. So did I. By the way, my 'punishment' for this offense was being returned to the United States and my family six months earlier than I would otherwise have been."[8]

Whether or not anti-Semitism played into Bourke's endorsement is impossible to ascertain. It is undeniable that the increasing publicity "The Purest Democracy" was receiving served to further infuriate the chaplains who originally protested Gittelsohn's selection to give the sermon in the first place. One of them wrote to Captain Dumstrey to complain vociferously about Gittelsohn and to accuse him of being "anti-Christian." The letter containing Dumstrey's response to the accusing chaplain was in Gittelsohn's personnel file, which Dumstrey had left for him to find. Gittelsohn read the letter, and it said a lot about Capt Herbert Dumstrey's character.

On May 11, 1945, Dumstrey replied to the complaining chaplain: "Following our recent conversation, I inquired into the other side of the point in question. It seems that you are not entirely without fault, that in both word and deed you have contradicted the high standards of a true Christian gentleman and the principles of freedom of religion so dear to the hearts of American citizens, which have been at stake in the European conflict."

Dumstrey's disappointment was evident as the letter concluded: "I deeply regret that one of your calling should take the stand which it appears you have taken. It serves no good purpose, especially in the service. We are a conglomerate group, a mixture of racial, religious and national antecedents. All have their constitutional rights and privileges. As a minister of religion, you should be among the first to champion rather than scorn them."[9]

———•———

While he was in Hawaii, Gittelsohn began receiving mail from the United States from citizens who had read "The Purest Democracy," as well as from Marines who he had served with at Iwo Jima. He saved much of this correspondence with his wartime notes; many pieces are, on one hand, inspiring and on the other hand, gut-wrenching. The outpouring of emotion to a total stranger that is revealed in these letters is a tribute to the powerfully meaningful message that his speech conveyed to many Americans.

On May 6, 1945, Mary McNeal of Kissimmee, Florida, wrote to Gittelsohn.[10] She began her letter by citing the *Time* magazine article of April 30 and Gittelsohn's sermon at the cemetery dedication. "Our son," she wrote, "PFC William J. McNeal, HqBn HQbr, 5th Marines, sleeps there with his buddies 'forever young' and at peace; no more suffering, no more fighting. It was his first action, I think. He was killed Feb 20. . . . Surely you spoke a great truth when you told what they might have given the world had they been spared. 'Theirs is indeed the highest and purest democracy.'" Mrs. McNeal went on to lament the futility of war, noting that it is "man-made misery," and not God's punishment "for our misdeeds." As in virtually every letter he received, she asked Gittelsohn if he could perhaps find out details about how her son died. As the *Time* magazine article contained only brief excerpts of the speech, she also wrote, "I wish that I might read all of your sermon—it would be like a service in honor of the boy we love so well. May I have a copy please?"

Mrs. McNeal went on, "Thank you for these beliefs—when these become the creed of the earth, there will be real lasting peace.

May God guide you in teaching them." In the rest of the letter, she revealed that William's brother Bernard was at the time in the Navy somewhere in the Pacific. In a heart-wrenching remembrance of her son William, she wrote, "He never got home on furlough after enlisting in August 1942. He went on until he could no longer endure there—now we can do no less here."

On May 26, 1945, Mrs. Alice Hartley wrote to Gittelsohn from Grass Valley, California.[11] "I have just finished reading over and over your address as a memorial to Marines who gave their lives on Iwo Jima. It was beautiful in the sense that it is a challenge to those alive . . . to see that 'Out of this, and from the suffering and sorrow of those who mourn this will come—we promise—the birth of a new freedom for the sons of men everywhere.' I quote your address.

"It meant a great deal to me and I shall re-read it many times more—for as you spoke, you were speaking of one very dear to me. My brother, PFC Bob McBurney, Co C, 1st Bn. 28th Marines, 5th Marine Div. gave his life on Mar. 10 on Iwo." Mrs. Hartley went on to describe Bob and his life at home and how hard it was to acknowledge that he would not be coming home. "As you said; 'Thus do we memorialize those who, having ceased living with us, now live within us.' How true that is, he is so much living within us."

"Bob has gone to his Maker . . . and I know will receive the glories of His Heaven. He never did a bad or mean act in all his nineteen years." She went on to ask Gittelsohn if he knew any details of Bob's death and burial: "I want to know if he was killed instantly or died of wounds—anything you can write about him! . . . You probably have received many letters such as mine—all grasping for direct information. Every little bit means so much."

———◆———

Gittelsohn's wartime notes also contain several letters from Marines he served with, thanking him for his friendship and compassion. Reading them, one can only conclude that he was an extremely effective chaplain to both his Jewish and Christian Marines, despite the pre- and post-battle conflicts with his fellow chaplains. When he was still at the Fifth Marine Division, he received a telegram dated June 12, 1945, from Private Walter Mirschinger.[12] Mirschinger was writing from Springfield, Massachusetts, where he was recovering from a severe combat injury received on Iwo Jima.

"It seems like a lifetime ago since our last meeting under very different circumstances. As it comes back to me, the door of our Higgins boat jammed as we were ordered over the side. As I scurried up the beach, the heavy equipment cause [sic] me to fall on my knees. As I was about to get up a very assuring voice said, 'Hello Walter.' I'd like to say that those two words were about the most encouraging words I heard on that hell hole."

After catching Gittelsohn up on his recovery from his surgeries, he closed by saying, "I hope you are well sir, and that you and the rest of the boys [unclear] anything like that to go through again before we meet again in the states. Thanks for everything. God speed and may He bless you all."

In addition to the original telegram, Gittelsohn's notes contain the cryptic entry: "never saw this boy on beach! Said goodbye to him on ship just before he went over the side!"[13]

In his wartime file is part of a letter from a Marine named Harold Gross.[14] The first page is missing, so the date he wrote to Gittelsohn is unclear. It is, however, apparent from the letter that Gross was from New York and was a member of Gittelsohn's synagogue. He described a religious experience that to him was a tribute to his rabbi. "The other night I joined a couple of the boys who were going to one of the local churches to listen to another fella play the organ. As I stood there in the church with the organ playing some beautiful old hymns I couldn't see the church before me but only the many times I have sat in our own temple listening to Betty Green playing our hymns and there I realized once more how much those services you gave, and worshipping with my own family and friends meant to me. Strange that one has to travel hundreds of miles from home, go to a different church before he realizes what his own means to him.—Why must it be that way?"

Gross closed his letter with news from home. "Last reports I got from home were that your children were cuter than ever, and I can readily imagine how anxious you must be to get home and share the joy of raising them with your 'swell' wife. Do hope it won't be much longer now."

# Chapter Twenty-Nine

# Why Pacifism Failed

Roland Gittelsohn's service on Hawaii after returning from Iwo Jima was marred by the petty jealousies of his fellow chaplains over the nationwide acclaim of "The Purest Democracy." His controversial (for the times) discussion groups had aroused the ire of the commanding general of the Fifth Marine Division, who would recommend his removal from the division and transfer him back to the staff of Fleet Marine Force, Pacific Fleet. Permeating throughout his tenure in the Pacific was the specter of anti-Semitism, both subtle and overt. On August 7, 1945, he received orders transferring him to the Sampson Naval Training Center on the shores of Lake Seneca in upstate New York. Shortly after, he learned of the dropping of the atomic bombs on Hiroshima and Nagasaki. The specter of nuclear war totally disgusted him. In his notes he jotted, "Utter insanity/war system. Nuclear destructive overkill. No life on planet. Disintegration, decay/our civ, No $ for schools, human needs, only for war."[1]

Sampson Naval Training Center was one of the Navy's boot camps. Gittelsohn worked with new recruits for the few months he was there. He would look back with some bitterness at this assignment, recalling he was there "to waste time for two months doing virtually nothing at Camp Sampson in upstate New York while collecting enough 'points' for discharge."[2] Not long after he arrived at the training center, he received an invitation from Dr. Julian Morgenstern, president of Hebrew Union College. The school was beginning a series of events to commemorate the seventieth anniversary of its founding, and the first event was a three day seminar to be held from October 16 through October 18 entitled "Judaism and American Democracy." Morgenstern extended an invitation to the school's distinguished alumnus to be one of the featured speakers.

Gittelsohn wrote back on October 19, expressing his sincere gratitude for the invitation. He would, however, not be able to attend. He explained to Morgenstern, "You undoubtedly received my message that naval duties would make it impossible for me to accept your invitation to speak from Cincinnati this week. I hope, however, that in the future it will be possible for me to do so; you know that I shall be delighted to do anything within my power for the College."[3] In the letter, he also took the time to compliment the work of rabbinical student Harold Waintrup for his fine work. Waintrup, who was studying at Hebrew Union College, had recently been filling in for Gittelsohn at the Central Synagogue of Nassau County. Gittelsohn was able to attend the Rosh Hashanah services that Waintrup had conducted when he was on Long Island taking rehabilitative leave after arriving home from the Pacific theater. He was very impressed with the young man's performance of his duties, and Gittelsohn felt compelled to let Morgenstern know that Waintrup was doing a "splendid job."

Several weeks later, Gittelsohn received another speaking invitation from the college. The school was planning a special seventieth anniversary dinner to be held on Saturday, December 8, and once again they were hoping that Roland Gittelsohn would be able to be one of the principal speakers. Gittelsohn replied to Rabbi Samuel Wohl in a letter dated November 12, in which he outlined the circumstances that would in all probability prevent him from attending. "My situation, briefly, is this: as of 1 December I shall be eligible on points for discharge from the Navy. It is necessary, however, for me to make formal application on that date, and then to await return of my papers from Washington. The probability is that I shall not be released before the dates of the Cincinnati celebration; my guess is that the middle of the month is the earliest I can expect to get out."[4] Among the guest speakers who were able to attend the December 8 dinner were Henry Morgenthau Jr., former secretary of the treasury, and Rabbi Stephen Wise, the prominent Zionist and personal friend of the late Pres. Franklin D. Roosevelt.

Gittelsohn submitted his paperwork for discharge from the service on December 1, and it took several weeks to work its way through the bureaucracy along with millions of other discharge requests. His official discharge date from the United States Naval Reserve was January 27, 1946.

After the war, the popularity of "The Purest Democracy" continued to resonate with the American public and would continue to do so for decades. Gittelsohn first publically described the controversy over his invitation to speak at the proposed joint religious service at the Fifth Marine Division Cemetery dedication in an article published in *The Reconstructionist* in February 1947. Over the years, the speech would also be referred to as the Gettysburg Address of World War II.[5] In his 1988 autobiography, Gittelsohn pondered how his sermon received such wide distribution in a quote that is now universally linked to the story of his famous speech. "I have often wondered whether anyone would ever have heard of my Iwo sermon had it not been for the bigoted attempt to ban it."[6]

At the end of the war, Gittelsohn wrote a memoir of his wartime experiences, but he never had it published. It had three proposed titles: "Pacifist to Padre," "Pacifist in Uniform," and "Pacifist No More." In the preface, he explained that it was not a "war book" or an account of the fighting on Iwo Jima. Instead, his reasons for writing the book were twofold. "One: to trace something of the cataclysmic changes which almost overnight converted a people of peace-lovers and pacifists into a military machine of deathly efficiency. Two: there is a warm,—beautiful and ugly,—thrilling but depressing story to be told from the memories and files of the chaplain. He has an unparalleled, unequaled opportunity to observe ordinary human beings, under far from ordinary circumstances, at close quarters."[7] The memoir is nearly two hundred pages long and begins on December 7, 1941, with his initial reaction of "I don't believe it!" He ended his book with a postscript entitled "Now I Believe It." In the postscript, he traces his evolution from pacifist to combat veteran. The reading provides a compelling story of a complex man, an intellect faced with a moral dilemma, and traces how that man, Roland Gittelsohn, evolved over the four year period.

He began the postscript by noting:

I suppose the story could have ended with the last chapter. That, however, would have left at least the author with a strange feeling of unfinished business. Sometimes, as I look backward and inward upon myself, I wonder whether I am the same "I" who found it so hard to believe on that fateful Sunday afternoon when, for an electric instant, the universe shook and God stopped breathing. I don't know which surprises me more, the stubborn pacifist of 1940 or the military chaplain of 1944. Perhaps the trouble is that I can't entirely forget the one, and I am not altogether adjusted to the other. But whatever the real cause, there are moments when, thinking of myself then and myself now I wonder if I have not suffered from a sort of spiritual schizophrenia.[8]

Gittelsohn pondered the question of what happened to the pacifism that was such an important part of his identity. Where had it gone, and why did it fail? He admitted that after his military experiences and the amount of thinking he had done in absorbing the lessons derived from these experiences, he had come up with some ideas of why his beloved philosophy of pacifism failed so dismally. It was, he concluded, compromised from the beginning and never had a chance. Pacifism perished, to use Gittelsohn's analogy, as a man having food withheld from him weakens and finally dies. "We allowed the nourishment it needed to be withdrawn from the world up to the point where we had on our hands an ideal which was no longer relevant in our new circumstance of international life."[9]

Pacifism could have been saved "if, at any one of a hundred points along the way, we had put down our foot stubbornly and said: 'No! We will not yield another inch! Inches add up to feet, and feet make yards. When yards are reached, it will be too late!'" Gittelsohn embellished this idea with an analogy to a building that has an adequate fire extinguisher. Over years, the building is expanded greatly but still has only the original fire extinguisher to handle possible fires. And when the building burns, who, he asks rhetorically, is to blame?[10]

By 1939, Gittelsohn concluded that pacifism had been forced into a corner where it could not work. "The cards were stacked against it. The cards were callous indifference in Manchuria, a winking of the eye in Ethiopia, outright deceit in Spain, and shameful appeasement of Berlin. Against such odds as these, what chance did pacifism or pacifists stand? In a world where two and two made four, we could have succeeded. But not in the world of Munich."[11]

He was still a pacifist down to the marrow of his bones, but by the time of Dunkirk, he realized that there were limited choices to deal with the reality of the situation. "By then, every choice but two had been eliminated, in part for the very reason that pacifism had been by-passed. It was then either slavery or war. What use, at such a time, to lament what might have been? Too late!"[12]

During the interwar years, men of "prophetic vision and faith" had been warning the world. "'If this and this and this is done, the sum total will unavoidably be war!' Their words went unheeded. Their warnings were ignored."[13] And now these people who had issued the warnings faced a dilemma. What must they do? While it may have represented some form of historic justice for these men and women to stand off, detached from the situation, and say, "I told you so," or "We warned you," the reality was much harsher than the theoretical finger-pointing. Gittelsohn expressed the sad irony of the situation. "And so—the grim irony of fate!—they who more than once had tried to stop this thing, they to whom the others would not listen, became colonels and corporals and chaplains."[14]

In the much broader sense, Gittelsohn concluded that their failure was religious. "Professing the beliefs of Christians and Jews, we pacifists had acted as though we were Romans and Greeks."[15] Noting that these ancient peoples believed that each separate human virtue could be deified by itself and followed for its own sake, "each became, if an end at all, purely an end by itself, without regard for the others." This he contrasted with the virtue of modern religions that view life as a whole. "There are times when either love or justice must prevail, not both. Our God is a God of all these virtues, not of any one or two or three. He is a God who combines and expresses all of our human ideals in one great pattern of perfection. God is truth and peace and justice and love; God is mercy and kindness and charity and order. All together. All parts of one whole. All related to and tempered by each other."[16]

It was at this point that Gittelsohn summarized the crux of his reason why pacifists had failed in their mission. For this he harkened back to the two-thousand-year-old teachings of Rabbi Simeon ben Gamliel, whom he first discussed in his powerful sermon of October 1, 1938. "Our mistake as pacifists was that we held peace up as our God and forgot that peace can come only along with the rest. Peace among nations, like the happiness of individuals, is something of a by-product, not a goal to be sought directly for itself. Our rabbis knew that. 'On three things does the world stand,' they said. 'On truth, on justice, and on peace.' So! First on truth! Second on justice! And only then on peace! Establish a world in which truth prevails, in which justice is triumphant, and then you shall have peace. Without truth and justice, your leagues will be empty shells, your pledges will be hollow mockeries, your pacifism will be a ghastly joke!"[17]

As he wrote this postscript, the war was still being fought. "The war will end, and peace—of a sort—will come again. Then our task will only have begun."[18] The sacrifices of those who had died in the war must not be in vain. Roland Gittelsohn used Yetta Weinberg's last thoughts about her late husband to express his feelings concerning the responsibility of mankind from this point forward. A world without war must be the ideal that every nation must strive for. "He held his ideals very high, and was willing to die for them. Should they ever be destroyed, I would lose all faith and trust in humanity!"[19]

Gittelsohn added an addendum to his postscript—a paragraph from Pearl Buck's book *Tell the People*. In it, Buck concluded, "These peace plans on which men consume their days and brains are useless. We must first think and plan how to remove oppressions and hunger and ignorance.... To work for peace, as though it were a thing in itself, without relation to causes, is the crowning folly of our foolish age."[20]

Like most antiwar activists of the 1930s, Roland Gittelsohn felt that his knowledge and understanding of the "lessons" of World War I helped him understand the international conflicts of the 1930s. The activists never stopped to consider that the insights gleaned from that war might not be relevant to the new and different international situation that prevailed during the Depression decade.[21] They tended to see the First World War as a product of economic imperialism, and they assumed that should war again break out, it would be a repeat of 1917, only accomplishing "the transfer of mines, mills and trade routes from one set of capitalists to another."[22] This rigid "economic determinism" left the antiwar activists unable to see the real nature of the upcoming war in Europe: a struggle not over capitalist spoils but over whether the world would fall under Nazi totalitarianism.[23]

In weighing absolute pacifism against what he learned over the years, especially with his World War II experiences, Roland Gittelsohn would reflect back in 1988 and summarize these lessons: "As the threat of nuclear catastrophe has loomed larger and more ominously on the horizon since 1945, I have been increasingly tempted to return to my erstwhile absolute pacifism." He realized that this was no longer possible, and like Rabbi Simeon ben Gamliel he reasoned that peace was only viable after truth and justice were first established. "We approach the perilous brink of war due to a multitude of factors—psychological, political, economic, ethical; because we have allowed monstrous immoralities to fester instead of eradicating them.... I am afraid that once these inequities have mounted, not even the refusal to fight by ten times Einstein's quota will help, especially as war becomes more and more fiendishly technological, with fewer combatants producing many more casualties."[24]

Chapter Thirty

# Once a Marine . . .

When examining the written record that he left behind, how is the reader able to interpret Roland Gittelsohn's true feelings concerning his service with the United States Marine Corps? Which more truly captures what he felt, his post-war memoir in which he seems both enthusiastic and positive about the experience, or his autobiography, which although is primarily a narrative of his experiences seems somewhat darker and at times resentful and bitter? The reality is that, to a degree, both accounts tell a true story, that perhaps as time went by and from the vantage point of a man in his seventies, he reflected more on some of the darker aspects of his Navy and Marine Corps service.

There are some definite facts that come through. The former pacifist was proud of his service, and this pride is evident throughout all of his writings. "Even as a pacifist," he wrote, "I noted more than once with manifest discomfort, that a good military band parading down the street set my foot a-tapping and my spirits a-marching."[1] In a pre-combat sermon that he delivered, he reminded the men that as they went into combat, they became members of the most honorable fraternity on earth, "the fraternity of those who have suffered and sacrificed so that humanity could move forward instead of backward. . . . Tonight you and I become members of that fraternity!"[2]

He was very candid in describing how his experience as a military chaplain influenced his own feelings on how it would affect religious life after the war. "How, then, has actual experience in the chaplaincy influenced my own thinking and feeling on this score? While I wish, above all else, to avoid glibness and easy optimism, there is little doubt in my own mind that men by the tens of thousands will return to civilian life after the war with a new respect for synagogue and church."[3] He enthusiastically described his belief that servicemen had discovered a new freshness and directness in religion, a new type of faith which helps them meet practical problems. They had listened to sermons that were short, simple, and to the point. He believed that was a positive development and that returning servicemen would respond in later years only to a similar kind of religion.[4]

Gittelsohn was buoyant over the effect that the interactions with their chaplains had on American servicemen, convinced that the chaplains had reintroduced religion into their lives, an important "brand" of religion that would be more relevant to these men. "Anyone who reads such views with understanding intelligence will see in them not only the greatest promise, but equally the highest challenge that organized religion has faced in a long time. Men will not return from wars willing to accept just any kind of religion. They will return ready to listen, ready to give civilian religion a chance. They will return ready to see if their minister, priest, or rabbi is a 'good Joe,' as their chaplain was, whether he speaks the same language and faces the same problems as they. If he does, and if toward the solution of those problems he brings them religion's message of eternity clothed simply in the language and needs of today, men will turn to religion in civilian life just as eagerly and hopefully as many of them have done in uniform."[5]

During his military service, Gittelsohn also observed a benefit to Judaism in regard to the longtime bickering that existed among the Orthodox, Conservative, and Reform branches of Judaism. In all branches of the military services, there were no Orthodox, Conservative, or Reform Jews. There were just Jews. Some prayed with their hats on, some prayed with their heads uncovered. Some prayed wearing the tallit (prayer shawl), some didn't. But all of them prayed together in the military. Roland Gittelsohn, a Reform Rabbi, wore a tallit and yarmulke at his services for the first time since his ordination. With enthusiasm, he noted, "We are learning from each other and with each other. Unless we muff the greatest opportunity either of us has had in centuries, out of this war we shall together forge a new unity in the religious life of the Jew!"[6]

Gittelsohn's admiration for the Marine Corps is obvious in his writings. Describing the courage that he witnessed at Iwo Jima, he stated, "Major General Julian Smith did not exaggerate in the least when he said: 'I can never again see a United States Marine without experiencing a feeling of reverence.'"[7] Describing the performance of the Marines on Iwo, he knew he would never be able to use the words "American" and "impossible" in the same sentence. Near the end of his memoir, he would, with obvious pride, record that "along with a humble respect for the average American's courage, I carried home with me from Iwo an admittedly egotistical pride in the fact that for him, nothing is impossible!"[8]

The more somber reflections of his later years in no way diminish the fact that Roland Gittelsohn took pride in his performance as a military chaplain. The reflections on the anti-Semitism and conflicts with fellow chaplains that are prominent in his autobiography in no way negate the fact that he believed that he performed critically important work during his military career and that he and his fellow military chaplains performed their duties in an extremely effective, positive manner. Significantly, he would conclude overall that his experience as a Navy chaplain was a very positive one. At the end of World War II, he wrote, "I have learned more about human behavior in twenty-four months as a chaplain than in an equal number of years as a student of psychology"[9] and "I think it would not be immodest or inaccurate to say that we shall—most of us—return one day to our civilian congregations considerably changed. We shall be better ministers, priests, and rabbis, because we have been chaplains."[10]

Gittelsohn's feelings regarding his military experience are best summarized in his autobiography when he wrote, "On the day of my return to civilian life, I said that I wouldn't take a million dollars for the military experience but wouldn't willingly repeat it for five million."[11]

In early 1946, Gittelsohn returned home to his wife, Ruth, son, David, and daughter, Judy. He promptly resumed his duties as the head of Central Synagogue of Nassau County in Rockville Center, New York. He had experienced both the glory and the horror that only people in combat will ever experience, and it was time to settle back down to the quiet life.

But Roland Gittelsohn's work was just beginning.

# Notes

**Chapter One**
1. "The Little Town That Is No More," letter dated 4 August 1956, 6, Roland Bertram Gittelsohn Papers, American Jewish Archives, Jacob Rader Marcus Center, Box 64, Folder 4.
2. Ibid., letter dated 9 January 1954, 4.
3. Ibid., 5.
4. Ibid., 4.
5. Ibid., letter dated 4 November 1932, 16.
6. Ibid., letter dated 18 November 1932, 17.
7. Ibid., letter dated 13 September 1941, 46.
8. Roland B. Gittelsohn, *Here Am I, Harnessed to Hope*, (New York: Vantage, 1988), 7.
9. Ibid., 15.
10. "The Little Town That Is No More," letter dated 7 January 1940, 21, Roland Bertram Gittelsohn Papers, American Jewish Archives, Jacob Rader Marcus Center, Box 64, Folder 4.
11. Ibid., 22.
12. Ibid., letter dated 13 September 1941, 47.
13. Ibid., 48.
14. Jane Avner, "Cleveland," *Encyclopaedia Judaica*, ed. Michael Berenbaum and Fred Skolnik, 2nd ed, vol. 4 (Detroit: Macmillan Reference USA, 2007), 755-59; *Gale Virtual Reference Library*, Web, 8 Jan. 2013, 24 March 2013.
15. Ibid.
16. Scott Cline, "Jews and Judaism," *Encyclopedia of Cleveland History*. Web, 1 Jul 2008, 24 March 2013.
17. U.S. Census Bureau (1900). Retrieved October 16, 2012, http://www.ancestry.com.
18. "Congregation Oer Chodosh Sfard records, 1910-1994." Western Reserve Historical Society, October 10, 2012.
19. "Benjamin Gittelsohn," The Encyclopedia of Cleveland History, Web, 10 July 1997, 20 October 2012.

20. Ibid.
21. Gittelsohn, *Here Am I, Harnessed to Hope*, 6-7.
22. Ibid., 6.
23. Ibid., 9.
24. Ibid., 7.
25. Ibid., 8.
26. Ibid., 12.
27. Ibid., 12; *Cleveland Jewish Independent*, 8 January 1932.
28. Gittelsohn, *Here Am I, Harnessed to Hope*, 14.
29. Ibid.
30. "The Little Town That Is No More," letter dated 28 July 1956, 8, Roland Bertram Gittelsohn Papers, American Jewish Archives, Jacob Rader Marcus Center, Box 64, Folder 4.
31. Ibid.
32. Gittelsohn, *Here Am I, Harnessed to Hope*, 17.
33. "The Little Town That Is No More," letter dated 28 July 1956, 9, Roland Bertram Gittelsohn Papers, American Jewish Archives, Jacob Rader Marcus Center, Box 64, Folder 4.
34. Ibid.
35. Gittelsohn, *Here Am I, Harnessed to Hope*, 18.
36. Ibid., 19.
37. Ibid., 22.
38. Ibid., 23.
39. Ibid.
40. Ibid., 24.
41. Ibid.
42. Ibid., 28.
43. Ibid., 30.
44. Ibid.
45. Ibid., 31.
46. Ibid., 26.
47. Ibid.
48. Ibid., 27.
49. Ibid., 30.

**Chapter Two**

1. Roland B. Gittelsohn, *Here Am I, Harnessed to Hope*, (New York: Vantage, 1988), 32.
2. Ibid., 33.
3. Ibid.
4. Ibid.
5. Ibid., 34.

6. Ibid., 147.
7. Ibid., 34.
8. Ibid.
9. A. Craig Baird, *Representative American Speeches: 1945-1946* (New York: H.W. Wilson Company, 1946), 17.
10. Gittelsohn, *Here Am I, Harnessed to Hope*, 35.
11. Ibid.
12. Ibid.
13. Ibid., 36.
14. Ibid., 17.
15. Ibid., 43.
16. Ibid.
17. Ibid.
18. Ibid., 44.
19. Ibid., 9.
20. Ibid.
21. "The Little Town That Is No More," letter dated 6 October 1936, 92, Roland Bertram Gittelsohn Papers, American Jewish Archives, Jacob Rader Marcus Center, Box 64, Folder 4.
22. Ibid.
23. Gittelsohn, *Here Am I, Harnessed to Hope*, 93.
24. Ibid., 94.
25. Ibid.
26. Lawrence Wittner, "Albert Einstein and World Peace," *JBooks.com*, accessed November 18, 2012.
27. Ibid.
28. David E. Rowe and Robert J. Schulmann, *Einstein on Politics: His Private Thoughts and Public Stands on Nationalism, Zionism, War, Peace, and the Bomb*, (Princeton: Princeton University Press, 2007), 240-42.
29. Gittelsohn, *Here Am I, Harnessed to Hope*, 93.
30. Robert Moats Miller, *Harry Emerson Fosdick: Preacher, Pastor, Prophet*, (New York: Oxford University Press, 1985), 76.
31. Ibid., 26.
32. Harry Emerson Fosdick, "The Unknown Soldier," in *Secrets of Victorious Living* (New York: Harper and Brothers, 1934), 88-98.
33. R. B. Gittelsohn, "Pacifist to Padre/Pacifist in Uniform/Pacifist No More" (unpublished manuscript, 1945).
34. Ibid.

**Chapter Three**
1. Robert Cohen, *When the Old Left Was Young*, (New York: Oxford University Press, 1993), 30.

2. Ibid., 39.
3. Ibid., 36.
4. Ibid., 86.
5. Ibid., 87.
6. Ibid., 88.
7. Ibid.
8. Ibid., 79.
9. Ibid., 82.
10. Ibid., 90.
11. Ibid., 82.
12. Ibid., 83.
13. Ibid., 95.
14. Ibid.
15. Ibid., 97.
16. Roland B. Gittelsohn, *Here Am I, Harnessed to Hope,* (New York: Vantage, 1988), 10.
17. "More Human Bondage," 9, Roland Bertram Gittelsohn Papers, American Jewish Archives, Jacob Rader Marcus Center, Box 53, Folder 4, Peace, 1930s.
18. Ibid., 1-2.
19. Ibid., 2.
20. Ibid., 2-3.
21. Ibid., 3.
22. Ibid., 4.
23. Ibid.
24. Ibid.
25. Ibid., 5.
26. Ibid.
27. Ibid., 6.
28. Ibid., 8.
29. Ibid., 7-8.
30. "Sermon for Chapel- Nov. 16, 1935," 4, Roland Bertram Gittelsohn Papers, American Jewish Archives, Jacob Rader Marcus Center, Box 53, Folder 4, Peace, 1930s.
31. Ibid., 4-5.
32. Ibid., 5.
33. Ibid.
34. Ibid.
35. Ibid., 6.
36. Ibid.
37. "The Fast That We Have Chosen," 1, Roland Bertram Gittelsohn Papers, American Jewish Archives, Jacob Rader Marcus Center, Box 61, Folder 6, Social Action 1934-1936.

38. Ibid.
39. Ibid., 2.
40. Ibid.
41. Ibid.
42. Ibid.
43. Ibid.
44. Ibid., 3.
45. Ibid.
46. Ibid.
47. Ibid., 3-4.
48. Ibid., 4.
49. Ibid., 5.
50. Ibid., 6.
51. Ibid.
52. Ibid., 8.
53. Ibid.

**Chapter Four**
1. National Federation of Temple Sisterhoods. "Minutes of First Meeting," (January 21, 1913).
2. Ibid.
3. Nadell, Pamela S., "National Federation of Temple Sisterhoods," in *Jewish Women: A Comprehensive Historical Encyclopedia,* last modified March 20, 2009, accessed December 6, 2012, http://jwa.org/encyclopedia/article/national-federation-of-temple-sisterhoods.
4. Rabbi Eric H. Yoffie, "In Memory of Jane Evans" (speech, Union for Reform Judaism, June 13, 2004), accessed December 7, 2012, http://urj.org/about/union/leadership/yoffie/evans/.
5. Nadell, "National Federation of Temple Sisterhoods."
6. National Federation of Temple Sisterhoods, "Resolution on Peace," Proceedings of the Ninth Assembly, (January 22, 1931).
7. Women of Reform Judaism, "Proceedings of the National Federation of Temple Sisterhoods, 1913-1955, Report of the National Committee on Peace," (March 1, 1933), American Jewish Archives, MS-73, Box 1, Vol 3, 85-89.
8. Women of Reform Judaism, "Sisterhood Publication Fund, June 17, 1933," (American Jewish Archives, Proceedings of the National Federation of Temple Sisterhoods, MS-73, Box 1, Vol 3.), 9-10.
9. Nadell, "National Federation of Temple Sisterhoods."
10. Women of Reform Judaism, "Report of the National Committee on Peace, February 1, 1935," (American Jewish Archives, Proceedings of the National Federation of Temple Sisterhoods, MS-73, Box 1, vol. 3.), 59-60.

11. Women of Reform Judaism, "Report of the National Committee on Peace, May 15, 1934," (American Jewish Archives, Proceedings of the National Federation of Temple Sisterhoods, MS-73, Box 1, vol. 3.), 63-67.

12. Women of Reform Judaism, "Report of the Executive Secretary, March 8, 1935," (American Jewish Archives, Proceedings of the National Federation of Temple Sisterhoods, MS-73, Box 1, vol. 3.), 20.

13. Roland B. Gittelsohn, "Balancing our War Books," in *The Jew Looks at War and Peace* (Cincinnati: National Federation of Temple Sisterhoods, 1935), book I, 2.

14. Ibid., 4.

15. Ibid., 8.

16. Roland B. Gittelsohn, "Religion on Trial," in *The Jew Looks at War and Peace*, (Cincinnati: National Federation of Temple Sisterhoods, 1935), book II, 3.

17. Ibid., 4.

18. Ibid.

19. Ibid.

20. Roland B. Gittelsohn, "Are Jews Pacifists?," in *The Jew Looks at War and Peace*, (Cincinnati: National Federation of Temple Sisterhoods, 1935), book III, 1.

21. Ibid., 2.

22. Ibid.

23. Ibid., 3.

24. Ibid., 5.

25. Roland B. Gittelsohn, "Can Jews Afford to be Pacifists?," in *The Jew Looks at War and Peace*, (Cincinnati: National Federation of Temple Sisterhoods, 1935), book IV, 1.

26. Ibid., 2.

27. Ibid., 3.

28. Ibid., 2.

29. Ibid., 5.

30. Ibid.

31. Ibid., 6.

32. Roland B. Gittelsohn, "If Women Wanted Peace," in *The Jew Looks at War and Peace*, (Cincinnati: National Federation of Temple Sisterhoods, 1935), book V, 1.

33. Ibid.

34. Ibid., 2.

35. Ibid.

36. Ibid., 3.

37. Ibid.

38. Ibid., 4.
39. Ibid.
40. Ibid., 5.
41. Women of Reform Judaism, "Report of the National Committee on Peace, December 15, 1936," (American Jewish Archives, Proceedings of the National Federation of Temple Sisterhoods, MS-73, Box 1, vol 3), 64.
42. Women of Reform Judaism, "Report of the National Committee on Programs, December 15, 1937," (American Jewish Archives, Proceedings of the National Federation of Temple Sisterhoods, MS-73, Box 1, vol. 3), 168.

**Chapter Five**
1. Roland Bertram Gittelsohn Papers, American Jewish Archives, Jacob Rader Marcus Center, Box 53, Folder 4, Peace, 1930s. "Rosh Hashonah Eve, 1935," 1.
2. Ibid., 2.
3. Ibid.
4. Ibid., 3.
5. Ibid., 4.
6. Ibid.
7. Ibid.
8. Ibid., 5
9. Ibid.
10. Ibid., 6.
11. Ibid., 5.
12. Ibid., 6.
13. Ibid.
14. Ibid., 7.
15. Ibid., 8.
16. Ibid.
17. Ibid.
18. Roland B. Gittelsohn, *Here Am I, Harnessed to Hope,* (New York: Vantage 1988), 40.
19. Ibid.
20. *Golden Jubilee Journal* (Rockville Centre, NY), Central Synagogue of Nassau County, 1986.
21. Ibid.
22. Ibid.
23. Gittelsohn, *Here Am I, Harnessed to Hope,* 45.
24. Ibid.
25. Ibid., 46.

26. Ibid.
27. "Rosh Hashonah Eve, 1936," 4-5, Roland Bertram Gittelsohn Papers, American Jewish Archives, Jacob Rader Marcus Center, Box 53, Folder 4, Peace 1930s.
28. "The Fast That We Have Chosen," 4, Roland Bertram Gittelsohn Papers, American Jewish Archives, Jacob Rader Marcus Center, Box 6, Folder 6, Social Action 1934-1936.

**Chapter Six**
1. "How Can We Stay Out of the Next War?" 2, Roland Bertram Gittelsohn Papers, American Jewish Archives, Jacob Rader Marcus Center, Box 53, folder 5, Peace 1939-1963.
2. Ibid., 3.
3. Ibid.
4. Ibid.
5. Ibid., 4.
6. Ibid.
7. Ibid.
8. Ibid., 5.
9. Ibid., 6.
10. Ibid., 6-7.
11. "Extemporaneous Lecture on: The Inter-American Peace Conference; Achievement or Illusion?" 1, Roland Bertram Gittelsohn Papers, American Jewish Archives, Jacob Rader Marcus Center, Box 53, Folder 4, Peace 1930s.
12. Ibid.
13. Ibid.
14. Ibid., 2.
15. Ibid.
16. *Golden Jubilee Journal* (Rockville Centre, NY), "Central Synagogue of Nassau County," 1986.
17. Ibid.
18. "Is There a Road Back?" 2, Roland Bertram Gittelsohn Papers, American Jewish Archives, Jacob Rader Marcus Center, Box 53, Folder 4, Peace 1930s.
19. Ibid.
20. Ibid., 3.
21. Ibid.
22. Ibid., 4.
23. Ibid., 5.
24. Ibid.
25. Ibid., 6.

26. Ibid.
27. Ibid., 7.

## Chapter Seven

1. Benjamin B. Goldstein, review of *Some of My Best Friends Are Jews*, by Robert Gessner, *New Masses*, 22, no. 10 (1937): 23-24.
2. N. L. Rothman, review of *Some of My Best Friends Are Jews*, by Robert Gessner, *Saturday Review*, 15, no. 15 (1937): 19.
3. *Kirkus Reviews,* review of *Some of My Best Friends Are Jews*, by Robert Gessner, December 7, 1936.
4. "Some of My Best Friends Are Jews," 1, Roland Bertram Gittelsohn Papers, American Jewish Archives, Jacob Rader Marcus Center, Box 57, Folder 5, Russia.
5. Ibid., 2.
6. Ibid.
7. Ibid.
8. Ibid., 3.
9. Ibid.
10. Ibid., 4.
11. Ibid.
12. Ibid., 5.
13. Ibid., 6.
14. Ibid.
15. Ibid.
16. Ibid., 7.

## Chapter Eight

1. Robert H. Wiebe, *Self Rule: Cultural History of American Democracy*, (Chicago: University of Chicago Press, 1996), 208.
2. Ole Rudolph Holsti, *Public Opinion and American Foreign Policy*, (Ann Arbor: University of Michigan Press, 2004), 17-18.
3. Conrad Black, *Franklin D. Roosevelt: Champion of Freedom*, (New York: PublicAffairs, 2003), 428.
4. United States Department of State, *Peace and War- United States Foreign Policy 1931-1941*, (Washington, DC: US Government Printing Office, 1943), 396.
5. Ibid., 543.
6. Arthur Schlesinger, *The Imperial Presidency*, (Boston: Mariner Books, 2004), 97-98.
7. United States Department of State, *Peace and War*, 400.
8. Ibid., 402.
9. Roland B. Gittelsohn, *Here Am I, Harnessed to Hope*, (New York: Vantage Press, 1988), 82.

10. "Why Was the American People Betrayed?" 1, Roland Bertram Gittelsohn Papers, American Jewish Archives, Jacob Rader Marcus Center, Box 53, Folder 4, Peace 1930s.
11. Ibid., 2.
12. Ibid., 4.
13. Ibid.
14. Ibid.
15. Ibid., 5.
16. Ibid.
17. Ibid., 6.
18. Ibid.
19. Ibid.
20. "Why Was the American People Betrayed?- Part II," 1, Roland Bertram Gittelsohn Papers, American Jewish Archives, Jacob Rader Marcus Center, Box 53, Folder 4, Peace 1930s.
21. Ibid., 2.
22. Ibid.
23. Ibid.
24. Ibid., 3.
25. Ibid., 5.
26. Ibid.
27. Ibid., 6.
28. Ibid.
29. Ibid., 7.

**Chapter Nine**
1. Robert Cohen, *When the Old Left Was Young,* (New York: Oxford University Press, 1993), 135.
2. Ibid., 142.
3. Ibid.
4. Ibid., 154.
5. Ibid.
6. Conrad Black, *Franklin Delano Roosevelt: Champion of Freedom,* (New York: PublicAffairs, 2003), 425.
7. Ibid., 426.
8. Ibid.
9. Ibid.
10. Cohen, *When the Old Left Was Young,* 171.
11. Ibid., 173.
12. Ibid.
13. Ibid., 175.
14. Ibid., 184-85.
15. Ibid., 186.

## Chapter Ten

1. "Should We fight For Democracy?" 2, Roland Bertram Gittelsohn Papers, American Jewish Archives, Jacob Rader Marcus Center, Box 53, Folder 4, Peace 1930s.
2. Ibid.
3. Ibid., 3.
4. Ibid.
5. Ibid.
6. Ibid.
7. Ibid., 4.
8. Ibid.
9. H. Struve Hensel and Richard G. McClung, "Profit Limitation Controls Prior to the Present War," *Law and Contemporary Problems* 10, no. 2, (1943): 209, http://scholarship.law.duke.edu/lcp/vol10/iss2/2.
10. Ibid.
11. "Should We fight For Democracy?" 5, Roland Bertram Gittelsohn Papers, American Jewish Archives, Jacob Rader Marcus Center, Box 53, Folder 4, Peace 1930s.
12. Gerald P. Nye, "A Bad Bargain for All Parties," *The Forum* 99.9 (1938): 276.
13. "May Bill Attacked in Minority Report," *Vassar Miscellany News* XXII, no. 40, (March 19, 1938): 5.
14. "Should We fight For Democracy?" 5, Roland Bertram Gittelsohn Papers, American Jewish Archives, Jacob Rader Marcus Center, Box 53, Folder 4, Peace 1930s.
15. Ibid., 6.
16. Ibid.

## Chapter Eleven

1. Carmela Karnoutsos, "Frank Hague 1876-1956," *Jersey City Past and Present*, accessed February 20, 2013, http://www.cityofjerseycity.org/hague/thirtyyears6.shtml.
2. Harvey Klehr, John Earl Haynes, and Kyrill M. Anderson, *The Soviet World of American Communism*, (New Haven: Yale University Press, 1998), 58-68.
3. "The Last of the Bosses: Mayor Frank Hague and his Jersey City," *Life*, (February 7, 1938), 44-51.
4. Daniel L. Schorr, "Congregation Ordered Out of Jewish Centre; Rabbi Sees Free Speech Issue," *The Canadian Jewish Chronicle*, (Montreal, May 20, 1938).
5. "A Rabbi is Dispossessed," 6, Roland Bertram Gittelsohn Papers, American Jewish Archives, Jacob Rader Marcus Center, Box 61, File 6, Social Action 1934-1936.

6. J. Owen Grundy, "Thirty Years War on Hagueism," *City of Jersey,* accessed February 22, 2013, http://www.cityofjerseycity.org/hague/thirtyyears6.shtml.
7. Schorr, "Congregation Ordered Out of Jewish Centre."
8. Ibid.
9. "A Rabbi is Dispossessed," 2, Roland Bertram Gittelsohn Papers, American Jewish Archives, Jacob Rader Marcus Center, Box 61, File 6, Social Action 1934-1936.
10. Ibid.
11. Ibid.
12. Ibid., 3.
13. Ibid., 4.
14. Ibid.
15. Ibid., 4-5.
16. Ibid., 5.
17. Ibid.
18. Ibid.
19. Ibid., 6.
20. Ibid.
21. Ibid., 7.
22. Ibid.

## Chapter Twelve

1. Gerhard L. Weinberg, *A World at Arms,* (New York: Cambridge University Press, 1994), 27.
2. "Shabbos Shuvah 5699—1938," 1, Roland Bertram Gittelsohn Papers, American Jewish Archives, Jacob Rader Marcus Center, Box 53, Folder 4, Peace 1930s.
3. Ibid., 2.
4. Ibid.
5. Ibid.
6. Ibid., 3.
7. Ibid., 4.
8. Ibid.
9. Ibid.
10. Ibid.
11. Walter Laqueur and Barry Rubin, *The Israel-Arab Reader* (New York: Penguin, 2001), 16.
12. Howard Grief, *The Legal Foundation and Borders of Israel under International Law* (Jerusalem: Mazo, 2008), 18.
13. Ibid., 19.
14. Ibid., 42.

15. Ibid., 45.
16. Shaw Commission, *Report of the Commission on the Palestine Disturbances of August 1929*, Command paper 3530, Great Britain, 1930.
17. Benny Morris, *Righteous Victims: A History of Zionist-Arab Conflict 1881-1999* (New York: Alfred A. Knopf, 2000), 133.
18. Laqueur and Rubin, *The Israel-Arab Reader*, 42.
19. Ibid.
20. "Shabbos Shuvah 5699—1938," 5, Roland Bertram Gittelsohn Papers, American Jewish Archives, Jacob Rader Marcus Center, Box 53, Folder 4, Peace 1930s.
21. Ibid., 5.
22. Ibid., 6.
23. *Report on the Administration of Palestine and Trans-Jordan, for the year 1938*, Great Britain, 1938.

**Chapter Thirteen**

1. David Faber, *Munich: The 1938 Appeasement Crises*, (New York: Simon & Schuster, 2008), 5-7.
2. Michael Keane, *Dictionary of Modern Strategy and Tactics*, (Annapolis: Naval Institute Press, 2005), 15.
3. William C. Adams, "Opinion and Foreign Policy," *Foreign Service Journal* 61, May 1984.
4. "Peace with Honor or Dishonor without Peace: Which is It?" 1, Roland Bertram Gittelsohn Papers, American Jewish Archives, Jacob Rader Marcus Center, Box 53, Folder 5, Peace 1939-1963.
5. Ibid., 2.
6. Ibid.
7. Ibid., 3.
8. Ibid.
9. Ibid., 4.
10. Ibid.
11. Ibid.
12. Ibid., 5.
13. Ibid.
14. Ibid., 6.
15. Ibid.
16. Ibid.
17. "Peace with Honor or Dishonor without Peace: Which is It? Part II" 1, Roland Bertram Gittelsohn Papers, American Jewish Archives, Jacob Rader Marcus Center, Box 53, Folder 5, Peace 1939-1963.
18. Ibid., 2.
19. Ibid.

20. Ibid.
21. Ibid., 3.
22. Robert J. Caputi, *Neville Chamberlain and Appeasement*, (Selinsgrove: Susquehanna University Press, 1999), 18.
23. Ibid., 19.
24. Ibid.
25. "Peace with Honor or Dishonor without Peace: Which is It? Part II" 4, Roland Bertram Gittelsohn Papers, American Jewish Archives, Jacob Rader Marcus Center, Box 53, Folder 5, Peace 1939-1963.
26. Ibid.
27. Ibid.
28. Robert J. Caputi, *Neville Chamberlain and Appeasement*, 166.
29. Richard Cockett, "Twilight of Truth: Chamberlain, Appeasement and the Manipulation of the Press" (PhD dissertation, University of London, 1989).
30. "Peace with Honor or Dishonor without Peace: Which is It? Part II" 5, Roland Bertram Gittelsohn Papers, American Jewish Archives, Jacob Rader Marcus Center, Box 53, Folder 5, Peace 1939-1963.
31. Ibid.
32. Ibid., 6.
33. Ibid.
34. Ibid.
35. Ibid., 7.
36. Ibid.
37. Gerhard L. Weinberg, *Visions of Victory*, (New York: Cambridge University Press, 2005), 8.
38. Ibid., 9.
39. Gerhard L. Weinberg, *Hitler's Second Book*, (New York: Enigma, 2006), 47.

**Chapter Fourteen**

1. Walter Laqueur and Barry Rubin, *The Israel-Arab Reader* (New York: Penguin, 2001), 43.
2. Ibid., 45.
3. Ibid., 44.
4. Ibid.
5. "Palestine: Historical Background," (report, Anglo-American Committee of Inquiry, Washington, DC, January 4, 1946).
6. "America and the Next War," 5-6, Roland Bertram Gittelsohn Papers, American Jewish Archives, Jacob Rader Marcus Center, Box 53, Folder 5, Peace 1939-1963.
7. Ibid., 6.
8. John Toland, *Adolf Hitler*, (New York: Ballantine, 1976), 712.

9. Neville Chamberlain, speech to the Birmingham Unionist Association, March 17, 1939.
10. John Toland, *Adolf Hitler*, 710.
11. Aleksandr M. Nekrich, , Gregory L. Freeze, *Pariahs, Partners, Predators: German–Soviet Relations, 1922–1941*, (New York: Columbia University Press, 1997), 115.
12. John Toland, *Adolf Hitler*, 753.
13. Robert Cohen, *When the Old Left Was Young* (New York: Oxford University Press, 1993), 279.
14. "Message of Israel Radio Address- August 26, 1939, WJZ," 1, Roland Bertram Gittelsohn Papers, American Jewish Archives, Jacob Rader Marcus Center, Box 53, Folder 5, Peace 1939-1963.
15. Ibid.
16. Ibid.
17. Ibid., 2.
18. Ibid.
19. Ibid., 3.
20. Ibid.
21. Ibid., 4.
22. Ibid.
23. Ibid., 5.
24. Ibid.

## Chapter Fifteen

1. John Toland, *Adolf Hitler*, (New York: Ballantine, 1976), 718.
2. Bradley Lightbody, *The Second World War: Ambitions to Nemesis*, (New York: Routledge, 2004), 39.
3. Neville Chamberlain, address to the House of Commons, September 3, 1939.
4. Robert Edwards, *White Death: Russia's War on Finland 1939–40*, (London: Weidenfeld & Nicolson, 2006), 18.
5. Ibid., 272-73.
6. *Golden Jubilee Journal* (Rockville Centre, NY), Central Synagogue of Nassau County, 1986.

## Chapter Sixteen

1. "The Riddle of Russia," 1, Roland Bertram Gittelsohn Papers, American Jewish Archives, Jacob Rader Marcus Center, Box 57 Folder 5, Russia.
2. Ibid.
3. Ibid.
4. Ibid.

5. Ibid., 2.
6. "Memo 8604, Russian Foreign Intelligence Service declassifies Munich Agreement papers," quoted in "Russia declassifies Munich Agreement papers," *Rianovosti*, September 29, 2008, http://www.unian.info/world/149430-russia-declassifies-munich-agreement-papers.html.
7. Ibid.
8. Ibid.
9. Ibid.
10. Ibid.
11. "The Riddle of Russia," 2, Roland Bertram Gittelsohn Papers, American Jewish Archives, Jacob Rader Marcus Center, Box 57 Folder 5, Russia.
12. Ibid.
13. Ibid., 3.
14. Laurence Rees, "Hitler's Invasion of Russia in World War Two," *BBC*, British Broadcasting System, last modified March 30, 2011, accessed February 26, 2013, http://www.bbc.co.uk/history/worldwars/wwtwo/hitler_russia_invasion_01.shtml.
15. "The Riddle of Russia," 3, Roland Bertram Gittelsohn Papers, American Jewish Archives, Jacob Rader Marcus Center, Box 57 Folder 5, Russia.
16. Ibid.
17. Ibid.
18. Ibid.
19. Ibid.
20. Ibid., 4.
21. Ibid.
22. US Army Center of Military History, *World War II: The War Against Germany and Italy*, (Department of the Army, 2006), 158, accessed via http://www.history.army.mil/html/books/030/30-22/index.html.
23. "The Riddle of Russia," 4, Roland Bertram Gittelsohn Papers, American Jewish Archives, Jacob Rader Marcus Center, Box 57 Folder 5, Russia.
24. Ibid.
25. Ibid.

**Chapter Seventeen**
1. Judy Gittelsohn Fales, telephone interview with author, March 17, 2013.
2. David Gittelsohn, telephone interview with author, March 15, 2013.
3. Donna Gittelsohn, telephone interview with author, April 1, 2013.
4. Roland B. Gittelsohn, *Here Am I, Harnessed to Hope*, (New York: Vantage, 1988), 49.
5. Ibid.

**Chapter Eighteen**
1. "Saturday Evening Post Americanism," 1, Roland Bertram Gittelsohn Papers, American Jewish Archives, Jacob Rader Marcus Center, Box 38, Folder 7, Capitalism, Socialism, and Communism.
2. Ibid.
3. Ibid.
4. Ben Hibbs, "Neo-Liberal Illusion: That Collectivism is Liberty," *Saturday Evening Post,* October 10, 1942.
5. Ibid.
6. Ibid.
7. Ibid.
8. Ibid.
9. Ibid.
10. "Saturday Evening Post Americanism," 2, Roland Bertram Gittelsohn Papers, American Jewish Archives, Jacob Rader Marcus Center, Box 38, Folder 7, Capitalism, Socialism, and Communism.
11. Ibid., 3.
12. Ibid.
13. Ibid.
14. Ibid.
15. Ibid., 4.
16. Ibid.
17. "Saturday Evening Post Americanism II," 1, Roland Bertram Gittelsohn Papers, American Jewish Archives, Jacob Rader Marcus Center, Box 38, Folder 7, Capitalism, Socialism, and Communism.
18. Ibid., 2.
19. Wendell Willkie, "Deliver the Materials of War- Define Our Peace Aims," (radio speech, October 1942).
20. Ibid.
21. "Saturday Evening Post Americanism II," 2, Roland Bertram Gittelsohn Papers, American Jewish Archives, Jacob Rader Marcus Center, Box 38, Folder 7, Capitalism, Socialism, and Communism.
22. Ibid.
23. Ibid.
24. Ibid., 3.
25. Ibid.
26. Ibid.
27. Ibid.
28. Ibid., 4.
29. Ibid.
30. Ibid.
31. Ibid.

32. "Ben Hibbs," Kansas Historical Society, last modified January 2013, accessed March 12, 2013, http://www.kshs.org/kansapedia/ben-hibbs/12086.

33. Stephen E. Ambrose, *D-Day, June 6, 1944: the Climactic Battle of World War II,* (New York: Simon and Schuster, 1994), 26.

**Chapter Nineteen**

1. Chaplain Roland B. Gittelsohn, USNR, "Pacifist to Padre/Pacifist in Uniform/Pacifist No More," (unpublished manuscript, 1945), 1.

2. Roland B. Gittelsohn, *Here Am I, Harnessed to Hope,* (New York: Vantage, 1988), 94.

3. Gittelsohn, "Pacifist to Padre," 2.

4. Ibid., 4.

5. Ibid.

6. William L. Shirer, *The Rise and Fall of the Third Reich: A History of Nazi Germany,* (New York: Simon and Schuster, 1959), 884.

7. Gittelsohn, "Pacifist to Padre," 5.

8. Harold I. Saperstein, *Witness from the Pulpit: Topical Sermons 1933-1980,* (Lanham: Lexington, 2001), 76.

9. Ibid., 102.

10. J. L. Magnes, *In the Perplexity of the Times,* (Jerusalem: Central, 1946), 19.

11. Ibid., 25.

12. Gittelsohn, "Pacifist to Padre," 83.

13. Ibid., 7.

14. Ibid., 8.

15. Gittelsohn, *Here Am I, Harnessed to Hope,* 96.

16. Jeremiah Snyder, "Let Us Die Bravely: United States Chaplains in World War II," *Undergraduate Research Journal at UCCS,* 2.1 (2009): 124.

17. Gittelsohn, "Pacifist to Padre," 8.

18. Ibid., 10.

19. Ibid., 11.

20. Ibid., 12.

21. Gittelsohn, *Here Am I, Harnessed to Hope,* 95.

22. Gittelsohn, "Pacifist to Padre," 14.

23. Clifford Merrill Drury, *United States Navy Chaplains 1778-1945,* (Washington, DC: United States Government Printing Office, 1948), 323.

24. Ibid., 42-43.

25. Ibid., 58.

26. Gittelsohn, "Pacifist to Padre," 158.

27. Ibid., 20; Ross H. Trower, interview by Paul Zarbock, "Military

Chaplains," University of North Carolina Wilmington, William Madison Randall Library Special Collections, Wilmington, NC, December 17, 2003; George W. Wickersham, *Marine Chaplain 1943-1946*, (Bennington: Merriam Press, 1997), 14.

28. Gittelsohn, "Pacifist to Padre," 21.
29. *Time*, "Religion: Seagoing Men of God," *Time*, June 21, 1943, http://content.time.com/time/magazine/article/0,9171,766782,00.html.
30. Gittelsohn, "Pacifist to Padre," 22.
31. Ibid., 18.
32. Ibid., 24.
33. Trower, "Military Chaplains."
34. *Time*, "Religion: Seagoing Men of God," http://content.time.com/time/magazine/article/0,9171,766782,00.html.
35. Gittelsohn, "Pacifist to Padre," 25.
36. Ibid., 27.

## Chapter Twenty

1. Benis M. Frank, Henry I. Shaw Jr., *History of U.S. Marine Corps Operations in World War II, Volume V: Victory and Occupation*, (Washington: United States Government Printing Office, 1968), 679.
2. Roland B. Gittelsohn, *Here Am I, Harnessed to Hope*, (New York: Vantage, 1988), 101.
3. David Gittelsohn, telephone interview with author, March 15, 2013.
4. Chaplain Roland B. Gittelsohn, USNR, "Pacifist to Padre/Pacifist in Uniform/Pacifist No More," (unpublished manuscript, 1945), 29.
5. Ibid., 34.
6. Ibid., 35.
7. Ibid., 39.
8. Ibid., 51.
9. Ibid., 136.
10. Gittelsohn, *Here Am I, Harnessed to Hope*, 125.
11. Gittelsohn, "Pacifist to Padre," 147.
12. Ibid., 158.
13. Ibid.
14. Ibid., 159; Gittelsohn, *Here Am I, Harnessed to Hope*, 142-43.
15. Gittelsohn, "Pacifist to Padre," 159; Gittelsohn, *Here Am I, Harnessed to Hope*, 143.
16. Jewish Telegraphic Agency, "Jews in Army and Navy Request Duty on Christmas to Relieve Non-jewish Comrades," Jewish Telegraphic Agency, December 24, 1943.
17. Gittelsohn, "Pacifist to Padre," 160.
18. Ibid., 162.

19. Gittelsohn, *Here Am I, Harnessed to Hope,* 191.
20. Gittelsohn, "Pacifist to Padre," 133.
21. Ibid., 164.
22. Ibid., 191; "Letter from Yetta Weinberg," undated, Roland Bertram Gittelsohn Papers, American Jewish Archives, Jacob Rader Marcus Center, Box 63, Folder 7, War, my experience.
23. Gittelsohn, "Pacifist to Padre," 164-65.
24. Bill D. Ross, *Iwo Jima: Legacy of Valor,* (New York: Vintage, 1986), 14.
25. Ibid., 17.
26. Ibid., 13.
27. Ibid., 26.
28. Ibid., 19.
29. Ibid., 20.
30. Ibid., 163.
31. Ibid., 28.
32. Ibid.
33. James Bradley, *Flags of Our Fathers,* (New York: Bantam, 2000), 102.
34. Gittelsohn, *Here Am I, Harnessed to Hope,* 125.
35. Ibid., 104.
36. James Bradley, *Flags of Our Fathers,* 107.

**Chapter Twenty-One**
1. Bill D. Ross, *Iwo Jima: Legacy of Valor,* (New York: Vintage, 1986), 31-32.
2. Ibid., 32.
3. "Headquarters letter to Jewish Marines," dated 8 August 1944, Roland Bertram Gittelsohn Papers, American Jewish Archives, Jacob Rader Marcus Center, Box 63, Folder 7, War, my experience.
4. Roland B. Gittelsohn, *Here Am I, Harnessed to Hope,* (New York: Vantage, 1988), 121.
5. Ibid.
6. Ibid.
7. Ibid., 105.
8. Chaplain Roland B. Gittelsohn, USNR, "Pacifist to Padre/Pacifist in Uniform/Pacifist No More," (unpublished manuscript, 1945), 161.
9. Gittelsohn, *Here Am I, Harnessed to Hope,* 125.
10. Ibid., 126.
11. "Negroes," dated 29 October 1944 and 25 December 1944, Roland Bertram Gittelsohn Papers, American Jewish Archives, Jacob Rader Marcus Center, Box 63, Folder 7, War, my experience.
12. Gittelsohn, *Here Am I, Harnessed to Hope,* 126.
13. Gittelsohn, "Pacifist to Padre," 85.

14. Gittelsohn, *Here Am I, Harnessed to Hope,* 128.
15. Gittelsohn, "Pacifist to Padre,"86.
16. Ibid., 87.
17. Gittelsohn, *Here Am I, Harnessed to Hope,* 128.
18. Ibid., 128-29.
19. Gittelsohn, "Pacifist to Padre," 89.
20. Deborah Dash Moore, *G. I. Jews,* (Cambridge: Harvard University Press, 2004), 27.
21. Seymour Brody, "American Jews Serve in World War II," *Jewish Virtual Library,* accessed October 29, 2012, http://dev.jewishvirtuallibrary.org/cgi-bin/itemPrintMode.pl?Id=4482.
22. Gittelsohn, *Here Am I, Harnessed to Hope,* (New York: Vantage, 1988), 127.
23. "Conference with Bauman, Ecker, and Bradley," dated 9 November 1944, Roland Bertram Gittelsohn Papers, American Jewish Archives, Jacob Rader Marcus Center, Box 63, Folder 7, War, my experience.
24. Arnold Forster, *Anti-Semitism in the United Stated in 1947*, (New York: Anti-Defamation League of B'nai B'rith, 1947), 25.
25. Gittelsohn, "Pacifist to Padre," 152.

**Chapter Twenty-Two**

1. Bill D. Ross, *Iwo Jima: Legacy of Valor,* (New York: Vintage, 1986), 39.
2. Ibid., 34.
3. Ibid.
4. Ibid., 35.
5. James Bradley, *Flags of Our Fathers,* (New York: Bantam, 2000), 137.
6. Chaplain Roland B. Gittelsohn, USNR, "Pacifist to Padre/Pacifist in Uniform/Pacifist No More," (unpublished manuscript, 1945), 165-o.
7. Ibid., 165-o – 165-p.
8. Ross, *Iwo Jima,* 42.
9. Ronald H. Spector, *Eagle Against the Sun,* (New York: Vintage, 1985), 498.
10. Ross, *Iwo Jima,* 49.
11. Ibid., 51.
12. "Heroism," undated note, Roland Bertram Gittelsohn Papers, American Jewish Archives, Jacob Rader Marcus Center, Box 63, Folder 7, War, my experience.
13. Bradley, *Flags of Our Fathers,* 147.
14. Spector, *Eagle Against the Sun,* 498.
15. Bradley, *Flags of Our Fathers,* 140.
16. Ibid., 142.
17. "Iwo Notes," 18 February 1945, Roland Bertram Gittelsohn Papers,

American Jewish Archives, Jacob Rader Marcus Center, Box 63, Folder 7, War, my experience.

18. Roland B. Gittelsohn, *Here Am I, Harnessed to Hope*, (New York: Vantage, 1988), 110-11.
19. Ibid., 106.
20. Ibid.; Gittelsohn, "Pacifist to Padre," 106.
21. Ibid., 106-7.

**Chapter Twenty-Three**
1. Bill D. Ross, *Iwo Jima: Legacy of Valor*, (New York: Vintage, 1986), 61.
2. Ibid., 62.
3. Roland B. Gittelsohn, *Here Am I, Harnessed to Hope*, (New York: Vantage, 1988), 108.
4. Ibid.
5. Ibid., 110. In his autobiography, Gittelsohn says the young man's hair turned white in three weeks; "General Notes," undated, Roland Bertram Gittelsohn Papers, American Jewish Archives, Jacob Rader Marcus Center, Box 63, Folder 7, War, my experience.
6. Roland B. Gittelsohn, *Here Am I, Harnessed to Hope*, 109.
7. Chaplain Roland B. Gittelsohn, USNR, "Pacifist to Padre/Pacifist in Uniform/Pacifist No More," (unpublished manuscript, 1945), 165-c.
8. Intelligence Section, Amphibious Forces Pacific and Assistant Chief of Staff, Fleet Marine Forces Pacific, *Beach Diagram, Southeastern Beaches, Iwo Jima*, July 4, 1944.
9. James Bradley, *Flags of Our Fathers*, (New York: Bantam, 2000), 154.
10. "General Notes," undated, Roland Bertram Gittelsohn Papers, American Jewish Archives, Jacob Rader Marcus Center, Box 63, Folder 7, War, my experience.
11. Bill D. Ross, *Iwo Jima*, 69.
12. Ibid., 80.
13. Ibid., 81.

**Chapter Twenty-Four**
1. Bill D. Ross, *Iwo Jima: Legacy of Valor*, (New York: Vintage, 1986), 80.
2. Chaplain Roland B. Gittelsohn, USNR, "Pacifist to Padre/Pacifist in Uniform/Pacifist No More," (unpublished manuscript, 1945), 165-g.
3. Roland B. Gittelsohn, *Here Am I, Harnessed to Hope*, (New York: Vantage, 1988), 109-10.
4. "Personal," undated note, Roland Bertram Gittelsohn Papers, American Jewish Archives, Jacob Rader Marcus Center, Box 63, Folder 7, War, my experience.
5. Rita H. Delorme, "Dr. Daniel McCarthy had everything to live for, but

gave his life for his country," *Southern Cross,* December 11, 2003, 3.

6. "General," undated note, Roland Bertram Gittelsohn Papers, American Jewish Archives, Jacob Rader Marcus Center, Box 63, Folder 7, War, my experience.
7. Gittelsohn, "Pacifist to Padre," 165-h.
8. "General," undated note, Roland Bertram Gittelsohn Papers, American Jewish Archives, Jacob Rader Marcus Center, Box 63, Folder 7, War, my experience.
9. Ibid.; Gittelsohn, *Here Am I, Harnessed to Hope,* 111.
10. Ibid.
11. "Personal," undated note, Roland Bertram Gittelsohn Papers, American Jewish Archives, Jacob Rader Marcus Center, Box 63, Folder 7, War, my experience.
12. Gittelsohn, *Here Am I, Harnessed to Hope,* 111.
13. Ross, *Iwo Jima,* 184.
14. Ibid.
15. Gittelsohn, *Here Am I, Harnessed to Hope,* 113.
16. Gittelsohn, "Pacifist to Padre," 165-f.
17. Ross, *Iwo Jima,* 185.
18. Gittelsohn, "Pacifist to Padre," 165-f – 165-g.
19. "General," undated note, Roland Bertram Gittelsohn Papers, American Jewish Archives, Jacob Rader Marcus Center, Box 63, Folder 7, War, my experience.
20. Gittelsohn, "Pacifist to Padre," 165-i.
21. Gittelsohn, *Here Am I, Harnessed to Hope,* 113.
22. "General," undated note, Roland Bertram Gittelsohn Papers, American Jewish Archives, Jacob Rader Marcus Center, Box 63, Folder 7, War, my experience.
23. James Bradley, *Flags of Our Fathers,* (New York: Bantam, 2000). 197.
24. Ibid.
25. Ross, *Iwo Jima,* 95.
26. Ibid.
27. James Bradley, *Flags of Our Fathers,* 202.
28. Ross, *Iwo Jima,* 96.
29. Ibid., 99.
30. James Bradley, *Flags of Our Fathers,* 207.
31. Ibid., 209.
32. Ibid.
33. "General," undated note, Roland Bertram Gittelsohn Papers, American Jewish Archives, Jacob Rader Marcus Center, Box 63, Folder 7, War, my experience.
34. Ross, *Iwo Jima,* 127.

35. Ibid.
36. "Humor," undated note, Roland Bertram Gittelsohn Papers, American Jewish Archives, Jacob Rader Marcus Center, Box 63, Folder 7, War, my experience.

**Chapter Twenty-Five**
1. Bill D. Ross, *Iwo Jima: Legacy of Valor*, (New York: Vintage, 1986), 108.
2. Ibid., 109.
3. Chaplain Roland B. Gittelsohn, USNR, "Pacifist to Padre/Pacifist in Uniform/Pacifist No More," (unpublished manuscript, 1945), 165-n.
4. Ross, *Iwo Jima*, 150.
5. Roland B. Gittelsohn, *Here Am I, Harnessed to Hope*, (New York: Vantage, 1988), 109.
6. Gittelsohn, "Pacifist to Padre," 165-b.
7. Gittelsohn, *Here Am I, Harnessed to Hope*, 113; "Heroism," undated note, Roland Bertram Gittelsohn Papers, American Jewish Archives, Jacob Rader Marcus Center, Box 63, Folder 7, War, my experience.
8. Gittelsohn, *Here Am I, Harnessed to Hope*, 119.
9. "General," undated note, Roland Bertram Gittelsohn Papers, American Jewish Archives, Jacob Rader Marcus Center, Box 63, Folder 7, War, my experience.
10. Ibid.
11. Gittelsohn, *Here Am I, Harnessed to Hope*, 114.
12. Gittelsohn, "Pacifist to Padre," 165-u.
13. Ibid.
14. Gittelsohn, *Here Am I, Harnessed to Hope*, 114.
15. James Bradley, *Flags of Our Fathers*, (New York: Bantam, 2000), 140.
16. "Heroism," undated note, Roland Bertram Gittelsohn Papers, American Jewish Archives, Jacob Rader Marcus Center, Box 63, Folder 7, War, my experience.
17. Ross, *Iwo Jima*, 185.
18. James Bradley, *Flags of Our Fathers*, 344.
19. Ibid., 345.
20. Ibid., 346.
21. "General," undated note, Roland Bertram Gittelsohn Papers, American Jewish Archives, Jacob Rader Marcus Center, Box 63, Folder 7, War, my experience.
22. Ibid.
23. Ibid.
24. Gittelsohn, "Pacifist to Padre," 165-g.
25. Gittelsohn, *Here Am I, Harnessed to Hope*, 115.
26. Gittelsohn, "Pacifist to Padre," 165-l.

27. Gittelsohn, *Here Am I, Harnessed to Hope*, 115.
28. Ibid.
29. "Iwo Humor," undated note, Roland Bertram Gittelsohn Papers, American Jewish Archives, Jacob Rader Marcus Center, Box 63, Folder 7, War, my experience.
30. Ross, *Iwo Jima*, 103.
31. Richard Holcomb, *Iwo Jima*, (New York: Henry Holt and Company, 2002), 106.
32. Ibid.

**Chapter Twenty-Six**
1. Bill D. Ross, *Iwo Jima: Legacy of Valor*, (New York: Vintage, 1986), 283.
2. Ibid., 296.
3. Ibid., 283.
4. "General," undated note, Roland Bertram Gittelsohn Papers, American Jewish Archives, Jacob Rader Marcus Center, Box 63, Folder 7, War, my experience.
5. Ross, *Iwo Jima*, 284.
6. Ibid., 276-77.
7. Ibid., 280.
8. James Bradley, *Flags of Our Fathers*, (New York: Bantam, 2000), 242.
9. Ross, *Iwo Jima*, 321.
10. Roland B. Gittelsohn, *Here Am I, Harnessed to Hope*, (New York: Vantage, 1988), 144.
11. Ibid.
12. Ibid., 145.

**Chapter Twenty-Seven**
1. Roland B. Gittelsohn, *Here Am I, Harnessed to Hope*, (New York: Vantage, 1988), 131.
2. Ibid.
3. Roland Gittelsohn, "Brothers all?," *The Reconstructionist*, 12, February 7, 1947, 10.
4. "We had just come through five weeks of miserable hell," undated, Roland Bertram Gittelsohn Papers, American Jewish Archives, Jacob Rader Marcus Center, Box 63, Folder 7, War, my experience.
5. Keller E. Rockey, "Address at the Dedication of the Fifth Marine Division Cemetery at Iwo Jima," *Togetherweserved.com*, accessed September 5, 2012.
6. "The Purest Democracy," March 21, 1945, Roland Bertram Gittelsohn Papers, American Jewish Archives, Jacob Rader Marcus Center, Box 63, Folder 7, War, my experience. Courtesy of the Jacob Rader Marcus Center of the American Jewish Archives, Cincinnati, Ohio, americanjewisharchives.org.

7. Gittelsohn, *Here Am I, Harnessed to Hope,* 145.
8. "General," undated memo, Roland Bertram Gittelsohn Papers, American Jewish Archives, Jacob Rader Marcus Center, Box 63, Folder 7, War, my experience.
9. Gittelsohn, *Here Am I, Harnessed to Hope,* 145-46.
10. Chaplain Roland B. Gittelsohn, USNR, "Pacifist to Padre/Pacifist in Uniform/Pacifist No More," (unpublished manuscript, 1945), 165-q.
11. Ibid.
12. Bill D. Ross, *Iwo Jima: Legacy of Valor,* (New York: Vintage, 1986), 336.
13. "General," undated note, Roland Bertram Gittelsohn Papers, American Jewish Archives, Jacob Rader Marcus Center, Box 63, Folder 7, War, my experience.
14. James Bradley, *Flags of Our Fathers,* (New York: Bantam, 2000), 246.
15. "General," undated note, Roland Bertram Gittelsohn Papers, American Jewish Archives, Jacob Rader Marcus Center, Box 63, Folder 7, War, my experience.
16. Gittelsohn, *Here Am I, Harnessed to Hope,* (New York: Vantage, 1988), 117.
17. Ibid., 116.
18. Ibid., 117.
19. Ibid.
20. Gittelsohn "Pacifist to Padre," 165-e.
21. "Personal," undated note, Roland Bertram Gittelsohn Papers, American Jewish Archives, Jacob Rader Marcus Center, Box 63, Folder 7, War, my experience.
22. Gittelsohn, *Here Am I, Harnessed to Hope,* 118.
23. Gittelsohn, *Here Am I, Harnessed to Hope,* 132.

## Chapter Twenty-Eight

1. *Time,* "Religion: The Purest Democracy." *Time,* April 30, 1945.
2. Roland B. Gittelsohn, *Here Am I, Harnessed to Hope,* (New York: Vantage, 1988), 129.
3. A. Craig Baird, "That Men Might Be Free," in *Representative American Speeches: 1945-1946,* (New York: H.W. Wilson Company, 1946), 16-17.
4. Gittelsohn, *Here Am I, Harnessed to Hope,* 132.
5. Ibid.
6. Ibid., 129.
7. Ibid., 129-30.
8. Ibid., 130.
9. Ibid., 142.
10. "Letter from Mary E. McNeal to Chaplain Roland Gittelsohn," 6 May 1945, Roland Bertram Gittelsohn Papers, American Jewish Archives, Jacob Rader Marcus Center, Box 63, Folder 7, War, my experience.

11. "Letter from Alice Hartley to Chaplain Roland Gittelsohn," 26 May 1945, Roland Bertram Gittelsohn Papers, American Jewish Archives, Jacob Rader Marcus Center, Box 63, Folder 7, War, my experience.
12. "Letter from Private Walter Mirschinger to Chaplain Gittelsohn," 12 June 1945, Roland Bertram Gittelsohn Papers, American Jewish Archives, Jacob Rader Marcus Center, Box 63, Folder 7, War, my experience.
13. "General," undated note, Roland Bertram Gittelsohn Papers, American Jewish Archives, Jacob Rader Marcus Center, Box 63, Folder 7, War, my experience.
14. "Letter from Harold Gross to Roland Gittelsohn," undated letter, Roland Bertram Gittelsohn Papers, American Jewish Archives, Jacob Rader Marcus Center, Box 63, Folder 7, War, my experience.

**Chapter Twenty-Nine**
1. "General," undated note, Roland Bertram Gittelsohn Papers, American Jewish Archives, Jacob Rader Marcus Center, Box 63, Folder 7, War, my experience.
2. Roland B. Gittelsohn, *Here Am I, Harnessed to Hope*, (New York: Vantage, 1988), 101.
3. Letter from Roland Gittelsohn to Julian Morgenstern, October 19, 1945.
4. Letter from Roland Gittelsohn to Samuel Wohl, November 12, 1945.
5. Bruce Braley, "Honoring the Life of Rabbi Roland B. Gittelsohn and His Stirring Eulogy on Iwo Jima," Congressional Record 153.85, h5688, May 23, 2007.
6. Gittelsohn, *Here Am I, Harnessed to Hope*, 132.
7. Chaplain Roland B. Gittelsohn, USNR, "Pacifist to Padre/Pacifist in Uniform/Pacifist No More," (unpublished manuscript, 1945), 1.
8. Ibid., 166.
9. Ibid., 167.
10. Ibid., 168.
11. Ibid.
12. Ibid.
13. Ibid.
14. Ibid., 169.
15. Ibid.
16. Ibid., 170.
17. Ibid.
18. Ibid.
19. Ibid.
20. Ibid., 170a.

21. Robert Cohen, *When the Old Left Was Young,* (New York: Oxford University Press, 1993), 95.
22. Ibid.
23. Ibid.
24. Gittelsohn, *Here Am I, Harnessed to Hope,* 95-96.

**Chapter Thirty**
1.  Chaplain Roland B. Gittelsohn, USNR, Pacifist to Padre/Pacifist in Uniform/Pacifist No More," (unpublished manuscript, 1945), 77.
2.  Ibid., 97.
3.  Ibid., 126.
4.  Ibid., 127.
5.  Ibid., 127-28.
6.  Ibid., 129-30.
7.  Ibid., 165-a.
8.  Ibid., 165-n.
9.  Ibid., i.
10. Ibid., ii.
11. Roland B. Gittelsohn, *Here Am I, Harnessed to Hope,* (New York: Vantage, 1988), 103.

# Index